Java™ Programming for the Absolute Beginner, Second Edition

JOHN P. FLYNT

THOMSON

COURSE TECHNOLOGY™

Professional ■ Technical ■ Reference

Important: Thomson Course Technology PTR cannot provide software support. Please contact the appropriate software manufacturer's technical support line or Web site for assistance.

Thomson Course Technology PTR and the author have attempted throughout this book to distinguish proprietary trademarks from descriptive terms by following the capitalization style used by the manufacturer.

Information contained in this book has been obtained by Thomson Course Technology PTR from sources believed to be reliable. However, because of the possibility of human or mechanical error by our sources, Thomson Course Technology PTR, or others, the Publisher does not guarantee the accuracy, adequacy, or completeness of any information and is not responsible for any errors or omissions or the results obtained from use of such information. Readers should be particularly aware of the fact that the Internet is an ever-changing entity. Some facts may have changed since this book went to press.

Educational facilities, companies, and organizations interested in multiple copies or licensing of this book should contact the Publisher for quantity discount information. Training manuals, CD-ROMs, and portions of this book are also available individually or can be tailored for specific needs.

ISBN-10: 1-59863-275-2

ISBN-13: 978-1-59863-275-0

Library of Congress Catalog Card Number: 2006923476

Printed in the United States of America

06 07 08 09 10 11 TW 10 9 8 7 6 5 4 3 2

THOMSON

COURSE TECHNOLOGY

Professional ■ Technical ■ Reference

Thomson Course Technology PTR,
a division of Thomson Learning Inc.
25 Thomson Place
Boston, MA 02210
http://www.courseptr.com

Publisher and General Manager, Thomson Course Technology PTR:
Stacy L. Hiquet

Associate Director of Marketing:
Sarah O'Donnell

Manager of Editorial Services:
Heather Talbot

Marketing Manager:
Mark Hughes

Acquisitions Editor:
Mitzi Koontz

Marketing Coordinator:
Meg Dunkerly

Project Editor:
Jennifer Davidson

Technical Reviewer:
Marcia Flynt

PTR Editorial Services Coordinator:
Elizabeth Furbish

Interior Layout Tech:
Digital Publishing Solutions

Cover Designer:
Mike Tanamachi

Indexer:
Kelly D. Henthorne

Proofreader:
Gene Redding

This book is dedicated to its readers.

ACKNOWLEDGMENTS

Thanks to Mitzi Koontz, Emi Smith, and Stacy Hiquet for arranging for the publication. To Jenny Davidson, for watching over the schedule and making it happen.

Also, many thanks to Kevin Claver and Professor Michael Main for their help and support along the way.

As always, thank you Marcia for your faith, hard work, trust, guidance, and support.

ABOUT THE AUTHOR

John **P. Flynt** has authored *Software Engineering for Game Developers*, *Simulation and Event Modeling for Game Developers* (with co-author Ben Vinson), *Perl Power!*, *UnrealScript Game Programming All In One*, and *In the Mind of a Game*. John lives in the foothills near Boulder, Colorado.

CONTENTS

CHAPTER 8 GRAPHIC USER INTERFACE ACTIVITIES......................305

CHAPTER 9 REFACTORING AND DATA CONTAINERS......................345

ABOUT THIS BOOK

This book provides you with an introduction to Java. It is not intended to fully explore the Java class hierarchy, nor does it offer a comprehensive view of Java. Instead, it works from an absolute beginner viewpoint and introduces you to the topics and techniques that prove essential to help you get started with Java as a hobby or as a part of your career.

The first chapters introduce you to the fundamentals of programming. Nothing is assumed. While all programs you create when you program with Java constitute exercises in object-oriented programming, for the first part of the book, you work with each program as though it has nothing to do with object-oriented programming. The focus remains on keeping things simple, so that you have a chance to enjoy learning how to program. After the first chapters, the book explores more advanced topics that incorporate explicitly defined work with object-oriented programming. Everything is explained as you go. The path is the same. You just see things from a more complex point of view.

WHO SHOULD READ THIS BOOK

This book is suitable for many purposes. If you are new to programming, it offers you a hands-on down-to-earth view of programming with Java. As time has gone on, the books on Java have become increasingly geared toward programmers who possess advanced knowledge of Java. The maturity of the language has in many ways made it inaccessible to beginners. This book replies to that trend by going back to the basics.

This book has been written to reflect lessons derived from both teaching and industry experience. You start on a simple basis, and as you go, the book continues to provide you with full discussions of all the particulars. The assumption is that it is better to repeat and review than to stall.

Because it offers full discussions of all its programs, this book provides a focus that tends to be fairly narrow. The approach is not that of the standard canon on Java, in which authors work in slow, painful, sedulous ways through hundreds of examples that reveal isolated uses and applications of a multitude of Java classes.

Instead, working through a number of starter programs, the approach this book takes involves creating a system of classes that you work with through the fundamental relationships the object-oriented programming paradigm provides. As you learn in the later chapters, these are association, composition, aggregation, and inheritance. To extend these relationships, the book also explores encapsulation and polymorphism. You learn how to build your own class hierarchy, complete with abstract classes and interfaces.

THE CHAPTERS

Chapter 1 allows you get started programming with Java. If you have never written a program before, you can start with Chapter 1 and stand a fairly good chance of succeeding.

In Chapter 2 you learn about the basic data types Java offers, and you have a chance to explore writing programs that accept input from you while they are running. This makes it possible to develop a few elementary games.

Chapter 3 offers you a context in which to explore the use of control statements. Along the way, you explore a few items related to numbers. One of these is the use of random numbers. Random numbers provide a basis for creating short programs that explore chance.

What you start in Chapter 3, you continue in Chapter 4. Chapter 4 involves you in work with repetition statements and allows you to write programs that grow in sophistication as you fold more knowledge into them.

In Chapter 5, you begin an adventure that takes you to the end of the book. Chapter 5 introduces the first few topics of object-oriented programming. Although all along you have been developing classes, you now learn to see your programs as classes and to begin thinking of programs in the language that object-oriented programming furnishes.

In Chapter 6, you develop your own class hierarchy. You learn how construction sequences work and how to override methods from parent classes.

With the activities in Chapter 7, you explore abstract classes and interfaces. You likewise investigate the workings of polymorphism.

The discussion in Chapter 8 involves using GUI components in Java. You make use of dialog components and start on a path of developing your own custom dialogs.

Chapter 9 allows you to explore the development of windows and main menus. By the time you reach Chapter 10, you are in the middle of a fairly large set of classes you have created on your own and understand in intimate detail.

OBTAINING THE CODE FOR THE BOOK

I t is important to have on hand the source code for the book if you want to fully benefit from the discussion the book offers of Java programming. You can obtain the source code from the publisher's website. Access www.courseptr.com/downloads and enter the title of the book. This provides you with a link to the source code and any resources associated the book that might be made available after the book's publication.

SETTING UP FILES

Create a directory as follows:

C:\JSource

You can then install the chapter folders in this directory and go to work. Code files for the book contain sets of Java source and class files. You can ignore the class files. For each chapter folder, start out by compiling all the source files in the directory (the *.java files). Then try to execute them. This might require a little patience, but in this way, you avoid problems that arise from dependencies. For files used in the first half of the book, no dependencies exist, so you have nothing to worry about. In later stages, however, you work with many files at once.

None of the files contain code relating to packages. A package is like a directory, and it creates problems for beginning programmers. While some advanced programmers might object to this approach, the fact remains that when you work with files without packages, you avoid a great deal of frustration and can spend more time concentrating on learning the basics rather than struggling with issues concerning how files fit together. This book avoids all of that. You can copy a directory to your computer, access the files, compile them, and then run them.

How to Use This Book

Work forward from Chapter 1. As you go, you start building up a collection of classes that you learn from because you have a chance to become familiar with them. As you go, however, remember that the classes increase in number, so it is a good idea to study the diagrams the book provides so that you understand how they work together and what dependencies exist among them.

The early chapters of the book assume you are working from a DOS prompt. By the time you reach Chapter 8, it is a good idea to investigate obtaining some type of development environment. The appendix provides you with an introduction to acquiring and installing ConTEXT. ConTEXT does not provide specific help with Java syntax, but it does make it easy for you to view and access many files at the same time. When you begin working with a system of ten or so files, then you need an editor.

CONVENTIONS

The coding conventions this book employs are based on practices common among Java programmers. These conventions receive discussion in different parts of the book. Every attempt has been made to present programs that are formatted so that you can easily read them.

GETTING STARTED

With this chapter, you begin to become familiar with the Java programming language and learn how to apply your knowledge to create Java applications and applets. Java applications are standalone programs that run on your system's operating system. Java applets are programs that run within a Web browser as part of a Web page. For example, if you search for "Java games" using Google, you see a list of links to games that were written as applets. You can play these games online within your Web browser. Everything you need to know to create your first simple application and applet can be found in this chapter. Topics include installing Sun's Java Development Kit (JDK 5.0) and writing, compiling, and running programs. The information this chapter contains provides you with a base of knowledge that you can call upon in later chapters. Topics in this chapter include the following:

- Learning what Java is
- Installing the Java Development Kit (JDK 5.0)
- Writing your first Java application
- Learning Java syntax basics
- Writing your first Java applet

THE HELLOWEB APPLET

The HelloWeb applet runs within your Web browser. It displays a message, "Hello, World Wide Web!" In Figure 1.1, you can see what this applet looks like when it runs. This is the HelloWeb applet as it appears while running in Internet Explorer. The text that reads "Hello, World Wide Web!" is provided by an applet that you create in this chapter.

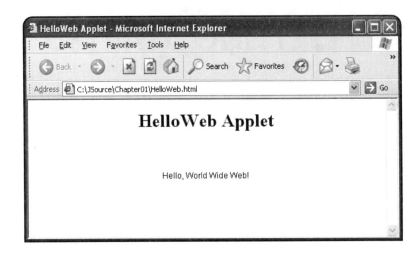

FIGURE 1.1

You learn to make an applet.

By the end of this chapter, you create this HelloWeb applet. More importantly, you understand the concepts behind it so that you can create similar programs on your own. By developing this applet, you learn how to write a Java program, how to compile it, and how to include it in an HTML document. Given this beginning, you are on your way to learning about more complex aspects of the Java programming language.

What Is Java?

Programmers at Sun Microsystems began developing Java behind closed doors in 1991. Java was initially developed as a way to make it possible to create small programs to run household appliances. It was the brainchild of a programmer named James Gosling. When developers at Sun released Java in 1995, the uses they envisioned for Java had expanded from operating appliances to addressing the needs of Internet developers. From that point, Java evolved into an established, exciting, and pervasive technology that programmers use to develop a multitude of different types of applications that run on practically every existing operating system, such as Linux, Mac (currently a version of Linux), Windows, and Unix, and form an integral part of the Internet.

In the tradition of several world-class programmers, James Gosling coauthored a book to introduce the language he pioneered. The name of the book is *The Java Programming Language*. It is coauthored by Ken Arnold and has gone through a few revisions since it was first printed. It provides an advanced overview of Java.

Some Java applications fall into the category of standalone programs, such as word processors, spreadsheets, and games. Such programs run on your desktop. Other programs involve servlets. *Servlets* are almost the opposite of desktop applications. They function in background roles that involve things like making it possible for different computers to communicate with each other. When you use Java in this way, you create what are known as *enterprise* applications. Such work lies beyond the scope of this book. This book addresses a more limited use of Java, one that involves writing simple applications and applets that run on your desktop or within a browser. An applet is essentially a program that executes inside another program—your browser. In this respect, it forms what you might view as the middle ground of working with Java.

How Did Java Get Its Name?

When you think of other programming languages names, such as BASIC, FORTRAN, COBOL, C, C++, and PASCAL, the name Java doesn't really fit in. The name itself is interesting enough to garner curiosity. So just how did Java get its name? The original name for Java was intended to be "OAK," but they couldn't use that name because it was already taken (by Oak Technologies). Other names floating around were "Silk" and "DNA." Apparently, the name "Java" was ultimately picked because it gave the Web a "jolt," and Sun wanted to avoid names that sounded nerdy. Java certainly does its part in making the Internet the interactive, dynamic, not to mention fun technology that it is. You can read more about this at http://www.javaworld.com/javaworld/jw-10-1996/jw-IG-javanarne.fullquote.html.

Java Is a Programming Language

It is beneficial to understand in general terms what a programming language is and what it should be able to do. A *compiler* defines a programming language. A compiler is a complex program that translates files you write into files that your computer can use.

A *programming language* contains a vocabulary that allows you to communicate a series of instructions to a computer in a form that the computer can understand. A fully implemented programming language allows you to control almost all aspects of a computer's operation. For example, you can use a programming language to make the computer communicate with telephone and printer devices. You can make it save data to a disc. You can tell the computer how to change images on a monitor. Java is such a language.

Java is a *high-level programming language*. A high-level programming language uses instructions that often closely resemble a written language (such as English). In contrast to high-level languages are *low-level* languages. A low-level language involves instructions in machine language, which involves groups of ones and zeros that the computer's operating system reads directly. High-level languages are much easier to understand. In fact, without formally learning the Java language, you can probably randomly flip to any program listing in this book, read the lines of code, and make pretty good guesses as to what the lines mean. This is hardly ever possible with low-level languages.

Java Is Platform Independent

Java is a *platform independent* programming language. When a programming language is platform independent, you can use it to write a program on one type of computer, such as a Windows-equipped PC, and then put it on a disc or transfer it over the Internet to another type of computer, such as a Linux-equipped PC (or Mac). It works on both computers without any changes.

A Java program can be platform independent because it does not directly communicate with your computer's operating system. Instead, it communicates with what is known as a *virtual machine*. A virtual machine is a program that runs other programs. More specifically, it *interprets* them. Because Java's virtual machine makes your programs platform independent, you enjoy a significant advantage as a programmer. Among other things, when you develop applets or applications that are downloaded from the Internet, almost anyone in the world can use them, regardless of what computer they use to connect to the Internet.

To run a Java application or applet on your computer, you install the *Java Runtime Environment* (JRE). The developers at Sun create special versions of the JRE for particular types of computers. In fact, they can make a JRE for any computer on which anyone wants to use a Java program. Professional developers regularly request that they do just that for different applications, such as those that run on handheld devices. Among the uses of handheld devices are air pressure gauges for tire maintenance, package delivery, data processing, and portable games.

The JRE communicates in a specific way with your type of computer, but on the other hand, it communicates with any Java program created on any type of computer. In this respect, all Java programs run independently of any specific operating system. It is universally *portable*.

A key factor in portability is what is known as an application programming interface (API). To picture an *API*, imagine a set of adapters for a screwdriver. You find different screws (computers), and the adapters (the API) allow you to continue working with the same screwdriver even though you must deal with different screws.

The API makes it so that a program you write on your Windows-equipped PC encounters the same API that resides on a Linux-equipped PC, a Sun Unix system, or among a multitude of others, an IBM RS6000 server. The API remains the same with respect to your program's communication with the JRE, but it is customized for the operating system. You see the side that does not change. The programmers at Sun worry about the other side. You do not need to change your program. You do not need to recompile it.

No matter what system you are programming for, your Java program remains the same. The technical name for the content of your program is *source code*. Java allows you to retain the same source code even if you move your program from one type of computer to another. On the other hand, the Java compiler still has to make it so that your source code communicates with the computer. To accomplish this, it creates what is known as *byte code*. Java byte code is a version of your source code that the JRE interprets as it communicates with your particular operating system. As mentioned already, the programmers at Sun create a JRE for each operating system. The function of the JRE involves interpreting your Java byte code to send instructions to your operating system.

JAVA IS OBJECT ORIENTED

Almost all programming languages developed over the past decade or so have been based on what is known as *object-oriented programming* (OOP). Java is among this group. It is an object-oriented programming language. As an object-oriented programming language, it makes use of *classes*. In fact, every program you create when you work with Java is a class.

A class is a pattern. The pattern is of anything you want to write a program about. You can use classes to create patterns of books, cars, tables, chairs, characters in games, whole games themselves, televisions, bank accounts, or anything else. In each case, you create a pattern. When you create a program, you use the pattern. You use the pattern to create a specific instance of the pattern. The specific instance of your pattern is an *object*. Your program ends up consisting of statements that change the object. In most cases, your programs make use of many classes and so many objects, and since your programs begin and end with controlling such objects, your are performing object-oriented programming.

Classes and Objects

The term *class* is short for *class of objects*. After all, one pattern can create many objects. A class is a pattern in the sense that it involves two basic types of information about the objects you can create with it. One type of information involves how you can define the object. The other type of information involves how you can change the object.

Consider a class that creates a pattern for a ball. With respect to its definition, the ball is spherical and can possess a specific color. A ball can be solid or hollow, large or small. With respect to how a ball changes, consider that someone might inflate a ball, so it grows in size. Someone might throw a ball, so its position changes. Someone might bounce a ball, so its speed can change relative to its position in the arc of the bounce.

The description of a ball is called its *state*. The state of a ball might be white, muddied, and "moving at 102 miles per hour out of the hand of a major league pitcher." The changes a ball makes are called its *behavior*. The behavior of a ball might consist of such actions as picking up speed, losing speed, or changing color. The behavior of a class changes its state. A class defines the state and the behavior of the objects it models.

Attributes and Methods

From a programming perspective, when you describe a ball, you do so through *attributes*. When you define the behavior of a class, you do so through what are known as *methods* or *member functions*. Consider the ball again. An attribute might be called `skinColor`. Another might be called `ballWeight`. Still another might be called `ballSpeed`. These are all states of a ball. On the other hand, a class method might be called `changeSkinColor`, `changeWeight`, or `changeSpeed`. In each case, the method allows you to change the value you assign to the attribute.

When you define a class, you define both attributes and methods. You create a class; you create a program that describes what a ball is and how you can change it. You then create an instance of the class, an object. You have the object perform actions or change states in the way you specify when you define it. That is the essence of object-oriented programming. How to go about actually creating classes with Java is covered in detail in Chapter 5, "Object-Oriented Programming."

WHY LEARN JAVA?

If you are learning your first programming language, Java is a good choice. Since Java is an object-oriented programming language, using it is intuitive. You understand how to use real objects in everyday life, so it isn't a big stretch for you to grasp how to use Java. Since Java is a high-level programming language, to learn to program with it, you do not need to go very far outside of your usual pathways of learning. You can read the code and often understand what it does.

In addition to being straightforward to learn, Java offers you significant potentials as a programmer. As mentioned previously, it addresses a wide range of applications. You can create standalone applications that run on your computer, applets for Internet solutions, or specialized applications that work on handheld devices. Such applications constitute the tip of an iceberg. Whether you are expanding your knowledge or trying to further your career, Java brings many benefits.

Pathways to Learning Java

If you already know languages like C, C++, or C#, learning Java from this book should not prove difficult for you at all. Java was designed to be similar to these languages. If you have not before tried to learn a programming language, this book is geared toward beginners. You do not need any programming experience, and from the start, Java's designers tried to make it easier to learn than other programming languages.

A key to its ease of use lies in the fact that James Gosling and his associates designed it to be used on a pure, object-oriented basis. It was not the first such language, of course, and other languages, such as C#, have come into existence since Java. Still, it remains a language that has been consistently designed to make your programming work involve use of standardized language features. Likewise, after you learn Java, you find that you can also readily begin to learn such languages as Visual Basic, C++, C#, Python, and any number of programming languages that incorporate the object-oriented paradigm. The concepts you learn with Java apply across the object-oriented programming spectrum.

Where to Start

There are two basic approaches to installing Java on your computer. One is as a developer. As a developer, you make use of the Java Development Kit (JDK), which consists of an extensive set of tools for programming. In its current manifestation, the JDK absorbs around 50 megabytes of disk space. The other approach is that of someone who just wants to run Java programs. In this instance, you make use of the Java Runtime Environment (JRE).

A JRE can involve only a few kilobytes of disk space. A JRE is designed to run programs, but at the same time, you can still use it for development purposes. In fact, the JDK incorporates a JRE. In this book, you are a developer, so your work involves using the JDK. In the next section, you investigate how to download the JRE along with the JDK.

INSTALLING AND SETTING UP THE JDK

Before you begin writing Java programs, you must first set up your system so that it can compile and run your programs. To accomplish this task, you must obtain and install the Java Development Kit (JDK).

Over time, the JDK has gone through many versions. Currently, Sun has released version 5 of the JDK. How Sun designates its different versions can prove somewhat confusing, but generally, all its versions have been named using a fairly simple approach. For example, Sun designates version 5.0 of the JDK as version 1.5. Version 4 of the JDK appears as version 1.4. This convention makes sense when you consider the complexity that regular updates of a software development environment used by millions of people involve.

In addition to version numbers, you also need to consider that you require the version of the JDK that addresses your particular computer. At Sun, your computer and the operating system you have on it are identified as a *platform*. A platform is something you can stand on, so the metaphor is based on your computer system as something you stand on as you develop applications. For this book, the assumption is that you are working on a version of Windows XP. (A few sections are set aside, however, to help you with other platforms.)

Accessing the Sun Site

To download the latest version of the JDK (1.5) for Windows XP, access the following Web site:

    http://java.sun.com/j2se/1.5.0/download.jsp

When you access this site, you see an advertisement for the Sun Development Network (SDN). This is a network you can join and access freely. For now, it is not necessary for you to do so, but if your interest in Java continues beyond this book, then one of your first tasks should involve navigating to the SDN pages and spending a few hours poking around.

In several places, you see Download JDK 5.0. You might see a number of updates or other features included with the wording for the download link. For purposes of this book, almost any recent update of the JDK 5.0 suffices. Professional developers concern themselves with cutting-edge features. You need only the stable, core features. Likewise, note that you see both the JRE and the JDK listed for downloading. Again, you need the JDK.

Click the Download JDK 5.0 link. This takes you to a page on which you are asked to indicate that you accept the license agreement. Click the button that indicates you accept the agreement. The page refreshes.

Now look for a black bar and wording along the following lines:

    Windows Platform – J2SE™ Development Kit 5.0

The J2SE designation might prove a little confusing. J2SE is Sun's way of designating the JDK and its accompanying tools. You might also see an "Update" designation. Again, you need not be concerned about that for this book. Any update will do. It's the base number, 5.0, that counts.

Beneath the Windows Platform banner, you see offline and online installations. These options appear on separate lines. For this book, select the offline option. This option allows you to download the complete JDK to your computer. Having the complete JDK allows you to more easily install it.

To download the JDK, create a directory in which you can store it temporarily. Here is an example:

    C:\downloads\JDK5

You can then place the Java installation file in this directory.

Click the download link for offline, designate the directory, and let the software do its work. Depending on the speed of the Internet, the process requires anywhere from a few seconds to several minutes.

The JDK Installation Executable

A fairly considerable difference in size exists between the JDK and the JRE, so if your download is less than a few megabytes, then you probably have the JRE. You require the JDK, which as of this writing is around 50 megabytes.

When you finish the download (for the Windows platform), you see a file with the following name:

    jdk-1_5_0_06-windows-i586-p.exe

Starting Your Windows Installation

To install on Windows XP, use the following steps:

1. After downloading the JDK 5.0 Windows installer program (jdk-1_5_0_06-windows-i586-p.exe, for example), select Start > Control Panel > Add or Remove Programs. In the Add or Remove Programs dialog, click Add New Programs. Then click CD or Floppy.
2. In the Install Program from Floppy Disk or CD dialog, click Next. Then click Browse and navigate to your download directory. From the Files of Type drop-down list, select All Files. You then see the jdk-1_5_0_06-windows-i586-p.exe file. Select this file and click Open.
3. In the Run Install Program dialog, click Finish.

4. You then see an Open File – Security Warning dialog. Click Run. This starts the Sun installation routine.

Windows Installation and Setup Continued

Use the following steps after the Sun installation program begins:

1. In the J2AE Development Kit dialog, click the I Accept option. Then click Next.
2. In the Custom Setup dialog, leave all the options as is and click Next.
   You then see a Progress dialog. The progress bar tracks the activity of the installation. After a time, the Custom Setup dialog appears. You see that the top item is highlighted (for the JRE). Leave everything as is and click Next.
3. You next see the Browser Registration dialog. Deselect the browser you do not want to use. Click Next.
4. You then see the Complete dialog. Click Finish.

Verifying and Copying the Path to Your JRE

This section requires that you first install the Java JDK. If you have not yet done so, refer to the section titled, "Starting Your Windows Installation."

After you complete the installation of the JDK, verify the location of your installation. To do so, use the following steps:

1. Open Windows Explorer and navigate to the following directory:

   C:\Program Files\Java

2. At this point, you see the actual version number of your Java installation. You see two folders. One is for the JDK. The other is for the JRE. Note the exact name of the JDK. For example, you see:

   `jdk1.5.0_06`

3. Click on this folder. You see a bin directory. If you look at the Address field in Windows Explorer, you see a path similar to the following:

   C:\Program Files\Java\jdk1.5.0_06

4. The only information that might differ for you is the version number. Copy what you see to a piece of paper. (Alternatively, type or copy and paste this path into a text file. One approach is to copy it to Notepad.)

Setting the Path Variable

This section assumes that you have performed the tasks detailed in the previous section, "Verifying and Copying the Path to Your JRE." If you have not completed the tasks designed in the previous section, do so before beginning the tasks in this section.

After the Sun installation completes, you need to set a system variable. This is the Path variable, and this variable tells Windows where to find the JRE when you want to run a Java program. To set the Path variable, follow these steps:

1. Select Start > Control Panel. In the Control Panel window, double-click System. The System Properties dialog appears. Click the Advanced tab. Click the Environment Variables button in the Advanced tab. The Environment Variables dialog appears.
2. In the Environment Variables dialog, inspect the System Variables pane. It is the lower of the two panes. In the System Variables pane, scroll down until you see the Path line.
3. Double-click the Path line. The Edit System Variable dialog appears.
4. Carefully click to activate the Variable Value field. Then use the right arrow to move the cursor to the end of the text in the field. At the end, add the path you copied or wrote down earlier and add a slash and the word "bin." The path designates the Java bin directory. For example:

    ;C:\Program Files\Java\jdk1.5.0_06\bin

    You add the semicolon at the beginning of the text. It separates this path from others in the list.
5. After confirming you have the correct path, click OK to exit the Edit System Variable dialog. Likewise, click OK to exit the Environment Variables dialog. And click OK to exit the System Properties dialog. Then close the Control Panel window.
6. When you finish with this set of actions, select Start > Turn Off Computer > Restart. Generally, you need to restart your computer to make new configurations take effect.

WRITING YOUR FIRST PROGRAM

In this section, you write a standalone application that can run on any system that has a Java interpreter. You write the source code for the program and then compile and run the program. Keep in mind as you do this that you will return to this program later and analyze it, so don't worry if you do not understand specific features.

Setting Up to Work with DOS

Before writing your first Java program, you might want to work with your system to make it easier to see what you are doing. To accomplish this, in Windows XP, you can set up a

Command Prompt window that has a white background and dark text. To accomplish this, use the following steps:

1. Access the Command Prompt. Begin on your Windows desktop with the Start menu. Select Start > All Programs > Accessories > Command Prompt. Figure 1.2 maps the path to the Command Prompt from the Windows Start menu.

FIGURE 1.2

From the Start menu, locate the Command Prompt.

2. After you locate the Command Prompt item in the Windows menu system, create a shortcut and place it on your Windows desktop.
   As shown in Figure 1.3, to create a shortcut, right-click the Command Prompt and then select Send To > Desktop (Create Shortcut).

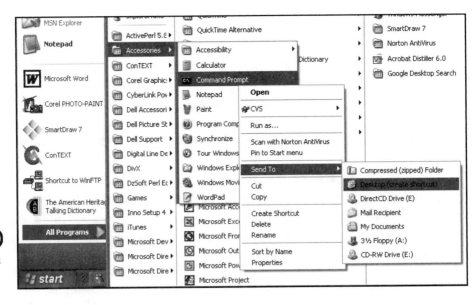

FIGURE 1.3

Create a shortcut and place it on your desktop.

Now set the Command Prompt window so that it has a light background and dark text (refer to Figure 1.4):

1. Start: Right-click on the top bar of the DOS window (Command Prompt).

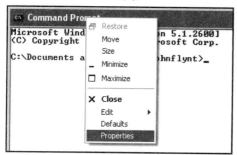

2. In the Colors tab, click the button for the Screen Background. Click the white box at the end of the color palette.

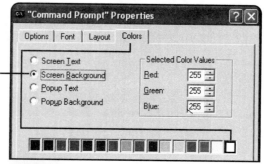

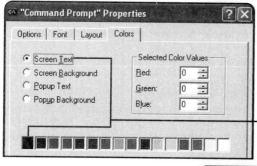

3. Click the button for the Screen Test. Click the black box at the end of the color palette.

4. Click the Modify Shortcut That Started This Window button.

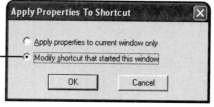

FIGURE 1.4

Set the properties of the DOS Command Prompt window so that you have dark text and a light background.

1. Right-click on the top of the window and select the Properties option from the drop-down menu. You see the Properties dialog, as Figure 1.4 illustrates.
2. Click the Colors tab. Then click the Screen Background radio button and set the value as shown in Figure 1.4 (255, 255, 255). To set the values, click the white box in the color palette.
3. To set the text, click the Screen Text radio button and set all of the values to zero (0, 0, 0) by clicking the black box in the color palette. When you finish setting the background and text colors, click OK.
4. When the OK dialog appears, click the radio button that corresponds to Modify Shortcut That Started This Window. Click OK once again.

Given that you have set up the DOS Command Prompt window with a light background and dark font, you see something along the lines of Figure 1.5. This window is now available to you on your desktop when you need to interact with the operating system.

To access the window, you click on the desktop icon. Also, you can select Start > Run. In the Open field, type **cmd**. Then click OK. You can use the procedure described previously to set the background and text colors of any DOS window you open.

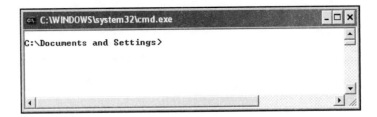

FIGURE 1.5

The Command Prompt is available through a DOS window.

DOS Commands

Table 1.1 provides a list of DOS commands you see after issuing the HELP command at the Command Prompt. Familiarize yourself with these commands if you've not used DOS before.

To create a file for a Java program, navigate to your working directory. To accomplish this, open your Command Prompt window. Use the CD command to change directories. Recall that if you type

```
cd ..
```

you move up one level of directory. If you are at the C: root, you can create a directory called JSource by typing

```
MKDIR JSource
```

TABLE 1.1   A FEW DOS COMMANDS

DOS Command	Discussion
*	This is a wildcard. You can use it to replace any character. For example, to check a directory for HelloWorld.uc, you can type DIR H*. The asterisk tells the system to look for any filename beginning with H.
CD	Displays the name of or changes the current directory. When you follow this command with two dots (periods), you navigate up a level (CD ..) To navigate up two or more levels, use dots in combination with slashes (CD ..\ .. or CD ../..).
CLS	Clears the screen.
COPY	Copies one or more files to another location or another name. To use this command, you type COPY *name_of_file new_name_of_file*. This command creates a copy under a new name. If you want to copy something to one directory above the one you are in, you can issue: COPY *name_of_file* ..*name_of_ file*. This command creates a copy of the same name in a different directory.
DEL	Deletes one or more files. Use this for files. Type DEL *file_name*.
DIR	Displays a list of files and subdirectories in a directory. A significant addition to the DIR command is DIR/P, which allows you to see the contents of a directory a page at a time.
HELP	Provides help information for Windows commands.
MKDIR	Creates a directory. Type the command and then the name of the directory you want to create. MKDIR *directory_name*.
RD	Removes a directory. Use with caution. To remove a directory, remove its contents first. The system prompts you to ensure that you want to delete the contents. You type RD *directory_name*.
RENAME	Renames a file or files. (Same as REN.)
TREE	Graphically displays the directory structure of a drive or path.
XCOPY	Copies files and directory trees.

You can then navigate to the directory by typing

```
CD JSource
```

You can then create a directory for this chapter called Chapter01, which corresponds to the directory found on the companion website.

```
MKDIR Chapter01
```

To navigate to the directory, you type

```
CD Chapter01
```

Creating a Hello World Program

To create a Hello World program for Java, as discussed in the previous section, begin by creating a directory to work in. When you create a directory, do not use spaces in the directory name. Also, keep the name short so that you can easily work with it. The files on the companion website use C:\JSource\Chapter01 (see Figure 1.6).

After you create a directory, use your Command Prompt window to navigate to the directory and then invoke Notepad to create your first Java file. As Figure 1.6 illustrates, type notepad and then the name of the file you want to create.

For the name of the file, type **HelloWorld.java**. Do not use any spaces in the name of the file. Likewise, the file type is *.java. All Java source files possess a *.java extension. Make certain you add the extension as shown in Figure 1.6. The trailing character is the cursor, not an underscore. When Notepad asks you if you want to create a new file, click Yes.

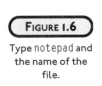

FIGURE 1.6

Type notepad and the name of the file.

With your Notepad document open, type the Hello World program exactly as follows:

```
/* HelloWorld.java
     The classic first program
*/

public class HelloWorld {
    public static void main(String args[]) {
        System.out.println("Hello, world!");
    }//end method definition
}//end class definition
```

Compare your work to verify that it appears as shown in Figure 1.7. Save your work when you finish. The next section discusses the meaning of the code.

The HelloWorld.java file and other source code files are available on the companion website, and you can copy and run them without having to type them. However, to get the most out of this book, create the file and type the source code yourself. After you finish typing this code, save the file. (See the sidebar later in this chapter, "Working with Java Files," for an overview of the routine you use for development.)

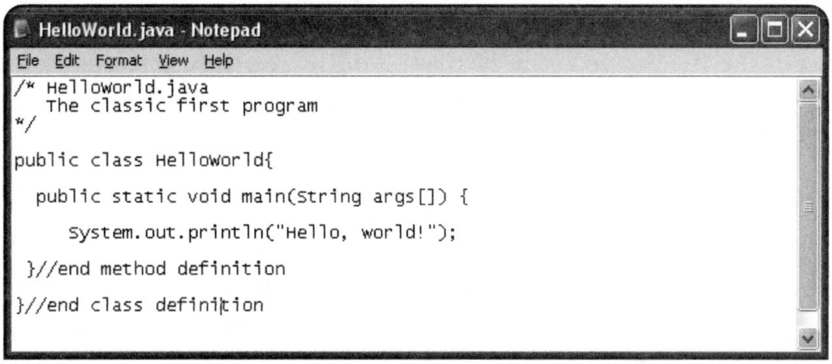
HelloWorld.java - Notepad
File Edit Format View Help
/* HelloWorld.java
The classic first program
*/
public class HelloWorld{
public static void main(String args[]) {
System.out.println("Hello, world!");
}//end method definition
}//end class definition

FIGURE 1.7

Use Notepad to compose your first Java program.

> **When you save the source code, pay close attention to the capitalization of the filename and the class. The filename must be the same as the name of the class. The source file has a *.java extension (HelloWorld.java). The filename is case sensitive, which means that uppercase letters are differentiated from lowercase letters. Your program does not compile if you type its name incorrectly.**

HelloWorld Syntax Basics

You've written your first Java program. Now you can step back and take a closer look at what you have accomplished. You have put the syntax of the Java language to work. The syntax is a set of rules you follow when writing a program. You can think of syntax as grammar for programming.

Comments

At the start of the HelloWorld.java file, the first syntax element you encounter involves a forward slash followed by an asterisk. Text then follows the asterisk. Following the text, you see an asterisk and a slash. Here are the lines:

```
/* HelloWorld.java
     The classic first program
*/
```

This is one way to add comments to your code. The compiler does not read comments. Comments are for human consumption and allow you to make notes in your program.

This form of comment requires you to have an opening and closing syntax element. The opening element is the slash and the star (/*). The closing element is the star and the slash (*/). Between these two elements, you can include as many lines of text as you want. The compiler does not read this text.

If you follow the lines of the file down to the last two, you see another form of comment element. This comment element consist of two slashes (//). Here are the lines:

```
        }//end method definition
    }//end class definition
```

This form of comment forces the compiler to ignore anything on the same line that *follows* the slashes. For this form of comment, you do not use closing elements, as you do with the asterisk-slash combination. If you were to rewrite the opening comments using the double slashes, they would appear as follows:

```
// Hello World
// The classic first program
```

A third form of comment is used in Java. This form of comment is related to the Java Document utility, which automatically generates Web pages for your code. The Web (HTML) pages provide documentation of the code in form you can easily read and access. A tool that is part of the JDK, known as javadoc, allows you to generate comments of this form.

Keywords and Defining a Class

After the comments, you find the beginning of a class definition:

```
public class HelloWorld {
```

You must define a class in every Java program. The word public is called a *keyword*. It is not necessary at this point to fully understand the public keyword. Still, you see it in almost every program in this book. It controls the extent to which other classes can access your class. (You learn much more about this in Chapter 5.) The word class is also a keyword. It identifies HelloWorld as a class. You use the class keyword in every Java file you create.

At the end of the line, you see a curly brace ({). The curly brace opens to the right, and it is known as an opening brace. The opening brace indicates the beginning of the contents of your *class definition*. For every opening brace there is a *closing brace*, so at the end of the class definition, you see a curly brace that faces to the left (}). It indicates the end of the class definition.

> Keywords are words used in Java to perform specific functions. You can use keywords only in their designated roles. You cannot use them for the names of classes, class attributes, or the methods of classes.

Defining a Method and a Statement

After the line that defines your HelloWorld class, you create a line of code that starts the main() method definition. Here's the code:

```
public static void main(String args[]) {
```

This is the *signature line* of the main() method. The main() method is the entry point of your program. In other words, it is where the execution of your program starts. You use the public keyword to designate that the main() method can be accessed outside the HelloWorld class. Discussion of the static keyword is beyond the scope of this chapter, but in general, it allows your program to run as a standalone application. The keyword void says that the main() method does not return a value. The name of the method is, of course, main.

Opening and closing parentheses follow the name of the method. Within these, you see what is known as the parameter of the method (String args[]). Every method in Java, as you learn later in this book, allows you to pass information to it. The parameter defines this information.

> Whenever the name of a method appears in this book, a pair of parentheses follow the name. For example, the method named main is designated as main(). This convention allows you to easily distinguish the names of methods from other names.

To define the main() method, you include one statement. A statement is an instruction to the computer. All statements end with a semicolon (;). The statement that defines the main() method occurs inside opening and closing braces, in the same way that you define a class definition. The statement instructs your computer to print the output. Here's the code:

```
System.out.println("Hello, world!");
```

The statement consists of a *call* to a method (println()) that is defined as part of the Java API. The words System and out are a special way to access methods that have to do with what are know as *streams*. Discussion of streams is outside the scope of this chapter, but suffice it to say that the `Standard.out.println()` call handles what you print to the screen. To designate the text you want to print to the screen, as an argument to the `println()` method, you place `Hello, World!` within quotes.

The last two lines of code provide the closing braces for the `main()` method and the `HelloWorld` class definition. You provide a comment following each of the closing braces to make it easier to recognize which block you are closing. The use of the expression `end...` is a convention. It designates the end of a block.

> To make it easier to remember to close your braces and also for purposes of readability, follow certain source code formatting conventions. Each time you open a new set of braces (a new block), indent the statements that compose the block. When you close a set of braces, position the closing brace so that it is even with the start of the line that contains the opening brace.

Compiling the Hello World Program

After you create the source code for HelloWorld.java, your next step is to compile it. To compile the code, first save and close your source code file so that it resides in your JSource directory. Issue the DOS `DIR` command to view your file. Verify that your file has a *.java extension. If it has another extension (such as *.txt), you can access Windows Explorer and easily change it.

Next, to compile your Java file, type the following command at the DOS prompt:

```
javac HelloWorld.java
```

The first term, `javac`, is a compiler command. It invokes the compiler for the program you name immediately after it. Figure 1.8 illustrates how you issue this command. When you issue the command, follow it with the name of the file you want to compile and include the *.java extension with the filename. (Again, the final character in Figure 1.8 is the cursor, not an underscore.)

FIGURE 1.8

Issue a `javac` command to compile your *.java (source code) file.

What happens when you *compile* Java programs? The Java compiler creates a new file, called a byte code file. As Figure 1.9 illustrates, if you issue a DIR command, you can recognize the byte code file because it has a *.class extension. The existence of the file indicates that your program has compiled correctly.

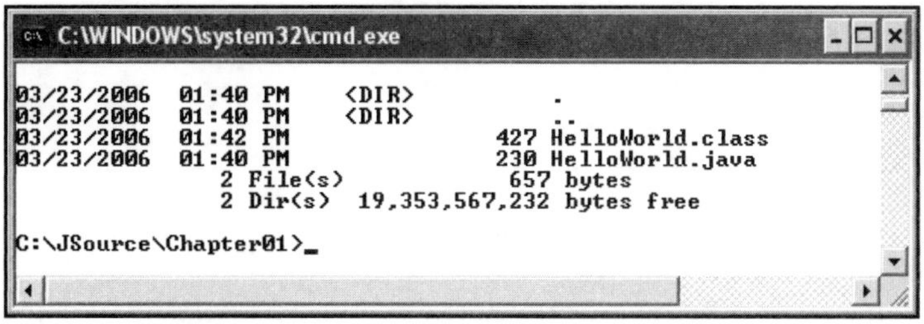

```
C:\WINDOWS\system32\cmd.exe                                    _ □ ×
03/23/2006   01:40 PM    <DIR>          .
03/23/2006   01:40 PM    <DIR>          ..
03/23/2006   01:42 PM              427 HelloWorld.class
03/23/2006   01:40 PM              230 HelloWorld.java
              2 File(s)             657 bytes
              2 Dir(s)   19,353,567,232 bytes free

C:\JSource\Chapter01>_
```

FIGURE 1.9

Issue a DIR command to see the new *.class (byte code) file.

As mentioned before, the Java Virtual Machine (JVM) reads the byte code and translates it so that your computer knows what operations it needs to perform. Each operating system has its own system-dependent Java interpreter, so it is able to compile your Java byte code into a specific machine language. For this reason, Java is known as the "Write once, run anywhere" language. You write and compile your code on whatever computer you are working on. You then run the byte code version of the code on any other computer. This way, among other things, you can link an applet to a Web page and have it run on any computer on which the Web page is opened.

Running the Hello World Program

Now that you have written and compiled your program, you can see the product of your efforts by running (or executing) it. To run your Java program in Windows, type the following command:

```
java HelloWorld
```

The first term, java, invokes the Java interpreter. The interpreter causes your file to execute. The second term is the name of your class. For this reason, you do not include a file extension. Figure 1.10 illustrates the command and the output.

Congratulations! You've just completed your first Java program. The output you see is the result of the execution of the byte code in the *.class file. As long as you place the *.class file in a folder with the same name as the folder in which it currently resides (Chapter01, for example), you can move the *.class file to any location on your hard drive and execute it if you issue the java HelloWord command.

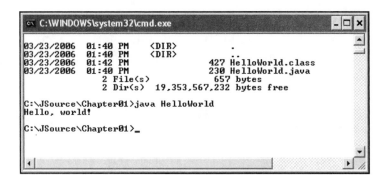

FIGURE 1.10

This is what your first application looks like when you run it.

Along the same lines, you can change the source code file (*.java) and use the javac command to compile it. Whenever you run the javac command, the previously existing version of your *.class file is automatically replaced.

WORKING WITH JAVA FILES

When you work with Java files, you perform a succession of three basic activities:

- **Create the *.java file.**
- **Use the javac command to compile the *.java file. This generates a *.class file.**
- **Use the java command to execute the *.class file.**

As you go, you are likely to make syntax and other programming errors. The compiler reports the errors, and you must fix them. In other cases, you encounter no errors but instead add code or features to your file.

Here is a sample of the commands you issue during a DOS session:

```
C:\JSource\Chapter01>notepad HelloWorld.java
C:\JSource\Chapter01>javac HelloWorld.java
C:\JSource\Chapter01>java HelloWorld
Hello, world!
C:\JSource\Chapter01>
```

After you have typed this set of commands once, use the arrow keys to retrieve them. This way, you do not have to retype commands. Likewise, you do not have to close Notepad if you edit your file. You must save your changes using Notepad, however, before you see them take effect.

WRITING YOUR FIRST APPLET

In this section, you learn to create the HelloWeb applet shown in Figure 1.1. This applet performs a task similar to that of the HelloWorld application, but it runs within your Web browser instead of as a standalone application.

Applets differ from standalone applications because, for one thing, they lack a main() function. Since they lack a main() function, they cannot execute by themselves, as does your HelloWorld application. To execute an applet, you must run it within a browser. To run it within a browser, you must call your applet from a Web page (also known as an HTML document). Special HTML syntax allows you to call an applet.

In this section, you write an applet and incorporate it into an HTML document. You then run the applet within your browser. In addition to such basics, you also use the Applet Viewer utility, which is built into the JDK. The Applet Viewer utility allows you to test your applets from the Command Prompt, outside of your browser.

Although this book does not focus on applets, it is useful at this point to create an applet and understand that an applet differs from an application. Applets add a great deal of life to Web documents. If you include an applet in a Web document and publish it on the Internet, anyone can run it without having to download it.

Applet Code

To create a HelloWeb applet, begin by once again using Notepad to create a file. This time, call the file HelloWeb.java. Save this file to your JSource\Chapter01 directory. Here's the code.

```
/*
    HelloWeb.java
*/
import java.awt.Graphics;
import javax.swing.JApplet;

public class HelloWeb extends JApplet {
    public void paint(Graphics g) {
    g.drawString("Hello, World Wide Web!", 10, 50);
    }//end paint
}//end class
```

The text of this program differs from the HelloWorld.java program in fairly significant ways, but for now just type the lines as shown. Save your work. Figure 1.11 illustrates the HelloWeb class after you have typed it.

```
HelloWeb.java - Notepad
File  Edit  Format  View  Help

/*
    HelloWeb.java
*/
import java.awt.Graphics;
import javax.swing.JApplet;
public class HelloWeb extends JApplet {
    public void paint(Graphics g) {
        g.drawString("Hello, world wide web!", 10, 50);
    }//end paint
}//end class |
```

FIGURE 1.11

Type the
HelloWeb class
and save it as a
*.java file.

After the comment at the top of the HelloWeb.java file, you see two `import` statements. An `import` statement allows you to access classes that are a part of the Java *class hierarchy*. The Java class hierarchy consists of hundreds of classes that are ready for you to use. In this case, you use the `Graphics` class, which allows you to draw text on the screen. The `Graphics` class is part of a *package* called the Abstract Windows Toolkit (`awt`), which is one of the main sets of classes that make up the Java class hierarchy. A package is like a directory.

You also use in `import` statement to access the `JApplet` class. This class is part of a package—or collection of classes—named `swing`. The `swing` package constitutes one of the major components of the Java class hierarchy.

To create the `HelloWeb` class, you use the `JApplet` class. You want to use the `JApplet` class because it contains several important methods that do things like make your text visible and control the size of your applet. To show that you want to use the class, you employ the `extends` keyword. The `extends` keyword allows you to have access to all the methods that have been defined in the `JApplet` class. As is explained later on in this book, you *inherit* all of these methods when you use the `extends` keyword. Here is the signature of the `HelloWeb` class:

```
public class HelloWeb extends JApplet {
```

When you make the `HelloWeb` class extend the `JApplet` class, the `HelloWeb` class is referred to as a *subclass*. The class it extends (`JApplet`) is called its *super class*.

The `JApplet` class defines a `paint()` method. Since you have use of the methods in the `JApplet` class, you can call this as a part of your `HelloWeb` class. The method returns no value (it is `void`), and it takes one argument, which is of the Java `Graphics` class. (You have access to this class due to the `import` operation discussed earlier.)

Within the paint() method, you call a method (drawString()). This method is defined in the Graphics class, not the JApplet class. Here is the call to drawString():

```
g.drawString("Hello, World Wide Web!", 10, 50); }
```

The g is called a *parameter argument*. It is an identifier or variable that represents the Graphics class. You use this identifier to call the drawString() method. When you call this method, you furnish it with three arguments. The first argument is a string ("Hello, World Wide Web!"). The second and third arguments position the string in your applet area when your applet displays. The two numbers designate the position of the bottom left corner of a rectangular box that contains the string. You'll learn more about positioning text and other such things in Chapter 8, "Graphic User Interface Activities."

IN THE REAL WORLD

In the real world, applications and applets typically do much more than simply print a message to the screen. Programmers tend to use methods in their programs that do not work in applets. One of these is the System.out.println() method, which you use extensively in the chapters to come.

The System.out.println() method is useful when debugging your code. As you develop a program, you can use this method to print information about the program. This way, you can see the state of the program at key locations in the code.

Compiling the Applet Code

Compile the HelloWeb.java file in exactly the same way that you compiled the HelloWorld.java file. Here is the command you type to compile it:

```
javac HelloWeb.java
```

After you compile the file, issue the DIR command. You see that the javac utility generates a *.class file, just as before.

In this case, you cannot do more with your program until you make use of it in a Web page. Recall that the HelloWeb class lacks a main() function. This makes it an *applet* rather than an *application*. As an applet, it cannot run by itself. If you try to execute it, the Java VM issues an error message. Try it yourself by typing java HelloWeb. Figure 1.12 shows you the VM message.

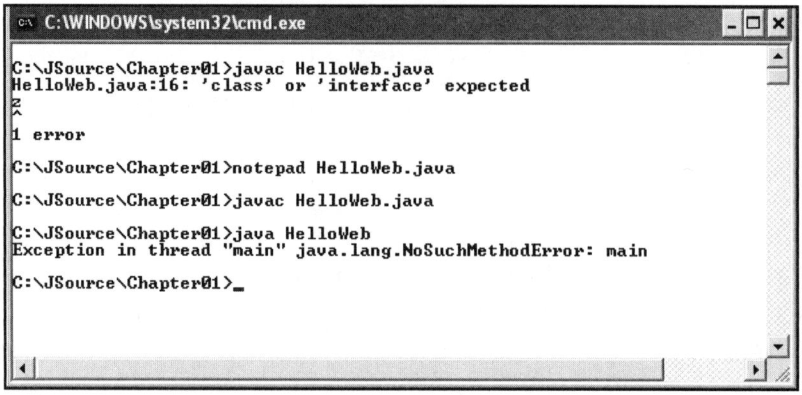

FIGURE 1.12

Since an applet lacks a main() function, trying to execute it with the java utility generates an error.

Writing an HTML File for an Applet

To test your applet, you need to create an HTML document. The HTML document allows you to perform two types of action. The first is to use a test utility, the Applet Viewer, to test your applet. The second allows you to run your applet within your browser.

You don't need to know much about HTML to create a page that accommodates your applet. To create the HTML document, use Notepad. Call the file HelloWeb.html. The *.html extension identifies the document so that your browser can read it. Save the file to your JSource directory. Type the following lines:

```
<html>
  <head>
    <title>HelloWeb Applet</title>
  </head>
  <body>
    <h1 align=center>HelloWeb Applet</h1>
     <center>
        <applet name="HelloWeb"
                code="HelloWeb.class"
                width=150
                height=100>
        </applet>
     </center>
  </body>
</html>
```

In the HelloWeb.html file, the words in the angle brackets (<>) are HTML tags. Table 1.2 provides you with a breakdown of what the tags mean. Opening and closing brackets must enclose each tag, but in the case of the applet tag, you also work with *tag attributes*. Tag attributes fit inside the opening and closing tag brackets. Tags also occur in sets, so for each opening tag, you must provide a closing tag. To create a closing tag, you precede the tag name with a slash (<\>).

Using the Applet Viewer

Before you try to run your applet in your browser, first test it. To test it, you can use the Applet Viewer. This is a utility program that you get with the JDK. Its name when you execute it at the command line is appletviewer. This utility allows you to test applets without having to invoke a browser. It displays only the output of your applet. To use it, type the following command at the Command Prompt:

```
appletviewer helloweb.html
```

	TABLE 1.2 HTML TAGS FOR APPLETS
Item	**Discussion**
html	This tag opens and closes an HTML document. Everything you want to include in an HTML document falls between the opening and closing html tags.
head	This tag provides an address space for an HTML document. You use the title tag within the head tag to make it so your browser can display the name of your document.
body	This designates the main part of your Web page. Within the body, you place the applet and text.
h1	This tag creates a heading, such as the one you see at the top of this section.
center	This tag causes anything that follows it (text or your applet) to be centered in the Web page.
applet	This tag identifies an applet. It has four required attributes: name, code, width, and height. Unless you assign values to these four attributes, your applet tag is not likely to successfully display. The units of measure are picture elements (pixels) of your monitor.
name	The name attribute is what you name your applet relative to the Web page. You can name your applet anything you want for use within your HTML document.
code	The code attribute is the name of your applet as you have compiled it. Since you have named your file HelloWeb.java and generated a class file named HelloWeb.class, you must assign HelloWeb.class to the code attribute.
width	This is the minimum width of your applet. If you do not make this large enough, your applet might not appear.
height	This is the minimum height of your applet. If you do not designate enough height, your applet might not appear.

Figure 1.13 shows the Applet Viewer window running your HelloWeb applet. If your program does not have errors, the messages you see in the viewer tells you that the applet is running. You see only the text that you use the Java code to generate. You see nothing of the HTML page. To close the Applet Viewer, click the control (X) button.

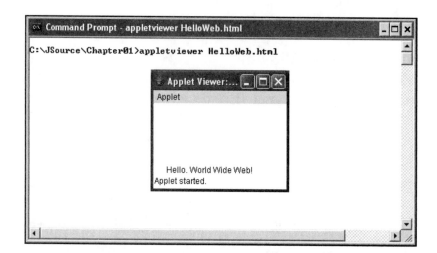

FIGURE 1.13

The Applet Viewer tests your applet without invoking the browser.

Running Your Applet in the Browser

Having tested your applet, you are ready to use your browser to display it. You can use one of several approaches to display your Web page. The easiest if you are working as a programmer is to use the Command Prompt window. To use the Command Prompt window, type the following line:

```
helloweb.html
```

Alternatively, in Windows Explorer, you can click on the name of the file. Your browser opens in response. If you are using Internet Explorer, you are likely to see a yellow bar at the top. Right-click the bar and select Allow Blocked Content. Then click Yes in the dialog box. You then see your applet, which you saw at the beginning of the chapter. For convenience, Figure 1.14 provides a second view of the applet.

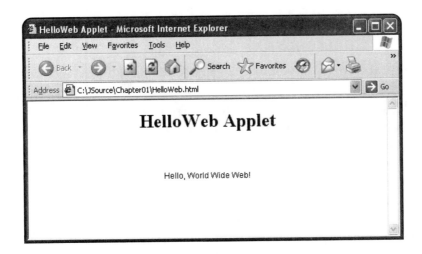

FIGURE 1.14

The browser
displays your
applet.

SUMMARY

You accomplished a lot in this chapter. You learned that Java is a platform-independent, object-oriented programming language that you can use to write applications and applets. You installed the Software Development Kit and set it up, giving your system the capability to compile and run Java programs. You wrote your first application, learned how to use the `javac` command to compile it and the `java` command to run it. After you successfully ran the HelloWorld application, you looked back and examined your code. You learned the basics of Java syntax. You also wrote your first applet and learned the basic differences between applications and applets. You learned how to include an applet within an HTML document. Finally, you learned how to run an applet by using the Applet Viewer utility and also how to run it in your browser. You are ready to take on some new challenges. In the next chapter you learn about variables, data types, mathematical operations, and how to accept simple user input.

CHALLENGES

1. Write a Java application that prints your first name to standard output.

2. Rewrite your Java application from challenge #1 to print your last name to standard output without deleting any lines by commenting out the line you don't need and adding the one that you do.

3. Write a Java application that prints two separate lines to standard output by repeating the `System.out.println()` statement using a different sentence.

4. Write an applet that displays your name and run it with both the Applet Viewer utility and with your browser.

VARIABLES, DATA TYPES, AND SIMPLE IO

I n this chapter, you learn how to use variables, data types, and standard input/output (IO) to create interactive applications. You start by learning what variables are and what you use them for. Then you learn about primitive data types and how you can employ them to define variables. After you understand variables, you learn how to work with numbers and mathematical operators. Following your work with numbers, you learn about the String data type. Using the String data type, among other things, you can write programs that accept user input. To cap things off, you put all this knowledge together to build an application that generates standard output, accepts user input, and processes strings and numbers. Topics in this chapter include the following:

- Creating a Name Game application
- Declaring and naming variables
- Using special characters
- Creating a Math Game application
- Creating a String Game application
- Accepting command-line arguments

THE NAME GAME APPLICATION

The skills you acquire in this chapter allow you to create an interactive application. Among other things, an interactive application allows you to process information that you type at the keyboard. This information is called *input*. The application processes this information and generates *output*, which in this instance you see displayed on your monitor. The two forms of interaction together are often called *IO* (for input/output). A class called NameGame supports the activity of your IO application, so it is appropriate to call the application Name Game. Figure 2.1 illustrates the session involving the Name Game application.

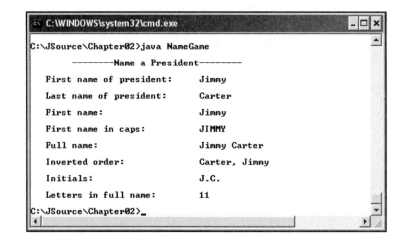

The Name Game application prompts you for your first and last names. It then changes the information you provide and generates output that shows the changes. To help you input information and see the results of the changes, it provides what is known as a *user interface*. A user interface is the part of an application that communicates with the users of the application. This portion of your application differs from what is known as the *core processing module*. The user interface takes care of IO; the core processing module takes care of changing the data. Together, these two activities characterize almost every Java application.

VARIABLES AND DATA TYPES

To work toward creating the Name Game application, a first step involves learning about *variables* and *data types*. A variable is a container that stores a specific form of data. Picture a variable as a box. Picture data as what you put in the box. You can put different things, of different sizes, in the box. When you work with a computer program, the situation is analogous, but there is a difference. When you work with a computer program, you must designate a specific size of box for every item of data you want to store. To accomplish this, you use a data type. A data type defines the size of the data a variable can store. Specific types of data include integers, floating-point numbers, and bytes, among others.

To designate the data type, you employ one of a select group of keywords to define the type of the identifier. The identifier is the word you use to name a given variable. After you assign a data type to an identifier, you create what programmers generally recognize as a variable. The activity of assigning the data type to an identifier is known as *declaring a variable*. Here are three declarations of variables:

```
int firstNumber;        //declarations of variables
float secondNumber;
byte thirdNumber;
```

The Java keywords `int`, `float`, and `byte` identify data types, and the three statements declare variables of the `int`, `float`, and `byte` types. The three expressions (`firstNumber`, `secondNumber`, and `thirdNumber`) constitute identifiers, but then after you associate them with data types, they become variables.

Having declared a set of variables, you can then *define* them. When you define a variable, you assign a value to it. Here are three statements that assign values to the three variables:

```
firstNumber = 1984;        //assignments of values to variables
secondNumber = 98.6;
thirdNumber = 8;
```

After you assign a value to a variable, you are free to change the value. For example, you can change the value you assign to `secondNumber` from `98.6` to `102.4`. To change the value in this way, you just assign the new number:

```
secondNumber = 102.4;        //change the value of the variables
```

On the other hand, you cannot change the data type you assign to a variable after you have declared the variable. The variable `secondNumber` remains defined by the `float` type for the life of your program.

Primitive Data Types

You must use a data type to define every variable you create when you program with Java. For this reason, Java is known as a *strictly typed* programming language. All variables have data types.

Java offers two forms of data types. One, which you see in the previous section, is known as *primitive data types*. Such data types are part of the core compiler definition of data that Java provides. Here are a few of the primitive data types, some of which you have seen before:

```
int, float, byte, bool, double, long, char
```

Primitive data types allow you to create another general data type. This other general form of data is known as a *reference data type*. This data type is also known as an abstract data type. You often use primitive data types to build reference data types, and the Java class hierarchy provides you with hundreds of ready-made reference data types. Here are a few of the reference data types:

```
Object, JApplet, Integer, Float, Byte, Double, Long, String
```

To master Java, you must master both types of data. Variables you declare using primitive data types store data of the type you use to define your variable. In other words, as you saw in the previous section, secondNumber stores the value 98.6. Reference data types prove more complex. They do not actually hold a value. Instead, they store information about the place in the memory of your computer at which a value can be found. The place in memory is known as an *address* or *reference*. This is where the name reference originates. Reference data types receive extended discussion later on. Table 2.1 provides information on the primitive data types in Java.

TABLE 2.I PRIMITIVE DATA TYPES		
Keyword	**Discussion**	**Size in Bits**
byte	small integer	8
short	short integer	16
int	integer	32
long	long integer	64
char	character	16
float	floating point	32
double	double floating point	64
boolean	Boolean (true or false)	1

Four of the data types Table 2.1 lists (byte, short, int, and long) are integers. An integer is a number that does not have a decimal point. You can assign positive or negative values to an integer. You can also assign zero (0) to an integer. A byte integer accommodates numbers in the range of roughly –128 to 127. You can use this data type to keep memory use at a minimum. The short integer type is larger than the byte and can accommodate a number approximately half as large as a regular int value. A variable of the long type, like a variable of the double type, can accommodate extremely large numbers. The only stipulation is that such numbers cannot contain decimal values.

The two data types that allow you to work with real numbers (numbers with decimal points) are known as floating-point types. These are the `float` and `double` data types. The `float` type is comparable in size to the `int` type. The `double` data type handles very large numbers. It is like the `long` data type in this respect.

A third form of primitive data is of the `char` type. This type of data allows you to deal with letters of the alphabet and a fairly large set of other symbols. A code, known as Unicode, establishes a unique numerical value for each letter or symbol. To use a variable of the `char` type, you assign a letter to it. You enclose the letter in single quotation marks to indicate that it is a character (for example, `'a'`, `'1'`, `'b'`, `'$'`).

The last type of data Table 2.1 lists, `boolean`, relates to true and false (Boolean) values. Java provides two keywords associated with this data type, `true` and `false`. The `true` keyword has a numerical value of 1. The `false` keyword has a numerical value of 0. You use the keywords in a literal way. Here's an example:

```
boolean testValue;
testValue = true;
```

Table 2.1 provides information relating to the size of the primitive data types. Generally, a bit is a 0 or a 1 in your computer's memory. Eight bits makes a byte. An integer in this scheme of things, then, can store a number that is four bytes long. What this means in specific values is that a variable of the `int` type can consist of roughly 15 digits. To store precise scientific calculations, you use a `double`. A `double` can store a very large number.

Understanding Literals

In the definitions shown previously, you assigned literal values to variables. Here are a few more examples:

```
dayOfMonth = 31;
firstLetter = 'c';
dogName = "Fido";
```

Identifiers allow you to create variables. You can assign literal values to these. Literal values are fixed values, the opposite of variables. If you type 31 to an identifier, Java interprets the number to mean the integer value 31. If you assign `'c'` to an identifier, Java determines the letter to be the character value c. Neither the number nor the letter stands for anything other than itself. Likewise, if you type the string `"Fido"`, the Java interpreter reads the words enclosed in the double quotations as Fido.

Even if the Java interpreter reads literal values literally, it remains that when it reads them, it identifies them according to specific data types. When you type 27, for example, the interpreter automatically interprets the number as a value of the type int. When you type 1.27, the interpreter automatically interprets the number as a value of the type double. Table 2.2 illustrates literal values and how the Java interpreter reads them. Note that the words true and false are read as Boolean values.

TABLE 2.2   HOW JAVA READS LITERALS

Literal	Discussion
27	int
0×2b	hexadecimal
27L	long
27.0	double
27.0e3	double (27.0 × 10 ^3)
27.0F	float
'b'	char
true	boolean
false	boolean First line

As Table 2.2 shows, Java by default considers literals such as 27 to be of the int type. If you want to designate that the interpreter should recognize a given integer as belonging to the long data type, you can append an uppercase L to the number. In this respect, then, you type 27L to designate that you want 27 to be recognized as a long data type.

> You can also use a lowercase l to designate numbers as long data values, but this practice leads to problems. For example, it proves difficult to tell 1.27l (an L is appended) from 271 (the number two-hundred and seventy-one).

Casting and Type Promotion

When you cast one type of data to another, you change the type of the data on a temporary basis. Here is an example of casting involving a value of an int type that you cast to a float type:

```
//declare two variables, one int and one float
int dayOfMonth;
```

```
float numOfDays;
//assign an integer value to the int
dayOfMonth = 31;
//cast the int value as a float value
numOfDays = (float) dayOfMonth;
```

When you complete this activity, if you print the value of dayOfMonth, you see 31.00, not 31. You have cast the value of an int (31) to a float (31.00). When you cast one data type to another, you temporarily convert the data so that you can use it in a specialized context. In the example involving days of the month, the casting operation involves an expression that consists of the data type keyword within opening and closing parentheses. You place this expression immediately before the value you want to cast:

```
(float) dayOfMonth
```

You can cast one type to another as long as you do so in a way that *promotes* the data type. Data type promotion involves making it so that when you cast the value, you cast it to a data type that is either the same size or larger. In Table 2.1 you see the sizes of the data types in bytes. Given the sizes, you can promote data of the int type to data of the float type or data of the float type to the double or long type. You cannot, however cast data of the long type to the byte type. In other words, you cannot make a large data type fit in a box designed for small data types.

When you cast a given value, you do not change the data type of the value. In other words, in the previous example, casting dayOfMonth does not permanently change its type from int to float.

As a final note, you can also cast literals. To cast a literal, you treat the literal in the same way that you treat a variable. Here's an example:

```
//cast a literal int as a float
numOfDays = (float) 31;
```

Strings and Character Escape Codes

Literals can be strings or characters. A string is a sequence of characters. To indicate that you want to create a string of characters, you enclose a series of characters in double quotation marks. Here is an example:

```
System.out.println("Hello World");
```

The expression "Hello World" is a string. You use it as a literal argument to the `println()` method. If you include this in an applet or application, as you know from Chapter 1, you see the following output:

```
Hello World
```

When you submit the literal string to the `println()` method, you employ double quotation marks to enclose the characters you want to include in the string. Suppose you want to include quotes as part of the string. Consider this line:

```
System.out.println("He said, ""Hello World" is an application."");
```

Use of the double quotations within the double quotations creates problems because the Java interpreter cannot read what amounts to a string within a string.

Such a problem creates the need to be able to indicate to the compiler that you want the compiler to process a character in a special way. You want it to process the character, not as a part of the syntax of the programming language, but as the character itself. To accomplish this task, you employ what is known as an *escape sequence*. An escape sequence consists of a backslash (\) immediately preceding the character you want to identify in a special way. Here's how to tell the compiler that you want it to process a given character (quotation marks) literally:

```
System.out.println("He said,\" \" Hello World \" is an application.\" ");
```

Each time you want the compiler to process the quotation marks as quotation marks, you precede the quotation marks with a backslash. There are four instances of this. Now the compiler knows that it is to read the quotation marks surrounding `Hello World` in a non-symbolic (or literal) way. It is escaping the normal use of the programming language. The output you see is as follows:

```
He said, " " Hello World " is an application."
```

Among other escape sequences you frequently use are the single quote (\'), the tab (\t), and the newline (\n). The newline escape sequence forces your string to start on a new line. Consider the following statement:

```
System.out.println("The projects were: \n Hello World \n Hello Web");
```

If you run a program with this statement, the output is as follows:

```
The projects were:
Hello World
Hello Web
```

Table 2.3 provides a partial list of the escape sequences available to you in Java.

TABLE 2.3 COMMON ESCAPE SEQUENCES	
Escape Sequence	**Discussion**
\n	The newline character forces the line on the screen to the next line.
\t	The tab character invokes a tab.
\r	The carriage return forces the line on the screen to a new line. (It's the same as \n.)
\\	If you want to show a slash (\), you can precede the slash with a slash.
*	To show an asterisk, you precede the asterisk with a slash.
\'	This shows a single quote.
\"	This shows a double quote.

Naming Variables

When you create identifiers (names) in Java, you must follow a few rules. For starters, when you create identifiers, you should, as a standard practice, use names that consist wholly of alphabetical characters. Here are some examples:

```
int newDay;      // okay to use
int oldDay;
int someDay;
```

Standard alphabetical characters are the letters of the alphabet (a through z or A through Z). That said, it is the case that you can use two other characters in the names of identifiers. These are the underscore (_) and the dollar sign ($). Here are a few examples of identifiers that use these characters:

```
int $oldDays;    //okay to use
int old_Days;    //okay to use
```

You can use numbers in the name of identifiers, but you may not begin identifiers with numbers. Here are some examples of identifier names that are okay to use:

```
int newDay2;     //okay to use
int new2Day;     //okay to use
```

On the other hand, you may not begin the name of an identifier with a number. Here are a few examples of improperly named identifiers:

```
int 1newDay       //not okay
int 5newDays      //not okay
```

When you begin the names of variables with numbers, the compiler assumes you are creating a number literal. For this reason, it tries to read 1newDay as a set of seven numbers.

Again, when you create identifiers, you cannot use most of the non-alphabetical, non-numeric characters you commonly encounter when you type at a keyboard. The reason for this is that these characters are reserved for other uses. Here are some of the most common characters:

```
# % & ' ( ) * + , - . / : ; < = > ? @ [ \ ] ^ ` { | } ~
```

Inclusion of these characters in an identifier generates a compiler error. Here are a few examples of improper identifiers:

```
int new#\Day      //not okay
int #new{}Day     //not okay
int new Day       //not okay
int newDay+=      //not okay
```

Likewise, as the third example shows, note that you may not include spaces in the names of identifiers.

Conventions

A *coding convention* differs from a syntax rule. A coding convention is a standard programmers adopt for formatting their code. Java programmers typically start the names of variable identifiers with a lowercase letter, as you've seen in the examples shown so far. For variables, a good practice is to combine two or more words. You leave the first letter in lowercase. You capitalize the first letter of each subsequent word. Here are a few more examples:

```
int numOfHits;
int levelOfPower;
```

As these examples emphasize, create variable names *mnemonically*. In other words, allow them to convey information about the data they store. Avoid using single letters, cryptic expressions, or odd case combinations. Here are some examples:

```
int a;
int aAaAaAaAa;
int myFaVoItThinG;
```

Java is a case-sensitive programming language. When you create identifier names, you must precisely designate a variable name each time you use it. To ensure that your job in this respect is easier, establish conventions that make it easy for you to type any given identifier repeatedly.

Assignment and Initialization

As mentioned previously, when you assign a value to an identifier, you define it. A general term for this activity is *initialization*. When you declare a variable, you associate a data type with an identifier. When you define or initialize a variable, you assign a value to it. Here is a set of declarations you see in VariableDemo.java:

```
int dayOfMonth;        // declaration
float numOfDays;       // declaration
dayOfMonth = 27;       // definition or initialization
numOfDays = 31.0F;     // definition or initialization
```

You declare two variables, dayOfMonth and numOfDays. One is of the int type. The other is of the float type. You then initialize the variable dayOfMonth using the value 27. You also initialize the variable numOfDays using the value 31.0F. In each case, to initialize the variable, you *assign* a value to it. To effect the assignment, you use the *assignment operator* (=). The VariableDemo.java program provides you with a number of examples of the initialization and use of variables.

After you assign a value to a variable, you are then in a position to retrieve the value for any number of purposes. In VariableDemo.java, your primary use of variable values involves printing. Consider the following:

```
System.out.println("The day of the month (int): \t " + dayOfMonth);
```

This statement uses the println() method in a way you have not yet seen. The plus sign (+) is called a *concatenation operator*. It makes it so that the expression "The day of the month (int): \t" is joined with the value stored in dayOfMonth. The plus sign does not add the two expressions. Rather, it joins them into a single string that is output to your terminal.

As Figure 2.2 shows, this line in the VariableDemo.java program outputs the following line to your monitor:

```
The day of month (int): 27
```

The effect of the concatenation operator is that the value you have assigned to dayOfMonth is retrieved and displayed. Rather than the name of the variable, you see the value stored in it. As Figure 2.2 shows, if you were to place the variable inside the quotation marks, then it would be treated as part of the string. Here's what you see:

```
The number of days is: dayOfMonth
```

VariableDemo.java also provides a few variations on the basic initialization routine. Consider the following lines:

```
//declaration and initialization
double doubleValue = 1500.00;
 char charValue = '?';
 boolean happyBool = true,
         sadBool = false;
```

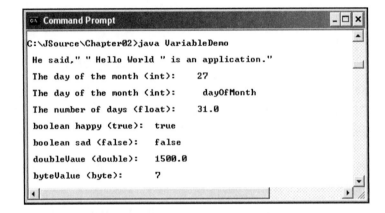

FIGURE 2.2

After declaring and initializing variables, you use the println() method to show their values.

In this instance, you both declare and initialize the variables. There are a couple of variations on this theme. In one case, you declare the variable and then assign a value to it. In another case, you create a comma-delimited list of variables that you also initialize. Although VariableDemo.java keeps things simple and so does not show any elaborations, you might see the following type of declaration on a fairly common basis:

```
int firstInt,
    secondInt,
    thirdInt;
```

Alternatively, the same approach can be used to declare the variables, in which case you see the variables laid out in much the same way that the Boolean values are laid out in the previous example:

```
int firstInt = 1,
    secondInt = 2,
    thirdInt = 3;
```

You can also use a comma-delimited list that includes both declarations and initializations—multiple variables on a single line:

```
int firstInt,           // not initialized
    secondInt = 2,      //initialized
    thirdInt = 3;
```

Here is the source code for VariableDemo.java. As with previous programs, you can find it on the companion website. To make the best use of it, however, it is best to type it for yourself.

```
/*
    VariableDemo.java
*/

public class VariableDemo {
    public static void main(String args[]) {
        // declarations
        byte byteValue;
        int dayOfMonth;
        float numOfDays;
        //initializations
        byteValue = 7;
        dayOfMonth = 27;
        numOfDays = 31.0F;

        //declaration and initialization
        double doubleValue = 1500.00;
            char charValue = '?';
            boolean happyBool = true,
                    sadBool = false;

        //Use of escape characters
        //Print a literal string with escape characters
        System.out.println(
                "\n He said,\" \" Hello World \" is an application.\" "
                    );
        //Print the values of the variables
        System.out.println("\n The day of the month (int):\t" + dayOfMonth);
        System.out.println("\n The day of the month (int):\t dayOfMonth");
        System.out.println("\n The number of days (float):\t" + numOfDays);
```

```
        System.out.println("\n boolean happy (true):\t" + happyBool );
        System.out.println("\n boolean sad (false):\t" + sadBool );
        System.out.println("\n doubleValue (double):\t" + doubleValue );
        System.out.println("\n byteValue (byte):\t" + byteValue);
    }//end main
}//end VariableDemo
```

To develop the VariableDemo.java program, you define the `VariableDemo` class. As mentioned in Chapter 1, a class is a data type that you define. This class consists of one method, `main()`. In the `main()` method, you include two main sections. In the upper part, you declare and initialize variables of the types discussed previously in this chapter. In the lower part, you make a series of calls to the `println()` method. For almost all uses of the `println()` method, you use the concatenation operator to join a variable with a literal string.

When you call the `println()` method, you make use of the \t escape sequences to line up some of the output, as Figure 2.2 shows. You also use the \" escape sequence to make it so that you can see quotations as a part of the string you print to the monitor. Likewise, to increase the distance between the lines, you use the newline (\n) escape sequence. Figure 2.2 shows the output of VariableDemo.java.

ABOUT PERIODS

A period can also be called a *dot operator*. As you have seen in previous programs, the dot operator serves to associate the names of classes, such as the `JApplet` class, with the names of packages. Packages are analogous to directories.

Dot operators also tell you when a method is part of a class. For example, when you use the `println()` method, you use dot operators to establish the identity of the class to which the `println()` method belongs. The form is as follows:

```
    System.out.println()
```

You used the same approach to accessing the `Graphics drawString()` method. In that case, you used an argument from the `paint()` method called g to call the `drawString()` method. Here's a review of the code:

```
    public void paint(Graphics g) {
        g.drawString("Hello, World Wide Web!", 10, 50);
    }//end paint
```

When you call the `drawString()` method, you do so using the dot operator and an identifier of a given class type (g is of the class type `Graphics`) with a method that the class contains (`Graphics` contains the `drawString()` method). This is standard procedure in Java. In subsequent chapters, the mechanics of such routines receive further elaboration. For now, it is important to notice only that when you put the dot operator to work in your code, you are associating a given class with a method that the class contains.

WORKING WITH NUMBERS

In this section, you learn how to use mathematical operations on numerical variables. As part of your work with numbers, you review the operators that apply to them. You also explore a Java class called `DecimalFormat` that lets you set the decimal precision of the numbers you use.

Operators and Operands

A variable is an *operand*. In other words, it is something you operate on. To operate on a variable, as you saw in part with the use of the plus sign for string concatenation, you use *operators*. When you learn arithmetic operators, you become acquainted with operators for addition, subtraction, multiplication, and division. The math operators you use in Java resemble these. There are some differences, however. Table 2.4 shows you some of the standard math operators that Java provides.

TABLE 2.4 COMMON MATH OPERATORS

Operator	Name	Variable	Literal Use
+	Addition	varA + varB	5 + 2
-	Subtraction	varA – varB	5 - 2
*	Multiplication	varA * varB	5 * 2
/	Division	varA / varB	5 / 2
%	Modulus	varA % varB	5 % 2

As Table 2.4 shows, for multiplication operations, you use an asterisk. You use a forward slash for division. You also make use of what is known as the *modulus* operator (%). The modulus operator allows you to divide one number by another and extract only the remainder. Here are some examples of the use of the modulus operator:

```
4 % 2 // The remainder is 0
5 % 2 // The remainder is 1
5 % 3 // The remainder is 2
10 % 1 // The remainder is 0
10 % 5 // The remainder is 0
```

How to Do Math

When you perform math operations with Java, you do not follow the same flow of activity you follow when you perform math manually. For instance, consider these basic math operations:

```
2 + 2 = 4
8 * 2 = 16
```

When you write a program in Java, you want the computer to perform the math operation. For this reason, you usually declare a variable to handle the result of the math operation. To perform the operation, you assign the result to the variables using an assignment operator. Here is an example of how to set up the addition and division operations just presented:

```
float sumOfNums;
float productOfNums;
sumOfNums = 2 + 2;
productOfNums = 8 * 2;
```

The flow of activity is from the right to the left. The logic remains the same, but the associativity of the assignment operator (the equals sign) dictates that you begin at the right and then move to the left. Also, use of literal values tends to be infrequent. Rather than literal values, you are likely to define variables and then use them in your math expression along the following lines:

```
float sumOfNums,
      firstNum = 2,
      secondNum =2;
      sumOfNums = firstNum + secondNum;
```

The TipAdder Program

The TipAdder.java program allows you to experiment with some basic math operations. You declare variables for the price of a meal and a tip percentage. You then calculate how much the tip should be if you set the tip to be 17 percent of the price of the meal. You also extend your work with the `println()` method to display the results of the calculations you perform.

```
/*
    TipAdder.java
*/

public class TipAdder {

    public static void main(String args[]) {
        // #1 Declare variable identifiers
        float mealPrice,
            percentToTip,
            tipAmount,
            totalMealPrice;
        //Assign values
            mealPrice = 33.50F;
            percentToTip = 0.17F;

        // #2 Get the amount of the tip
        tipAmount = mealPrice * percentToTip;

        //Add tip to the price of the meal
        totalMealPrice = tipAmount + mealPrice;

        //#3 Display results
        System.out.println("\n  ------  $$$ Tip Adder $$$  --------");

        System.out.println("\n Cost of Meal: \t $" + mealPrice);
        System.out.println("\n " + percentToTip
                            + "% tip is: \t $" + tipAmount);

        System.out.println("\n -------------------------------------");
        System.out.println("\n The total bill: \t $" + totalMealPrice);
    }
}
```

The TipAdder.java program performs a few math operations using floating-point numbers. The main body of the program is in the main() method. At comment #1, you begin by declaring a number of variables of the float type. You then initialize the variables that store information on the percent of the tip (percentToTip) and the price of the meal (mealPrice). In both cases, you append an F to the values you assign to the variables to ensure that the compiler reads them as `float` values.

Having set up your basic data in the lines following comment #2 to determine the amount of the tip, you multiply the price of the meal by the percentage designated for the tip. You assign the result of this calculation to the `float` variable `tipAmount`. Given that you have obtained the amount of the tip, you can then add this to the price of the meal to determine the total price of the meal, which you assign to the `float` variable `totalMealPrice`.

In the lines associated with comment #3, as Figure 2.3 illustrates, you use the `println()` method to display the price of the meal alone, the amount of the tip, and the full price of the meal with the tip. As part of this set of operations, you use the concatenation operator and escape characters to apply formatting to the display of your data. When you use a few character graphics, such as horizontal lines, you render the data more readable than it would be otherwise.

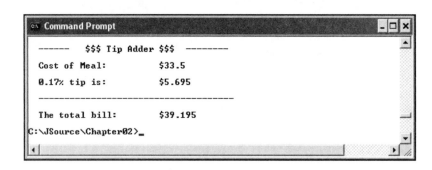

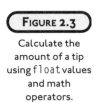

FIGURE 2.3

Calculate the amount of a tip using `float` values and math operators.

As Figure 2.3 illustrates, when you make use of numerical values, you cannot immediately control the precision of the decimal points. In this case, the amount of the tip and the total price of the meal run into three digit places. To solve this problem, you must find a way to assert the precision of the decimal values you display. The next section reviews how you can accomplish this task.

Formatting Decimal Precision

To format the precision of your data, you use a Java class called `DecimalFormat`. To use the `DecimalFormat` class, you follow the same approach you followed when you accessed the `JApplet` class in Chapter 1. You first employ an `import` statement at the top of your file to access the `DecimalFormat` class. The `import` statement is as follows:

```
import java.text.DecimalFormat;
```

Next, you declare and initialize an instance of the DecimalFormat class. As you see in the TipAdderFormatted.java program, you accomplish this using the following line:

```
DecimalFormat twoDigits = new DecimalFormat("0.00");
```

As is discussed later on, this statement involves a method called a *constructor* to initialize the identifier (twoDigits) of the DecimalFormat data type.

Given that you have declared and initialized an instance of the DecimalFormat class, then just as you did when you worked with the applet program in Chapter 1, you can call methods from the class. In this case, you call the format() method, which formats your numbers so that they have a specific decimal precision. Here's the code from the TipAdder.java program revised as TipAdderFormatted.java. Comments indicate where you add lines to make the formatting possible.

```
/*
    TipAdderFormatted.java
*/
//#1 Access the package for the formatter
import java.text.DecimalFormat;

public class TipAdderFormatted {

    public static void main(String args[]) {
        float mealPrice,
            percentToTip,
            tipAmount,
            totalMealPrice;

        mealPrice = 33.50F;
        percentToTip = 0.17F;

        //#2 declare and initialize a formatter
        //This is for precision of two decimal places
        DecimalFormat twoDigits = new DecimalFormat("0.00");
        //Get the amount of the tip
        tipAmount = mealPrice * percentToTip;
        //Add tip to the price of the meal
        totalMealPrice = tipAmount + mealPrice;
```

```
System.out.println("\n ------ $$$ Tip Adder $$$ --------");
System.out.println("\n Cost of Meal: \t $" + mealPrice);

//#3 Call the method for formatting
System.out.println("\n " + percentToTip
                    + "% tip is: \t $"
                    + twoDigits.format(tipAmount));
System.out.println("\n -----------------------------------");
System.out.println("\n The total bill: \t $"
                    + twoDigits.format(totalMealPrice));
    }
}
```

To develop the TipAdderFormatted.java program, your actions involve only a few changes. Your goal is to make it so you can designate the decimal precision of the numbers you display. At comment #2, you use a constructor to define a *formatter*. A formatter is a variable or instance of the DecimalFormat class. To create the formatter, you supply a mask to the DecimalFormat constructor. The mask consists of zeros and a decimal point that show how many decimal places you want to use. To create the mask, you supply the argument of 0.00 surrounded by double quotation marks:

```
DecimalFormat twoDigits = new DecimalFormat("0.00");
```

When you employ two zeros following the decimal point, you define a mask for standard currency. To designate three decimal places, you use the following expression:

```
DecimalFormat twoDigits = new DecimalFormat("0.000");
```

Figure 2.4 illustrates the result of the formatting. The values you display now have only two decimal places. To apply the formatting to your data, you call the format() method.

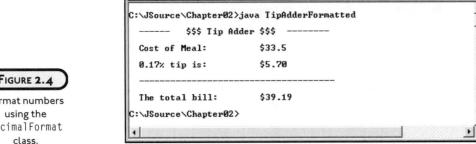

FIGURE 2.4

Format numbers using the DecimalFormat class.

```
twoDigits.format(tipAmount)
```

As with the `drawString()` method of the `Graphics` class in your HelloWeb.java program, you use the instance of the class (in this case `twoDigits`) to call the `format()` method of the `DecimalFormat` class. The `format()` method takes one argument—the number you want to format.

Later in this chapter, you undertake steps similar to those you used with the `DecimalFormat` class with the `BufferedReader` class. The Java class hierarchy provides a multitude of classes that are set up to make it easy for you to accomplish common programming tasks. Later chapters investigate the hierarchy in much greater detail.

Operator Precedence

Operator precedence determines the order in which operations are applied to numbers. In general, multiplication (*), division (/), and modulus (%) have precedence over addition (+) and subtraction (-). This means that multiplication, division, and modulus operations are evaluated before addition and subtraction. When operator precedence is the same, operations occur from left to right. Take the following line of code for example:

```
int x = 10 - 4 + 14 / 2;
```

When the compiler evaluates this expression, the first operation it attends to is the division. The result of the division of 14 / 2 is 7. The second operation it attends to is the subtraction of 4 from 10, leaving 6. It then adds 6 and 7, resulting in 13, which is then assigned to x. Here is the process that unfolds:

```
int x = 10 - 4 + 14 / 2
int x = 10 - 4 + 7
int x = 6 + 7
int x = 13
```

You can alter the order in which the compiler evaluates operations if you use parentheses. Generally, parentheses take precedence over almost all other operations. Consider what happens if you create the following expression:

```
int y = (10 - 4 + 14) / 2;
```

In this case, the first operation to be performed is the subtraction of 4 from 10, which results in 6. The compiler then adds 6 and 14, resulting in 20. With this, the operations in the parentheses end, and the compiler proceeds to divide 20 by 2, resulting in 10. Here's how the process unfolds:

```
int x = (10 - 4 + 14) / 2
int x = (6 + 14) / 2
int x = (20) / 2
int x = 10
```

The ParenMath.java program allows you to experiment with operator precedence and how parentheses affect arithmetic operations:

```java
/*

    ParenMath.java

*/


public class ParenMath {
    public static void main(String args[]) {

        System.out.println("\n Using parentheses in different ways");

        int mathResult = 10 - 4 + 14 / 2;
        System.out.println("\n A. 10 - 4 + 14 / 2 \t = \t" + mathResult);


        mathResult = (10 - 4) + 14 / 2;
        System.out.println("\n B. (10 - 4) + 14 / 2 \t = \t" + mathResult);


        //The addition occurs first because of the parentheses
        //Next the division and then the subtraction.
        mathResult = 10 - (4 + 14) / 2;
        System.out.println("\n C. 10 - (4 + 14) / 2 \t = \t" + mathResult);


        mathResult = 10 - (4 + 14 / 2);
        System.out.println("\n D. 10 - (4 + 14 / 2) \t = \t" + mathResult);


        mathResult = (10 - 4 + 14) / 2;
        System.out.println("\n E. (10 - 4 + 14) / 2 \t = \t" + mathResult);
    }
}
```

Figure 2.5 illustrates the output of the ParenMath.java program. For each of the math equations set up in ParenMath.java, you use the mathResult variable, which is of the float type. When you assign a value to the variable, the value you assign overwrites the previously assigned value. For math expression for item A, you allow the default order of operations to unfold, and this results in 13, as previously discussed. For item B, the result is also 13. In the math expression for item B, when you use the parentheses to group 10 - 4, you do not alter the regular flow of operations.

For item C, the parentheses cause 4 to be added to 14, resulting in 18. Then 18 is divided by 2, resulting in 9. The last operation to be performed is the subtraction of 9 from 10, resulting in 1. For item D, the first operation performed is the division of 14 by 2, which results in 7. Then 7 is added to 4, resulting in 11. The last operation involves the subtraction of 11 from 10, resulting in -1. As discussed previously, for item E, the first operation performed results in 6, which is added to 14. Then the division takes place.

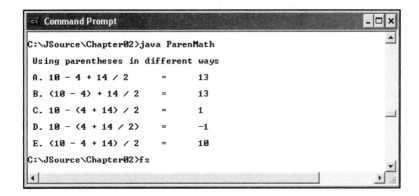

FIGURE 2.5

Parentheses affect the outcome of your math operations.

GETTING USER INPUT

Thus far, the programs you have written do not accept user input. Such programs can be useful in many situations, especially if you are in a position, as a programmer, to alter the code in the programs. If you cannot alter the code, however, you must supply your programs with data through a user interface. Command-line interaction is the oldest and most basic form of user interface. With this form of interaction, when you run your program, a message at the terminal prompts you for data. You type the data you want to supply. The program processes the data you enter and usually displays the results.

A key to accepting input is what is known as a *buffer*. A buffer is a space in the memory of your computer in which you temporarily store data. Your program requires a buffer if it is to accept information you supply from the keyboard. It allocates a buffer when it executes. Java provides a class called BufferedReader that allows you to incorporate this activity into your program. The HelloUser.java program reworks the TipAdderFormatted.java program. The rework allows you to supply the price of a meal and the percentage you want to tip. The sections following the program provide discussion of its features.

```java
/*
    HelloUser.java
*/
    //#1
import java.io.*;
import java.text.DecimalFormat;

public class HelloUser{
    public static void main(String args[]) {
    float    mealPrice = 0,
             percentToTip = 0,
             tipAmount = 0,
             totalMealPrice = 0;
    //String data type
    String value;
    //#2
    //Declaration of a buffer
    BufferedReader reader;
    //Create an instance of the buffer
    reader = new BufferedReader(new InputStreamReader(System.in));
    //Format the data
    DecimalFormat twoDigits = new DecimalFormat("0.00");
    //Prompt for input
    //#3
    //A try block
        try {
    //#4
            System.out.print("\n Price of the meal: ");
            value= reader.readLine();
            //convert the input to a float
            mealPrice = Float.parseFloat(value);

            System.out.print("\n Percent of type (17% suggested): ");
            value= reader.readLine();
```

```
        //convert the input to a float
        percentToTip = Float.parseFloat(value);
    }
    catch (IOException ioe) {
        System.out.println("I O Exception Occurred");
    }


//#5
    tipAmount = mealPrice * percentToTip;
    totalMealPrice = tipAmount + mealPrice;

    //output the information entered
    System.out.println("\n ------ $$$ Tip Adder $$$ --------");
    System.out.println("\n Cost of Meal: \t $"
                                + twoDigits.format(mealPrice));
    //#3 Call the method for formatting
    System.out.println("\n " + 100 * percentToTip
                            + "% tip is: \t $"
                            + twoDigits.format(tipAmount));
    System.out.println("\n -------------------------------------");
    System.out.println("\n The total bill: \t $"
                                + twoDigits.format(totalMealPrice));
    }//end main
}// end HelloUser
```

The BufferedReader Class

Figure 2.7 illustrates the output of the HelloUser.java program. At comment #1, you use an import statement to allow you to access the Java io package, which contains the BufferedReader class. The use of the import statement involves the same syntax you have used with the JApplet class and the DecimalFormat class. The periods between the terms describe a package or directory path within the Java class hierarchy. When you use io.*, you designate everything in the io package.

At comment #2, you declare a BufferedReader identifier (reader). You also declare a variable of the String type (value). As mentioned before, a string is a series of characters. The String data type accommodates strings. You can assign the data you input to your application from the keyboard using a BufferedReader to a String variable.

After declaring the BufferedReader and String variables, you then use a complex form of constructor to create an instance of a BufferedReader. Here's the code:

```
BufferedReader reader;
reader = new BufferedReader(new InputStreamReader(System.in));
```

As an argument to the constructor for the BufferedReader, you use the constructor for the InputStreamReader class. A stream is analogous to a pipe of data to or from your program. When the stream is an input stream, it is coming to your program. In this case, it is coming from the keyboard. To indicate that it is an input stream, you use an attribute of a class called System. The System class takes care of operations that relate to the overall functioning of your computer. The name of the attribute is in. After this preliminary work, you initialize the reader identifier with the result.

At this point, it is worthwhile to mention the new keyword. The new keyword tells the compiler to create an instance of the class that immediately follows it. You use it only with reference data types. Subsequent chapters elaborate on the use of the new keyword.

To make use of the reader identifier to get input from the keyboard, in the lines trailing comment #3, you use a call to the readLine() method. This method halts the execution of the program until you type something and press the Enter key.

```
value = reader.readLine();
```

The readLine() returns a character string, and you can assign this the value variable, which is of the String type. At this point, you could output this value directly to the terminal using the println() method. You do not do this, however, because your program processes the information as a float value.

To convert the string into a number, you make calls to a method called parseFloat(). This method call converts the input you get form the keyboard into a float value. Here's the code:

```
//convert the input to a float
mealPrice = Float.parseFloat(value);
```

When you call the parseFloat() method, you make a call to a method in the Float class. The Float class is a Java class that corresponds to the primitive float data type. Your call to the parseFloat() method allows you to convert the String value you have received from the BufferedReader readLine() method into a value of the Float type. You assign the returned value of the method call to mealPrice. You use the same approach to retrieve the value for the percentToTip variable. See the section titled "Parsing Strings to Numbers" for a more detailed discussion.

> The print() and println() methods differ. The println() method appends a newline char-
> acter to its output. The print() method does not append a newline character. Use the print
> () method if you want to prompt the user for input and then see the cursor remain at the end
> of the prompt line. See Figure 2.7 for an example of this approach to prompting for input.

The try...catch Block

In the lines trailing comment #3, in the HelloUser.java program, you make use of a try block. A try block has opening and closing braces just like a method. Within the try block you call methods that can return (or *throw*) *exceptions*. The BufferedReader readLine() method is a method of this type. An exception is a special type of message that reports that something has gone wrong when you call the method with which the message is associated.

In the lines trailing comment #4, you follow the try block with a catch block. The flow of your program enters the catch block if your call to the readLine() method results in an exception. If no exception occurs, then the flow of the program skips the catch block. You define a catch block by providing it with an argument type in the parentheses following the catch keyword. In this instance, the argument type is IOException. You use this type of argument because it is the type of the value (or exception) that the readLine() method returns (or throws).

When you define the argument type of the catch block as IOException, you designate that this block processes exceptions of this type. As Figure 2.6 illustrates, if you set up a try block with methods that return several different types of exceptions, you can create several catch blocks in a row following the try block, each defined with a different exception type. In this way, if an exception of a particular type is thrown, the flow of the program enters only the catch block you have defined to process this type of exception. The flow of the program skips the other catch blocks. In this way, you can deal with each type of exception in a unique way.

Within the catch block, you write statements that tell the interpreter how to respond if problems occur. In this instance, the response is a message your program writes to the terminal: "I O Exception Occurred." Given normal execution of your program, you are unlikely to see the error message.

The lines trailing comment #5 are the same as those you have seen before. You calculate the amount of the tip based on the price of the meal and the percentage of the tip and then use calls to the println() method to display the results at the terminal. Figure 2.7 illustrates the results.

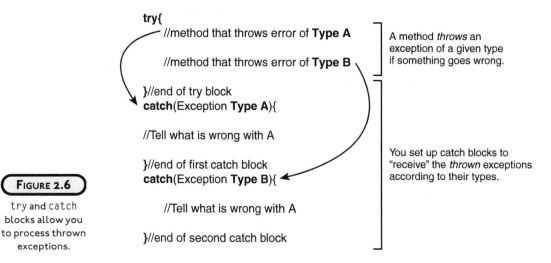

```
try{
    //method that throws error of Type A        A method throws an
                                                 exception of a given type
    //method that throws error of Type B         if something goes wrong.

}//end of try block
catch(Exception Type A){

    //Tell what is wrong with A
                                                 You set up catch blocks to
}//end of first catch block                      "receive" the thrown exceptions
catch(Exception Type B){                         according to their types.

    //Tell what is wrong with A

}//end of second catch block
```

FIGURE 2.6

try and catch blocks allow you to process thrown exceptions.

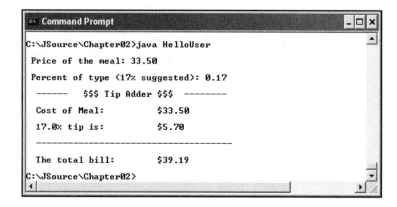

FIGURE 2.7

Interaction allows you to enter the price and the tip percentage.

PARSING STRINGS TO NUMBERS

The HelloUser.java program included static calls to the Float class that allow you to convert the string input you provide from the command line into a float value. Here is an example of one of the calls:

```
value = reader.readLine(); //Value is of the String type
//convert the input to a float
percentToTip = Float.parseFloat(value);
```

The call to the parseFloat() method allows you to convert a string of characters that represent a number into a number. To accomplish this, the method parses the characters in the string.

Parsing, like casting, involves changing the data type of the value of a variable or literal. The BufferedReader.readLine() method accepts the input in string form. If you attempt to assign the input you get from the readLine() method directly to the percentToTip variable, the compiler reports an error. To see how this is so, suppose that instead of the previous lines, you composed the following:

```
percentToTip = reader.readLine();     //creates error
```

You attempt here to assign a character string to the percentToTip variable. Since the compiler cannot assign the character string to the float variable, it issues the following error message:

```
HelloUser.java:44: incompatible types
found    : java.lang.String
required: float
          percentToTip = reader.readLine();
```

The report of incompatible types tells you that the compiler found a returned value of the String type and a variable of the float type. The message then shows you the problem line.

To avoid this problem, you make use of one of the classes in Java that provide you with the reference equivalent of the float data type. The Float class is one of several classes that are derived from the Number class in the Java class hierarchy. Here are the classes derived from the Number class:

```
Float    Byte    Short    Integer    Double    Long
```

All of the classes derived from the Number class offer a core set of methods. Table 2.5 lists some of the methods.

The methods in Table 2.5 are available for all the Number data types. In other words, if you call Float.toString() for a Float object, you can also call Integer.toString() for an Integer object. Table 2.4 might include the parseFloat() method, but to make it clearer that Java provides you with parsing methods for all the Number types, Table 2.6 lists the methods as they are associated with the different Number data types.

The NumberGame.java program provides you with a demonstration of the uses of the various parsing methods.

TABLE 2.5   REPRESENTATIVE FLOAT (NUMBER) METHODS

Method	Use
`floatValue()`	This method returns the `float` value of a `Float` object.
`intValue()`	This method allows you to convert a `Float` value to an `int` value by casting the value to type `int`.
`longValue()`	This method allows you convert a `Float` value to a `long` value by casting the value to type `long`.
`toString()`	This method converts a `Float` object to a `String` representation.
`valueOf(String)`	This method returns a `Float` object that stores the `float` value represented by the `String` argument.
`toString(float)`	This method returns a `String` representation of the `float` argument.
`equals(Object)`	This method allows you to compare one `Float` object with another.
`compareTo(Float)`	This method allows you to determine whether two `Float` objects are numerically equal.

TABLE 2.6   NUMBER DATA TYPES AND PARSING METHODS

Method	Use
`Byte.parseByte(String)`	Converts the characters in a `String` variable to a `byte` value.
`Short.parseShort(String)`	Converts the characters in a `String` variable to a `short` value.
`Integer.parseInt(String)`	Converts the characters in a `String` variable to an `int` value.
`Long.parseLong(String)`	Converts the characters in a `String` variable to a `long` value.
`Float.parseFloat(String)`	Converts the characters in a `String` variable to a `float` value.
`Double.parseDouble(String)`	Converts the characters in a `String` variable to a `double` value.

```
/*
    NumberGame.java
*/
import java.io.*;
public class NumberGame {
    public static void main(String args[]) {
        //Declaration of a buffer
        BufferedReader reader;
        //Create an instance of the buffer
```

```java
reader = new BufferedReader(new InputStreamReader(System.in));
String sourceString = "7";
double cumulativeNumber = 0;
try{
    System.out.print("\n Type a number: ");
    //accepted as a String
    sourceString = reader.readLine();
}
catch (IOException ioe) {
    System.out.println("I O Exception Occurred");
}
//Convert from a string primitive data type
//using the Number classes
System.out.println("\n ------ Cumulative Values --------");
cumulativeNumber += Byte.parseByte(sourceString);
System.out.println("\n Add " + sourceString
                            + "\t \t" + cumulativeNumber);
cumulativeNumber += Short.parseShort(sourceString);
System.out.println("\n Add " + sourceString
                            + "\t \t" + cumulativeNumber);
cumulativeNumber += Integer.parseInt(sourceString);
System.out.println("\n Add " + sourceString
                            + "\t \t" + cumulativeNumber);
cumulativeNumber += Long.parseLong(sourceString);
System.out.println("\n Add " + sourceString
                            + "\t \t" + cumulativeNumber);
cumulativeNumber += Float.parseFloat(sourceString);
System.out.println("\n Add " + sourceString
                            + "\t \t" + cumulativeNumber);
cumulativeNumber += Double.parseDouble(sourceString);
System.out.println("\n Add " + sourceString
                            + "\t \t" + cumulativeNumber);
    }
}
```

Figure 2.8 illustrates the output of the NumberGame.java program. At the top of this program, you declare a `BufferedReader` identifier (reader), a `String` identifier (sourceString), and a `float` variable (cumulativeNumber). You then prompt the user to enter a value at the keyboard and call the readLine() method to assign the value, as a character sting, to the sourceString variable.

Following the assignment of the character string to the sourceString variable, you proceed to make calls to the parsing methods for each of the Number data types to convert the string to primitive data types. When you convert the data to primitive data types, you can then use the addition assignment operator to accumulatively assign the converted values to the cumulativeNumber variable.

The addition assignment operator (+=) allows you to take the value stored in the variable to the left of the operator, add it to the value stored in the variable on the right, and then assign the sum back to the variable on the left. Consider the following expression:

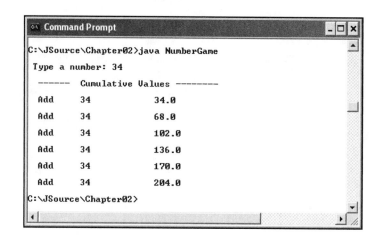

FIGURE 2.8

You can use the Number classes to parse a string so that it becomes a number.

```
cumulativeNumber += Double.parseDouble(sourceString);
```

You could also write this expression as follows:

```
cumulativeNumber = cumulativeNumber + Double.parseDouble(sourceString);
```

ACCEPTING COMMAND-LINE ARGUMENTS

A *command-line argument* is an argument that you pass to a program when you use the java command to execute it at the Command Prompt. The command-line argument immediately follows the name of your program. You can provide as many command-line arguments as you want. They must be separated by spaces. Here is an example of how you execute the HelloArg.java program using the java command:

```
java HelloArg Washington
```

The term Washington is passed to the args[] array of the main() method. You can then retrieve arguments from this array by using what is known as an index argument for the array. An index argument is simply an integer that you insert between the square brackets that follow the name of the array. Here is how you retrieve the first and second items in the args array:

```
args[0]
args[1]
```

Arrays receive more attention in Chapter 3. The HelloArg.java program allows you to experiment with the basics of command-line arguments.

```
/* HelloArg.java
     Uses command-line arguments
*/


public class HelloArg {
    public static void main(String args[]) {
        System.out.println("Argument from array: \t" + args[0] + " ");
    }
}
```

Figure 2.9 illustrates the execution and output of the HelloArgs.java program. Such programs have value in a number of contexts. One involves being able to channel the output of one program into another. Another is testing.

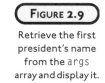

FIGURE 2.9

Retrieve the first president's name from the args array and display it.

Arguments are separated by spaces. HellolArg.java accepts only one argument, but many command-line programs involve multiple arguments. To process multiple arguments, you call the arguments using the indexes of the args array (args[0], args[1], args[2], and so on). When you type multiple arguments at the prompt, you separate them with spaces. If you want two or more words separated by white spaces to count as one argument, then you enclose them with double quotation marks. Here are a few examples:

```
java multiArgProgram first_argument
java multiArgProgram first_argument second_argument
java multiArgProgram "first argument" "second argument"
```

STRINGS AND STRING OPERATIONS

A *string* is a succession of characters strung together. The String class provides methods that allow you to examine and operate on the characters that compose a string. Included among these methods are those for searching, comparing, and concatenating strings, among many others. Table 2.7 provides a partial list of the String methods.

Java treats all string literals as String objects. String literals are always surrounded by quotation marks. On the other hand, as the programs in this chapter demonstrate, you can use the String data type to create String objects (or variables). You can use the String class methods with both literal strings and String objects. Consider the following lines:

```
//Create a String Object
String str = "Cranberry";
//the next two lines of code do basically the same thing
char strChar = str.charAt(4);
char cranChar = "Cranberry".charAt(4);
```

After declaring a String object (str), you first call the charAt() method and provide it with an argument of 4, indicating the fourth position in the string. The fourth position in the string retrieves the fifth character in the string because a string is an array of characters, and arrays position their elements starting with position (or *index*) 0. The index of the first character in a String is 0, the index of the second character is 1, and the next index of the third character is 2.

The character at index 4 of the String variable str is b, and this character you assign to strChar. In the following line, you again call the charAt() method, but this time you do so using the literal string "Cranberry". The charAt() method works just as before. The fourth position is occupied by b, so this is the character assigned to cranChar.

You have already been introduced to the use of the plus (+) sign or concatenation operator to join numbers and strings together for display purposes. You can also use the concatenation operation in conjunction with the assignment operator to join small strings into a large string. Consider the following:

```
String largerString = "In the spring " + "the rain is heavy.";
```

The concatenation operation in this instance joins the two strings that surround it into one string that the assignment operator stores in the largerString variable.

TABLE 2.7   THE STRING CLASS METHODS

Item	Discussion
charAt(int)	This method takes a single argument, an integer that indicates a character position in a string. The first position is 0. The method returns the character at the specified position.
concat(String)	This method takes a string as an argument and joins or concatenates the string to the end of the calling String object.
endsWith(String)	Tests if a string ends with a specified suffix. This method returns a true or false (Boolean) value.
equals(Object)	Compares this string to the specified object. It returns a true or false (Boolean) value.
equalsIgnoreCase(String)	Compares this string to another string. The comparison ignores the cases of the letters in the strings compared. It returns a true or false (Boolean) value.
indexOf(char)	Returns the integer that indicates the position of a character in a string. It takes a single character (in single quotes or of the char type) as an argument. It searches from the start of the string (position 0).
indexOf(char, int)	Returns the index within this string of the first occurrence of the specified character. In this case, you designate the position in the string from which you want to initiate the search.
indexOf(String)	Returns the starting position of a string within a string.
indexOf(String, int)	Returns the starting position of a string within a string. For the first argument, you provide the string you want to search for. For the second argument, you designate the position at which you want to initiate the search.
length()	Returns an integer that tells you the length of the string.
replace(char, char)	Replaces all the occurrences of a given letter in a string. The first argument is the character (in single quotes or as a char variable) that you want to replace. The second argument designates the replacement character. This argument must also be in single quotes or of the char type.
substring(int)	Returns a substring beginning at the position the argument designates and continuing to the end of the string.
substring(int, int)	Returns a substring that begins at the position the first argument designates and ends at the position the second argument designates.
toLowerCase()	Converts all the characters in the string to lowercase.
toUpperCase()	Converts all of the characters in the string to uppercase.
trim()	Removes any white space characters that might be at the beginning or end of a string. Returns a string without leading and trailing white spaces.
valueOf(int)	One of several methods that attend to all the primitive data types. This version of the method returns the argument in the form of a string. It converts it to a string.

THE NAME GAME

The Name Game application introduced at the beginning of this chapter uses some `String` methods to play around with the user's name. Now that you're almost at the end of the chapter and have already learned so much about the Java language, you should be able to understand the source code. Try writing this application and running it:

```java
/*
    NameGame.java
*/
import java.io.*; public class NameGame {
    public static void main(String args[]) {
        //#1
        String firstName = "",
                lastName = "",
                fullName = "",
                initials= "";
        int numLetters = 0;
        BufferedReader reader;
        reader = new BufferedReader(new InputStreamReader(System.in));

        System.out.println("\n\t\t--------Name a President--------");
        //#2
        try {
            System.out.print("\n First name of president: \t");
            firstName = reader.readLine();
            System.out.print("\n Last name of president: \t");
            lastName = reader.readLine();
        }
        catch (IOException ioe) {
            System.out.println("I/O Exception Occurred");
        }

        System.out.println("\n First name: \t\t" + firstName);
        //#3
        System.out.println("\n First name in caps: \t\t"
                    + firstName.toUpperCase() );
        //#4
        fullName = firstName;
```

```
fullName = fullName.concat(" ").concat(lastName);
System.out.println("\n Full name: \t\t\t" + fullName);
            System.out.println("\n Inverted order: \t\t"
            + lastName + ", " + firstName);
//#5
initials = firstName.charAt(0) + "."
            + lastName.charAt(0) + ".";
System.out.println("\n Initials: \t\t\t" + initials);

//#6
firstName = firstName.trim();
lastName = lastName.trim();
numLetters = firstName.length() + lastName.length();
System.out.println("\n Letters in full name: \t"
            + numLetters ); }
}
```

At comment #1 in the NameGame.java program, you work in the scope of the main() function and declare a series of String variables (firstName, lastName, fullName, initials) that you initialize with null strings (strings without content). This can eliminate compiler errors if the actions of the program do not initialize the variable prior to their use. In addition, you declare an int variable, numLetters, and a BufferedReader object, reader.

After setting up the variables for the program, in the lines associated with comment #2, you create a try block in which you call the print() method to prompt the user for the first and last name of a president. For each prompt you also call the readLine() method. You assign the input for the first call to the readLine() method directly to the firstName variable. To the second variable, lastName, you assign the input of the second call to the readLine() method. The catch block following these calls to the readLine() method checks for an exception of the IOException type.

At comment #3, after calling the println() method to display the name of the president as input by the user, you make use of the toUpperCase() method to convert the characters assigned to the firstName variable to uppercase. Figure 2.10 illustrates the output of this line as BILL, which differs from the previous line because the last three characters of the name now appear capitalized. When you call the toUpperCase() function, only the returned form of the string is capitalized. The original string remains as entered at the terminal. To permanently change the string, you would have to assign the string back to itself, as follows:

```
firstName = firstName.toUpperCase()
```

In the lines associated with comment #4, you concatenate two strings. To accomplish this, you first assign the characters of the firstName variable to the fullName variable. You then call the concat() method and provide it with an argument that consists of open and close double quotation marks separated by one white space (" "). Since a white space constitutes a character like any other character when presented in this way, the concat() operation adds a white space to the end of the character string you have assigned to fullName. After concatenating the white space, you then call the concat() method again, this time to append the characters stored in the lastName variable. When you complete these concatenation operations, you call the println() method to display the contents of fullName. As Figure 2.10 illustrates, this now consists of the first and last name of a president, separated by a white space.

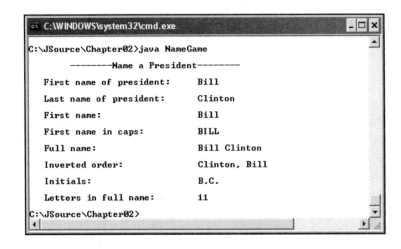

FIGURE 2.10

Use various String methods to obtain information about a president's name.

In the line trailing comment #5, you again perform a concatenation operation, this time using the plus (+) sign instead of the concat() method. The goal is to access initials of the president. To access the initial of the first name, you employ the firstName identifier to call the charAt() function, providing it with an argument of 0. This action retrieves the character in the first index position of the string. You then use the concatenation operator to append a period (".") to the first initial. Having appended the period, you use the concatenation operator to add the last initial. You repeat the call to the charAt() method using the lastName identifier, and you follow by concatenating another period. To make the information you have retrieved convenient to use, you assign it all to the initials variable.

At comment #6, you call the trim() function to remove any white spaces that might have been added accidentally to the firstName and lastName variables. You then call the length() function using both the firstName and lastName variables. In each instance the returned value of the length() method is an integer value that designates the length in characters of the variable you have used to call the `length()` function. Since the returned values are integers, when you employ the plus sign this time, the result is that the integer values are added. You assign the sum to `numLetters`.

SUMMARY

In this chapter, you learned about variables and data types and how to use them in your applications. You learned how to obtain user input to create interactive applications by employing the `BufferedReader` class and the `readLine()` method. To use this method, you learned about `try...catch` blocks. To make use of the input to your programs, you examined how to convert characters to numerical values using the parse function. You also examined the fundamentals of operator precedence in arithmetic operations. To extend your work with numbers and characters, you examined how to use some of the methods associated with the `Number` classes (`Float`, `Integer`, and so on) and the `String` class. Many of the activities in this chapter introduce advanced topics, and in subsequent chapters you have a chance to more fully develop your knowledge of these topics. In the next chapter, you learn how to generate random numbers and conditional statements and how to work with arrays.

CHALLENGES

1. Write an application that calculates a 5% tax for any given price and displays the total cost.
2. Write an application that prints the multiplication table for integers 1 through 12.
3. Write an application that accepts a number from the user and prints its multiplication table values (multiply it by 1 through 12 and print the results).
4. Write an application that reads in an expression the user provides, possibly consisting of mixed upper- and lowercase letters. Have the application capitalize the first letter of the sentence and make all other letters lowercase. Also, add a period at the end. Display the result.
5. Write an application that searches for your first name in a string and replaces it with your last name.

THE FORTUNE TELLER: RANDOM NUMBERS, CONDITIONS, AND ARRAYS

So far, all the programs in this book have been predictable. Every time they run, they do exactly the same thing. They vary only based on user input or command-line arguments. To extend this routine, you can write programs that produce unpredictable output each time you run them. To make this possible, you generate random numbers. In addition to working with random numbers, you explore control statements. Control statements allow you to write programs that behave differently based on decisions that take place as they execute. There are two basic forms of control statement. One is called *selection*. The other is call *repetition*. In this chapter you learn about selection. To top things off, in this chapter you also explore arrays. Java offers you two forms of array. One extends the set of primitive data types you explored in Chapter 2. The other is a class in the Java class hierarchy. In this chapter, you explore only the primitive type of array. Future chapters afford opportunities to explore the Array data type. As you go, you explore the following topics, among others:

- How to use the Math.random() method to generate random numbers
- How to use the java.util* package and the resources it offers
- How to use if and if…else and if…else if…else selection statements
- How to use the switch selection structure

- How to use the ternary operator (? :)
- How to declare, initialize, and traverse arrays

THE FORTUNE TELLER APPLICATION

The final project of this chapter involves the Fortune Teller application. The Fortune Teller application allows you to generate random numbers, use a selection structure, and retrieve strings from an array to create a program that simulates the predictions of a fortune teller. Figure 3.1 illustrates a session with this application.

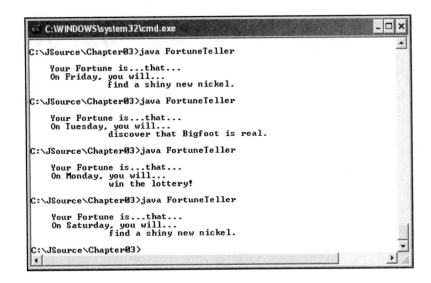

FIGURE 3.1

Random numbers, a selection structure, and an array allow you to create a program that tells fortunes.

When you run the Fortune Teller application, it generates a random prediction for each day of the week. The predictions are drawn from an array. The application uses a random number to select the prediction and the day of the week.

GENERATING RANDOM NUMBERS

A *random number* is a number that you choose from a range of numbers. When you choose a given number randomly from a range of numbers, the chance that you are going to choose any given number is equal to the chance that you are going to choose any other number. The fact that all numbers in the group stand the same chance of being chosen makes the numbers random.

To gain a sense of randomness, flip a coin. If you flip the coin repeatedly and record whether the flips result in heads or tails, you find approximately half the time you see the head of the coin. The other half of the time you see the tail of the coin. The chances of seeing either are equal. For this reason, the flip of the coin renders a random result.

To generate random numbers with Java, you employ methods from the Math and Random classes in the Java class hierarchy. These two classes provide you with different ways to generate random numbers.

THE MATH CLASS

Java provides you with a *random number generator* that you access through the Math class. The random number generator is the random() method. When you call the random() method, it generates a real number value in the range extending from 0 up to (but not including) 1.0. To make use of such numbers, you *interpolate* or *shift* them. The NumberMaker.java program demonstrates the use of the random() method and these associated procedures:

```
/*
  NumberMaker.java
*/


public class NumberMaker {
    public static void main(String args[]) {
        double randNum = 0;
        //generate a random number
      System.out.println("\n Here is a series of random numbers: \n ");
          for(int ctrl = 0; ctrl < 6; ctrl++){
      //#1
            randNum = Math.random();
            System.out.println("\n Raw: \t\t\t\t" + randNum);
      //#2
              System.out.println(" Translated (10): \t\t"
                                        + (int)(randNum * 10));
        //#3
              System.out.println(" Shifted (+1) and interpolated: "
                                        + (int)(1+ randNum * 10));
          }//end loop
      }//end main
}//end NumberMaker
```

The NumberMaker.java program features what is known as a for repetition block. Chapter 4 provides detailed discussion of repetition blocks. For now, just observe that the repetition block makes it so that you can call the `random()` method six times over, generating the random numbers Figure 3.2 illustrates.

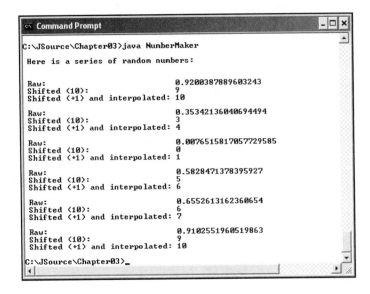

```
C:\JSource\Chapter03>java NumberMaker

Here is a series of random numbers:

Raw:                             0.9200387889603243
Shifted (10):                    9
Shifted (+1) and interpolated:   10

Raw:                             0.35342136040694494
Shifted (10):                    3
Shifted (+1) and interpolated:   4

Raw:                             0.0076515817057729585
Shifted (10):                    0
Shifted (+1) and interpolated:   1

Raw:                             0.5828471378395927
Shifted (10):                    5
Shifted (+1) and interpolated:   6

Raw:                             0.6552613162360654
Shifted (10):                    6
Shifted (+1) and interpolated:   7

Raw:                             0.9102551960519863
Shifted (10):                    9
Shifted (+1) and interpolated:   10

C:\JSource\Chapter03>_
```

FIGURE 3.2

The `Math` class provides a random number generator.

Figure 3.2 displays a set of random numbers interpolated and shifted in different ways. To see how this happens, begin with the statements following comment #1 in the NumberMaker.java program. First, you call the `random()` method of the `Math` class. The repetition block makes it so that you call this method six times, and with each call, it returns a value of the `double` type in a range that extends from 0 up to 1.0. You assign the returned value to the `randNum` variable. You then call the `println()` method to display this "raw" form of the random number. As Figure 3.2 illustrates, this number offers a large degree of decimal precision.

The raw form of the value the `random()` method returns proves difficult to handle if you are trying to do something like simulate the throw of dice. For such an activity, you require whole numbers (1 through 6). To change a decimal number into a whole number, you shift and cast it.

In the lines associated with comment #2, you multiply the raw decimal the `random()` method generates by 10. This has the effect of shifting the value to a whole number range. The value 0.2, for example, becomes 2.0. To eliminate the decimal point, you cast the shifted number to the `int` data type. To accomplish this, you directly precede the `randNum` variable with the keyword `int` enclosed in parentheses.

At comment #3, you cast, shift, and interpolate the raw value the `random()` method returns. Interpolation makes it so that the number is always greater than 0. To interpolate the number, you add 1 to the raw value prior to casting it. As Figure 3.2 illustrates, 0 becomes 1, and 6 becomes 7.

If you run the NumberMaker.java program repeatedly, you see that the values you obtain vary with each run. As mentioned previously, even if you see repeated numbers during a given run, it remains that the chances that any given number appears remain the same for all numbers in the range. It is as though you are repeatedly flipping a coin.

THE RANDOM CLASS

As the NumberMaker.java program illustrates, you can use the `Math random()` method without having to incorporate an `import` statement in your program. The `Math` class provides you with access to general methods relating to math, and the generic `random()` method is included among these as a matter of convenience. If you want to deal specifically with random number operations, Java provides the `Random` class. To use this class you must include a package `import` statement: `java.util.Random`.

The `Random` class differs from the `Math` class because it has one area of responsibility: generation and use of random numbers. Toward this end, it makes it possible to generate random numbers of different types, so that you do not have to shift, cast, and interpolate raw values to obtain those you require for your programming work. Table 3.1 provides descriptions of some of the `Random` methods that provide these services.

TABLE 3.1   SELECTED METHODS OF THE RANDOM CLASS

Method	Discussion
nextBoolean()	Returns a Boolean value.
nextFloat()	Returns a float value between 0.0 and 1.0.
nextInt()	Returns a number of the `int` type that ranges over the entire range of possible `int` values. The numbers returned include positive and negative values.
nextInt(int)	You supply this method with a single argument of the `int` type. Returns a number of the `int` type in the range extending from 0 up to the number you supply as an argument.
nextLong()	Returns a number of the `long` type. This number can be positive or negative in the range that includes all possible value of the `long` type.
nextDouble()	Returns a value of the `double` type in the range from 0.0 up to 1.0.
setSeed(long)	The method had no return type (it is void). You use it if you want to designate a starting value as you generate random numbers. See the section titled "Seeding Values," later in this chapter.

Generating Different Types of Random Numbers

To call the methods in Table 3.1, you create a new Random object. Then you use the Random object to call the Random methods. The NumberMakerUtil.java program allows you to explore such activities.

```
/*
NumberMakerUtil.java
*/
import java.util.Random;
public class NumberMakerUtil{
    public static void main(String args[]) {

    //Create an instance of the Random class -- an object
//#1
    int iLimit = 10;
    Random rand = new Random();

//#2
    System.out.println("\n Random Numbers with the Random Class \n");
    System.out.println(" Integer    Int (0-10)\tFloat\t\tDouble\t\t\tBoolean" );
    System.out.println("-----------------------------------"+
                       "----------------------------------" );
        for(int ctrl = 0; ctrl < 10; ctrl++){
//#3
            System.out.println( " "       + rand.nextInt()
                        +"\t"    + rand.nextInt(iLimit)
                        +"\t"    + rand.nextFloat()
                        +"\t"    + rand.nextDouble()
                        +"\t"    + rand.nextBoolean()
                    );
        }//end for
    }//end main
} //end NumberMakerUtil
```

At the top of the NumberMakerUtil.java program, you use an import statement to access the java.util package and within that package the Random class. Next, at comment #1, you declare an int variable (iLimit) that you use to control the range of integers you generate. You also use the new keyword and the constructor for the Random class to create a Random object (rand).

Given these preliminary actions, as Figure 3.3 illustrates, you then proceed in the lines associated with comment #2 to create a table heading. Creation of the heading involves making use of the tab escape character (\t). You set up column headings for integer values that span the possible integer range, integer values that range from 0 up to 10, float values, double values, and boolean values.

In the lines trailing comment #3, you again use the approach shown in the previous program to generate a series of random numbers. This time the repetition block repeats 10 times, generating 10 rows. To generate items for the rows, you make calls to five of the Random methods. In each instance, you append the method to the Random object (rand) using the dot operator.

To generate integer values that span the integer range, you call nextInt(). To generate integers in a range that spans from 0 to 10, you call nextInt() and employ the iLimit variable as its argument. When you have two methods with the same name but different arguments, the methods are said to be *overloaded*. The compiler can tell them apart because they have different arguments.

To generate values of the float type in the range that spans from 0 up to 1.0, you call the nextFloat() method. To generate values of the boolean type, you call the nextBoolean() method. To generate numbers of the double type, you call the nextDouble() method. If you compare Figure 3.2 with Figure 3.3, you can see that the Math.random() and Random.nextDouble() methods generate numbers in the same range. After numbers of the double type, you then call the nextBoolean() method to access random Boolean values. This method returns values that consist of false and true.

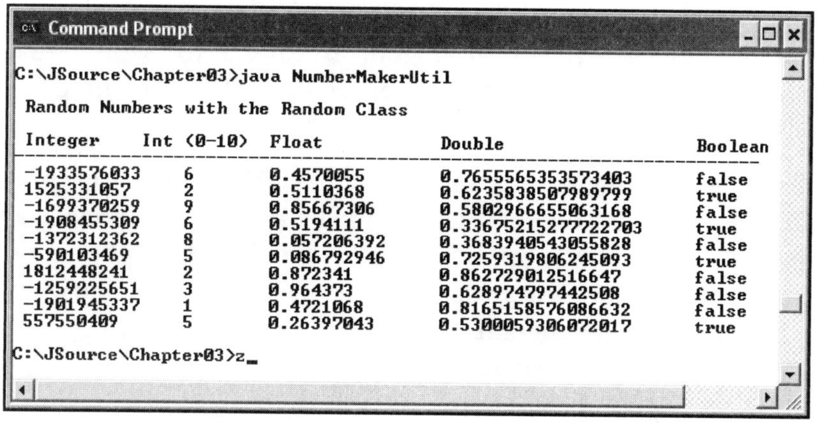

```
C:\JSource\Chapter03>java NumberMakerUtil

Random Numbers with the Random Class

Integer      Int (0-10)  Float         Double                  Boolean
--------------------------------------------------------------------------
-1933576033      6       0.4570055     0.7655565353573403      false
1525331057       2       0.5110368     0.6235838507989799      true
-1699370259      9       0.85667306    0.5802966655063168      false
-1908455309      6       0.5194111     0.33675215277722703     true
-1372312362      8       0.057206392   0.3683940543055828      false
-590103469       5       0.086792946   0.7259319806245093      true
1812448241       2       0.872341      0.862729012516647       false
-1259225651      3       0.964373      0.628974797442508       false
-1901945337      1       0.4721068     0.8165158576086632      false
557550409        5       0.26397043    0.5300059306072017      true

C:\JSource\Chapter03>z_
```

FIGURE 3.3

Use the Random class to generate numbers of various types.

Seeding Values

Computers cannot generate numbers that are wholly random. The reason for this is that a computer is not infinite. A wholly random number would be indeterminate, and to generate such a number, you would have to have at hand a machine capable of being infinite. No such machine exists. For this reason, computer scientists refer to random numbers a computer generates as *pseudorandom* numbers. *Pseudo* is derived from the ancient Greek term for "lie."

The pseudorandom numbers you obtain through the Math and Random classes serve in almost any imaginable programming context as genuine random numbers, but to make it so that the numbers you have access to through the Random object possess especially strong random characteristics, Java allows you to supply the Random object with what is known as a seed value. A seed value is a value Java uses as it starts to calculate random numbers for you.

By default, Java begins the process of generating random values by obtaining a starter value from your computer's clock. Your computer's clock works on a system that is based on milliseconds. A millisecond is a thousandth of a second. Because the random number program (or algorithm) generates numbers in this way, every time you run your program, Java has a new starter value to work with.

> Because Java repeatedly calls on the "next" millisecond time count when it provides you with a random number, the Random methods Table 3.1 lists all start with the expression next.

Although by default Java appropriates the date in milliseconds as the starting point of its random number generation activities, you can vary this routine. You can set the starting value so that it is the same (or different) each time your program executes. If you set it so that it is the same, your program always generates the same set of random values each time the program executes.

Java provides two approaches to setting the starting seed values. The first involves using the setSeed() method, shown in Table 3.1. The setSeed() method enables you to provide a seed value to a Random object any time after you have created the object. The other approach involves using a Random class constructor to provide an argument for the seed value when you first create the object. The SetSeed.java program allows you to experiment with the default, constructor, and setSeed() approaches to setting starter values.

```
/*
  SetSeed.java
*/
import java.util.Random;
public class SetSeed{
public static void main(String args[]) {
/*
  SetSeed.java
*/

import java.util.Random;
public class SetSeed{
public static void main(String args[]) {
//#1
    //Allow the default to be used in milliseconds
    Random rand1 = new Random();
//#2
    //Use the Random constructor
    Random rand2 = new Random(12345);
//#3
    //call the setSeed() method
    Random rand3 = new Random();
    rand3.setSeed(232345);


  System.out.println("\n Different Seed Values for Random \n");
  System.out.println(" Default \t Random(12345)\t setSeed(232345)" );
  System.out.println("--------------------------"+
                     "--------------------------" );
    for(int ctrl = 0; ctrl < 5; ctrl++){
//#4
        System.out.println( " "      + rand1.nextInt() //Random()
                    +"\t"    + rand2.nextInt() //(12345)
                    +"\t  "  + rand3.nextInt() //(232345)
        );
      }//end for
    }//end main
 }//end SetSeed
```

At the top of the SetSeed.java program, you use the import statement to access the Random class in the Java class hierarchy. You then proceed at comment #1 to declare an instance (rand1) of the Random class using the default constructor. This constructor requires no argument and uses the current system time in milliseconds as a starting seed value.

At comment #2, you use the overloaded version of the Random constructor to set the seed value as 12345. The name of the Random object in this instance is rand2.

At comment #3, you first create an instance of the Random class (rand3) using the default constructor and then call the setSeed() method to assign a value of 12345 as the starting seed value. This value is the same as the value you see for rand2.

After setting up a table heading that allows you to audit three columns of values, the first for rand1, the second for rand2, and the third for rand3, you proceed at comment #4 to create a for statement to generate five rows of random values for each of the random objects. For each row, you use the Random objects to call the nextInt() method. This method generates positive and negative integers in the permissible integer range.

As Figure 3.4 illustrates, through two successive runs of the SetSeed.java program, if you allow the default Random constructor to perform its work, you obtain a unique set of numbers each time. On the other hand, when you use the overloaded constructor or the setSeed() method to set the starter value at 12345, then the program generates the same set of numbers each time.

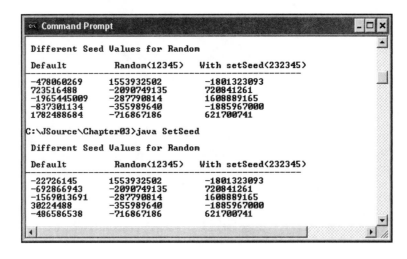

FIGURE 3.4

Seeding starter values allows you to generate the same set of numbers with each run of your program.

MORE OF THE MATH CLASS

In addition to the `random()` method, the `Math` class provides a variety of methods that attend to standard mathematical operations. Among these operations are calculating absolute values, exponents, logarithms, and square roots. Table 3.2 lists some of the `Math` methods. Java provides overloaded versions of several `Math` methods to accommodate different data types, such as `int`, `long`, `float`, and `double`.

TABLE 3.2 METHODS OF THE MATH CLASS	
Item	**Discussion**
`PI`	Not a method. This is an attribute of the `Math` class. You can use it in calculations in which you require a value for B.
`static double abs(double)`	Returns the absolute value of a `double` value.
`float abs(float)`	Returns the absolute value of a `float` value. Similar methods are `int abs(int)`, which returns the absolute value of an integer and `abs(long )`, which returns the absolute value of a `long` type.
`acos(double)`	Returns the arc cosine of an angle, in the range of 0.0 through pi. The return type is `double`.
`asin(double)`	Returns the arc sine of an angle. The range is -pi/2 through pi/2.
`atan(double)`	Returns the arc tangent of an angle. The range is -pi/2 through pi/2. The return type is `double`.
`ceil(double)`	Returns a value of the `double` type. The value is the smallest `double` value that is not less than the argument. The value is equal to a mathematical integer.
`cos(double)`	Returns the trigonometric cosine of an angle. The return type is `double`.
`floor(double)`	Returns the largest `double` value that is not greater than the number. The value is equal to a mathematical integer. The return type is `double`.
`log(double)`	Returns the natural logarithm of a `double` value. The return type is `double`.
`max(double, double)`	Returns the greater of two `double` values. The return type is `double`. Similar methods are `max(float, float)`, `max(int a, int b)`, and `max(long, long)`.
`min(double, double)`	Returns the smaller of two `double` values. The return type is a `double`. Similar methods are `float min(float, float)`, `min(int, int)`, and `min(long, long)`.

pow(double, double)	Returns the value of the first argument raised to the power of the second argument. The return type is double.
static double random()	Returns a double value with a positive sign. The range is from 0.0 to 1.0.
round(double)	A value of the long type closest to the argument. A similar method is round(float), which returns a value of the int type.
sin(double)	Returns the trigonometric sine of an angle.
sqrt(double)	Returns the correctly rounded positive square root of a double value.
tan(double)	Returns the trigonometric tangent of an angle.
toDegrees(double)	Takes an argument of the double type in radians. Converts an angle measured in radians to an approximately equivalent angle measured in degrees.
toRadians(double)	Takes an argument of the double type in degrees. Converts an angle measured in degrees to an approximately equivalent angle measured in radians.

To use the methods in the Math class, you make *static* calls to the Math class. A static call involves using the name of the class and then the name of the method you want to call. You then submit the number you want to operate on as the argument to the method. The MathMethods.java program allows you to experiment with some of the Math class methods.

```
/*
 MathMethods.java
*/
public class MathMethods{
    public static void main(String args[]){
//#1
        double firstNumber = -120.45,
               secondNumber = 232.30;
        String tableBar = "--------------------";
        tableBar += tableBar;
        System.out.println("\n\n   A Few Math Class Methods" );
        System.out.println(tableBar);
        System.out.println("  Starting number:\t\t" + firstNumber );
//#2
        System.out.println("  Absolute value (" + firstNumber + ")\t"
                              + Math.abs(firstNumber));
        System.out.println("  Absolute value (" + secondNumber + ")\t"
```

```
                                      + Math.abs(secondNumber));
        System.out.println("  Rounded (" + firstNumber + ") \t\t"
                                      + Math.round(firstNumber));
        System.out.println("  Rounded (" + secondNumber + ") \t\t"
                                      + Math.round(secondNumber));
//#3
        System.out.println("\n" + tableBar);
        System.out.println("  Ceiling of " + firstNumber + "\t\t"
                                      + Math.ceil(firstNumber));
        System.out.println("  Floor of " + firstNumber + "\t\t"
                                      + Math.floor(firstNumber));
        System.out.println("  Ceiling of " + secondNumber + "\t\t"
                                      + Math.ceil(secondNumber));
        System.out.println("  Floor of " + secondNumber + "\t\t"
                                      + Math.floor(secondNumber));
//#4
        System.out.println("\n" + tableBar);
        System.out.println("\n  Square root of 100 \t\t"
                                      + Math.sqrt(100));
        System.out.println("  3 to the power of  2 \t\t "
                                      + Math.pow(3, 2));
//#5
        System.out.println("\n" + tableBar);
        System.out.println("\n  Max of " + firstNumber
                                          + " and " + secondNumber + "\t"
                                  + Math.max(firstNumber, secondNumber));
        System.out.println("  Min of " + firstNumber
                                          + " and " + secondNumber + "\t"
                                  + Math.min(firstNumber, secondNumber));
                                  + Math.min(firstNumber, secondNumber));
        System.out.println("  Value of PI\t\t" + Math.PI);
    }
}
```

In the lines accompanying comment #1 of the MathMethods.java program, you declare two variables of the double type, firstNumber and secondNumber. You initialize firstNumber to a negative value, -123.45. You initialize secondNumber to a positive value, 232.30. You then set up a variable of the String type and use concatenation operators to create a separator bar for a table of values. Given these preliminaries, you then call the println() method to print a table heading and a bar.

In the lines associated with comment #2, you call the abs() method for firstNumber and secondNumber. The absolute value method returns the absolute distance of the numbers from 0. In Figure 3.5, you see both numbers rendered as positive numbers. You then call the round() method for both numbers. When you round the value stored in firstNumber, since the decimal portion of the number is less than 0.5, the number is rounded to -120, and in Figure 3.5 you see an integer value. When you round 232.3, you see that value rounded to 232, again as an integer.

In the lines associated with comment #3, you call the ceil() and floor() methods. As Figure 3.5 illustrates, when you call the ceil() method and supply it with firstNumber as an argument, the ceiling is the number greater in value relative to 0. In this respect, -120 is greater than (the ceiling of) -120.45. When you call the ceil() method for 232.0, you get the next highest whole number, 233.0.

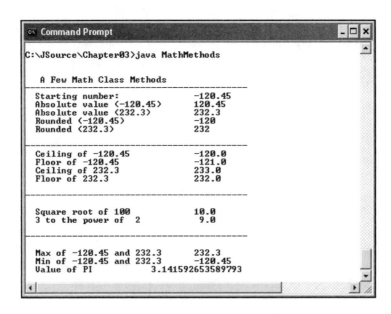

FIGURE 3.5

Call the Math class methods statically.

In the lines trailing comment #4 you call the sqrt() method to extract the square root of 100. Even though you provide an integer argument, the method returns a real (double) value. You then call the pow() method to raise 3 to the power of 2. The method requires two arguments. The first is the base number, and the second is the power.

At comment #5, you call the max() method. This method takes two arguments in any order and returns the larger of the two values. You also call the min() method, which takes two values in any order and returns the lower of the two values. As a final venture, you call the PI attribute. As the number of decimal places for PI in Figure 3.5 illustrates, the Math class defines B as a double value.

FLOW AND SELECTION

Points of decision you include in your programs allow your programs to take alternate courses of action. Selection statements prove central to this type of activity. Selection statements provide gateways to conditional blocks. A selection statement begins with a keyword that designates the type of selection you want to apply to a given block of statements. Figure 3.6 illustrates the if keyword. Following the keyword is a logical expression enclosed by parentheses. The logical expression sets a condition that the flow of the program must satisfy before it can enter the block.

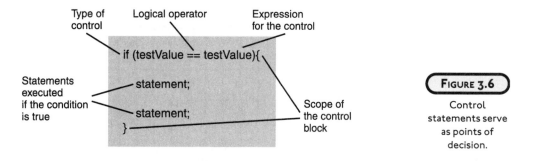

FIGURE 3.6

Control statements serve as points of decision.

To define the block of a selection statement, you use opening and closing braces. In the block you include all the statements your program is to perform if the selection expression is true. If the selection expression proves false, then the flow of the program skips the block.

In the most rudimentary type of control statement, your program can take only one alternative course of action. Either the program performs a given action or it does not. Figure 3.7 illustrates this form of selection statement. In more complex selection statements, you select from among a range of alternatives.

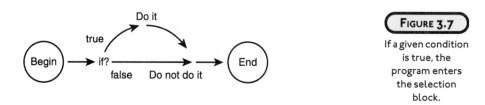

FIGURE 3.7

If a given condition is true, the program enters the selection block.

Java provides you with several forms of selection statement. The more involved forms of selection allow you to take several courses of action. Table 3.3 lists the selection statements Java provides.

TABLE 3.3	SUMMARY OF SELECTION STATEMENTS
Term	**Discussion**
if	The if control statement is known as a *single-entry/single-exit control statement*. You follow it with an expression in parentheses to be evaluated. Then in a block defined by curly braces you provide a statement or set of statements to be performed if the expression evaluates to true.
if else	The if else statement provides a categorical form of selection. If one course of action is not taken, then another course of action is taken. You are limited to two mutually exclusive actions.
If...else if...else	You can test several cases or alternative courses of action. If one course of action is not taken, then any among several others might be taken.
switch	This is known as a *multiple-case selection statement*. It provides you with a number of case statements. Each case can be entered, depending on whether its control expression evaluates to true.

Conditions and Conditional Operators

Control statements depend on two sets of operators. One set of operators involves numbers and relations of equality. The other set involves Boolean relations. Operators that involve numbers are called *relational operators*. When you use these operators, you can apply them only to literal numbers or variables you have defined using primitive data types, such as int, long, float, or double. The items you compare are called operands, and the operator compares the operand on the right side of the operator to the operand on the left and returns a Boolean value that indicates whether the comparison holds true. Table 3.4 discusses the relational operators.

Some examples of how relational operators work are as follows:

- The expression 1 < 2 evaluates to true because one is less than two.
- The expression 2 < 1 evaluates to false because 2 is not less than 1.
- The expression 1 < 1 evaluates to false because 1 is not less than 1.
- The expressions 1 <= 1 and 1 >= 1 evaluate to true because 1 is equal to 1.
- The expression 1 != 1 evaluates to false because 1 is equal to 1.
- The expression 1 == 1 evaluates to true because 1 is equal to 1.

TABLE 3.4   RELATIONAL OPERATORS

Operator	Syntax	Discussion
==	x != y	When you test operands for equality, you use two equal signs. This expression is translated as "x equals y." The operator evaluates the expression as true if x equals y. Otherwise, it evaluates it as false.
<	x < y	This expression is translated as "x is less than y." The operator evaluates the expression as true if x is less than y; otherwise, it evaluates it as false.
<=	x<= y	This expression is translated as "x is less than or equal to y." The operator evaluates the expression as true if x is less than y or if x is equal to y; otherwise, it evaluates it as false.
<	x > y	This expression is translated as "x is greater than y." The operator evaluates the expression as true if x is greater than y; otherwise, it evaluates it as false.
<=	x >= y	This expression is translated as "x is greater than or equal to y." The operator evaluates the expression as true if x is greater than y or if x is equal to y; otherwise, it evaluates it as false.
!=	x != y	This expression is translated as "x is not equal to y." The operator evaluates the expression as true if x does not equal y; otherwise, it evaluate it as false.
?	exp ? a : b;	This expression is translated as "if a is true, do a; if a is not true, then do b." The question mark is known as the ternary, or conditional, operator.

Single-Entry Selection

The if control statement is known as a *single-entry, single-exit selection statement*. The reason for this is that it sets one condition and allows you to access one block of statements. The if statement tests this condition. If the expression the statement evaluates does not turn out to be true, then the statements that follow in the control block are not performed. The if statement can handle expressions that test numbers, Boolean values, and strings. The SelectionAndRelation.java program allows you to explore a few uses of the if selection statement.

```
/*
    SelectionAndRelation.java
*/
class SelectionAndRelation{
```

```java
public static void main(String Args[]){
  //#1
  int firstNumber = 18 , secondNumber = 25;
  float realNumber    = 35.15F;
  boolean boolValue = true;
  String firstNation = "China", secondNation = "India";
  //#2
  if(firstNumber < secondNumber){
    System.out.println("\n   " +  firstNumber
                              + " is less than " + secondNumber);

  }
  if(realNumber != firstNumber){
    System.out.println("\n   " +  realNumber
                              + " is not equal to " + firstNumber);

  }
  //# 3
  if(boolValue){
    System.out.println("\n   " + boolValue + " is true.");
  }
  if(!boolValue == false){
    System.out.println("\n   !" + boolValue + " is false.");
  }
  //#4
  if("China" == firstNation){
      System.out.println("\n  \"China\"  is the same as "  + firstNation);
  }
  if(firstNation !=  secondNation){
    System.out.println("\n   " +  firstNation
                              + " is different from "  + secondNation);

  }
}//end main
}//end SelectionAndRelation
```

In the lines accompanying comment #1, you declare variables of the int, boolean, float, and String types. You then proceed at comment #2 to use relational operators to set up tests involving numbers. To use the if selection statement, you place the expression you want to test within opening and closing parentheses. For the first test, you use the less than (<) operator to determine if the value of firstNumber is less than secondNumber. As Figure 3.8

shows, since 18 is less than 25, the selection expression tests to true, so the flow of the program enters the block, and the `println()` statement is executed.

Associated with comment #2, you use the inequality operator (!=) to test a real number in relation to an integer. As the following "Precision Problems" sidebar discusses, you can run into problems with such operations. In this case, the statement proves true, since `realNumber` is not equal to `firstNumber`, but evaluating variables of different types for equality is likely to generate errors. It is best to evaluate numbers of the same type and precision.

In the lines trailing comment #3, you make use of `boolean` values. The first test evaluates whether the `boolean` variable `boolValue` is true. In this case, you evaluate only the `boolean` value itself. Generally, any variable with a value equal to 0 evaluates to false, as does the `false` keyword. Likewise, any variable that is not equal to 0 (either positive or negative) evaluates to true, as does the `true` keyword. Since you have assigned the value of the `true` keyword to `boolValue`, this expression evaluates to true.

The second test associated with comment #3 involves the negation of the truth of the `boolean` variable. To negate a value, you use the *not* operator, which is an exclamation mark (!). In this expression, even though you have assigned the value of the `true` keyword to `boolValue`, when you precede `boolValue` with the not operator, you assert the opposite of true. The expression evaluates to true since "not true" is equal to false.

The lines following comment #5 allow you to use relational operators with values of the `String` type. In the first instance, you use a literal string value (`"China"`) and test it against a variable (`firstNation`) to which you have assigned the string `"China"`. The expression evaluates to true because the literal and variable forms of `"China"` are equal. In the next selection statement, you test for the inequality (!=) of the two `String` variables. The expression results in true because the values assigned to the variables `"China"` and `"India"` are not equal.

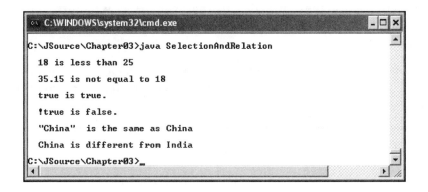

FIGURE 3.8

Relational operators allow you to create a variety of selection actions.

PRECISION PROBLEMS

Evaluations involving integers usually pose no problems. For this reason, if you set up the following operation, you are not likely to encounter problems:

```
// 22 × 2 == 44 is true
(22F * 2 == 44)    //This evaluates to true
```

On the other hand, your computer does not store floating-point numbers precisely. For this reason, when you create expressions that evaluate variables of the float or double type, you find the following:

```
// 22.5 × 0.15 == 3.375 is true
(22.5F * 0.15F) == 3.375F //This evaluates to false
```

Java calculates the left result as 3.3750002, which is not equal to 3.375. This is a precision error. A precision error arises when the number of decimal points for two operands differ.

To avoid precision errors, format your numbers or compare values within acceptable ranges. In Chapter 2, you made use of the DecimalFormat class. When you call the format() method, you can control the precision of decimals. To work with acceptable ranges, instead of testing that the calculated value on the right is *exactly* equal to 3.375, you can test that it is greater than 0.3749 and less than 0.3751. Here's an example:

```
// 22.5 × 0.15 == 3.375 is true
(22.5F * 0.15F) >= 3.375F //This evaluates to false due to precision
```

Consider the following expression:

```
2 == 2 == 2
```

Does it evaluate to true or false? The fact is that it does not evaluate at all. Instead, it causes a compiler error. Take a closer look and you can see why. The compiler first evaluates the operator on the left, so the first step of the compiler's action might be viewed as follows:

```
(2 == 2) == 2
```

The left side of this expression is (2 == 2). This evaluates to true, so you are left with the expression true == 2. The data types of the two operands are incomparable; thus the compiler will generate errors.

The Ternary Operator

In addition to the other operators listed in Table 3.4, Java provides you with the conditional, or ternary, operator. The conditional operator allows you to test a condition and then on the basis of its result, follow with one of two actions. The syntax is as follows:

```
condition ? firstAction : secondAction;
```

To use the conditional operator, you create an expression that evaluates to true or false. This expression immediately precedes the question mark. You then follow the question mark with two expressions that define two courses of action. These expressions are separated by a colon. The courses of action can be anything that you normally define as a statement within the block of a selection statement.

If the condition tests true, then the first action is taken. If the condition tests false, then the second action is taken. Consider this example:

```
String result = x < y ? "x is less than y" : "x is not less than y";
```

In this statement, assume that x is equal to 4 and y is equal to 5. The expression 4 < 5 proves true, so the first expression, "x is less than y" is assigned to the String variable result.

On the other hand, assume that x is equal to 5 and y is equal to 4. In this case, the expression 5 < 4 is false, and "x is not less than y" is assigned to the String variable result.

Boolean Operators

The mathematician George Boole created a system of mathematics that became known by his name. This system of mathematics lay largely in the background for a century until Edward Shannon (1916–2001) reintroduced Boole's work as a part of information theory. Today, Boolean relational operators constitute a common feature of every programming language. Relational operators involve knowing how to group statements. Table 3.5 provides a summary of the Boolean operators.

TABLE 3.5 BOOLEAN OPERATORS	
Item	**Discussion**
&&	The Boolean AND operators establish a condition in which both of the items tested are true for the expression that contains them to be true.
||	The Boolean OR operator establishes that one or both of the items to be tested must be true for the expression that contains them to be true.

The Boolean AND (&&) operator considers two items. It finds the resulting statement true if both constituent items are true. In addition to the AND operation, you can also use the OR statement. The OR statement (||) can be true if either or both of its constituent statements are true. Figure 3.9 summarizes the Boolean operators.

AND &&

T	T	Two true statements are **true**.	T
T	F	A true statement and a false statement are **false**.	F
F	F	A false statement and a false statement are **false**.	F

OR ||

T	T	Two true statements are **true**.	T
T	F	A true statement or a false statement is **true**.	T
F	F	A false statement or a false statement is **false**.	F

FIGURE 3.9

AND and OR operators allow you to combine statements.

BoolWork.java allows you to experiment with AND and OR operators involving a few integers.

```
/*
  BoolWork.java
*/

class BoolWork{
    public static void main(String Arg[])
    {
//#1
        int iIntA = 5, iIntB = 5,
            iIntC = 4, iIntD = 4;
System.out.println("\n  Boolean operations \n");
System.out.println("------------------------"+
                   "------------------------" );
//#2  Test using AND
        if(iIntA >= iIntD && iIntD == iIntC){
            System.out.println("\n  A. " + iIntA
                        + " is greater than or equal to " + iIntD
```

```
                               + " AND " + iIntD + " is equal to "
                               + iIntC + ": true.");

            }
//#3 Test using OR
        if(iIntA >= iIntD || iIntC == iIntB){
            System.out.println("\n  B. " + iIntA
                               + " is greater than or equal to " + iIntD
                               + " OR " + iIntC + " is equal to "
                               + iIntB + ": true.");

            }
//#4 Test using OR and negation
        if(iIntA != iIntC && iIntB == iIntA){
            System.out.println("\n  C. " + iIntA
                               + " is not equal to " + iIntC
                               + " AND " + iIntB + " is equal to "
                               + iIntA + ": true.");

            }
        }//end main
}//end BoolWork
```

In the lines associated with comment #1 in BoolWork.java, you declare two sets of int variables. To the first set (iIntA and iIntB) you assign the integer value of 5. To the second set (iIntC and iIntD) you assign the integer value of 4. At comment #2, you create a compound expression using the Boolean AND (&&) operator. You make use of the if selection statement to test the compound expression.

Since AND expressions render true if both of the compounded relational statements are true (see Figure 3.10), when you test to determine if 5 is greater than or equal to 4 AND 4 is equal to 4, the selection statement evaluates the compound statement as true.

In the lines trailing comment #3, you work with a Boolean OR (||) expression. In this case, one of the two compounded expressions must be true if the selection statement is to be true. The first part of the statement (5 >= 4) proves true, while the second part (4 == 5) is not true. Given that one expression evaluates to true, the OR statement returns true, as you see in item B of Figure 3.10.

In the final test, at comment #4, you invoke the exclusive AND operator once again. In this case, you again test whether 5 is not equal to 4 and whether 5 is equal to 5. With AND statements, both of the expressions must be true for the statement to be true, and in this case, this condition is satisfied.

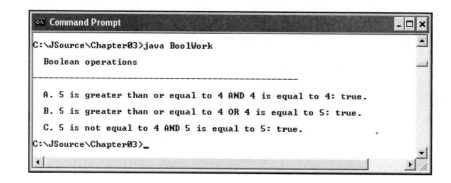

FIGURE 3.10

Use Boolean operators to compound expressions that involve relational operators.

THE if...else STATEMENT

The if selection statement allows you to set up a condition to test whether your program should execute a statement or a set of statements. If the conditional expression evaluates to true, the program executes the statements contained within the block of the if statement. If the conditional expression does not evaluate to true, then the flow of your program skips the statement in the block. Consider what happens if you want to set up your program so that you include an either/or condition in it. Here is an example of how you might handle the situation using if selection statements:

```java
boolean Shoes;
// Shoes assigned can be true or false. . .
//#1
if(Shoes == false){
    System.out.println("Sorry, no service.");
}
//#2
if(Shoes == true){
    System.out.println("Please be seated.");
    }
```

If the Shoes variable is set to false, then the flow of the program enters block #1. If the Shoes variable is set to true, then the flow of the program enters block #2. The program works just fine with this way of processing information, but then it is necessary to create redundant tests. A way to avoid such redundancy involves the if...else selection statement. The if...else selection statement processes the choice categorically, allowing you to designate that if Shoes is not set to true, then it must be set to false. Here is the form the code assumes using the categorical form of selection statement:

```
if(Shoes == false){
    System.out.println("Sorry, no service.");
}else{
    System.out.println("Please be seated.");
}
```

Using a categorical form of selection statement, if the value of Shoes is not false, then the structure provides that it must be true. As a result, you test the expression only once. If Shoes is set to false, then it enters the first block. If it is set to true, then it enters the else block.

THE TEMPERATURE CONVERSION PROGRAM

The TempConversion.java program allows you to explore the use of the categorical selection statement. This program uses the if...else selection statement to determine whether you want to convert degrees Fahrenheit to degrees Celsius or degrees Celsius to degrees Fahrenheit. At the same time, it allows you to work with the conditional operator to help with user interaction:

```
/*
    TempConversion.java
*/
import java.io.*;
import java.text.DecimalFormat;
public class TempConversion{
    public static void main(String Ags[]){
        BufferedReader reader;
        String value = "", tempType = "";
//#1
        float basicTemp = 0, tempCelsius = 0, tempFahrenheit = 0;
        int choice = 0;
        DecimalFormat twoDigits = new DecimalFormat("0.00");
        reader = new BufferedReader(new InputStreamReader(System.in));
//#2
        System.out.print("\n  Select an option: "
                        + "\n \t 1 - Convert from Fahrenheit to Celsius"
                        + "\n \t 2 - Convert from Celsius to Fahrenheit"
                        + "\n >>");
        try {
//#3
```

```
            value = reader.readLine();
            choice = Integer.parseInt(value);
    //#4 Conditional
            tempType = (choice == 1) ? "Fahrenheit" : "Celsius";
            System.out.print("\n Enter the temperature: ("
                                    + tempType + "): ");
            value= reader.readLine();
            basicTemp = Float.parseFloat(value);
        }
        catch (IOException ioe) {
            System.out.println("I O Exception Occurred");
        }


        //categorical selection for either Fahrenheit or Celsius
        System.out.println("\n  Temperature entered: ("
                                    + tempType + ") "
                                    + twoDigits.format(basicTemp));
    //#5
    if(choice == 1){
            //convert to Celsius
            tempCelsius = 5.0F/9.0F * (basicTemp - 32);
            System.out.println("\n  Temperature Celsius: "
                                    + twoDigits.format(tempCelsius));
    }else{
            tempFahrenheit = (9.0F/5.0F) * basicTemp + 32;
            System.out.println("\n  Temperature Fahrenheit: "
                                    + twoDigits.format(tempFahrenheit));
    }//end else
    }//end main
}//end class
```

In the lines associated with comment #1, you declare variables of the float type to accommodate user input and conversions between Celsius and Fahrenheit temperature values. You also declare a String variable that you use as part of the interface to guide user input. Returning to themes introduced in Chapter 2, you declare and define BufferedReader and Decimal-Format objects.

As Figure 3.11 illustrates, in the lines accompanying comment #2, you call the println() method to display a menu of options for the reader. The menu prompts the reader to input

1 or 2 as options, but as you see in the following lines, you make decisions based on whether the input is 1 or not 1.

At comment #3, you call the readLine() method to retrieve input from the user. You assign the input to the String value variable and then call the parseInt() method to convert the String value into an integer value (choice). Given that you assign a value to choice, you then use a conditional statement (at comment #4) to determine whether to assign Celsius or Fahrenheit to the String tempType variable. You then employ the tempType to help the user to enter the temperature.

In the lines identified by comment #5, you use a categorical form of selection (if…else) to evaluate whether the user has input a 1. If the user has input a 1, then the flow of the program enters the first block of the selection statement, where you calculate the temperature in Celsius degrees. If the number entered is 2 (or anything else), the flow of the program skips the first block and enters the else block, and you calculate the temperature in Fahrenheit degrees. Figure 3.11 shows you two executions of the program, and the values input are those for the normal body temperature of a healthy human being.

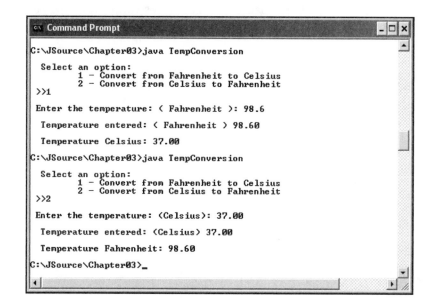

FIGURE 3.11

A categorical selection statement allows you to convert temperatures.

The if…else if…else Statement

In addition to the basic form of categorical selection, Java provides you with an extended selection structure that uses a pattern of if…else if…else. This type of selection statement is known as a *cascading* or *multiple-case* selection structure. When it encounters this type of structure, the flow of the program enters the if statement that heads the structure. If the control expression for the if expression evaluates to true, then the first block executes. Following the execution of this block, the flow of the program exits the structure.

If the evaluation of the if expression renders a false outcome, then the flow of the program passes to the first of a possibly long series of else if control statements. If the expression of the first else if control statement evaluates to true, then the flow of the program enters its block. As before, the flow of the program exits the structure after the statements in the block are executed.

After a series of else if blocks, you can set up concluding else statements for this structure. This is known as a *default* condition. Since the default condition does not support an evaluation expression, the flow of structure enters it when all the explicit evaluations the structure supports have rendered false.

You can place as many else if statements in a cascading structure as you want, and you do not have to have an else statement at the end of the structure. If you do not include a default condition, it is a good idea to provide an else if selection that covers exceptions. The PoetList.java program is a random number routine that generates values that the selection structure evaluates. Evaluation of different values leads to the display of information on different poets of the nineteenth century.

```java
// PoetList.java
import java.io.*;
import java.util.Random;

class PoetList{
    public static void main(String Args[]){
// #1
String strRWE, strHDT, strSMF,
       strCST, strChar,
       strToPrint;
int iItr = 0;
Random rand = new Random();

// Define information for poets
//Ralph Waldo Emerson
strRWE =    "\n   Ralph Waldo Emerson -- "    +
            "\n   The Apology, Uriel, Destiny"    +
            "\n   Each and All, The Eternal Pan"    +
```

```
                    "\n    Hamatreya, Earth-Song, Brahma";
//Henry D. Thoreau
strHDT =        "\n    Henry D. Thoreau -- "                +
                "\n    Sympathy  , Sic Vita"                +
                "\n    Friendship, Prayer"                  +
                "\n    Independence, The Inward Morning" +
                "\n    My Love Must Be as Free";


//Sarah Margaret Fuller
strSMF =        "\n    Sarah Margaret Fuller -- "          +
                "\n    Encouragement, Dryad Song"           +
                "\n    The Highlands, Winged Sphinx"       +
                "\n    The Passion-Flower";


//Caroline Sturgis Tappan
strCST =        "\n    Caroline Sturgis Tappan -- "        +
                "\n    Lyric , Life"                         +
                "\n    Art and Artist"                       +
                "\n    Lines , The Hero";


// #2
 iItr = rand.nextInt(4);


System.out.println("\n------Poet List"  + "("
                        + iItr + ")" + "------");
//#3
if(iItr == 1){
    strToPrint =  strRWE;
 }
 else if(iItr == 2){    // if Fuller
    strToPrint =  strSMF;
 }
 else if(iItr == 3){
    strToPrint = strHDT;
 }
  else{
    strToPrint = strCST;
 }
```

```
System.out.print( strToPrint + "\n");
  }//end main
}//end PoetList
```

In the lines comment #1 identifies, you declare and initialize the identifiers the program requires. You require variables to hold lists of poems by different poets. The String variables you create for this purpose also hold the names of the poets. In addition to String variables, you also create an instance of the Random object, rand. At comment #2, you call the nextInt() method to generate random values ranging from 0 to 3 to use in the selection structure that follows. You assign this value to the iItr variable.

At comment #3, you create a selection structure. The structure consists of an if statement followed by two if…else statements and concluded with a default else statement. The if selection statement tests the value assigned to the iItr variable against 1. If the statement evaluates to true, the flow of the program passes into the first block, and you assign the value of strRWE to strToPrint. The flow of the program then exits the structure, and the next statement encountered includes the print() method, which outputs the information (on Emerson) assigned to strToPrint.

If the first selection statement results in an evaluation of false, the control passes to the first else if statement. The control expression of this statement evaluates the value assigned to the iItr variable against 2. If the evaluation renders a true outcome, then control passes into the first else if block, and the string associated with Margaret Fuller is assigned to strToPrint. Following the assignment, the flow of the program exits the selection structure, and the print() method is called.

If the first else if statement renders a false result, the flow of the program passes to the second else if statement. The same action takes place with this statement that took place with the first, except that the evaluation for 3 and the information assigned to strToPrint concerns Henry David Thoreau. As before, after the statement in the block executes, the flow of the program exits the structure.

The flow of the program reaches the else statement only if the random character generated for the program is 0. The else statement accepts the flow as a default because it possesses no control expression. Figure 3.12 illustrates the output of the PoetList.java program for three sequential runs.

The switch Structure

The if…else structure provides one approach to creating cascading selection statements in your programs. Another is the switch selection structure. The switch statement tests for "cases." As Figure 3.13 illustrates, when you set up a switch structure, you open with the keyword `switch` and follow up with parentheses containing a test condition. After this, you include open and closing curly braces enclosing the set of cases.

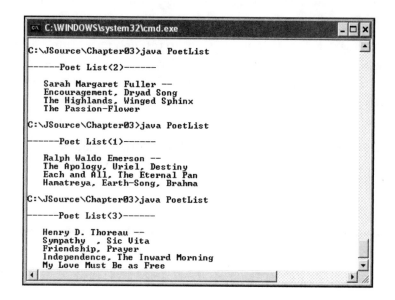

FIGURE 3.12

Multiple-case selections accommodate extensive bodies of information.

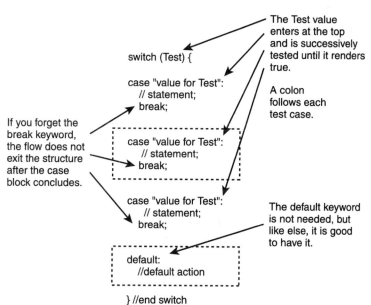

FIGURE 3.13

The `switch` structure has a number of components that you must attend to.

The keywords you use in the switch statement are switch, case, break, and default. The switch keyword names the selection structure. You follow the switch keyword with a test expression enclosed in parentheses. This expression consists of a term that is evaluated against a series of case statements.

You use the case keyword to set up expressions you want to test as a part of the switch structure. Each of these expressions is called a *case*. You can set up as many cases as you want. For each case, you follow the case keyword immediately with the expression you want to test. The line that contains the test expression concludes with a colon. The colon opens a block that executes if the test condition for the case proves true.

Each case block closes with the break keyword. The break keyword is analogous to a closing brace. Within the block the colon and the break keyword create, you include any statements you want to perform for the case.

At the end of the series of cases you include in your switch structure, you can use the default keyword to set up a case that executes in the event that no tested cases prove true for the value you have used for testing.

THE DICE ROLLER PROGRAM

This DiceRoller.java program allows you to experiment with a switch structure to print the faces of a die rendered with character graphics. To determine which face to display, you randomly generate a number in the range from 1 to 6. The cases evaluate the number to determine which face to display:

```
/*
  DiceRoller.java
*/

import java.util.Random;
public class DiceRoller{
    public static void main(String args[]) {
    //#1
    Random random = new Random();
    int die;
    String dieFace;
    System.out.println("Rolling die...");
    die = random.nextInt(6) + 1;
    dieFace = "\n      -------------";
    //#2
```

```
switch (die) {
//#3
case 1:
    dieFace += "\n    |            |";
    dieFace += "\n    |      *     |";
    dieFace += "\n    |            |";
    break;
case 2:
    dieFace += "\n    |        *   |";
    dieFace += "\n    |            |";
    dieFace += "\n    | *          |";
    break;
case 3:
    dieFace += "\n    |        *   |";
    dieFace += "\n    |     *      |";
    dieFace += "\n    | *          |";
    break;
case 4:
    dieFace += "\n    | *        * |";
    dieFace += "\n    |            |";
    dieFace += "\n    | *        * |";
    break;
case 5:
    dieFace += "\n    | *        * |";
    dieFace += "\n    |     *      |";
    dieFace += "\n    | *        * |";
    break;
case 6:
    dieFace += "\n    | *        * |";
    dieFace += "\n    | *        * |";
    dieFace += "\n    | *        * |";
    break;
default:
    //dieFace should never get here
    dieFace += "\n    |            |";
    dieFace += "\n    |            |";
    dieFace += "\n    |            |"; }
    dieFace += "\n     ------------";
```

```
        System.out.println(dieFace);
    }//end main
}//end FuzzyDice
```

In the lines accompanying comment #1 in the DiceRoller.java program, you create an instance of the `Random` class (`rand`). You declare the `dieFace String` variable to contain character representations of the faces of the die. You use the `Random` class constructor and assign the generated values to the `die` variable. At comment #2, you begin the `switch` structure. As the argument for the structure, you provide the `die` variable.

In the lines following comment #3, you set up the first case for the structure. This case tests for the value of 1. If the case renders true, then you use a process of concatenation to create a string that represents the face of a die with a value of 1 (see the first item in Figure 3.14). In the next five cases, you perform similar operations, testing for the values from 2 through 6.

Although no default case is likely to be needed, you set up a default case with a blank die face. An alternative might be to issue a message, such as "Number not found." Figure 3.14 illustrates three "rolls" of the die.

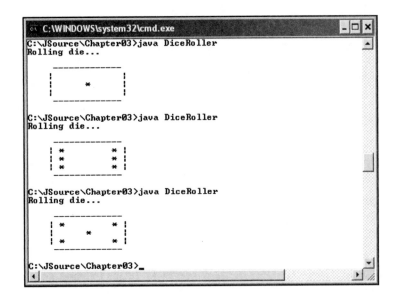

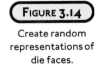

FIGURE 3.14

Create random representations of die faces.

ARRAYS

An array is analogous to a set of drawers. Consider the following items with relation to a set of drawers:

- Each drawer is part of a larger entity.
- You cannot easily change the way the drawers are organized.
- You can change the contents of each drawer.
- You open and close each drawer in the same way.
- Each drawer is similar in size to the other drawers.

Figure 3.15 illustrates a file cabinet and highlights a few of its features with respect to the previous list. Consider, for example, that if you identify a file cabinet storing information on a play by Shakespeare, then each drawer might bear a label that identifies a character. The cabinet might be thought of as the Macbeth Cabinet. You could then go to it when you needed information on *Macbeth*.

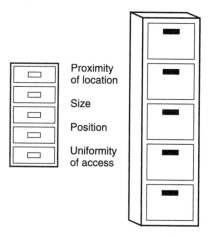

FIGURE 3.15

Think of an array as a file cabinet.

An array consists of a set of items associated with a single name. The items in an array are called *elements*. You can know each element in the array according to its *index*. Each index marks what might be viewed as a place in your computer's memory.

When you define an array, you associate it with a given data type. You can create an array using almost all of the reference and primitive data types Java provides. When you associate an array with a given data type, you create a situation in which a number of items of the same type of data are stored sequentially in your computer's memory.

If you consider the amount of memory a given data type requires as a basic counting unit, you can understand how the elements in an array are arranged. Consider Figure 3.16. When you create an array, you can think of each of its indexes as a number that can be multiplied by the length (or size) of the data type that defines the array. For the first item in an array, then, the index is 0. It is as though you are starting at the bottom of a class. Its beginning is at point 0. The array item Duncan is then located (or starts) at the 0 index. The next element, Malcolm, starts where Duncan ends. If you were seeking the starting position of Duncan, then, you would look for 1 times the unit of measure.

Since an element represents a unit of the data type with which you define the array, each index designates a multiplication of this unit. Index 3 is the place in memory that 3 times the unit represents. At this position, you find the beginning of the memory unit for Donalbain.

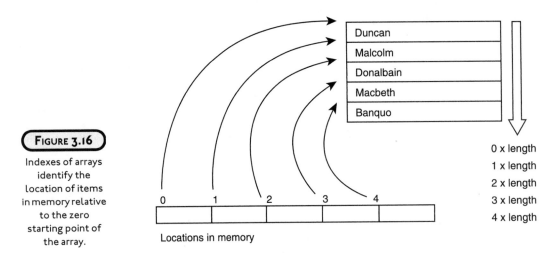

FIGURE 3.16

Indexes of arrays identify the location of items in memory relative to the zero starting point of the array.

Arrays are containers that store units of data sequentially. For this reason, you can access one element of an array after another by just incrementing the value of the index. To access elements in an array, you employ brackets at the end of the array name. The number you place in the brackets indicates the index of the item in the array. Here's an example of how you might access a name from an array named Macbeth:

```
String character = Macbeth[3];
```

Declaring Arrays

When you declare an array, you specify the data type of the array. To designate that you are declaring an array, you follow the name of the array with square brackets. Here are some examples of a few array declarations:

```
String macbethCharacters[];
int intList[];
double mealPrices[];
```

After you declare an array identifier, you assign an array object to it. To accomplish this, you use only the name of the array without the square brackets to identify the array. Then you assign an array reference to the identifier. To create the reference, you use the new keyword followed by the name of the data type you are using for the array. To the name of the data type, you append square brackets and within the brackets define the number of elements you want to store in the array. Here are array definitions for the previously defined arrays:

```
macbethCharacters = new String[10];
intList = new int[100];
mealPrices= new double[6];
```

Generally, every data type in Java provides an array constructor. You always create arrays in the same way. After you create an array, you cannot readily change the number of items it contains. Likewise, the number you provide when you define an array designates the number of elements it contains. The macbethCharacters array stores 10 elements. On the other hand, since the single largest index of an array is one less than its number of elements, the largest index of the macbethCharacters array is 9. The intList array stores 100 elements, and its largest index is 99. The mealPrice array stores 6 elements, but its largest index is 5. (See the following sidebar titled "Array Overflow" for more information on array lengths and indexes.)

Assigning Values to Arrays

After you declare an array and assign an array reference to it, you can assign values to it. To assign a value to an array, you identify the index number of the element to which you want to assign a value. Then you employ the assignment operator and a literal or variable value that provides the value you want to assign to the element. Here are a few examples:

```
String characterA = "Duncan",
        characterB = "Malcolm",
        characterC = "Lady Macbeth";
//assignments made in any order
macbethCharacters[0] = characterA;
macbethCharacters[2] = characterB;
macbethCharacters[1] = characterC;
macbethCharacters[3] = "Banquo";
mealPrice[0] = 9.99;
mealPrice[1] = 23.22;
```

Combined Declaration and Initialization

As with other variables, you can declare and initialize arrays with the same statement. To accomplish this task, you use a data type keyword to designate the data type of the array. You follow this with the array constructor. Then you create a list of comma-delimited items you want to assign to the array. You enclose them in curly braces and assign it to the array identifier. Here's an example:

```
String[] hamletCharacters[] = {"Claudius", "Hamlet",
                               "Polonius", "Horatio",
                               "Laertes",  "Voltimand"};
```

When you initialize an array in this way, the values in the list are added to the array in the order in which you present them. The fist value, `"Claudius"`, is assigned to array element 0. `"Hamlet"` is assigned to array element 1. `"Voltimand"` is assigned to array element 5.

Accessing Array Values

To access the values in an array, you employ the index number of the element you want to access. To access `"Hamlet"` in the `hamletCharacters` array, for example, you use the following statement:

```
characterOfPlay = hamletCharacters[1];
```

ARRAY OVERFLOW

When you access the elements in an array, you use an index number to do so. A danger accompanies this activity. If you use a number larger than the largest index you have defined for the array, then you go *outside the bounds* of the array. When this happens, the interpreter issues an error message. The error message tells you that your program has an array *overflow* problem or an *access violation*.

Overflow and access problems occur because each index of an array designates a place in the memory of your computer. The starting point of the array is 0. This is a fixed place in memory. All other elements are located relative to this place in memory (recall the discussion of how the size of the data you designate for an array is multiplied by the index). By using a negative number or too large a number, you cause the interpreter to try to find a place in the memory of your computer that is not within the bounds of the array.

You usually do not see overflow problems when you compile a program. The reason for this is that the compiler checks your syntax but does not actually execute your program. When you run the `java` command, however, the situation changes. Then the interpreter tries to access memory. Then you see the problem. Here is a slightly modified version of a typical overflow or out-of-bounds error message.

```
Exception in thread "main"
java.lang.ArrayIndexOutOfBoundsException: 6
    at ArrayUse.main(ArrayUse.java:31)
```

When you define an array to contain five elements and then try to access a sixth, the interpreter reports an error, or exception. The error is that the index is out of bounds, as the message indicates. Again, you usually see such messages only when you try to run your program, which is one reason that programmers usually both compile and run their programs before they conclude that they lack defects.

The Array Use Program

The ArrayUse.java program allows you to explore different approaches to declaring and defining arrays and accessing the values they contain. The program involves creating two arrays that contain the names of characters of Shakespeare's *Macbeth* and *Hamlet*. In this program, you make use of a for structure to *traverse* the elements of the arrays. When you traverse the elements of an array, you sequentially visit each element in the array. In most cases, you begin with the element at index 0 and then *iterate* through the array an element at a time until you reach the end.

```
/*
    ArrayUse.java
*/
import java.util.*;
class ArrayUse{
    public static void main(String Args[]){
        //final makes the value so it cannot change
        //#1
        final int  MCHARS = 10, HCHARS;
        HCHARS = 6;
        //#2
        //Declaration
        String macbethCharacters[];
        macbethCharacters = new String[MCHARS];

        String characterA = "Duncan",
               characterB = "Malcolm",
               characterC = "Lady Macbeth";
```

```
    macbethCharacters[0] = characterA;
    macbethCharacters[2] = characterB;
    macbethCharacters[1] = characterC;
    macbethCharacters[3] = "Banquo";
    macbethCharacters[5] = "Lady Macbeth";


    //#3
    String[] hamletCharacters = {"Claudius",
                                 "Hamlet", "Polonius",
                                 "Horatio", "Laertes",
                                 "Voltimand"};
    System.out.println("\n  Characters of Macbeth:");
    //#4
    for (int itr = 0; itr < MCHARS; itr++){
        System.out.print("\n    " + itr + ". " + macbethCharacters[itr]);
        if(macbethCharacters[itr] == null){
            System.out.print("\t\t    No character assigned.");
        }//end if
    }//end for
    //#5
    System.out.println("\n\n  Characters of Hamlet:");
    for (int itr=0; itr < HCHARS; itr++){
        System.out.print("\n    " + itr + ". " + hamletCharacters[itr]);
    }//end for
  }//end main
}//end ArrayUse
```

At comment #1 in the ArrayUse.java program, you make use of the final keyword to declare and define MCHARS and HCHARS identifiers. The final keyword makes it so that the variable with which you use it cannot be changed. Such an identifier is known as a *constant*. Programmers usually employ capital letters to identify constants. Since you cannot change the value of a constant, when you declare a constant, you usually also define it. For demonstration purposes, the program illustrates that you can declare a constant on one line and then on a later line define it. Still, the compiler prevents you from *redefining* a constant. In other words, after assigning 6 to HCHARS, you cannot then assign 4 to it a few lines later.

You define final identifiers, or constants, so that you have at hand identifiers you can use as arguments when you designate the size of your arrays and access elements within them. You do not want such values to vary. If they do, then you risk memory violations (refer to the previous sidebar titled "Array Overflow").

In the lines trailing comment #2, you employ two approaches to declaring arrays. The first approach involves declaring an array, macbethCharacters, with no index value. This approach to declaring an array makes it more or less just an array identifier, a starting point in memory. The compiler waits for you to furnish more details, such as how many elements you want to assign to the array. To assign the elements, on the line following the declaration, you use the new keyword and the MCHARS constant. You use the MCHARS constant to have the new keyword (which is an operator) set aside enough memory to hold a group of elements of the String type equal in size to the value assigned to MCHARS. (Later chapters provide more discussion of this activity.)

Following the definition of the macbethCharacters array, you then assign values to its elements. You do not have to assign the values sequentially. To demonstrate this, the program shows that you can initialize the elements in the order 0, 2, 1. Likewise, you can initialize the elements using literal values or variables.

At comment #3, you employ a second approach to defining an array. This approach involves assigning a list of items to the array. To create the list, you use opening and closing curly braces, and within the braces, you provide a comma-delimited list of items you want to assign to the array. When you assign the list to the hamletCharacters array, the compiler places them in the array in the order you provide. "Claudius", for example, is assigned to index 0, and "Hamlet" is assigned to index 1.

In the lines associated with comment #4, you use a for repetition statement to traverse the elements in the array. As the discussion in Chapter 4 makes clear, a control governs the number of times a for statement repeats. In this case, to control the number of repetitions, you use the MCHARS constant. You also make use of the value of the itr variable, which increases by 1 with each repetition of the loop. This allows you to traverse all the indexes of the hamletCharacters array, which, as Figure 3.17 illustrates, begins at the 0 index and then proceeds to index 9 (which is the tenth element).

Figure 3.17 also shows that some of the elements have "No character assigned." To display this message, you use an if selection statement and test an expression that uses the null keyword. When you create an array, the interpreter uses the null keyword to automatically initialize elements you have not formally defined. For this reason, when you traverse an array, you can test the values of the elements in the array against the null keyword to discover if any of the elements have not been initialized. As Figure 3.17 illustrates, elements 4, 6, 7, 8, and 9 have not been initialized.

At comment #5, you traverse the hamletCharacters array. Since you have initialized this array using the list technique, it lacks any null elements. As the output in Figure 3.17 reveals, the list contains 6 elements. Since the elements begin at 0, the largest index value is 5.

```
C:\WINDOWS\system32\cmd.exe                                       - □ ×
C:\JSource\Chapter03>java ArrayUse
  Characters of Macbeth:

  0. Duncan
  1. Lady Macbeth
  2. Malcolm
  3. Banquo
  4. null                      No character assigned.
  5. Lady Macbeth
  6. null                      No character assigned.
  7. null                      No character assigned.
  8. null                      No character assigned.
  9. null                      No character assigned.

  Characters of Hamlet:

  0. Claudius
  1. Hamlet
  2. Polonius
  3. Horatio
  4. Laertes
  5. Voltimand
C:\JSource\Chapter03>
```

FIGURE 3.17

You can use different approaches to defining and initializing arrays.

THE FORTUNE TELLER REVISITED

This section explores the Fortune Teller application introduced at the beginning of the chapter. This program makes use of the features of Java you have explored in this chapter and adds a few more. One feature is the use of the split() method of the String class, which allows you to divide a string into parts that you can insert into an array. Another feature is the length attribute associated with arrays, which allows you to easily obtain the length of an array.

The FortuneTeller.java program generates random numbers in two ranges. One range covers the days of the week and stems from 0 through 6. You establish this range using a constant value. The other range covers all the predictions of the fortune teller, and you establish this range using the length attribute associated with arrays.

```
/*
  FortuneTeller.java
*/
import java.util.Random;
public class FortuneTeller {
    public static void main(String args[]) {
    //#1
```

```
Random rand = new Random();
String day = "";
int sayIndex = 0;
final int DAYSOFWEEK = 7;
//#2
 String sayings =
   "stub your toe.  find a shiny new nickel."
 + "  talk to someone who has bad breath."
 + "  get a hug from someone you love."
 + "  remember that day for the rest of your life!"
 + "  get an unexpected phone call."
 + "  find nothing significant has happened."
 + "  bump into someone you haven't seen in a while."
 + "  be publicly humiliated.  find forty dollars."
 + "  find others have discovered your secret."
 + "  be mistaken for a god by a small country."
 + "  win the lottery!  move to Alaska."
 + "  discover that Bigfoot is real."
 + "  succeed at everything you do."
 + "  learn something new.  have friends buy you lunch."
 + "  meet someone famous.  be very bored."
 + "  hear your new favorite song.";

  //You split the string whenever you find two
  //consecutive white spaces.
  String[] predictions = sayings.split("\\  ");

  System.out.println("\n    Your Fortune is...that... ");
//#3
  switch (rand.nextInt(DAYSOFWEEK)) {
     case 0:
         day = "Sunday";
         break;
     case 1:
         day = "Monday";
         break;
     case 2:
         day = "Tuesday";
```

```
            break;
        case 3:
            day = "Wednesday";
            break;
        case 4:
            day = "Thursday";
            break;
        case 5:
            day = "Friday";
            break;
        case 6:
            day = "Saturday";
            break;
        default:
            day = "Tomorrow";
    }//end switch
//#4
    System.out.println("    On " + day + ", you will...");
    sayIndex = rand.nextInt(predictions.length);
    System.out.print("                    " + predictions[sayIndex] + "\n");
    }//end main
}// end class
```

In the lines associated with comment #1 in the FortuneTeller.java program, you declare an instance of the Random number class. Then you declare a variable to which you can assign random numbers for predictions (sayIndex), and you define a constant to designate the number of days in the week (DAYSOFWEEK). You then proceed to create a long string (sayings) that contains all of the predictions you want to be able to store in your array. To define the string, you use a convention that stipulates that two spaces must separate each of the predictions. You precede the first prediction with no space. The concatenation operator joins the lines of the string.

After you have defined the sayings string, you then call the String split() method to divide (or tokenize) the string so its separate predictions can be assigned to an array. The argument for the split() method consists of two backslashes (which creates what is known as a *regular expression*) followed by two white spaces. The two white spaces indicate that you want to divide the sayings string into elements based on the occurrence of two consecutive white spaces. You assign the returned value of the split() method to the predictions array, which is of the string type.

At comment #3, you create a `switch` statement that allows you to determine days of the week. As an argument for the `switch` statement, you call the `Random nextInt()` method. For the argument of the `nextInt()` method, you use the `DAYSOFWEEK` constant. The result is that the method generates numbers ranging from 0 through 6. For each case in the `switch` structure, you assign a string naming a different day of the week to the `day` variable.

In the lines associated with comment #4, as Figure 3.18 illustrates, you call the `print()` method to display predictions. To select a prediction from the `predictions` array, you again call the `nextInt()` method. This time, you also access the `length` attribute that Java associates with arrays. The `length` attribute tells you the number of items in an array. It identifies the number according to the index count, so in this way you avoid the risk of choosing an index value that can cause an out-of-bounds exception. You assign the random number the `nextInt()` method generates to the `sayIndex` variable and then use this variable to select a prediction from the `predictions` array.

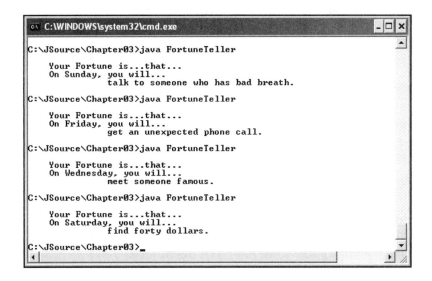

FIGURE 3.18

Use random numbers and an array to generate fortunes.

SUMMARY

In this chapter, you learned about random numbers and how to generate them. You explored how to generate random numbers of different types, such as integers and doubles. You learned about the `Math` class and the methods it contains. In addition, you explored the use of selection statements in conjunction with relational and Boolean operators. Along with selection statements, you learned about arrays. Among other things, you learned that you can declare arrays in two basic ways and access the elements in arrays using array indexes. Given your knowledge of arrays and selection structures, you were able to use the `Random` class to create an application that imitated a fortune teller. Some of the work you have performed in this chapter put you in a position to anticipate your work in the next chapter, which explores repetition structures.

CHALLENGES

1. Use the MathMethods.java program as a starting point. Set up a series of five calculations involving division of an odd starting number. Use the ceil() method on the result of each calculation and then submit the result to the next calculation. Set up a second series of five calculations using the round() method. Do you end up with different results?

2. Set up a structure with four if…else…if tests that test for the names of states. Set a default block so that it prints "Not found." Set up an array with eight state names. Use a random number generator to access a name in the array and assign it to an identifier that you test in the if...else...if structure. Output the name of the state if the generated state matches one of the states you test for in the selection structure.

3. Set up a switch selection statement with 12 cases, one for each month of the year. Accept input from the user in the form of an integer value greater than 0 and less than 13. Return the name of the month corresponding to the number.

4. Use the ternary operator four times in a row to make comments about a given number. Take input from the user and then evaluate the number using ternary operations only. Here is a scenario: n (the number) is one less that n+1, double n/2, the square of n(n), is not equal to n - 1, and so on.

REPETITION STATEMENTS AND EXCEPTION HANDLING

In this chapter, you learn how to work with repetition statements. Repetition statements are also called looping statements or simply loops. Repetition statements resemble selection statements because they govern blocks of statements that enter and remain in the flow of your program, depending on the truth or falsehood of an expression you include in the repetition statement. You have already had a chance to work with the for repetition statement when you dealt with arrays in Chapter 3. Now this beginning is extended to increase your understanding of the specific items involved in creating and using for statements. In addition to for statements, you also examine while and do...while statements. To complement your work with repetition statements, you also extend the work you have done in previous chapters with exception handling. The work you perform merges in the end in the Guess-a-Number program. Among the topics in this chapter are the following:

- Understanding the need for repetition blocks
- The uses of for, while, an do...while repetition statements
- Innovations, such as iterating backward and at varying intervals
- Using special terms that allow you to escape repetition blocks
- Further examining the use of try and catch blocks to handle exceptions

THE GUESS-A-NUMBER APPLICATION

The Guess-a-Number application generates a number in the range extending from 1 to 100 and then prompts users to guess the number. The application allows users as many guesses as they need. To make this possible, you include a repetition block in the application. The block allows the flow of the program to repeatedly prompt the user for a number and evaluate the number to determine whether it matches the target number. To make the guessing less of an ordeal for the user, the application tells the user whether each number is higher or lower than the target number, as shown in Figure 4.1.

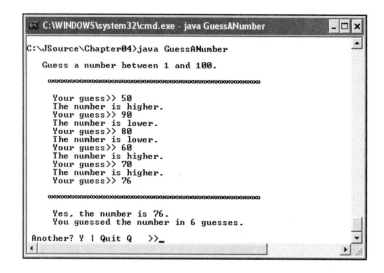

FIGURE 4.1

Repetition allows you to create the Guess-a-Number application.

FLOW AS REPETITION

In many programming contexts, you must develop your program so that at some point a given statement or set of statements repeatedly executes. In such situations, you require a repetition control statement. A simple repetition control statement involves a single block. This block allows you to define a statement or set of statements that your program repeatedly executes. The same mechanics introduced for selection blocks also apply to repetition blocks. In some instances, the control statement precedes the repetition block and includes an expression that is evaluated as the flow of the program enters the block. In other cases, the control statement comes at the end of the block. Opening and closing braces define the block. As Figure 4.2 illustrates, as long as the expression evaluates true, the flow of the program continues to iterate through the loop.

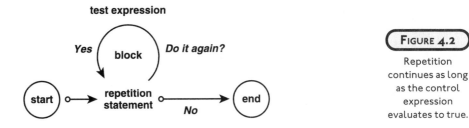

FIGURE 4.2

Repetition continues as long as the control expression evaluates to true.

Repetition statements become more complex when they involve embedded repetition and selection statements. Later sections of this chapter examine such involved structures. Table 4.1 provides general discussion of a few of the keywords related to repetition statements.

TABLE 4.1   DISCUSSION OF REPETITION TERMS

Term	Discussion
while	This statement precedes the block it governs. You accompany the while keyword with a test expression enclosed in parentheses. If the expression tests true, the flow of the program enters the block. The block then repeats, testing the expression before each repetition. The block continues to repeat as long as the expression evaluates to true.
do...while	The do keyword precedes the block. The while keyword follows the block. Braces define the block. You accompany the while keyword with a test expression enclosed in parentheses. The flow of the program enters the block without being tested. After it has passed through the block once, the expression accompanying the while keyword is tested. If the expression evaluates to true, then the flow jumps back to the start of the block and repeats.
for	The Java for repetition statement involves three control expressions. One is a counter. A second sets a limit. A third establishes the increments in which you want to count as you repeatedly execute the block following the for statement. You have a great deal of flexibility in how you use these control expressions. You can put them in the block or in your program outside the repetition statement and its block.
break	This keyword allows you to exit a repetition block. You usually make this keyword a part of a selection statement you embed within the repetition block.
continue	This keyword allows you to skip a portion of a block and return to the start or top of the block. To use the this keyword, you can employ a selection statement that supplements the work of the repetition statement.

THE FOR STATEMENT

You had a chance to work with the for repetition statement in several of the programs featured in Chapter 3. Now it is time to take a closer look of the some of the features of the for statement. Given an understanding of these features, you can begin to use `for` statements in many ways that complement and extend the uses you encountered in Chapter 3.

Generally, the `for` statement (or `for` loop) provides the quintessential vehicle for elementary repetition. To use it, you employ three arguments, which the following list summarizes. Refer to Figure 4.3 as you review the items in the list:

- **The control value.** The control value is an integer identifier that establishes a starting value for the counter you use to control the number of times the `for` block repeats. Programmers often set the starting value to 0, but you can use any range of numbers that fits your need. For example, you can use 100 or 1,000 as an initial value.

- **The limit.** The second expression in the `for` statement uses a relational operator to compare the value of the control identifier with a another value, one that you can provide as a constant value or as an identifier. Normally, the counter you establish as the first expression increases in value with each repetition of the block. This expression tests the increasing value. You can use any of the relational operators in this expression.

- **The incremental expression.** The incremental expression usually consists of the control value suffixed or prefixed by an increment operator. This value grows with each iteration of the loop. You can use assignment operators and other expressions instead of the increment operators to change the control value.

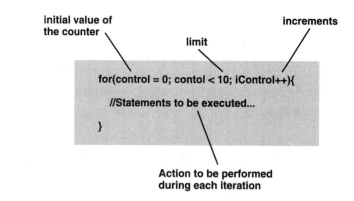

FIGURE 4.3

The basic `for` control allows three arguments.

THE RACER PROGRAM

The Racer.java program provides you with a context in which to experiment with different forms of the `for` repetition statement. The basic form of the statement involves using three control expressions inside parentheses, as you glimpsed in the programs included in Chapter 3.

```
/*
Racer.java
*/
public class Racer{
    public static void main(String args[]){
//#1
// Standard control forms
// Build a string
        String raceTrack = "";
        for (int track = 1; track <= 78; track++) {
            raceTrack += "#";
            //Track goes to --
            if(track == 78){
                System.out.println("\n\tTrack units (=): "+ track );
            }
        }
//#2
        System.out.println("\n\tGO!");
        raceTrack += "\n";
        System.out.print(raceTrack);
//#3
        System.out.print("\n Race One:\t");
        for (int lap = 0; lap <=10; lap++) {
            System.out.print(lap + ")->");
        }
        System.out.println("Finish!\n");
        System.out.print(raceTrack);
//#4
// Shift the range
        System.out.print("\n Race Two:\t");
        for (int lap = 10; lap <21; lap++) {
            System.out.print(lap + ")->");
        }
        System.out.println("Finish!\n");
        System.out.print(raceTrack);
    }//end main
}//end Racer
```

Basic Repetition Activities

In the lines accompanying comment #1 in the Racer.java program, you define a standard for statement. Within the parentheses of this statement, you declare a variable, track, and assign it an initial value of 1 (track = 1). After defining track, you then create a test expression (track <= 78). The test expression allows the block to repeat only as long as the value of track is less than or equal to 78.

The flow of your program encounters the definition expression first. It then moves on to the test expression. If the value of track is less than or equal to 78, the flow of the program moves into the block of the statement. When the flow of the program enters the block, it encounters a statement similar to one you saw in Chapter 2. This statement uses a String concatenation operator (+=) to assign a character ("#") to raceTrack. With each repetition of the block, a character is appended to the string raceTrack stores.

In addition to building a string, the block contains an if selection statement. This statement evaluates whether the value of track has reached 78. It is tested each time the block repeats. It evaluates to true only once, the last time the block repeats.

After adding the character to the raceTrack string and testing the value of track, the flow of the program returns to the for statement. Its first action is to increase (increment) the value of track by 1 (track++). It then goes to the second expression (track <= 78), which evaluates this new value of track against 78. Given that the value of track has been increased to 2, it is less than 78, so the flow of the program now enters the repetition block. Within the repetition block, the concatenation and selection statements are again executed.

How many times does the flow of the program execute the statements in the block? As Figure 4.4. illustrates, the answer is 78. It executes the statements 78 times because it enters the block as long as the middle expression renders a true result. To verify that the count reaches 78, the action of the if selection statement prints the value of track. It prints it only when it equals 78. It equals it during the last iteration of the block. Likewise, if you count the number of pound signs used to make up the raceTrack line, you find that there are 78 of them.

The last iteration of the block allows the flow of the program to enter, once again, the repetition statement. The statement allows the value of track to be increased to 79. However, when the flow of the program moves to the control expression, the expression results in false. At this point, the flow of the program exits the repetition statement without entering the repetition block. It proceeds to the next sequential statement in your program, which is a call to the println() method.

At comment #2, you call the println() method. The result of this call is that you print the expression GO!. You then call the print() method to print the contents of raceTrack, which is the top line of pound signs you see in Figure 4.4.

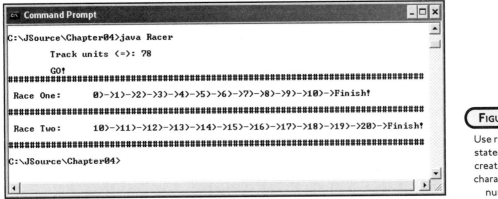

FIGURE 4.4

Use repetition statements to create lines of characters and numbers.

In the lines trailing comment #3, after calling the println() function to display the words Race One, you create a second for statement. This one is simpler than the first. It involves the same type of control expressions. You begin by defining the lap control variable, to which you assign a starting value of 0. You then test the lap variable in the same way that you tested the track variable, but in this case, the limit is 10 rather than 78.

After defining lap, the flow of the program tests lap using the less-than-or-equal-to relational operator (<=). Since the initial value of lap is 0, the flow of the program enters the statement block. Within the block, you call the println() method to print the current value of lap and a couple of characters to simulate the progress of a race (")->"). As Figure 4.4 illustrates, the first value of lap is 0, and the last value is 10. When the value of lap reaches 11, lap cannot test true in the middle expression, so the flow of the program does not again enter the repetition block. Instead, it goes on to call the println() method to print Finished!. You then call the print() method to print another line of pound signs.

Redefinition of Control Variables

Following comment #4 of the Racer.java program, you call the print() method to display the words Race Two. You then create a third for statement. When you create the third for statement, you *redefine* the variable lap. As you recall from Chapter 2, when you define a variable, the definition consists of a data type keyword, the variable identifier, an assignment operator, and the value assigned. Here is the definition for the lap variable that follows comment #3:

```
int lap = 10;
```

On the other hand, following comment #4, you see another definition:

```
int lap = 0;
```

In the main flow of a program, you may not redefine a variable. To do so creates a compiler error. You can certainly changes its value, but you cannot repeatedly declare it. If the variable is part of a `for` repetition statement, however, you can redefine it. You can do this because the definition lies within the *scopes* of different `for` statements. The expressions between the opening and closing parentheses of the `for` statements are within the scopes of the statements, as is all the activity that takes place between the opening and closing curly braces of the repetition blocks that follow the statements. Since you define two repetition blocks, you can define two versions of `lap`.

For the second definition, you assign a starting value of 10 to `lap`, and you evaluate its value using a less than operator (`<`). The limit in this case is 21. As with the previous `for` statement, the block repeats 10 times. After the tenth iteration concludes, the flow of the program increments `lap` to a value of 21. It then tests this value and finds that it is no longer less than 21. At that point, the flow of the program skips the block and goes to the `println()` and `print()` methods that follow.

CONTROL AND UNARY OPERATORS

The two plus signs you use in succession following the counter (`lap++`) in the Racer.java program are among the *unary* operators that Java furnishes. A unary operator is an operator that requires only one operand. The operators you explored in Chapters 2 and 3 consist mainly of binary operators—operators that require two operands. Here are some examples of unary operators and equivalent binary expressions:

```
a = a + 1;     // binary
a++;           // unary
b = b - 1;     // binary
b--;           // unary
```

The unary operators increase or decrease the value of the operands (or variables) to which they are applied by a value of 1 each time they are called. This is equivalent to adding 1 to the variable using a binary plus (+) operator and then assigning the variable back to itself.

Decrement and increment operators offer you options that the binary operations do not. You can use *prefix* and *postfix* forms of unary operators. Here are some examples:

```
b++;
++b;
a--;
--a;
```

Whether you use a prefix increment operator or a postfix increment operator, the operator increments or decrements the value of the variable by 1 each time you call it. However, there is a difference between prefix and postfix operators. The postfix operator is evaluated *after* assignments or operations are performed, whereas the prefix increment is evaluated *before* assignments or operations are performed. In the following example, the value assigned to y is 2:

```
int y,
x = 1;
y = ++x;      // predict operation: 2 is assigned to y
```

The reason that a value of 2 is assigned to y is that the flow of the program increments the value of x before the assignment operation is carried out. In the following example, the situation changes. In this case, a postfix operator is used, so the value assigned to y is 1:

```
int y,
x = 1;
y = x++;      // postfix operation: 1 is assigned to y
```

The value of 1 is assigned to x because the flow of the program first assigns the value of x as initialized to 1 to y. Then it increments x. The PrePost.java program allows you to explore the use of such operations:

```
/*
     PrePost.java
*/
public class PrePost{
    public static void main(String args[]) {
        int x = 0, y = 0, a = 0, b = 0;
        System.out.println("\n\t y and x both = 0");
        y = x++;

        System.out.println("\t The expression y = x++ "
                    + " results in y = " + y
                    + " and x = " + x);
        System.out.println("\t The assignment takes place before "
```

```
                               + " x is incremented");
          System.out.println("\n\t a and b both = 0");
          b = ++a;
          System.out.println("\t The expression b = ++a "
                               + " results in b = " + b
                               + " and a = " + a);
          System.out.println("\t The assignment takes place after "
                               + " a is incremented");
    }
}
```

Figure 4.5 illustrates the output of the PrePost.java program. In the opening of the program, you assign the variables y and x values of 0. You then use the prefix operator with x and assign its value to y. When you display the value of y, you see that it is still 0. On the other hand, the value of x has increased to 1. The value of y remains 0 because you have assigned it the value of x while using the postfix operator with x. The value of x is assigned before x is incremented.

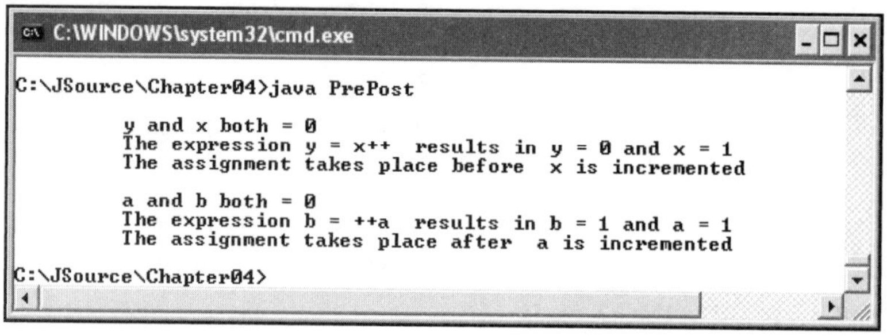

FIGURE 4.5

With postfix and prefix operators, results differ.

The results change with the use of the prefix operator. With the prefix operator, you again start by assigning values of 0 to both variables. This time the variables are named a and b. You apply the prefix operator to variable a and assign its value to variable b. The result is that you see that the values of variable a and variable b are both 1. This occurs because you use the prefix increment operator with the a variable, which increments the value of the a variable prior to the assignment of its value to b.

Variations on Intervals

In some situations, it is necessary to use different approaches to augmenting values as you work with repetition structures. For example, your programming tasks might require that you create a repetition block that generates only even or odd values. In other instances, you might have to move though a series of numbers at some other intervals. The

DifferentIntervals.java program allows you to employ a `for` repetition statement that repeats 10 times to generate four columns of data that represent different intervals:

```
/*
 DifferentIntervals.java
*/
public class DifferentIntervals{
    public static void main(String args[]){
//#1
        int valueA = 0,
            valueB = 0,
            valueC = 0,
            valueD = 0;

        String line = "\n";
        for (int ctr = 1; ctr <= 60; ctr++){
            line += "-";
        }
        line += "\n";
//#2
        System.out.println(line);
        System.out.println(" By 1\t\tBy 2\t\tBy 5\t\tBy 10");
        System.out.println(line);
        for(int ctr = 0; ctr <=10; ctr++){
            valueA++;
            valueB = valueB + 2;
            valueC = valueC + 5;
            valueD = valueD + 10;
            System.out.println("   "  +   valueA    + "\t\t"
                                     +   valueB    + "\t\t"
                                     +   valueC    + "\t\t"
                                     +   valueD    + "\t\t");
        }//end for
    }//end main
}//end DifferentIntervals
```

In the lines associated with comment #1, you declare and initialize a series of variables of the `int` type. All these variables are set to 0. Then in the lines following comment #2, you set up a table heading to identify the different counting intervals. After that, you create a `for` repetition block. The counter allows the block to repeat 10 times. Within the block you use different forms of incremental operations to advance the values of the different variables. Using the unary increment operator, you advance by a value of 1 each time the block repeats. The other operations increase the values by 2, 5, and 10. Figure 4.6 illustrates the table of values that results.

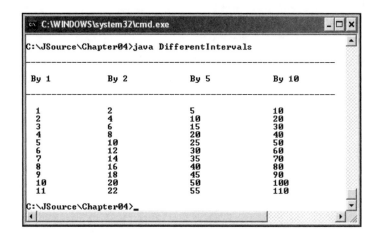

FIGURE 4.6

You can advance a count by using different increment operations.

Compound Assignment Operators

You can abbreviate the binary operations in the DifferentIntervals.java program. To accomplish this, you use *compound assignment operators*. The compound assignment operators all work in the same way. Here is an example of how the operations in the DifferentIntervals.java program are abbreviated using compound operators:

```
valueB = valueB + 2;
valueB += 2;                //compound assignment
valueC = valueC + 5;
valueB += 5;                //compound assignment
valueD = valueD + 10;
valueB += 10;               //compound assignment
```

In each instance, the compound assignment operator takes the value to its right, adds it to the value on its left, and then assigns the result back to the value on the left. You have already seen this type of operation at work with the String concatenation operator. In that case, however, the operator is customized so that rather than trying to effect an arithmetic operation, it appends characters. Along with the String concatenation operator, Java provides compound assignment operators for the common math operations. Table 4.2 provides discussion of these operators.

TABLE 4.2	COMPOUND ASSIGNMENT OPERATORS	
Operator	**Example**	**Discussion**
+=	a += b	Adds a to b and assigns the sum back to b
-=	a -= b	Subtracts b from a and assigns the difference back to a
*=	a *= b	Multiplies a by b and assigns the product back to a
/=	a /= b	Divides a by b and assigns the result back to a
%=	a %= b	Takes the remainder of the division of a by b and assigns it back to a

The CompoundIntervals.java program reworks the DifferentIntervals.java program to enable you to explore the uses of the compound assignment operators. This program features a `for` repetition statement that allows its block to iterate six times. With each iteration, a series of compound operations is performed.

```
/*
 CompoundIntervals.java
*/
public class CompoundIntervals{
   public static void main(String args[]){
//#1
      int valueA = 0;
      long valueB = 2;
      float valueC = 12F;
      double valueD = 10000.00;

      String line = "\n";
      for (int ctr = 1; ctr <= 60; ctr++){
          line += "-";
      }
      line += "\n";
//#2
      System.out.println(line);
      System.out.println(" += 2\t\t*= 2\t\t-= 2\t\t/= 2");
      System.out.println(line);
      for(int ctr = 0; ctr <=5; ctr++){
         valueA += 2;
         valueB *= 2;
```

```
        valueC -= 2;
        valueD /= 2;
        System.out.println("   "  +    valueA   + "\t\t"
                                  +    valueB   + "\t\t"
                                  +    valueC   + "\t\t"
                                  +    valueD   + "\t\t");
    }//end for
  }//end main
}//end CompoundIntervals
```

In the lines trailing comment #1 in the CompoundIntervals.java program, you declare and define variables of four types: int, float, long, and double. Incremental and compound assignment operations work with all these data types. To show how this is so, at comment #2 you set up a table heading that identifies four types of compound assignment operators. You then set up a for repetition statement that allows a block to repeat six times.

Within the scope of the block, you use the compound assignment operators to alter the values of the variables in different ways. As Figure 4.7 illustrates, the compound operator for addition adds 2 to the value of the variable of the int type with each iteration of the block. The compound operator for multiplication doubles the value of the variable of the long type with each iteration. Beginning with a value of 10, the compound operator for subtraction decreases the value of the variable of the float type with each iteration. For the compound operator for division, when you start with a value of 5000 assigned to the variable of the double type, you decrease it through successive divisions to 156.25 after six iterations of the block.

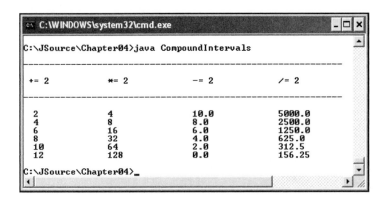

FIGURE 4.7

Compound operators combine math operators with the assignment operator.

VARIATIONS ON THE USE OF THE FOR STRUCTURE

You can use unary and compounded operators with all the primitive data types, and you can vary the approaches you use to declare and define the control variables you use. The Increments.java program allows you to explore four general topics in this respect. First, you can use counters of different data types to control repetition statements. Second, you can decrement the control values of a repetition statement. You can also use random intervals, and this you accomplish by calling the nextInt() method of the Random class. Finally, you can vary the way you structure your for statements. For example, you can declare your counter prior to the start of the repetition statement while incrementing it within the block of the statement.

```java
/*
 Increments.java
*/
import java.util.Random;
public class Increments{
    public static void main(String args[]){
//#1
        Random rand = new Random();
        String mineralNames = "Covelite Galena " +
                    "Molybdenite Graphite Basalt";
        String Minerals[] = mineralNames.split("\\ ");
        final int LIMIT = Minerals.length;

        String line = "\n";
        for (int ctr = 1; ctr <= 56; ctr++) {
            line += "-";
        }
        line += "\n";


//#2

        System.out.println("\n" + line);
        System.out.print(" Double:\t");
        for (double doubleValue = 0; doubleValue <=5; doubleValue++) {
            System.out.print(doubleValue + " ");
        }
        System.out.println("\n" + line);
```

```
//#3
        System.out.print(" Long:\t");
        for (long longValue = 0; longValue <=5; longValue++) {
            System.out.print(longValue + " ");
        }
        System.out.println("\n" + line);
//#4
        System.out.print(" Decrement:\n");
        for(int ctr = LIMIT-1; ctr >=0; ctr--){
            System.out.print(" " + ctr + " " + Minerals[ctr]);
        }
        System.out.println("\n" + line);
//#5
        System.out.print(" Random:\n");
        for(int ctr = 0; ctr < LIMIT ; ctr += (rand.nextInt(LIMIT) + 1)){
            System.out.print(" " + ctr + " " + Minerals[ctr]);
        }
        System.out.println("\n" + line);
//#6
        System.out.print(" Outside and Inside:\n");
        int control = 0;
       ,for(;control < LIMIT ; ){
            System.out.print(" " + control
                                    + " " + Minerals[control]);
            control += (rand.nextInt(LIMIT) + 1);
        }
        System.out.println("\n" + line);
    }//end main
}//end Increments
```

In the lines associated with comment #1 of the Increments.java program, you create
an instance of the Random class and assign it to the rand identifier. You then define a
String variable, mineralNames, and assign a set of mineral names to it. After defining the
mineralNames variable, you call the split() method to separate the names into elements that
you assign to the Minerals array. Given the definition of the Minerals array, you access the
length attribute to obtain the number of elements in the array, which you use to initialize
the LIMIT constant.

In the lines trailing comments #2 and #3, you use counters of the `double` and `long` types to control repetition statements. The increment operator works for both of the data types, as has been shown previously. In this instance, as Figure 4.8 illustrates, you call the `print()` method to display the values of the counters (`doubleValue` and `longValue`) as the blocks iterate.

In the lines accompanying comment #4, you use the decrement operator with the `ctr` control variable to traverse the indexes of the `Minerals` array. To make the traversal work, it is necessary to start with the number of elements in the array (`LIMIT`) and subtract 1 from this value to ensue that you do not exceed the bounds of the array. You then decrement the value of the control while it is greater than or equal to 0. As Figure 4.8 reveals, the last element of the string, `Basalt`, has an index of 4 but is the first mineral name to be printed.

The operations associated with comment #5 involve calling the `nextInt()` method of the `Rand` class. In this instance, you use a compound addition operation to add a random value to the control. You use the `LIMIT` constant to set the range of the random numbers the `nextInt()` method generates, but you also shift the value by 1 to ensure that you obtain a value at some point that forces the repetition action to terminate. As Figure 4.8 illustrates, the action of the block displays the mineral names sequentially, but how many names you see remains a matter of chance.

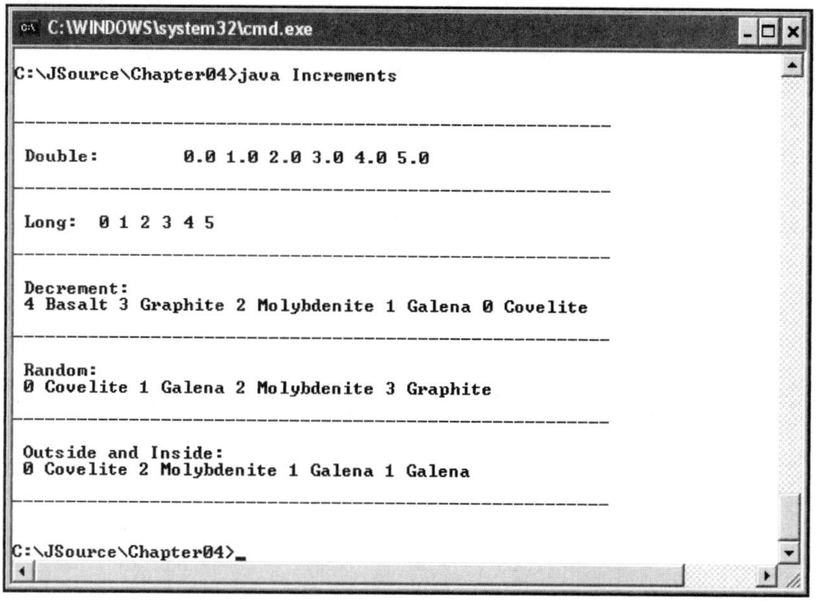

```
C:\WINDOWS\system32\cmd.exe                                    _ □ ✕

C:\JSource\Chapter04>java Increments

---------------------------------------------------------------
 Double:        0.0 1.0 2.0 3.0 4.0 5.0
---------------------------------------------------------------
 Long:   0  1  2  3  4  5
---------------------------------------------------------------
 Decrement:
 4 Basalt 3 Graphite 2 Molybdenite 1 Galena 0 Covelite
---------------------------------------------------------------
 Random:
 0 Covelite 1 Galena 2 Molybdenite 3 Graphite
---------------------------------------------------------------
 Outside and Inside:
 0 Covelite 2 Molybdenite 1 Galena 1 Galena
---------------------------------------------------------------

C:\JSource\Chapter04>_
```

FIGURE 4.8

You can use the for repetition statement to achieve a number of different results.

At comment #6, you declare a control variable (control) prior to the definition of the for repetition statement. This allows you to leave the first control expression blank. For this reason, the definition of the controls for the statement begins with a semicolon. For the control limit, you use the LIMIT constant and evaluate it using the less than relational operator (<). Inside the block you attend to incrementing the value of the control. You accomplish this by calling the nextInt() method of the Random class. As the block iterates, the value of the control variable increases randomly.

Since the definition of the control variable precedes the definition of the repetition state- ment, the first mineral name you see displayed is always Covelite (index 0). On the other hand, the mineral names you see after that depend on the value that the nextInt() method gener- ates. This value is reset during each iteration of the block. The counter is not incremented. Instead, it is reset. The block continues to iterate until the value generated exceeds the value of the limit. As a result, even though you are working with a repetition statement, the mineral names appear randomly.

NESTED REPETITION BLOCKS

In the programs you have worked with so far, in a few instances you have placed selection blocks inside repetition blocks. You can also place repetition blocks inside repetition blocks. Programmers commonly refer to such structures as *nested blocks* or *nested loops*. As Figure 4.9 illustrates, when you implement a nested block, the main flow of the program first encoun- ters the outer repetition statement. The condition you have set for the repetition statement evaluates to true, and the flow of the program enters the *outer block*. Within the scope of the outer block, you position a second repetition statement. This is the *inner block*. The flow of the program then enters the inner block. The statements there are executed, and after the pro- gram completes the execution of these statements, it then returns to the outer block. From the outer block, the flow of the program then returns to the main flow of the program.

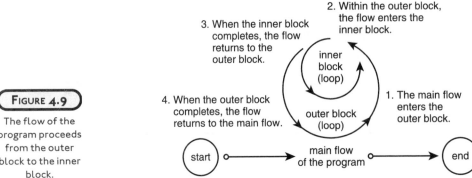

FIGURE 4.9

The flow of the program proceeds from the outer block to the inner block.

When you set up an inner block, it continues to repeat until its test condition proves false. If you set up several inner blocks in succession, then, a full cycle of the outer block does not complete until all the inner blocks have completed. The MultiplicationTable.java program provides you with a familiar application of nested blocks. The outer block successively identifies the number of rows you want to create. The inner block generates the rows to be multiplied and the rows of the table. Figure 4.10 illustrates the flow of activity that generates the table.

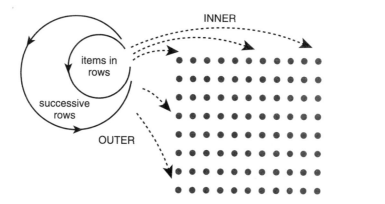

FIGURE 4.10

Inner and outer repetition statements generate a table of values.

To create a table of multiplication values for the numbers 1 through 12, you create two for repetition statements, one nested within the other. The outer block allows you to designate the numbers for which you want to generate multiplication values. The inner block performs the multiplications and generates the rows and columns of the table. The outer block serves only to increment the starting point of the work of the inner block.

```
/*
  MultiplicationTable.java
*/

public class MultiplicationTable{
    public static void main(String args[]) {
        //#1
        String line = "\n    ";
        for (int ctr = 1; ctr <= 61; ctr++) {
            line += "-";
        }
        System.out.println(line);
        //#2
```

```
    for (int outer= 1; outer <= 12; outer++) {
        System.out.print(" |");
        //#3
        for (int inner=1; inner <= 12; inner++) {
            //#4
            String rowItem = " " + outer * inner + " ";
            System.out.print(rowItem.substring(0, 4) + "|" );
        }//end inner block
        //#5
        System.out.println(line);
    }//end outer block
  }//end main
}//end class
```

In the lines following comment #1 of the MultiplicationTable.java program, you create a string variable, line, that contains the horizontal dashed line that separates the rows of numbers shown in Figure 4.11. Creating the line involves experimenting with the width of the table after you have generated it. A line that consists of 61 dashes and 4 white spaces fits the table that results from the actions of the repetition blocks.

Having created the horizontal divider line, you call the println() method to print the top line of the table. You then create a nested set of for repetition statements. At #2, you create the outer for statement. To define this statement, you set the control (outer) to start at 1 and repeat until it equals 12. In this way, you generate 12 rows for the table, each row starting with an incrementally greater value.

Within the outer loop, you call the print() method and print the left border character of the table. You then proceed at comment #3 to define the inner for statement to generate the values that occupy the columns of the row. You set the inner for statement to repeat 12 times, like the outer for statement, and in this way you generate 12 columns of data.

Generating a row of 12 formatted columns involves first creating a String variable, rowItem, which you join together to make the row. You attend to this in the lines associated with comment #4. First, to define the rowItem variable, you concatenate a space, the product of the outer and inner control variables, and two trailing spaces. The total number of characters for the String variable grows as the values involved in the multiplications increase. When you multiply 1 by 1, for example, you obtain a one-character product. When you multiply 12 by 12, you obtain a three-character product. For this reason, the number of characters that constitute rowItem ranges from 4 to 7 as the table is being built.

To make it so that the columns are of the same width, you use `rowItem` to call the `substring()` method of the `String` class. The `substring()` method returns a selected number of characters (a substring) from the string with which you call it. It requires two arguments. The first argument designates the starting position of the substring to extract from the source string. The second argument designates the number of characters to extract. In this instance, you designate 0 as the starting point and 4 as the number of characters to extract. This results in cells four characters wide. You then use the concatenation operator to add a vertical bar to the end of each cell string.

The inner block performs 12 successive multiplications and places the products in cells positioned horizontally one after the other. Each product rests in a cell four characters wide. A horizontal bar separates each cell. Each time the inner `for` statement iterates, it starts its actions with a value one greater than it started with during the previous iteration. This is the value obtained from `outer`. On the other hand, it always multiplies `outer` by numbers ranging from 1 to 12, the values of `inner`. Each time the inner `for` statement concludes, the flow of the program passes back into the outer block and calls the `println()` method, which prints a horizontal line for the table. Then the flow of the program returns to the start of the outer block, where a call to the `print()` method prints the left border of the table.

```
C:\WINDOWS\system32\cmd.exe                                          - □ ×

C:\JSource\Chapter04>java MultiplicationTable

  -----------------------------------------------------------------------
  ! 1  ! 2  ! 3  ! 4  ! 5  ! 6  ! 7  ! 8  ! 9  ! 10 ! 11 ! 12 !
  -----------------------------------------------------------------------
  ! 2  ! 4  ! 6  ! 8  ! 10 ! 12 ! 14 ! 16 ! 18 ! 20 ! 22 ! 24 !
  -----------------------------------------------------------------------
  ! 3  ! 6  ! 9  ! 12 ! 15 ! 18 ! 21 ! 24 ! 27 ! 30 ! 33 ! 36 !
  -----------------------------------------------------------------------
  ! 4  ! 8  ! 12 ! 16 ! 20 ! 24 ! 28 ! 32 ! 36 ! 40 ! 44 ! 48 !
  -----------------------------------------------------------------------
  ! 5  ! 10 ! 15 ! 20 ! 25 ! 30 ! 35 ! 40 ! 45 ! 50 ! 55 ! 60 !
  -----------------------------------------------------------------------
  ! 6  ! 12 ! 18 ! 24 ! 30 ! 36 ! 42 ! 48 ! 54 ! 60 ! 66 ! 72 !
  -----------------------------------------------------------------------
  ! 7  ! 14 ! 21 ! 28 ! 35 ! 42 ! 49 ! 56 ! 63 ! 70 ! 77 ! 84 !
  -----------------------------------------------------------------------
  ! 8  ! 16 ! 24 ! 32 ! 40 ! 48 ! 56 ! 64 ! 72 ! 80 ! 88 ! 96 !
  -----------------------------------------------------------------------
  ! 9  ! 18 ! 27 ! 36 ! 45 ! 54 ! 63 ! 72 ! 81 ! 90 ! 99 ! 108!
  -----------------------------------------------------------------------
  ! 10 ! 20 ! 30 ! 40 ! 50 ! 60 ! 70 ! 80 ! 90 ! 100! 110! 120!
  -----------------------------------------------------------------------
  ! 11 ! 22 ! 33 ! 44 ! 55 ! 66 ! 77 ! 88 ! 99 ! 110! 121! 132!
  -----------------------------------------------------------------------
  ! 12 ! 24 ! 36 ! 48 ! 60 ! 72 ! 84 ! 96 ! 108! 120! 132! 144!
  -----------------------------------------------------------------------
C:\JSource\Chapter04>_
```

FIGURE 4.11

Inner and outer blocks create rows and columns.

THE WHILE STATEMENT

The while repetition statement resembles the for repetition statement. As with the for statement, the control condition you assign to it determines whether the flow of your program can enter the block the while statement governs. Having entered the block, the flow of the program continues to repeat the actions the block defines until the control expression evaluates to false.

The while statement differs from the for statement because it does not explicitly provide slots for the definition, testing, and incremental change of the control. You must design the control from scratch. You can design the control so that it works in a way similar to that of the for statement. Figure 4.12 illustrates such an approach. In this case, you implement selection statements within the scope of the while block. As the while block repeats, this selection statement audits a condition. At some point, the condition changes, and the selection statement changes the repetition control to false. When the while control expression evaluates the control and renders a false report, the flow of the program exits the while block.

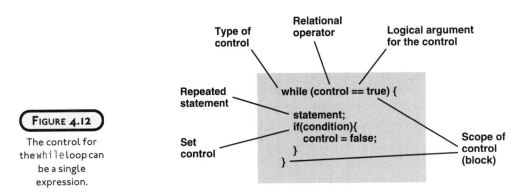

FIGURE 4.12

The control for the while loop can be a single expression.

The MineralChance.java program provides you with a context in which to explore the use of the while repetition statement. With each iteration of the block, the program user sees a mineral and its description. At the end the block, the user decides whether to continue to view another mineral and its description.

```
/*
MineralChance.java
*/
import java.util.Random;
import java.io.*;
public class MineralChance{
    public static void main(String Args[]){
```

```
    Random rand = new Random();
    BufferedReader reader;
    //Create an instance of the buffer
    reader = new BufferedReader(new InputStreamReader(System.in));

//#1
    String choice = "Y";
    String mineralDescriptions[]  =
            {"Natrolite \n    Colorless, white; nonmetallic luster",
            "Colemanite \n    Colorless, white; nonmetallic luster",
            "Corundum   \n    Bluish gray; nonmetallic luster",
            "Topaz      \n    Colorless, yellow, blue; nonmetallic luster",
            "Vanadinite \n    Orange; nonmetallic luster",
            "Serpentine \n    Green; nonmetallic luster",
            "Turquoise  \n    Blue, green; nonmetallic, luster",
            };
    final int LIMIT = mineralDescriptions.length;
    int n = 236;
    char c = (char )n;
    String line = "\n    ";
    for (int ctr = 1; ctr <= 61; ctr++) {
        line += c;
    }
    line += "\n";

    System.out.println("       View the properties of minerals.   ");
    System.out.println(line);

//#2
    while(choice.equalsIgnoreCase("Y")){
        int index = rand.nextInt(LIMIT);

        System.out.println("              "
                            + mineralDescriptions[index]);
        System.out.println(line);
      try {
        System.out.print("\n     View another (y n)>>");
        choice= reader.readLine();
```

```
            System.out.print("\r");
        }
        catch (IOException ioe) {
            System.out.println("I O Exception Occurred");
        }
        choice.trim();
    }//end while
  }//end main
}//end class
```

In the lines accompanying comment #1 of the MineralChance.java program, you declare and define a repetition control called control. It is of the String type, and you initialize it to the letter Y. You then define an array of the String type, mineralDescription. This array stores the names and descriptions of a group of minerals. A line return separates each mineral name from the description of the mineral. You also define a constant, LIMIT. To assign value to this constant, you access the limit array attribute.

To create a formatting element for the display, you use a casting technique to access the ASCII value (236) for the infinity sign (4). When you cast an ASCII value as a character and assign it to a string, you can access a character that it is not possible for you to input from the keyboard. You use the concatenation operator to create a line of infinity signs.

In lines associated with comment #2, you create a while block. To implement the control expression for the while block, you call the String equalsIgnoreCase() method. This method takes as its argument any character of the alphabet in lower- or uppercase form. It evaluates the value of the String variable you use to call it in relation to this character. The case of the characters you use for the evaluation does not affect the outcome. The method tests the value of choice against the upper- and lowercases of the letter y. The user enters the value of choice with each iteration of the while block.

To access minerals to display from the mineralDescription array, you call the Random nextInt() method and generate a random number in the range set by LIMIT, which is the number of elements in the array. You then display the results of the random selection using a call to the println() method. As Figure 4.13 illustrates, you follow the display of the mineral information with one of the formatted lines.

To assess whether the user wants to repeatedly view mineral information, you implement a try...catch structure. In the try block, you call the BufferedReader readLine() method and assign the input to the choice variable. After obtaining the input, you call the String trim() method to remove white spaces from the input. With this action, you reach the end of the while block. As long as the user enters a lower- or uppercase y at the prompt, the while block continues to repeat. Any other character causes the flow of the program to exit the while block and the program to terminate. Figure 4.13 illustrates two iterations of the while block.

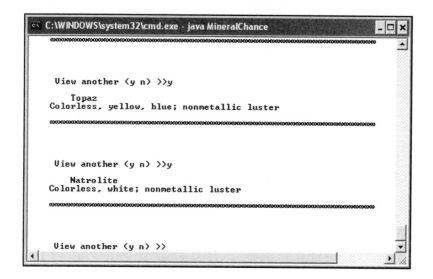

FIGURE 4.13

The while block repeats when the user prompts it to do so.

THE DO...WHILE STATEMENT

The do...while repetition statement differs in a few fundamental ways from the while repetition statement. For starters, the control expression of the do...while statement follows the closing brace of the do...while block. Placement of the control statement at the end of the block allows the flow of the program to enter the block without being tested. This can make it easier to implement user interfaces such as the one in the previous program. There, it was necessary to declare and define a control variable so that the flow of the program could enter the repetition block. With the do...while control, the flow of the program enters the block by default.

A second feature of the do...while block is that keywords both precede and follow it. The do keyword, followed by the opening brace, opens the block. The while keyword, followed by the control expression in parentheses, follows the bock. You terminate the while statement with a semicolon.

Within the do...while block, you can implement a selection statement or some other mechanism to change the value of the repetition control so that it allows the block to continue to repeat or to exit. The ElementWeights.java program allows you to experiment with employing user input as a way to control the do...while loop.

```
/*
 ElementWeights.java
*/
import java.util.Random;
import java.io.*;
 public class ElementWeights{
    public static void main(String Args[]){
        Random rand = new Random();
        BufferedReader reader;
        //Create an instance of the buffer
        reader = new BufferedReader(new InputStreamReader(System.in));
    //#1
        String choice = "Y";
        String elementsAtomicWeights =
                        "Oxygen 15.9994, Fluorine 18.9984032, "    +
                        "Neon 20.1797, Sodium 22.989770, "         +
                        "Magnesium 24.3050, Aluminum 26.981538, "  +
                        "Silicon 28.0855, Phosphorus 30.973761, "  +
                        "Sulfur 32.065, Chlorine 35.453, "         +
                        "Potassium 39.0983, Calcium 40.078, "      +
                        "Vanadium 50.9415, Manganese 54.938049";

        String elementsAndWeights[] = elementsAtomicWeights.split("\\, ");
        final int LIMIT = elementsAndWeights.length;
        int n = 236;
        char c = (char )n;
        String line = "\n     ";
        for (int ctr = 1; ctr <= 61; ctr++) {
            line += c;
        }
        line += "\n";
        System.out.println("\n" +line);
        System.out.println("      View the properties of minerals.  ");

    //#2
        do{
                System.out.println(line);
                int index = rand.nextInt(LIMIT);
```

```
        System.out.println("\n           "
                              + elementsAndWeights[index]);
        System.out.println(line);
    try {
        System.out.print("\n\n\n      View another (y n) >>");
        choice= reader.readLine();
        System.out.print("\n\n\n");
    }
    catch (IOException ioe) {
        System.out.println("I O Exception Occurred");
    }
    choice.trim();
//#3
    }while(choice.equalsIgnoreCase("Y"));//end while
}//end main
}//end class
```

At comment #1 of the ElementWeights.java program, you declare a String variable, choice, which you use to control the do...while block. You then declare another String variable, elementsAtomicWeights, and assign a list of elements and their atomic weights to it. After defining the elementsAtomicWeights string, you call the String split() method to divide the string into the elements of an array. As an argument for the split() method, you employ a space followed by a comma. You assign the elements to the elementsAndWeights array, which is of the String type. To set up a constant to control the generation of random numbers, you access the array limit attribute and assign the result to the LIMIT constant.

After creating a line to use in the display, you print the title to the application, as Figure 4.14 illustrates. You then implement the do...while block. To implement the block, you follow the do keyword with the opening brace of the block. Within the block, you implement a try...catch block and call the nextInt() method of the Random class to generate a random number within the range set by LIMIT. You assign the random number to the int variable index and use index to access an element in the elementsAndWeights array. This you display with a call to the println() method.

Within the try block that follows the display of the element and its atomic weight, you prompt the user for input. The input governs whether the application displays another element and its atomic weight. The message prompts the user to input a y to view another element and its weight. The catch block attends to problems that might occur with input. After the close of the catch block, just before the closing brace of the block, you employ the trim() method to remove any blank characters the user might include with the input.

To process the user's input, you call the `String equalsIgnoreCase()` method as the control expression for the `while` statement. This method evaluates the user's input to determine whether it equals either lowercase or uppercase y. If the test renders true, then the flow of the program returns to the top of the block. If not, then the flow of the program exits the block, and the program terminates.

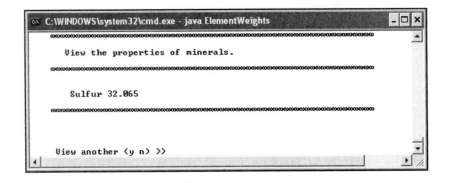

FIGURE 4.14

The `do…while` block repeats as the `equalsIgnoreCa se()` method evaluates user input.

THE CONTINUE AND BREAK KEYWORDS

The `continue` and `break` keywords allow you to exert greater control over repetition statements. The `continue` keyword causes the flow of your program to return immediately to the top of the block in which you use it. The `break` keyword causes the flow of your program to exit the block. The ChooseWeightView.java program allows you to experiment with the use of the `break` and `continue` keywords. The experimentation involves creation of an `if…else if…else` selection structure within an infinite repetition block (or loop). An infinite loop is one that continues to repeat indefinitely.

To create an infinite repetition statement, you assign the `true` token to the `while` test expression. The flow of your program enters the `while` block and then stays within it, repeating endlessly, unless you provide some way that it can exit the block. The `break` keyword provides a means to accomplish this task. You set up an `if` selection statement that evaluates user input. Given a true evaluation, the flow of the program enters the selection block, and the `break` keyword causes it to exit the repetition block.

The ChooseWeightView.java program also allows you to experiment with the `continue` keyword. When you use the `continue` keyword, you cause the flow of your program to jump back to the beginning of the repetition block in which you use it. If statements follow the `continue` keyword, the flow of the program never reaches them. In the ChooseWeightView.java program, you embed the `continue` keyword in an `if` selection block. If the user's input allows the flow of the program to enter a block that contains this keyword, then when the flow of the program reaches the keyword, it jumps back to the beginning of the block. The flow of the program does not reach statements that might follow it within the block. (See Figure 4.15.)

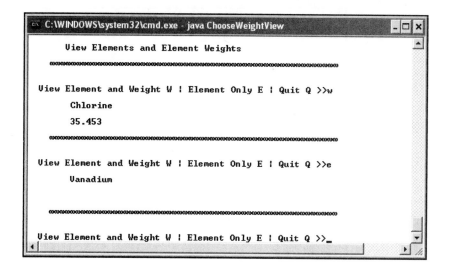

FIGURE 4.15

Use break and continue to allow users different options.

```
/*
ChooseWeightView.java
*/

import java.util.Random;
import java.io.*;
 public class ChooseWeightView{
    public static void main(String Args[]){
        Random rand = new Random();
        BufferedReader reader;
        //Create an instance of the buffer
        reader = new BufferedReader(new InputStreamReader(System.in));
    //#1
        String choice = "";
        String elementsAtomicWeights =
                    "Oxygen 15.9994, Fluorine 18.9984032, "   +
                    "Neon 20.1797, Sodium 22.989770, "        +
                    "Magnesium 24.3050, Aluminum 26.981538, " +
                    "Silicon 28.0855, Phosphorus 30.973761, " +
                    "Sulfur 32.065, Chlorine 35.453, "        +
```

```java
                    "Potassium 39.0983, Calcium 40.078, "     +
                    "Vanadium 50.9415, Manganese 54.938049";
   String elementsAndWeights[]  =
                         elementsAtomicWeights.split("\\, ");
   final int LIMIT = elementsAndWeights.length;
//#2
   int n = 236;
   char c = (char )n;
   String line = "\n     ";
   for (int ctr = 1; ctr <= 54; ctr++) {
       line += c;
   }
   line += "\n";
   System.out.println("\n        "
                 + "View Elements and Element Weights      ");
   System.out.println(line);
//#3 //Create an infinite loop
   while(true){
     //Generate a random number and choose an element
       int index = rand.nextInt(LIMIT);
       String answerString = elementsAndWeights[index];
       //split the element into two parts: name and weight
       String elementAnswers[] = answerString.split("\\ ");
//#4
     try {
       System.out.print(
          "\n  View Element and Weight W " +
                "| Element Only E | Quit Q >>");
       choice= reader.readLine();
     }
     catch (IOException ioe) {
        System.out.println("I O Exception Occurred");
     }//end catch
     //Show the element
     System.out.println("\n        " + elementAnswers[0]);
     choice.trim();
   //#5
     if( choice.equalsIgnoreCase("W") ){
```

```
        //Pass on to display the number
        }
        else if( choice.equalsIgnoreCase("E") ){
            System.out.println("\n" + line);
//#6     //returns to the top -- no number
            continue;
        }
        else if( choice.equalsIgnoreCase("Q") ){
//#7                 //exits program
            break;
        }
        System.out.println("\n       " + elementAnswers[1]);
        System.out.println(line);
    }//end while
  }//end main
}//end class
```

In the lines trailing comment #1 of the ChooseWeightView.java program, you define a string to store a number of element names and their associated atomic weights (elementsAtomicWeights). You then call the split() function, using a comma and a white space as the argument that separates the items in the string. You assign the resulting elements to the elementsAndWeights array, which is of the String type. To ascertain the length of the array, you access the array length attribute and assign the result to the constant LIMIT.

At comment #2, you define a String variable, line, that you use for display purposes. To create the character string you assign to the variable, you cast the ASCII number 236 as a character, which creates the infinity sign. You employ the String concatenation operator (+) to create a string of infinity signs 54 characters long. As Figure 4.15 illustrates, you then call the println() method to display the application title, followed by the line of infinity signs.

In the lines associated with comment #3, you implement the opening of an infinite while repetition statement. To implement the statement, you employ the true token as the sole argument of the test expression. This causes the expression to test true indefinitely.

After the opening brace of the block, you call the nextInt() method of the Random class. As the argument of this method, you employ the LIMIT constant. You assign the resulting random number to the index variable. You then use the index variable to access an element in the elementsAndWeights array, which you assign to the answerString variable. This variable is of the String type.

Having assigned a string consisting of the name of a chemical element and its associated atomic weight to the answerString variable, you again call the split() method to separate the chemical element name and the atomic weight into elements of an array. The name of the array is elementAnswers. This is the second array you define in the ChooseWeightView.java program. It consists of only two pieces of data corresponding to its 0 and 1 indexes.

At comment #4, you set up a try...catch structure to obtain user input. You prompt the user for input that reflects three paths of activity:

- **W or w.** View the element and its corresponding atomic weight.
- **E or e.** View the element only.
- **Q or q.** Quit the application.

After soliciting the input, at comment #5 you immediately call the println() method to print the first (0) of the elementAnswers array. This is the name of the chemical element. Following the display of the name of this element, you then initiate a selection structure to process the user's input.

For the first phase of the selection structure, you test for w. To test for this letter, you use the choice variable to call the equalsIgnoreCase() method. If the user has typed a w, the flow of the program enters the selection block for this option. Since the block contains no statements, the effect is that the flow of the program exits the selection structure and moves to the portion of the program just prior to the end of the while block. There, you call the println() method to print the atomic weight of the chemical element, which is stored in the 1 index of the elementAnswers array.

For the second test of the selection structure, you again call the equalsIgnoreCase() method. This time you test for e. If this test renders true, then the flow of the program enters the selection block associated with the test, and you call the println() method to print a line of infinity characters to close the action of the block. As Figure 4.15 illustrates, this option allows the user to see only the name of the chemical element, not the atomic weight.

To prevent the program from exiting the selection structure as it does with the w selection option, at comment #6, you use the continue keyword The continue keyword causes the flow of the program to jump back to the top of the repetition block. The flow never reaches the lines in the remaining portion of the block, so the atomic weight is not printed.

For the final test of the selection structure, you call the equalsIgnoreCase() method to test for q. If the expression evaluates true for this statement, then the flow of the program enters the selection block and encounters the break keyword. The break keyword causes the flow of the program to exit the while block. With this action, the program ends.

USING THROW AND FINALLY WITH TRY...CATCH STRUCTURES

Chapter 2 provides a discussion of error processing using try...catch structures. In the try block, you use a method that can *throw* an exception of a specific type. You then define a catch block to process the exception. If you call more than one method in a try block and the methods throw exceptions of different types, then you can implement several catch blocks, each to process an exception of a different type.

To this basic scheme you can add one further type of catch block. When you define a catch block and designate a specific type of exception as its argument, it processes exceptions only of the type you have defined. For exceptions of types you cannot define or anticipate, you can use the finally keyword.

Unlike the catch keyword, the finally keyword requires no argument. The flow of your program always enters the finally block. For this reason, you can use it either to confirm that your program is functioning properly or to clean up activities you have initiated in previous portions of your program. The DivisionException.java program allows you to experiment with a try...catch...finally structure that processes exceptions relating to division by zero and improper formatting of numbers.

In addition to the finally keyword, this program also allows you to use the throw keyword. To employ the throw keyword, you develop a class that contains two static methods. The first is the main() method you have developed repeatedly. The second is the divideNumber() method. Within the divideNumber() method, you test for whether the denominator of an expression that performs division is equal to 0. If it is equal to 0, then you use the following statement:

```
throw new ArithmeticException();
```

The throw keyword causes the divideNumber() method to immediately issue (you can say *throw* or *return*) an object of the ArithmeticException type. This object can then be processed by any catch statement that you define using ArithmeticException as the type of its argument. In this way, you define a customized exception action for your program. Figure 4.16 provides a basic sketch of the relations that pertain between the statement you define in divideNumber() method and the catch block you define with the ArithmeticException data type.

Chapter 5, "Object-Oriented Programming", and subsequent chapters provide more discussion of throwing exceptions and creating static methods, but for now it suffices to point out that when you use the static keyword to define the divideNumber() method, you make it so that you can call this method without creating an instance of the DivisionException class.

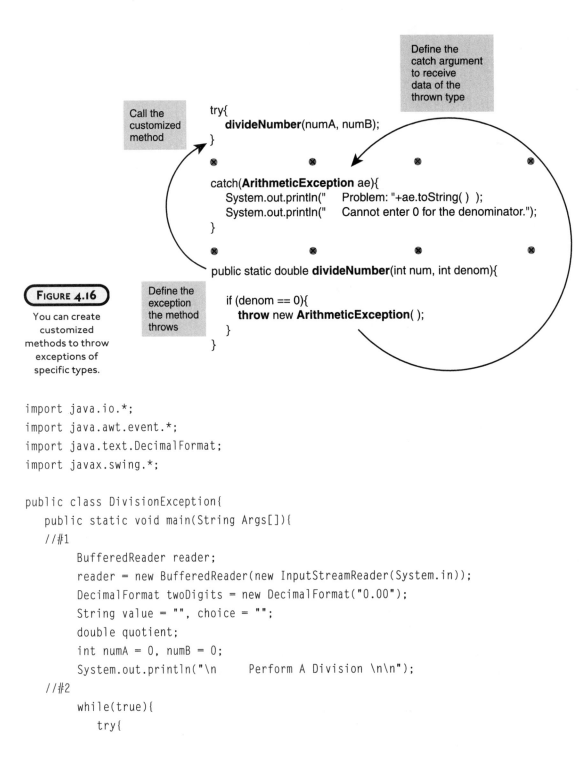

Define the catch argument to receive data of the thrown type

Call the customized method

```
try{
    divideNumber(numA, numB);
}


catch(ArithmeticException ae){
    System.out.println("    Problem: "+ae.toString( ) );
    System.out.println("    Cannot enter 0 for the denominator.");
}


public static double divideNumber(int num, int denom){

    if (denom == 0){
        throw new ArithmeticException( );
    }
}
```

Define the exception the method throws

FIGURE 4.16

You can create customized methods to throw exceptions of specific types.

```java
import java.io.*;
import java.awt.event.*;
import java.text.DecimalFormat;
import javax.swing.*;

public class DivisionException{
    public static void main(String Args[]){
    //#1
        BufferedReader reader;
        reader = new BufferedReader(new InputStreamReader(System.in));
        DecimalFormat twoDigits = new DecimalFormat("0.00");
        String value = "", choice = "";
        double quotient;
        int numA = 0, numB = 0;
        System.out.println("\n    Perform A Division \n\n");
    //#2
        while(true){
            try{
```

```
                System.out.print("   Type the numerator>>\t\t");
                value = reader.readLine();
                numA = Integer.parseInt(value);
                System.out.print("   Type the denominator>>\t");
                value = reader.readLine();
                numB = Integer.parseInt(value);
//See comment #5
                quotient = divideNumber(numA, numB);
                System.out.println("   Quotient>>\t\t\t"
                                    + twoDigits.format(quotient) );

          }
//#3

          catch(IOException ioe){
              System.out.println(ioe.toString() );
          }
          catch(ArithmeticException ae){
              System.out.println("   Problem: " + ae.toString() );
              System.out.println("   Cannot enter 0 for the denominator.");
          }
          catch(NumberFormatException nfe){
              System.out.println( nfe.toString() );
          }
          finally{
              System.out.println("---------------------" +
                                   "---------------------\n");
          }
//#4

          //-------------------------------------------------
          //Check user preference
          try{
              System.out.print("\n Another? Y | Quit Q   >>");
              choice= reader.readLine();
          }
          catch (IOException ioe) {
              System.out.println("I O Exception Occurred");
          }//end catch

          if( choice.equalsIgnoreCase("Q") ){
```

```
                //exits program
                  break;
        }
     }//end while
   }//end main method

//#5
//custom method for DivisionException
  public static double divideNumber(int num, int denom){
    if (denom == 0){
      //You construct the error message
      throw new ArithmeticException();
    }
    //perform the division
    return (double) num / denom;
  }//end divideNumber method
}//end class
```

In the lines trailing comment #1 in the DivisionException.java program, you define BufferedReader and DecimalFormat objects to process user input. Also, along the same lines, you define String value and choice variables. Finally, you define a variable of the double type (quotient) to process the results of division operations.

At comment #2, you define an infinite while block by using the true token as the argument of the while statement. You then create a try block in which you prompt the user for the numerator and denominator of a division operation. The initial input operations involving the readLine() method assign both values to the value variable. You use the Integer parseInt() method to convert the contents of value to an integer. You assign the numerator input to numA and the denominator input to numB.

To process the division, you call the divideNumber() method, which you define in the lines associated with comment #5. Definition of the divideNumber() method begins with use of the static keyword, which makes this method so that you can call it without having to declare an instance of the DivisionException class. The method has a return type of double and accepts two arguments of the int type for the numerator and denominator of the division problem.

Within the scope of the divideNumber() method, you implement an if selection statement that tests whether the value of the denominator (denom) equals 0. Division by 0 is undefined, so if the selection test evaluates to true, you employ the throw keyword to throw an exception.

The throw keyword causes the method to immediately return (or throw) an object of the ArithmeticException type. This data type is an Exception type you obtain from the Java class hierarchy. You can use it to identify exceptions relating to math problems. If the user tries to divide by 0, then, the method throws the ArithmeticException object, and the flow of the program exits the method. If the user does not try to divide by 0, the selection statement does not evaluate to true, the numerator is divided by the denominator, and the quotient value of the double type is returned.

You call the divideNumber() method in the lines following comment #2 using the numA and numB variables as arguments. You assign the returned value of the divideNumber() method to the quotient variable. You then call the println() method to display the output, as Figure 4.17 illustrates.

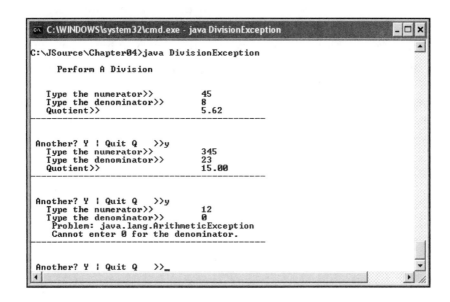

FIGURE 4.17

Processing exceptions gives you greater control over the flow of your program.

In the lines trailing comment #3, you implement a set of catch blocks. The first block processes exceptions of the IOException type, which the BufferedReader readLine() method is likely to generate. When you process the ioe argument of this block, you call the toString() method of the IOException type. Every Java class defines the toString() method for all classes. It returns a string bearing the name of the data type of the object you use to call it.

For the argument of the second catch block, you use the ArithmeticException class. As the error message in Figure 4.17 shows, you catch errors from the divideNumber() method, and the message you implement in the scope of the catch block informs the user that division by 0 is not permitted.

For the last phase of the catch sequence, you use a finally block. The sole activity you perform in the finally block involves printing a horizontal line. As Figure 4.17 illustrates, the finally block executes with every cycle of the application, even if no method generates an exception.

At comment #4, you process user control input in the same manner that you have pursued in previous programs. The user has the options of pressing Y to continue on to perform another division problem or Q to exit. You call the readLine() method to retrieve input. You call the equalsIgnoreCase() method in the selection statement to test the input. If the selection tests true for Q, then you use the break keyword to exit the program.

BACK TO GUESSING A NUMBER

The GuessANumber.java program provides you with a way to draw together the activities you have explored in this chapter to develop an application that prompts you to guess the value of a randomly generated number. This application extends the work you have performed so far by using a series of fairly involved embedded statements. You use both embedded selection statements and embedded repetition statements. By using a while block within a do...while block, you allow the user to repeatedly try to guess the values of randomly generated numbers. When you use this approach, you spare the user from having to again and again execute the program to play it.

```
/*
  GuessANumber.java
*/
import java.io.*;
import java.util.Random;

public class GuessANumber {
    public static void main(String args[]){
        BufferedReader reader;
        Random rand = new Random();
//#1
        int numberToGuess = 0;
        int guess = 0;
        boolean invalid; int nGuesses = 0;
        String choice = "";
        reader = new BufferedReader(new InputStreamReader(System.in));

            int n = 236;
```

```
                char c = (char )n;
                String line = "\n      ";
                for (int ctr = 1; ctr <= 40; ctr++) {
                    line += c;
                }
                line += "\n";


        while(true){
          numberToGuess = rand.nextInt(100) + 1;
          guess = -1;
          nGuesses = 0;
          System.out.println("\n   Guess a number between 1 and 100.");
          System.out.println(line);
//#2
          //-------------------------------------------------------------
            do {
                nGuesses++;
                System.out.print("     Your guess>> ");
                invalid = false;
                try{
                    guess = Integer.parseInt(reader.readLine());
                 }
                 catch (IOException ioe){
                    System.out.println("     Problem: " + ioe.toString());
                 }
//#3
                 catch (NumberFormatException nfe){
                    System.out.println("     Problem: " + nfe.toString());
                    System.out.println("     Not an integer value.");
                    guess = -1;
                    invalid = true;
                 }
//#4
                 if (guess >= 1 && guess <= 100){
                    if (guess == numberToGuess){
                       System.out.println(line);
                       System.out.println("     Yes, the number is "
                           + numberToGuess + ".");
```

```
                System.out.println("     You guessed the number in "
                    + nGuesses + " guesses.");
            }
            else if (guess < numberToGuess){
                System.out.println("     The number is higher.");
            }else{
                System.out.println("     The number is lower.");
            }
        }
        else if (!invalid){
            System.out.println("     Remember, the number lies between "
                        + "1 and 100.");
        }
    }while (guess != numberToGuess);  //end do while
    //------------------------------------------------------------
//#5
    //Check user preference
    try{
        System.out.print("\n Another? Y | Quit Q   >>");
        choice= reader.readLine();
        System.out.print("\n\n");
    }
    catch (IOException ioe) {
        System.out.println("I O Exception Occurred");
    }//end catch

    if( choice.equalsIgnoreCase("Q") ){
        //exits program
        break;
    }
}//end while
//------------------------------------------------------------
} //end main
}//end class
```

At comment #1 you declare two integer variables, numToGuess and guess. The numToGuess variable stores a randomly generated number the user guesses. The guess variable stores the guesses the user makes while playing the game. You initialize the variables in the lines immediately preceding comment #2, where you begin the outer repetition block. This block defines an entire guessing session for the user.

At the start of the outer block, you call the Random nextInt() method to generate random numbers in the range spanning 1 to 100. You shift the raw random numbers by 1 to avoid 0 and include 100 in the range. Also, you set guess to -1 to initially exclude it as legitimate. You also set nGuesses to 0. Following these initializations, you call the println() method to prompt the user to enter a guess.

To make it possible for the user to repeatedly enter guesses during each session of play, in the lines immediately following comment #2 you implement an inner do...while repetition block. Immediately after the opening brace of the inner block, you increment the nGuesses variable using the increment operator. Each time the do...while block repeats, the user makes a new guess. This variable tracks the number of guesses. You also set the invalid variable to false so that it can be reset in the event that the appropriate selection statement discovers that the user has entered a value less than 1 or greater than 100.

In the catch blocks immediately preceding and following comment #3, you process number and IO exceptions. After that, at comment #4, you implement a set of embedded selection statements. At the outer level of selection, you implement an if...else statement that employs a Boolean expression to evaluate whether the number the user has entered is greater than or equal to 1 and less than or equal to 100.

If the number the user has entered falls within the legitimate range, you then go to a second level of selection to help the user with the next guess. On the other hand, as part of the outer selection structure, if the guess has not fallen within the legitimate range, then in the else block you report that the number must be in the correct range.

At the second level of selection, as you see in the lines following comment #4, if the user has guessed the randomly generated number (guess == numberToGuess), then the session must end. You then call the println() method to display a concluding message. The selection block exits, and the flow of the program goes to the test expression for the do...while block (which allows for repeated guessing). This expression evaluates to false. The flow of the program then goes to the outer block, where the user can choose to play again or quit.

If the number guessed is not equal to the randomly generated number, then at the second level of selection you use else...if and else blocks to help the user along. In the else...if expression, you test for whether the user's guess is less than the randomly generated number. If this is so, then you call the println() method to prompt the user to enter a higher number.

The flow of the program reaches the nested else block if other conditions do not evaluate to true, and in this case the user has guessed too high. You call the println() method to prompt the user to guess a lower number.

In the lines trailing comment #5, you process the user's preferences concerning whether to engage in another round of guessing. As Figure 4.18 reveals, the procedures used involve calling the readLine() method to accept input and then using the equalsIgnoreCase() method to test for Y (to go another round) or Q (to quit). If the user elects to go another round, then the flow of the program jumps to the while statement preceding comment #2, the relevant variables are reset, and the inner repetition block again begins to execute, allowing the user to guess the value of yet another number.

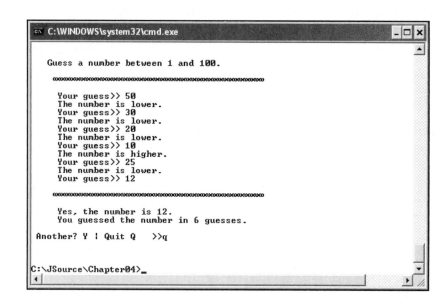

FIGURE 4.18

Combining selection and repetition statements with exception handling allows you to process input in a comprehensive manner.

SUMMARY

In this chapter, you have explored uses of the for, while, and do…while repetition statements. The for repetition statement involves the use of three controls, and you can use these in a variety of ways. For example, you can declare a counter before you implement the for statement. You can also increment a counter with the block of the statement. With respect to the while and do…while repetition statements, you explored ways to use controls you place within the block of the statement. Two keywords that prove especially useful with such operations are continue and break. The continue keyword causes the flow of the program to jump back to the start of the block. The break keyword cause the flow of the program to exit the bock.

In addition to repetition control statements, you also explored a few extended aspects of try...catch structures. Two new keywords were finally and throw. Using the throw keyword, you defined your own static method and used it in a try block to generate a customized exception. With the finally keyword, you created a default exception processing block.

CHALLENGES

1. Create a table with five columns. Make the columns 20 rows long. In each column, create a succession of numbers that show successive summations. Have one column progress by increments of 2, 3, 4, 5, and 6.

2. Calculate how much a loan of 100 dollars costs if you have it for 12 months. To accomplish this, set up a repetition block that repeats 12 times. For each repetition, multiply 100 by 0.12 and use a compound operation (+I) to assign this to a variable called interestAmt. Display the results.

3. Alter the program you write for Challenge 2 so that you can calculate the cost of any loan over any number of months at any rate you assign. You can accomplish this with a while, do...while, or for statement. Prompt the user to input the values.

4. Create a program that generates a table that shows the amount of loan at the start of its life. Assume that you make payments of a fixed rate. Output data to show how the loan decreases over time as you make more payments. Assume, for instance, a loan of $12,000. Divide this by 200, as though that is the monthly payment. That gives you the number of months. Go from there to create a table so that you can say how much you have paid and how much you still owe for any given month.

OBJECT-ORIENTED PROGRAMMING

K nowledge of the principles and practices of object-oriented programming (OOP) proves essential to your success as a Java programmer because Java is an object-oriented programming language. In every Java program you have written thus far, you have explored the rudiments of object-oriented programming, because you have defined classes. In this chapter, you extend your exploration of classes to include a few of the formal practices of object-oriented programming. Among these are encapsulation and the use of class composition. In later chapters, you explore inheritance and polymorphism. These concepts lie at the basis of all object-oriented programming activities. At the end of this chapter, you'll work with composition to create an application that deals cards from a deck. Among the topics this chapter covers are the following:

- Understanding objects
- State and behavior of classes
- Encapsulation and class design
- Data hiding
- Accessor and mutator members
- Constructing objects
- How classes are polymorphic

OBJECT-ORIENTED CONCEPTS

In previous chapters, you have worked with class definitions, largely though the creation of a static `main()` method. The characteristics of the classes that contain only a `main()` method tend to be background features because the focus of the classes is on the logic and syntax of the lines within the `main()` method. Now it is time to look at things differently. Rather than working with a class as a vehicle for being able to write a single method that serves largely as a program, you look at a class as an *abstract data type*. You take this work so far that the classes you create do not contain a `main()` method. To make use of a `main()` method, you create other classes, testing classes, in which you create instances of your abstract data types.

States and Attributes

An abstract data type is a data type that you formally define to model an entity you derive from the real world. This entity can be anything you care to name. It can be a process or a thing. A good starting point is that you can designate the entity as a noun. Here are a few nouns that designate entities that can be used as the basis of classes:

Human Heart
Book
Car
Card Deck
Bank Account

In each case, the entities named have two general characteristics. If you assess the characteristics of the entity, you discover the *state* of the entity. Table 5.1 provides an analysis of a few of the characteristics of the entities named above relating to their states:

As Table 5.1 reveals, in every case you can picture an entity as a collection of characteristics. These characteristics describe the current state of the entity. When these characteristics change, the state of the entity changes. Likewise, if two entities of the same type possess different characteristics, then you know they are different entities, and both of the entities can be described as possessing a distinct state.

Behaviors

You can picture a change of the state of an entity as the *behavior* of the entity. Consider, for example, the ways that the state of an automobile might change. You can address its motions. It moves along the highway at different rates. You can distinguish it by its fuel consumption or the amount of fuel in its tank. You can address it in terms of its interior and exterior colors. All of these characteristics can change. If a car is standing still and then accelerates

TABLE 5.1   ENTITIES AND STATES

Entities	States
Human heart	Considered in medical terms, a heart *beats* at a given rate and pumps a given *quantity* of blood. A heart has levels of *blockage*. The *age* of your heart is the same as your age, generally. **Questions to assess the state:** How many times per minute is a heart beating? How old is the person whose heart you are interested in examining? If there is blockage, how much is the flow of blood restricted?
Card deck	A card deck can be for learning vocabulary or multiplication. It can be a poker or pinochle deck. It can be a set of Tarot cards. Card decks differ in size, shape, back pattern, and front pattern, among other things. **Questions to assess the state:** What is on the face of the cards (math, vocabulary, standard suits)? What is the back design of the cards? What colors are used on the back and front?
Book	A book possesses a given number of *pages*, a specific type of *cover*, and a *size*. It can also be considered as a *fiction* or *nonfiction* work and according to *genre*. **Questions to assess the state:** How many pages does the book contain? What color is the cover of the book?
Car	A car might be defined in terms of how much *gasoline it consumes* and the *quality of stereo* installed in it. It can be viewed as a *sedan* or a *compact*. It is of a given *color*. **Questions to assess the state:** How much fuel is in the tank? How expensive is the stereo that comes with it? What is the color of the car?
Bank account	A bank account can be identified according to the *name* of the person owning the account, the account *number*, whether the account is a *savings* or *checking* account, and how much the account holds. **Questions to assess the state:** How much is in a bank account? What is the interest rate paid?

to 100 kilometers per hour, then this is a change in its behavior. On the other hand, as Figure 5.1 illustrates, if you see two cars standing on a car lot, you can often distinguish them according to their color, make, and model. Such differences, again, constitute forms of behavior. The behavior in this respect is their appearance to someone who looks at them.

States	Behaviors
Exterior color	Change of exterior color
Interior color	Change of interior color
Speed	Change of speed
Stereo	Quality of stereo
Fuel	Change of fuel level
Make	Change of manufacturer
Model	Change of model name

FIGURE 5.1

A class models states and behaviors.

Attributes and Methods

In the terms provided by object-oriented programming, an entity is an object. A class models an object. Attributes represent the state of a class object. Methods allow you to change the state of the class object, so they represent behavior. Table 5.2 recapitulates the terms used so far in this chapter as they relate to classes, objects, attributes, and methods.

TABLE 5.2	TERMS RELATED TO ATTRIBUTES AND METHODS
Item	**Discussion**
Class	A model of an entity. You can view a class as a pattern. The class creates an abstract data type that allows you to create objects. Objects are also known as instances of the class.
Object	An instance of a class. You create objects using an abstract data type. The abstract data type is a class. You create many objects from any given class. Each object is distinct from the others.
State	Every object is known according to its state. The state of an object can change. Likewise, you can tell two objects of the same class apart because they possess different states.
Attributes	The state of an object is known through the values you assign to its attributes. The attributes of an object are the identifiers you use to define the class.
Behavior	Every object is known according to how it changes or appears. This is the behavior of the object. When the state of an object changes, the change constitutes the behavior of the object. You use methods to allow for an object to change.
Methods	Methods of a class allow you to change the objects you create using the class.

The methods you include in a class represent changes of behavior. Well-designed classes allow you to change the state of a class only by using methods. You never access the attributes directly, only through the methods that pertain to them. This practice relates to *encapsulation* and *scope*. These topics receive extensive discussion later on in this chapter.

Picturing Classes

One of the most convenient ways to picture classes in Java involves using a Unified Modeling Language (UML) *class diagram*. A class diagram begins with a rectangle divided into three parts. As Figure 5.2 illustrates, in the top division, you name the class. In the next division, you name the attributes of the class. In the lower division, you name the methods of the class. As Table 5.3 discusses, the minus signs preceding the attributes and methods signify that they are *private*, so they cannot be used outside the scope of the class. The plus signs preceding the names of attributes and methods signify that they are *public*, which means that they can be used outside the scope of the class. (These topics receive further discussion later on in this chapter.)

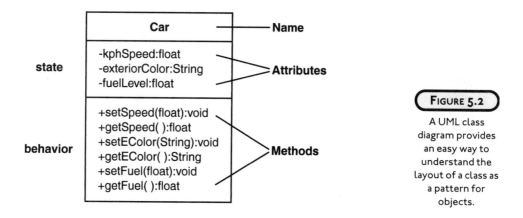

FIGURE 5.2

A UML class diagram provides an easy way to understand the layout of a class as a pattern for objects.

Table 5.3 provides a summary of the features of the UML diagram Figure 5.2 presents. The Car class represents but one of many definitions you might create for such a class. The features of the class are kept to a minimum to make it easier to discuss them. Every class definition can be represented in this way.

ACCESSING INFORMATION ON JAVA CLASSES

You can obtain comprehensive documentation of the Java classes from the Sun Internet site. You have a couple of options. You can download this set of documentation in the same way that you download the JDK. Since the amount of disk space the Java documentation requires can equal the disk space required by the JDK, however, you might consider a second option. Using this option, access the documentation as it is presented on the Internet and then create a "favorites" item for your browser. Here is a link that covers much of the version of the JDK used in this book:

http://java.sun.com/j2se/1.5.0/docs/api/index.html

This link provides you with a list of all the classes in the Java hierarchy set up in frames. As an example of how to proceed, click in the left frame and use the Find utility of your browser to search for the Number class. You must click Find Next a few times before you reach it. When you see Number in the list, click it to view the features of the Number class in the main viewing frame. In many cases, the classes are defined so that you cannot see their attributes. For this reason, you see only a list of methods. However, in cases in which public attributes occur, you usually see them listed first.

TABLE 5.3   UML CLASS DIAGRAM FEATURES

Item	Discussion
Class name	The name of the class appears in the top division of the rectangle. Java programmers often use two or more words to name classes. To accomplish this, you join the words into a single term and capitalize the first character of each word used in the name (CardGame, CardDeck, and so on).
Attributes	The names and types of attributes appear in the second division. Attributes define the state of the class, as discussed previously.
Colon (:) after attributes	If a colon follows the name of an attribute, then the term following the colon identifies the data type of the attribute. In many cases, these data types are primitive. In others, however, you see abstract data types, especially those you obtain from the Java class hierarchy.
Colon (:) after methods	If a colon follows the name of a method, then the term or expression following it designates the return type of the method. The getFuel() method returns a numerical value of the float type.
Methods	The names, return types, and parameter definitions of methods appear in the lower division of the rectangle.
Parameter lists	You can include method parameter (or argument) lists in UML class diagrams. For the setSpeed() method, you use a value of the float type.
+ - #	The plus and minus signs tell you about the scope of an attribute or method. The plus means *public*. The minus means *private*. A third sign, the pound sign (#) indicates *protected*. These terms relate to scope.

Implementing a Class

Although you have implemented many classes in previous chapters, formal implementation of a class that reflects the model Figure 5.2 provides involves attending to the layout of the class. Likewise, implementation of a formally defined class allows you to discuss your Java classes, not as Java *programs*, but as Java *classes*. Accordingly, you can then refer to methods and attributes in relation to their class definitions. (See the sidebar later in this chapter, "Formal References to Class Methods and Attributes.")

When you formally implement a class, you can use one of two basic approaches. You can define the class attributes first, at the top of the class, and then define the methods at the bottom. Alternatively, you can define the methods at the top of the class and then define the attributes at the bottom. For learning purposes, if is often best to stick with a pattern that involves defining the attributes first and then defining the methods. In this way, you can more easily translate the view you gain from a class diagram into the implementation of the code. This presentation of classes also tends to characterize most of the documentation Sun provides of the classes in the hierarchy.

To create a formal class definition, follow the same approach you have followed in previous chapters. Create a file named Car.java. Implement the code as shown in the listing. When you compile the file, use the `javac` command. Having gone that far, you must then proceed to the section titled "Creating a Test Driver" to find information on how to develop a program that allows you to create an instance of your class and explore its features. Specific discussion of the features of the Car class is provided in the four topics that immediately follow the Car listing. Here is the listing for the Car class:

```
/*
 Car
*/


public class Car{
//# 1 Attributes
  private float kphSpeed;
  private String exteriorColor;
  private float fuelLevel;


//#4 Default Constructor
// If you define any constructors with arguments, you must
// also define an explicit default constructor if you want
// to continue to have such a constructor
```

```java
 Car(){
     kphSpeed = 0.0F;
     exteriorColor = "Not set.";
     fuelLevel = 0.0F;
 }
//#5
//Overloaded Constructor
 Car(String color){
     kphSpeed = 0.0F;
     exteriorColor = color;
     fuelLevel = 0.0F;
  }


//Methods
//#2 Mutator
//----------------setSpeed------------------------
//Assign a speed in kph to the Car object as a float
 public void setSpeed(float speed){
     kphSpeed = speed;
  }
  //#3 Accessor
//----------------getSpeed------------------------
//Obtain the speed of the car in kph as a float
 public float getSpeed(){
     return kphSpeed;
  }
//----------------setEColor------------------------
//Assign a color as a String
 public void setEColor(String eColor){
       exteriorColor = eColor;
   }
//----------------getEColor------------------------
//Retrieve the color as a String
 public String getEColor(){
       return exteriorColor;
   }
```

```
//--------------setFuel-----------------------
//Assign a level of fuel as a float
 public void setFuel(float fuel){
     fuelLevel = fuel;
 }
//--------------getFuel-----------------------
//Obtain a float value designated the level of fuel
 public float getFuel(){
     return fuelLevel;
 }
}//end class
```

The definition of the Car class begins with the public keyword. This keyword makes the class accessible when you want to create an instance of it in another class. As you have done many times before, you then use the class keyword to designate that you want to define an abstract data type. The name of the abstract data type follows: Car. The next few sections address specific implementation details of the Car class. After that, as previously mentioned, you find the test driver (CarDriver) class for the Car class.

Defining Attributes

At comment #1 in the Car class, you formally define the attributes of the class. The class contains three attributes. As Figure 5.1 illustrates, you might define many more attributes. The attributes define the state of an object you create using a class. In this case, Car objects have a speed (kphSpeed), possess an exterior color (exteriorColor), and at any given moment have a specific amount of fuel in their tanks (fuelLevel).

In each case, you define the characteristics as private. This word relates to scope. In the next section and sections that follow, specific attention is given to the notion of scope, but for now concentrate on the idea that when you use an object of this class, you cannot access its attributes directly. You must access them through mutator and accessor methods.

Java programmers often use attribute naming conventions that call for names that consist of at least two words. You do not capitalize the first of the words. You capitalize all subsequent words. In the instance of an abbreviation, such as kph (kilometers per hour), you improvise.

Defining Methods

Following the definition of the attributes of a Car object, at comment #2 you define the methods of the class. (The code shows comments #4 and #5 right after comment #1. For now, skip them. They are discussed further on.) The methods of a class allow you to shape the behavior of the class. Generally, you implement two types of methods for almost all the classes you create. One type of method, which you see associated with comment #2, allows you to assign a value to an attribute of a class. Such a method is called a mutator. (A *mutation* is a *change*.)

To create a mutator method, you begin by declaring it as a public method. The `public` keyword allows you to accomplish this task. This keyword makes it so that users of your class can access the mutator method. You then designate the return type of the method. The return type in this case is `void`, which means that the method does not allow you to retrieve a value. It only allows you to set a value.

The name of the method consists of a combination of the term "set" and part of the name of the attribute that it applies to. Java programmers commonly name mutator methods in this way. The convention is so common that some programmers use the expression "set method" instead of mutator to designate such a method.

Between the parentheses following the name of the method, you provide the argument list for the method. The argument list consists of values you can submit to the method when you call it. For the `setSpeed()` method, you are concerned with only one value: the speed of the car (`speed`). For the type of the `speed` argument, you use `float`. Given this definition, you say that the method has one parameter (or one argument).

The purpose of the `setSpeed()` method is to assign the value of the `speed` argument to the `kphSpeed` class attribute. To accomplish this, you employ the assignment operator. The effect of the assignment operation is to allow you to use a public method (`setSpeed()`) to access a private attribute (`kphSpeed`).

At comment #3, you create an accessor method, `getSpeed()`. The accessor method allows you to access the value you have stored in the `kphSpeed` attribute. To implement the method, you first designate the scope of the method using the `public` keyword. The `public` keyword allows users of the `Car` class to access the method. Next, you identify the type of the data the method returns (`float`). After that, you name the method. To name the method, you compound the word "get" with a name that resembles that of the attribute it allows the user to access (`kphSpeed`). As with the use of "set" for mutator methods, programmers often refer to accessor methods as "get" methods.

When you define the `getSpeed()` method, you make use of the `return` keyword. This keyword creates a copy of whatever variable follows it. When you use the `return` keyword, the method allows the user of the method to access a copy of whatever value follows the `return` keyword. In this instance, the user obtains a copy of the value residing in the `kphSpeed` attribute.

The `kphSpeed` attribute is of the `float` type. The type of the identifier that follows the `return` keyword can be a variable in the method or an attribute. The type of the identifier should match the return type you define for the method that contains the return keyword. In this case, you see that the first line of the method reads as follows:

```
public float getSpeed(){
```

The return type of the method is float, so in this instance, the value of the identifier following the return keyword in the definition of the method matches the type of the return value for the method.

After you define the setSpeed() and getSpeed() methods, you define mutator and accessor methods for the exteriorColor and fuelLevel attributes. The approaches you employ for the definition of those methods are the same as those you employ for the setSpeed() and getSpeed() methods. For the mutator methods, you define the type of the argument and then assign the value you obtain through the argument to the class attribute. For the accessor method, you use the return keyword to create a copy of the class attribute that the user of the method can access by calling the method.

Default Constructors

When you create an instance of a class (a class object), another term for the action is *construction*. To make possible the construction of an object, you can do one of two things. You can allow Java to construct your object using the built-in constructor, known as an *implicit default constructor*. Alternatively, you can create your own constructor. In fact, you can create several versions of constructors. Such constructors are known as *explicit default constructors* and *overloaded constructors*.

A constructor is a special method that attends to the construction of a class object. It has the same name as the class and does not return a value. By default, whenever you create a class definition, Java includes a constructor that you do not have to define. You need only to call it. This is the implicit default constructor. It takes no arguments. Its use takes the following form:

```
ClassName classObject = new ClassName()
```

In this statement, ClassName designates any class you might create. The classObject identifier is an identifier you supply. The new keyword is an operator that tells the compiler to create an object of the type you name. The constructor follows the new keyword. It designates the type of object you want to use. When you have not defined a constructor and the constructor you use lacks arguments, then it is an implicit default constructor.

In the lines associated with comment #4 in the Car class definition, you create a constructor for the Car class. The constructor in this instance is a default constructor because it takes no arguments. Here's how you use it:

```
Car carA = new Car();
```

In the same way that the default ClassName class constructor allows you to create an instance of the ClassName class, the default Car class constructor allows you to create an instance of the Car class. To carry out the construction activities, you follow the new keyword with the constructor. You then assign the constructed object to an identifier of the Car type (carA). The constructor requires no arguments because you do not define it so that it requires arguments. Because it lacks any arguments, it is known as a default constructor. However, in this instance, it is not an *implicit* default constructor that Java provides. Instead, it is an *explicit* default constructor—one that you define.

You define your explicit default constructor in the lines trailing comment #4 in the Car class definition. For convenience, here are the lines for this constructor:

```
//#4 Default Constructor
  Car(){
      kphSpeed = 0.0F;
      exteriorColor = "Not set.";
      fuelLevel = 0.0F;
  }
```

When you use this constructor, you explicitly set the kphSpeed attribute to 0, the exteriorColor attribute to "Not set", and the fuelLevel attribute to 0. Every object you create using this constructor has the same initial state.

If you do not define a default constructor, you then have no option but to employ Java's default constructor. When you use this approach, since you have not explicitly defined the default initialization conditions, the constructor does not set the initial values of the class attributes in other than default ways.

You do not have to define a default constructor for a class unless you define one or more constructors that are not default constructors. If a constructor is not a default constructor (no arguments), then it is known as an overloaded constructor (it has arguments). The difference between your constructors (default or overloaded) and the one Java creates for you lies in the initial state of the objects you create with the constructors. The next section covers overloaded constructors.

Overloaded Constructors

At comment #5 in the definition of the Car class, you define an *overloaded* constructor. An overloaded constructor requires one or more arguments. The arguments allow you to set the initial state of the objects of a class in customized ways. In this instance, you define the overloaded constructor so that it requires the user to supply the color of the Car object. You define an overloaded constructor much along the lines that you used when you defined the mutator methods of the Car class. For convenience, here are the lines you use to define the overloaded constructor:

```
//#5
//Overloaded Constructor
 Car(String color){
     kphSpeed = 0.0F;
     exteriorColor = color;
     fuelLevel = 0.0F;
 }
```

The difference between the default constructor and the overloaded constructor is that the overloaded constructor requires the user of the constructor to set one or more of the values assigned to the class attributes. In this case, the required value relates to the exteriorColor attribute. Use of the constructor takes the following form:

```
    Car carA = new Car("Blue");
```

The result of calling the overloaded constructor is that the initial state of the Car object is set, as is the case with the defined version of the default constructor. The kphSpeed and fuelLevel attributes are set to 0. However, in this case, rather than assigning "Not set." to the exteriorColor attribute, this constructor assigns a value supplied as an argument ("Blue"). When you employ this constructor, you can initialize every Car object you create using a different set of values for the attributes.

FORMAL REFERENCES TO CLASS METHODS AND ATTRIBUTES

When you develop classes formally, you almost never refer to them or the attributes or methods they contain according to the files that contain them. Instead, you use a notation system that involves using colons, the names of methods, and the names of classes.

Consider, for example, the Car class and the getSpeed() and setSpeed() methods in this class (see Figure 5.2). To designate these methods as associated with the Car class, you employ the following notation:

```
     Car::getSpeed()
     Car::setSpeed()
```

In this way, you can indicate that these methods belong to the Car class. For methods named getSpeed() and setSpeed(), it might not seem that such specificity is necessary.

However, within the Java class hierarchy, this approach to identifying methods becomes necessary due to the consistent way the developers of Java have named methods for the classes in the hierarchy. For example, there are roughly 2,500 classes in the Java class hierarchy. At the base of this hierarchy is a class called Object. The Object class provides a method called toString().

Because all classes in the Java hierarchy are derived from the Object class, every class has a toString() method. Given the use of the set of colons, you can easily indicate which toString() method you want to designate.

Creating a Test Driver Class

When you formally define classes as abstract data types, you make it so that they are used as part of a structure of classes rather than standalone programs. You do not usually include a main() method with such classes. Instead, you create a target or driver class. A driver class can make use of a multitude of other classes. Such a class contains a main() method. The main() method of the driver class is a *static* method. It is a method that you can call from within the class definition that contains it. Such a method provides the *entrance point* to your application.

For the Car class, you create the CarDriver class. This class allows you to explore how to create instances of the Car class using the default and overloaded versions of the Car class constructors. Then it allows you to call all of the accessor and mutator methods you have defined for the Car class. Calling these methods allows you to change the state of the car objects you create.

To make a set of classes work, you must first create, compile, and debug the *source* classes. Only when these compile correctly can you make use of them in the dependent class. The CarDriver in this case is a dependent class. Even then, however, you still have to anticipate a great deal of *regression testing*. Regression testing involves working from dependent to source classes to remove defects in the source classes. Such defects often remain hidden until you use the source classes in dependent classes. Here is the definition of the CarDriver class:

```
/*
 CarDriver.java
 Depends on Car
*/
public class CarDriver{
     public static void main(String Args[]){
     // Set up a formatting line
       String line = "";
```

```
        for (int ctr = 1; ctr <= 56; ctr++) {
            line += "-";
        }
//#1 use the default Car constructor
    Car carA = new Car();
// Use the overloaded Car constructor
    Car carB = new Car("Red");
    Car carC = new Car("Blue");


//#2 Call the accessor methods
        System.out.println("\n" + line);
        System.out.println("\t\tCar A\t\tCar B\t\tCar C");
        System.out.println(line);
        System.out.println(" Color --    "
                                + " "    + carA.getEColor()
                                + " \t"   + carB.getEColor()
                                + " \t\t" + carC.getEColor() );
        System.out.println("\n Speed --    "
                                + " "    + carA.getSpeed()
                                + " \t\t" + carB.getSpeed()
                                + " \t\t" + carC.getSpeed() );
        System.out.println("\n Fuel --    "
                                + " "    + carA.getFuel()
                                + " \t\t" + carB.getFuel()
                                + " \t\t" + carC.getFuel() );
//#3 Call the mutator methods
        //Reset the state of carA
        carA.setFuel(27.50F);
        carA.setSpeed(140.0F);
        carA.setEColor("Purple");
        //Reset the state of carB
        carB.setFuel(25.0F);
        carB.setSpeed(180.0F);
        carB.setEColor("Red");
        //Reset the state of carC
        carC.setFuel(30.0F);
        carC.setSpeed(160.0F);
        carC.setEColor("Green");
```

```
//#4 Call the accessor methods
    System.out.println("\n" + line);
    System.out.println(" Color --    "
                            + " "      + carA.getEColor()
                            + " \t\t"  + carB.getEColor()
                            + " \t\t"  + carC.getEColor() );
    System.out.println("\n Speed --    "
                            + " "      + carA.getSpeed()
                            + " \t\t"  + carB.getSpeed()
                            + " \t\t"  + carC.getSpeed() );

    System.out.println("\n Fuel --   "
                            + " "      + carA.getFuel()
                            + " \t\t"  + carB.getFuel()
                            + " \t\t"  + carC.getFuel() );
    }
}
```

You set up the CarDriver class in the same way that you set up many of the classes in previous chapters. It contains a main() method. Within the main() method, you implement all the functionality of the class. In the lines accompanying comment #1 of the CarDriver class, you call the default constructor of the Car class. As discussed previously, the default constructor sets the kphSpeed and fuelLevel attributes to 0 and the exteriorColor attribute to "Not set.". (Figure 5.3 shows the initial values in the top cell of the table.) You assign the object you create to the carA identifier.

After calling the default constructor for the Car class, you call the overloaded version of the constructor to create instances of the Car class to assign to the carB and carC identifiers. As mentioned previously, you can develop any number of overloaded constructors. In this instance, you have implemented only one overloaded constructor. It requires only one argument, which you use to define the exteriorColor attribute of the Car class. With the first call to the overloaded constructor, you set the value of the exteriorColor attribute to Red. With the second call to the overloaded constructor, you set the value of Blue. (Figure 5.3 shows these values in the top cell of the table.) You assign the resulting class instances to the carA and carB identifiers.

At comment #2, you call the accessor methods you have defined for the Car class. To call the accessor methods, you use the Car objects you have created (carA, carB, and carC). In each instance, to call a method, you use the name of the object, a dot operator, and the name of the method. Given these calls, the println() method and the tab escape sequence allow you to create the cells of the table shown in Figure 5.3.

For the first cells of the first row of the table, you use three successive calls to the getEColor() method. Using the three Car objects you have created, you obtain the color state of the objects. Accordingly, the cell under "Car A" contains "Not set.", which is the value the default constructor provides to carA. In the remaining two cells, Red and Green, you see the arguments you have provided to the carB and carC objects using the overloaded constructor.

In each case, the call to the method returns a value of the String type. You employ the concatenation operator (+) to insert the values returned into the string that forms the table row.

To display the speed and fuel attributes of the three Car objects, you again use calls to accessor methods. For the speed, you call the getSpeed() method. For the level of fuel, you call the getFuel() method. Using the println() method as before, you generate two table rows, both of which show the work of the default and overloaded constructors. Both of these constructors assign values of 0 to the speed and fuel attributes.

In the lines trailing comment #3, you call the mutator methods of the Car class. To call these methods, you use three instances of the Car objects you have created. In each instance, you provide the appropriate values. To ensure that the numerical values you provide are read as float values, you append the letter F to the end of each of the numbers you supply as arguments.

In the lines associated with comment #4, you once again call the accessor methods of the Car class. The procedures you use are the same as those accompanying comment #2. As Figure 5.3 illustrates, the result is that you see different values for the three Car objects. The state of each object in this respect has been changed. The state of the object has been changed as a manifestation of the behavior that its methods embody.

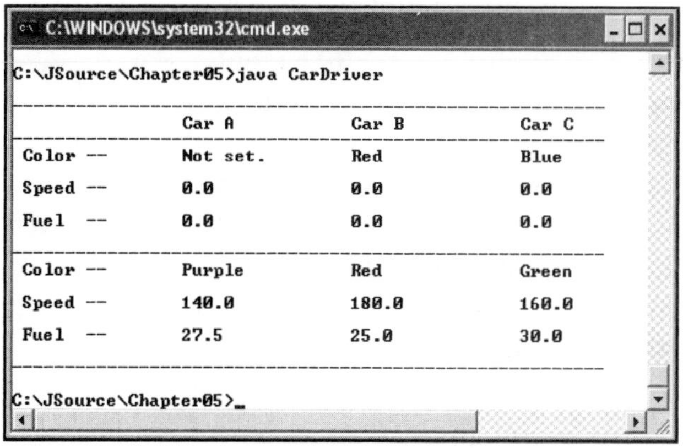

FIGURE 5.3

The test driver class allows you to test the constructors, accessors, and mutators of the Car class.

ENCAPSULATION

The methods you develop in the Car class represent a standard approach to implementing a class. Each method accesses or alters the value of one of the class attributes. Such methods constitute the *interface* of the Car class. The interface of a class consists of its public methods. To create the interface of a class, you employ the public keyword to define the methods you want to make part of the interface. The public keyword enables you to make it so that users can access the methods the class provides.

When a class provides an interface, it *encapsulates* the functionality of a class. Encapsulation constitutes one of the three primary aspects of object-oriented programming. Encapsulation has to do with how you use the features of a programming language to define entities (classes, methods, attributes) that represent *abstractions*.

As Figure 5.4 illustrates, when you define a class, you use abstraction to reduce the state and behavior of the real-world entity in which the class is based from a large number of possibilities to a narrowly defined set of attributes and methods that address a specific set of *responsibilities* you designate for the class. In the case of the Car class, the responsibilities of the class involve allowing the user of the class to track the fuel levels, speeds, and colors of Car objects. The class encapsulates methods and attributes that address its responsibilities.

Encapsulation relates to the features of a programming language that allow you to define a class with relation to its responsibilities. When you use the public keyword to define accessor and mutator methods, you pursue one form of encapsulation. This form of encapsulation involves the definition of the interface.

Another manifestation of encapsulation lies in the use of the private keyword to limit access of the attributes of the class. When you make it so that users of the class cannot access the attributes of the class other than through the accessor and mutator methods, you are exercising what is known as the principle of *data hiding*. For a class like the Car class, data hiding involves making it so that the user cannot directly view or change the kphSpeed, exteriorColor, or fuelLevel attributes.

You practice data hiding when you restrict access to the attributes of a class. The interface methods force the user to relate to the attributes at a specified level of abstraction. The integrity of the objects the class embodies is in this way preserved. When you use "get" and "set" in the names of methods, you push this theme a step further. Such interface features induce users to change the values assigned to attributes in specific ways. Users cannot add to the number of attributes or rename or redefine the attributes. As Figure 5.5 emphasizes, they relate to objects according to the uses you have defined for the objects.

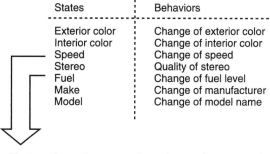

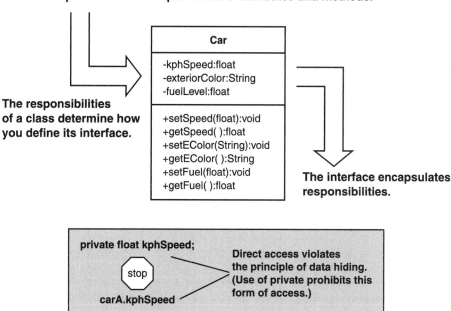

FIGURE 5.4

Abstraction and class responsibility guide the use of encapsulation.

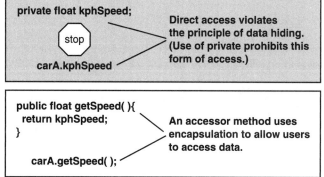

FIGURE 5.5

Encapsulation is made possible by language features that allow you to control the visibility and use of the entities you create.

Scope Considerations

The Scope and ScopeTest classes provide examples of a number of operations related to encapsulation and the this keyword. Some of this discussion extends to topics not covered in this chapter, but it does not hurt to present the information here in a preliminary form. Later chapters develop themes presented in greater detail. Table 5.4 provides discussion of terms that relate to scope. The this keyword is not itself an access control term. Instead, it is a means by which you identify and access an object.

	TABLE 5.4 TERMS RELATING TO SCOPE	

Term	Discussion
public	You use the public keyword to make it so that users of your classes can access methods and attributes using calls initiated by objects of the class type. You can directly access an attribute or method of the public type if you call it with an object of the class.
private	You use the private keyword to make it so that users of your classes cannot access its methods and attributes using calls initiated by objects of the class type. You can access private attributes and methods only within the classes in which they are defined, not elsewhere.
protected	The protected keyword is more complex than the private and public keywords because to effectively use it you must have experience with deriving classes. The next chapter dwells on this topic. Formally, the protected keyword makes it so that you cannot access attributes or methods using calls initiated by objects of your class, but you can access them if you derive a class from the class in which they are defined. Again, specific discussion of class derivations lies beyond the scope of the current chapter.
this	The this keyword allows you to call methods and attributes within the scope of the class in which they are defined. It is used to identify a specific object. It allows you to access "this" instance of the class (this object). It is a keyword that does not work in static methods because static methods do not require that you create instances of a class.

The Scope and ScopeTest Classes

The Scope and ScopeTest classes provide you with a context in which to experiment with the private, public, protected, and this keywords. The Scope class defines attributes and methods using three access control keywords. You cannot access private or protected attributes or methods using calls from objects you create using the class data type. However, if you first encapsulate calls to private and protected attributes and methods in a public method, you can then call the public method to access them.

```
/*
Scope.java
*/
public class Scope{
```

```
//#1
//Can be accessed
public String firstWord = "Public scope ";
private String secondWord = "Private scope ";
protected String thirdWord = "Protected scope ";
//#2
public void showFirst(){
    System.out.println("   showFirst(): " + firstWord);
}
private void showSecond(){
    System.out.println("   showSecond(): " + secondWord);
}
protected void showThird(){
    System.out.println("   showThird(): " + thirdWord);
}
//#3
public void showAllMethods(){
        showFirst();
        showSecond();
        showThird();
}
//#4
public void useThis(){
        this.showFirst();
        this.showSecond();
        this.showThird();
    System.out.println(" this.toString(): " + this.toString());
}
}//end class
```

In the lines associated with comment #1 of the Scope class, you define three class attributes of the String type: firstWord, secondWord, and thirdWord. You define each term using a different access modifier (public, private, and protected). Likewise, you initialize each of the attributes with an expression that identifies its scope.

After defining the attributes for the Scope class, you then move on to define public, private, and protected methods. The showFirst() method calls the println() method to print the value of the firstWord attribute. Both the method and the attribute are public. The showSecond() method calls the println() method to print the value of the secondWord attribute. Both the method and the attribute are private. For the showThird() method, you use the protected keyword to define its scope. In this method, you call the println() method to print the value of the thirdWord attribute, which like the showThird() method is protected.

Since you cannot use Scope class objects to call the showSecond() and showThird() methods, it is necessary to wrap or encapsulate calls of them in a public method. Toward this end, you create the showAllMethods() method. This method wraps calls to the first three. Its scope is public.

As a demonstration of the this keyword, you create the useThis() method. The useThis() method possesses a public scope. It employs the this keyword to make calls to the first three methods of the Scope class. Then it uses the this keyword a fourth time to call the toString() method, which returns the name of the class along with an address identifier for the object the this keyword identifies. As Figure 5.6 illustrates, the result is that you see the Scope class followed by a hexadecimal memory address.

The ScopeTest class provides a context in which you can experiment with different calls to the attributes and methods you define in the Scope class.

```java
/*
ScopeTest.java
*/
public class ScopeTest{
    public static void main(String Args[]){
        Scope testScope = new Scope();
//#1 Call public method
        System.out.println(
                "\n A. Call a public method: testScope.showFirst(): ");
                testScope.showFirst();
//#2 Call an attribute defined as public
      System.out.println("\n B. Call an attribute defined as public: "
                + " testScope.firstWord: \n      "
                + testScope.firstWord);
//#3
        //This statement generates an error
        //secondWord is not a public attribute
        //System.out.println("\n    Public attribute: "
        //                 + testScope.secondWord);
        //System.out.println("\n    Public attribute: "
        //                 + testScope.thirdWord);
```

```
    //#4 Call a method that is defined to call public,
    //   private, and protected methods
        System.out.println("\n    C. Public, private, protected: "
                      + "testScope.showAllMethods(): ");
                      testScope.showAllMethods();
    //#5 Call a method that calls methods using
    //   the this keyword
      System.out.println(
                  " \n    D. The this keyword: testScope.useThis(): ");
                  testScope.useThis();
        }//end main
}//end class
```

To test the Scope class attributes and methods, at comment #1 in the ScopeTest class definition, you call the public showFirst() method. As item A in Figure 5.6 shows, you see the
Public scope message the method issues. In the lines associated with comment #2, you use
the dot operator to call the firstWord attribute of the class. While this approach to accessing
data violates the principle of data hiding, it serves to illustrate that you can access attributes
defined to have public scope.

At comment #3, in contrast, the calls to secondWord and third, private, and protected
attributes, are commented out. If you remove the comments and attempt to compile the
program, the compiler issues error messages indicating that you cannot access the attributes.

In the lines trailing comment #4, you use the testScope object to call the showAllMethods()
method. As item C in Figure 5.6 illustrates, the effect of this call is to access the public, private,
and protected methods in the Scope class. The compiler does not issue an error message
because wrapping calls to the non-public methods in a public method removes scope
violations.

At comment #5, you call the useThis() method. The result is that the non-public methods are
again called. This time you add to the displayed data the message the toString() method
returns.

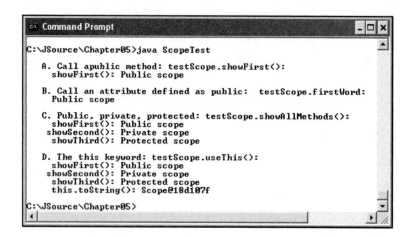

Figure 5.6

You can employ public, private, and protected attributes in a method definition, but you cannot call private and public attributes directly.

More on Methods

When you define methods, you can expand your programming options in fairly significant ways by using method overloading and developing some methods as utility methods. It is also useful to further investigate the use of static methods.

Method Overloading

When you overload the constructor for the Car class, you create a version of a constructor that differs from the default form of the constructor. This form of constructor allows you to initialize an object to a customized state. In the instance of the Car class, you use an overloaded constructor to initialize a Car object with the color of the car set when the Car object is created.

Creating methods with the same name but different argument parameters is referred to as *method overloading*. Java allows you to define any number of methods with the same name as long as you vary the number or types of the arguments that characterize the methods. The Math class example provides examples of an overloaded add() method. You see three versions of the method.

```
/*
Math.java
*/
public class Math{
    public static void main(String Args[]){
        //#1 define variables
            double numberE = 3.4,
                    numberF = 5.6;
            int numberB = 3,
```

```
            numberC = 6,
            numberD = 5;

        String line = "";
        for (int ctr = 1; ctr <= 56; ctr++) {
            line += "-";
        }

        System.out.println("\n    " +
                    "Overloaded forms of the add() method    ");
        System.out.println(line);
//#2 Calls to overloaded methods
        add(numberB, numberC);
        add(numberB, numberC, numberD);
        add(numberE, numberF);

        System.out.println("\n" + line);
    }//end main

    //#3 -------------add(int a, int b)-----------------------
    //method accepts two int arguments
    public static void add(int a, int b){
        a += b;
        System.out.println("   add(int, int) : \t\t " + a);
    }
    //#4-----------add(int a, int b, int c)---------------------
    //method accepts three int arguments
    public static void add(int a, int b, int c){
        a += b + c;
        System.out.println("   add(int, int, int) : \t\t " + a);
    }
//#5--------------add(double, double)----------------------
//method accepts two double arguments
public static void add(double a, double b) {
        a += b;
        System.out.println("   add(double, double) : \t " + a);
    }
}//end Math
```

At comment #1 of the Math class, you work with the scope of the main() method and create a number of variables you use when you call the different versions of the add() method. You also create a formatting line, which creates the brief table you see in Figure 5.7.

At comment #2, you call the three version of the add() method that you define in the Math class. The first call requires two integer values. The second requires three integer values. The final call requires two double values.

In the lines associated with comment #3, you define the version of the add() method that requires two arguments of the int type. In the implementation of the method, you add the value of the first argument to the value of the second argument and assign the result back to the first argument. You then call the println() method to display the result.

For the method you define in association with comment #4, you require three arguments of the int type. In this operation, you first add the values of the second and third arguments. You then use a compound addition operator to add this sum to the value of the first argument. The final sum you assign back to the first argument.

For the definition of the overloaded version of the add() method that trails comment #5, you define two arguments of the double type. You then use a compound addition operator to add the value of the second argument to the value of the first argument. You assign the result back to the first argument.

FIGURE 5.7

Method overloading allows you to define multiple methods of the same name within a single class.

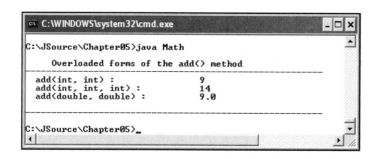

Method Signatures and Return Operations

The line in which you define the return type, name, and arguments of a method is called the *signature line* of the method. In many instances, in the documentation for Java, you see only the signature lines. Use of signature lines allows you to understand the definition of a class interface without worrying about the details of implementation.

To make it so that a method can return a value, you define a return type in the signature line of the method and employ the return keyword in the implementation of the method. The return type can be any type that Java supports, primitive or abstract. If a method returns no value, then you employ the void keyword. The void keyword prevents the method from accidentally returning a value. Likewise, if you use the void keyword, then you cannot also employ the return keyword.

As mentioned previously, the return keyword allows the method to return a copy of the variable that follows it within the scope of the method. When a method returns a value, the type of the variable that follows the return keyword should correspond to the return value you define in the method signature. Still, it remains that the type of the identifier that follows the return keyword does not have to be the same as the type of the return value. Consider the implementation of the highNumber() method. (To view this method, open the MoreMath.java file):

```
///From MoreMath.java
//The return type should be int. However the
//return type is double. No compiler error results. See MoreMath.java
//Values of the int type are promoted to a value of the double type
//------------------------- highNumber --------------------------------
  public static double highNumber(int a, int b) {
    int higher;
    if (a > b){
        higher = a;
    }
    else{
        higher = b;
    }
    return higher;    //int value
}
```

This implementation of the highNumber() method creates no compiler errors because the compiler can promote values of the int, long, and float types to double values.

However, if you define an overloaded version of the highNumber() method that involves arguments of the double type and a returned value of the int type, then the compiler issues an error message. Consider this implementation (see the MoreMath.java file for an example of how to include the highNumber() method in a working program):

```
//Compiler error results -- see MoreMath.java
//Values of the double type cannot be demoted to the int type
public static int highNumber(double a, double b) {
    int higher;
```

```
    if (a > b){
        higher = a;
    }
    else{
        higher = b;
    }
    return higher;
}
```

This implementation generates an error. The points of trouble in this second version of the highNumber() method arise when you attempt to assign a and b to higher. This type of implicit casting does not work. Just as you cannot implicitly cast a double to the int type, so you cannot use the return keyword to effect the conversion.

Assignments and Cascading Calls

You can use the value a method returns as part of a variable definition. Assume that the signature line for the highNumber method reads as follows:

```
public int highNumber(int a, int b)
```

This method takes two integer values as arguments and returns an integer value. Given that the method returns an integer value, you can use it to initialize a variable of the int type, just as though it were a literal integer value. Here is an example:

```
int maxNumber = highNumber(2, 4);
```

The highNumber() method returns the higher value (in this case 4), and the assignment operator then allows you to define the maxNumber variable using the returned value.

Along the same lines, you can insert method calls in any slot in which you might otherwise use a literal variable value. When you use one method call to return a value that you use for another method call, the approach is referred to as a *cascading* method call. The following cascading call uses the returned value of the highNumber() method as an argument for a second call to the highNumber() method:

```
int maxNumber = highNumber(6, highNumber(2, 4) );
```

In this instance, the "outer" call to the highNumber() method involves two arguments. The first argument is 6. The second argument is the value that an "inner" call to the highNumber() method provides. The inner call returns 4. This returned value is then compared with 6. The result is that the value assigned to maxNumber by the outer call is 6.

Points of Return

In addition to assignment operations and cascading method calls is the use of a single point of return in the implementation of your methods. A single point of return involves following a practice characteristic of *structural programming*. According to this practice, a method should have one *point of entry* and one *point of exit*. Accordingly, the point of entry is the argument list of the method. The point of exit is the return keyword. Here is a version of a method called lowNumber() that offers one point of entrance and one point of exit:

```
//one point of entry
public static int lowNumber(int a, int b) {
    int lower;
    if (a < b){
        lower = a;
    }
    else{
        lower = b;
    }
    return lower; //one point of exit
}//end lower
```

In this implementation of the lowNumber() method, the point of entrance consists of two arguments, a and b. To process the values of these arguments, you declare a local variable of the int type (lower). You then use an if...else selection structure. If the value of a is less than the value of b, you assign the value of a to lower. Then you skip the else block and return the value of lower. On the other hand, if a is not less than b, then the flow of the program goes to the else block, and the value of b is assigned to lower. You then pass to the return statement and return the value of lower. In either case, the flow of the program proceeds from one point of entrance to one point of exit. One use of the return keyword marks the point of exit.

In contrast, consider the following implementation of the same set of functionality. This implementation offers one point of entrance and two points of exit:

```
public int lowNumber(int a, int b){ //one point of entrance
    if (a < b){
        return a; // two points of return
    }
    return b;
}
```

In this second form of implementation, the flow of the program proceeds from the argument list to the if selection statement. If a is less than b, then the flow of the program enters the selection statement block, and the return statement is invoked to return the value of a. At this point, the flow of the program exits the lowNumber() method. It never encounters the second return statement.

If the if selection statement evaluates to false, the flow of the program does not enter the if selection block. Instead, it skips to the return statement that immediately precedes the closing brace of the method.

While this second form of implementation does not generate an error, it is considered questionable because it has two points of return. A method with two points of return can sometimes cause problems because it can make it difficult to trace the flow of your program.

Static Methods and Attributes

In a number of instances in this and previous chapters, you have made use of the static keyword to define attributes and methods. In the instance of the main() method, you always use it. With other methods, you use it in situations in which you do not want to create an instance of the class in which you define the method. Because you do not need to create an instance of the class in which they are defined, static methods and attributes are referred to as *class* methods and attributes. Table 5.5 provides a summary discussion of some of the terms related to class methods and attributes.

The signature lines of static methods usually follow the same pattern. Here is the signature line of one of the add() methods defined in the Math class:

```
public static void add(double a, double b)
```

As has been mentioned previously, the main() method is always static. The Java interpreter calls the main() method to identify the entry point of your application. An application, regardless of the number of classes it uses, must have at least one static main() method. On the other hand, applets require no main() method because your browser is itself an application.

To call a static method outside the scope of the class in which it is defined, you can use the name of the class or an object of the type of the class. As you see in the StaticUseTest class, a call to the useStatic() method takes the following forms:

```
StaticUse.useStatic();
testStaticUse.staticUtility();
```

TABLE 5.5 TERMS RELATING TO STATIC ATTRIBUTES AND METHODS

Term	Discussion
static final	A static final attribute is a constant value. You call it using the class name and the name of the attribute. It does not represent a specific instance of a class.
final (methods)	Use of final methods lies beyond the scope of the current discussion. Formally, when you qualify a method with the final keyword, it cannot be overridden. In other words, if you derive a class from the class in which the final method is defined, then you must use the method as defined.
static (attributes)	A static attribute is not a constant. In other words, you can change it. You call it using the class name. It does not represent a specific instance of a class. You can also access it using an object of the class in which it is defined.
static (methods)	A static method does not represent a specific instance of a class. It is known as a class method. You can call it using only the class name. You can also call it using an object to the class that defines it.

Static attributes behave in ways similar to static methods. To define a static attribute as a constant, you use the final keyword. You also usually define such attributes as public. When you declare a constant (final) static value, you initialize it. As the StaticUse class illustrates, it is not necessary to declare static attributes as final. A static attribute is a class attribute (associated with a class rather than the object of a class), so you can access it without the use of a class object. The StaticUse class provides examples of how to declare attributes and methods involving the static keyword.

```
/*
  StaticUse.java
*/
public class StaticUse{
    //#1
    public static String staticWord = "Static public";
    public final static String staticFinalWord = "Static final public";
    //#2
    static void useStatic(){
        //Cannot call a non-static method in a static method
        //You can call a static method using a static method
        System.out.println("\n    useStatic() calling staticUtility().");
        staticUtility();
```

```
    }
    //#3
    static void staticUtility(){
        System.out.println("\n     This is staticUtility().");
    }
}
```

At comment #1 of the StaticUse class definition, you create two static attributes: staticWord and staticFinalWord. Both are public. For the second attribute, you use the final keyword, making it a constant. To each of the attributes, you assign a string that identifies its defined characteristics.

In the lines associated with comment #2, you define the useStatic() method. To define this method, you use the static keyword. Within the scope of the method, you call the staticUtility() method. In the lines following comment #3, you define the staticUtility() method. The useStatic() method can incorporate a call to the staticUtility() method. A static method may not, however, incorporate a call to a non-static method.

```
/*
    StaticUseTest.java
*/
public class StaticUseTest{

    public static void main(String Args[]){
        StaticUse testStaticUse = new StaticUse();

    //#1
        //Call a static method using the name of the class
        //not an object of the class
        System.out.println("\n Call using -- StaticUse.useStatic(): ");
        System.out.print(" ");
        StaticUse.useStatic();

    //#2 Call a static method with an object of the class
        System.out.println("\n Call using -- testStaticUse.staticUtility: ");
        System.out.print(" ");
        testStaticUse.staticUtility();

    //#3 Call static and static final attributes with
    // The name of the class
```

```
            System.out.println("\n Call using -- StaticUse.staticWord: ");
            System.out.print(" " + StaticUse.staticWord);
            System.out.println("\n Call using -- testStaticUse.staticWord: ");
            System.out.print(" " + testStaticUse.staticWord);
            System.out.println("\n Call using -- StaticUse.staticFinalWord: ");
            System.out.print(" " + StaticUse.staticFinalWord);
            System.out.println("\n Call using -- testStaticUse.staticFinalWord:
");
            System.out.print(" " + testStaticUse.staticFinalWord);
      }//end main
}//end class
```

At comment #1 in the StaticUseTest class, you employ the StaticUse class name to make a call to the useStatic() method. Following this call, at comment #2, you use the testStaticUse object to call the staticUtility() method. You repeat this activity in the lines following comment #3, but now you access the values provided by the staticWord and staticFinalWord attributes. As Figure 5.8 reveals, calling them with either the testStaticUse object or the StaticUse class name renders the same result.

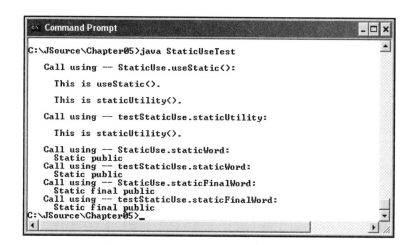

FIGURE 5.8

Use of the static and final keywords allows you to create constants, class attributes, and methods.

More on Constructors and the this Keyword

Using the this keyword, as you saw with the call to the toString() method in the Scope class, you can access the reference identity of an object. The this keyword identifies any object in which you use it. Because it identifies an object, you cannot use the this keyword in static contexts. Static contexts characterize static method definitions and the calling of static attributes.

At the same time, the this keyword helps elucidate the use of constructors. The Construction class allows you to explore a set of three constructors. You create an explicit default constructor. You also create two overloaded constructors. The two overloaded constructors take different arguments. However, within one of these you employ the this keyword to implicitly call to the other. When you employ this approach to calling a constructor, the this keyword invokes any constructor that possesses the number arguments you place in parentheses following it.

```
/*
Construction
*/
public class Construction{

    //#1
    private int firstNum, secondNum, thirdNum;

    public Construction(){
        System.out.println(" Default constructor....");
    }
    //#2 First overloaded constructor
    public Construction(int fN, int sN){
    //The this keyword calls
    //a constructor that has three parameters
        this(fN, sN, sN);
        System.out.println(" Construction using this....");
    }
    //#3 Second overloaded constructor
    public Construction(int fN, int sN, int tN){
        firstNum = fN;
        secondNum = sN;
        thirdNum = tN;
        System.out.println(" Construction using three parameters....");
    }
}//end class
```

In the lines accompanying comment #1, you define three class attributes of the int type. You then create a default constructor. When you define overloaded constructors, as you do in the lines accompanying comments #2 and #3, it becomes necessary to explicitly define a default constructor if you are to use a default constructor.

Putting aside discussion of the second constructor for a moment, at comment #3 you create a constructor that involves the use of three parameters. You use the values you obtain from the argument list to initialize the three class attributes. Having defined this constructor, you are then in a position to use the `this` keyword in the definition of the constructor trailing comment #2.

In the definition of the constructor that trails comment #2, you define two parameters. You then use the `this` keyword, followed by a set of parentheses that contain identifiers from the argument list of the constructor. The effect of using the `this` keyword followed by three argument identifiers is to invoke the three-argument constructor. The `this` keyword invokes any constructor that contains arguments that correspond in number to the number of identifiers contained within the parentheses.

In the `ConstructionTest` class, you make use of the three constructors. As Figure 5.9 reveals, the two-argument constructor invokes the three-argument constructor. Such is the work of the `this` keyword.

```
public class ConstructionTest{

    public static void main(String Args[]){
        //Default
        Construction testConA = new Construction();
        Construction testConB = new Construction(1, 2);
        Construction testConC = new Construction(1, 2, 3);
        }//end main
}//end class
```

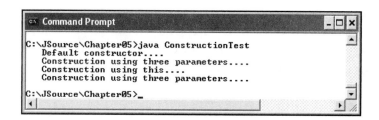

FIGURE 5.9

Using the `this` keyword followed by parentheses, you can invoke constructors.

COMPOSITION

Two primary types of relation exist between classes. One is called inheritance. The other is called association. You will explore the topic of inheritance a little later. To explore association, it is necessary to slightly extend the work you have already performed. Composition involves creating an instance of one class within another. The Unified Modeling Language

(UML) allows you to represent composition using an expanded version of the class diagram introduced earlier in this chapter. In this instance, to illustrate the project at hand, consider Figure 5.10.

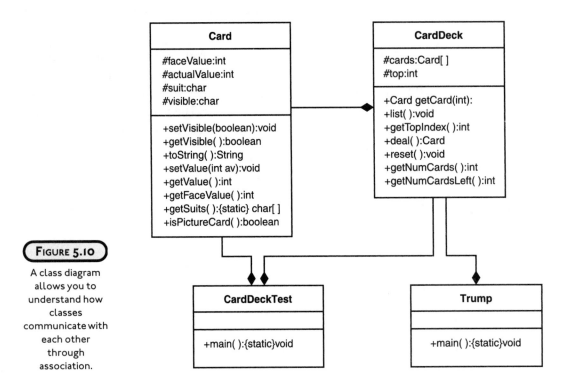

FIGURE 5.10

A class diagram allows you to understand how classes communicate with each other through association.

The shaded diamond that creates the tip of the line points to the class that contains an object of the type that lies at the tail of the line. A shaded diamond indicates that a relationship of composition always exists between the two classes involved. In this respect, then, an object of the Card type is always created within an object of the CardDeck type. Likewise, an object of the CardDeck class is always created within an object of the CardDeckTest type.

With the Card, CardDeck, CardDeckTest, and Trump classes, you develop a system of classes in which one class is dependent on one or more other classes. When you test the system, you create instances of the Card and CardDeck classes in the CardDeckTest class. When you develop the Trump class, the dependency cascades from the CardDeck class to the Card class.

The Card Class

The Card class represents playing cards in terms of an actual value and a face value. The actual value, stored in the actualValue attribute, designates an arbitrary card value that you determine based on the game you are playing.

The face value, stored in the faceValue attribute, designates the fixed numerical value of the card as defined in the two ranges of low and high cards. Accordingly, these value are not arbitrary. Valid values for low cards are restricted to 2 through 10. Valid values for high cards are restricted to 11 for a Jack, 12 for a Queen, 13 for a King, and 14 for an Ace. The Card class provides constants of the int type to implement the high cards: JACK, QUEEN, KING, and ACE. As Figure 5.11 illustrates, single letters indicate the suits: C signifies clubs, D diamonds, H hearts, and S spades.

When a card is visible, it is turned so that you can see its value. It is face up. To indicate whether you can see the value of a card, you use a boolean attribute (visible). If set to true, this attribute designates that the card is face up. If set to false, this attribute designates that the card is face down.

The Card class features two constructors. You define one using three arguments. You define the other using four arguments. The three-argument constructor allows you to set up a card so that its face value and its actual value are the same. Use of the this keyword in the definition of the three-argument constructor allows you to call the four-argument constructor, to which you supply the same face and actual values. The four-argument constructor allows you to designate different values for the face and actual values. To implement the three-argument constructor, you use the this keyword.

```
/*
   * Card
*/
// A class that defines playing cards that you
// low cards: 2, 3, 4, 5, 6, 7, 8, 9, 10,
// high cards Jack, Queen, King, and Ace
// suits: clubs, diamonds, hearts, and spades
// faceValue: int value representing the face value of the card
//            low cards 2 - 10; high cards 11 - 14
// actualValue: an arbitrary point value -- depends on the game
//

public class Card {
    public static final int JACK = 11, QUEEN = 12,
```

```
                        KING = 13, ACE = 14,
                        MIN = 2, MAX = 14;
    protected int faceValue;
    protected int actualValue;
    protected char suit;
    protected boolean visible;
//#1
//-----------------Card constructor--------------------------
    public Card(int fv, char s, boolean v){
        //Use the fully implemented constructor
        //Use the fv argument to set both the
        //face value and the actual value
        this(fv, fv, s, v);
    }
//------------------Card constructor-------------------------
    public Card(int fv, int av, char s, boolean v){
        //if the value is in the acceptable range
        //of 2 to 14, use it as is
        //otherwise, give it a value of 2
        faceValue = (fv >= MIN && fv <= MAX) ? fv : 2;
        actualValue = av;
        if (s == 'C' || s == 'D' || s == 'H' || s == 'S'){
            suit = s;
        }
        else{
                suit = 'C';
        }//end else if
            visible = v;
    }//end constructor
//#2
//------------------toString--------------------------------
    public String toString(){
        if (!visible){
            return "??";
        }
        String face;
        //Convert the number to a string if it is
        //Not a high card or an ace
```

```
        if (faceValue >= 2 && faceValue <=10){
            face = String.valueOf(faceValue);
        }
        //if 1 or a value greater than 10
        //assign a letter
        else{
            switch (faceValue){
                case JACK:
                    face = "J";
                    break;
                case QUEEN:
                    face = "Q";
                    break;
                case KING:
                    face = "K";
                    break;
                case ACE:
                    face = "A";
                    break;
                default:
                    face = "2";
            }//end switch
        }//end else
        face += suit;
        return face;
    }//end toString


//#3
//-----------------setVisible-----------------------------
    public void setVisible(boolean v){
        visible = v;
    }
//-----------------getVisible-----------------------------
    public boolean getVisible(){
        return visible;
    }
//-----------------setValue-----------------------------
    public void setValue(int av) {
```

```
            actualValue = av;
        }
//------------------getValue------------------------------
        public int getValue() {
            return actualValue;
        }
//------------------getFaceValue---------------------------
        public int getFaceValue() {
            return faceValue;
        }
//#4
//------------------ getSuits ----------------------------
        public static char[] getSuits(){
            char[] suits = { 'C', 'D', 'H', 'S' };
            return suits;
        }
//#5
//------------------isPictureCard--------------------------
// returns true if this card is a picture card
// For example, jack, queen, or king
        public boolean isPictureCard(){
            if (faceValue >= JACK && faceValue <= KING) {
                return true;
            }
                return false;
        }//end isPictureCard
}//end class
```

Preceding comment #1 in the Card class, you declare four class attributes. They are all of the protected scope, which allows them to be used only by classes that you derive from the Card class. Derivation of classes is a topic of the next chapter. The significance of the protected form of access in the current context rests on the fact that you cannot call these attributes directly using objects of the Card class.

Following comment #1, you create two constructors. As mentioned previously, the first constructor takes three arguments and uses the this keyword to supply these arguments to the four-argument constructor. In the definition of the four-argument constructor, you check the value of the fv (face value) argument to ensure that it lies within the range extending from 2 to 14. You also verify that the value provided by the s (suit) argument is one of the defined suits (C, D, H, or S). If it is, you assign it to the suit attribute. If not, you assign a default value of C to the suit attribute. You do not check the av (actual value) and v (visible) arguments.

In the lines trailing comment #2, you define the Card::toString() method. The purpose of this method involves converting the numerical value of the a card to a string representation. To make the conversion, you begin with the low cards. You create a selection statement in which you verify that the card value lies in the range extending from 2 to 10. If the card lies within this range, then you call the String::valueOf() method to convert the value you have assigned to the faceValue attribute of the Card object into a string. You assign the string to the face variable. To convert the values assigned to the high cards into strings, you create a switch selection statement. You develop cases that test the value of faceValue against the JACK, QUEEN, KING, and ACE constants. For each case, to the face variable you assign a letter that designates the card's identity.

To create the character string that the toString() method returns, you employ the String concatenation operator to join the values you obtain from the face variable with the value you obtain from the Card suit attribute.

In the lines associated with comment #3, you set up a series of accessor and mutator methods. These methods allow you to set and get the actual value and face value of cards. They also allow you to set and get the visibility of cards.

The method you define at comment #4 allows you to return an array that provides character identifiers for each of the card suits. The array is of the char type. The index 0 of the array corresponds to the C (club) suit.

In the lines accompanying comment #5, you implement the isPictureCard() method. This method uses the constants you define as Card class attributes to determine whether the card you are working with is a high card. It returns a Boolean value of true if the card is a high card. If not, it returns a Boolean value of false.

The CardDeck Class

The CardDeck class simulates a deck of cards by organizing a group of Card objects. It maintains this group of Card objects in a protected Card array and defines methods that allow you to perform such operations as selecting a specific card from the deck (getCard()) and ascertaining the number of cards the deck contains (getNumOfCards()).

```
/*
    CardDeck
*/
```

```java
public class CardDeck {
    protected Card[] cards;
    protected int top;
//#1
//-------------------CardDeck constructor-------------------
//Creates a deck of cards
    public CardDeck(){
        top = 0;
        char[] suits = Card.getSuits();
        //Number of possible cards is number of suits * number of
        //high and low values
        //MIN is 2; MAX is 14
        int numValues = Card.MAX - Card.MIN + 1;
        //create a card array using an array constructor
        //with the number of cards: Number of suits
        //times the number of cards for each suit
        cards = new Card[suits.length * numValues];
        int cIndex;
        //For the 4 suit of cards...
        for(int s=0; s < suits.length; s++){
          //iterate from 1 through 14...
          for(int v=Card.MIN; v <= Card.MAX; v++){
            cIndex = s * numValues + v - Card.MIN;
            //And assign a card for each to the card array
            cards[cIndex] = new Card(v, suits[s], true);
          }//end inner for
        }//end outer for
    }//end constructor


//-------------------getCard-------------------------------
//Retrieves card according to its position in the card array
    public Card getCard(int index){
        return cards[index];
    }
//#2
//-------------------list----------------------------------
//Displays cards in rows according to suit
```

```java
    public void list(){
        for (int ctrl=0; ctrl < cards.length; ctrl++) {
            if(ctrl % 13 == 0){
                    System.out.print("\n ");
            }
            System.out.print(cards[ctrl].toString() + " ");
        }
    }
//#3
//-----------------getTopIndex-----------------------------
    public int getTopIndex(){
        return top;
    }
//#4
//-----------------deal------------------------------------
// returns the card at top index and moves the index
    public Card deal(){
        Card dealt = cards[top];
        top++;
    //if last card dealt, reset the top card
        if (top >= cards.length){
            reset();
        }
        return dealt;
    }
//-----------------reset-----------------------------------
    public void reset(){
        top = 0;
    }
//#5
//-----------------getNumCards-----------------------------
    public int getNumCards(){
        return cards.length;
    }
//#6
//-----------------getNumCardsLeft-------------------------
    public int getNumCardsLeft(){
```

```
        return cards.length - top;
    }
}
```

Just prior to comment #1 in the CardDeck class, you define two attributes. The first is an array of the Card type (cards). The second is an identifier of the int type (top). The value of top varies as you work with the deck. Initially, this value is 0, representing the 0 index of the cards array.

Following comment #1, you define the default constructor for the CardDeck class. To define the constructor, you first assign 0 to the top attribute. You then call the static Card.getSuits() method, which returns a char array containing the valid suits. You assign this array to the suits variable.

You then calculate the number of possible face values. To accomplish this, you subtract the Card.MIN constant (2) from the Card.MAX constant. The Card.MAX constant represents the highest possible face value (14). You then add 1 to the difference, which results in 13. You assign this value to the numValues variable.

Given the assignment of a value to numValues, you then create an array of the Card type. To set the length of the array, you access the length attribute of the suits array and multiply it by the value assigned to numValues. The number of suits times the number of face values produces the total number of cards (52). This is the initial set of elements in the cards array.

To create Card objects to assign to the cards array, you develop nested for statements. For the outer statement, you traverse the elements of the suits array (there are 4 elements). For the inner for statement, you start by multiplying the number of cards in a suit by the current index of the suits array (beginning with 0). You then add the value of the inner for statement control (v) to this number and subtract the value of Card.MIN (2). As the array iterates, then, the numbers proceed as follows:

```
0 1 2 3 4 5 6 7 8 9 10 11 12
13 14 15 16 17 18 19 20 21 22 23 24 25
26 27 28 29 30 31 32 33 34 35 36 37 38
39 40 41 42 43 44 45 46 47 48 49 50 51
```

You assign these values to cIndex and use cIndex to identify indexes of the cards array, to which you assign Card objects. As you move through the array, you call the three-argument Card constructor to create the Card objects. For the first argument of this constructor, you provide the value of v, which is the value of the card in a given suit. For the second argument, you retrieve the suit from the suits array using the s control from the outer for statement. For the final argument, you provide the true token to make all cards face up. Figure 5.11 illustrates the alphanumerical values assigned to the cards.

Immediately after the definition of the CardDeck constructor, you define the getCard() method. This method allows you to retrieve a card from the cards array. Its return type is Card, and it takes as an argument the index of the Card object you want to retrieve from the cards array.

At comment #2, you define the list() method. Figure 5.11 illustrates the output of the list() method in the upper part of the window. To implement the method, you traverse the cards array. As you traverse the array, you employ the modulus operator (%) to determine when the number of items in the rows reaches 13. At this point, you invoke a line return. To print the character values of the cards, you call the Card::toString() method for each Card object the cards array contains.

After defining an accessor method to obtain the value of the top attribute (comment #3), you define the deal() method, which returns a Card object from the cards array each time it is called. To return a Card object from the cards array, you first use the current value of the top attribute (which is initially set to 0 by the class constructor) to retrieve a Card object. You assign the object to the dealt variable, which is of the Card type. You then increment the top attribute by 1. After incrementing the top attribute, you then check to determine whether it is greater than or equal to the length of the cards array. If it is greater than or equal to the cards array, you then call the reset() method. If the value of the top attribute does not satisfy this condition, then you return the Card object you have assigned to the dealt variable.

Immediately preceding comment #5, to define the reset() method, you assign 0 to the top attribute. Following comment #5, to define the getNumCards() method, you employ the length attribute of the array data type to obtain the length of the cards array. For the final bit of work in the CardDeck class, at comment #6 you define the getNumCardsLeft() method. To implement the method, you subtract the value of top from the length of the cards array.

Testing the Associated Classes

Testing a class thoroughly involves calling every method it contains. The CardDeckText class does not thoroughly test the Card and CardDeck classes. Instead, addressing only a few methods, it serves as a framework you can expand if you want to test all the methods on your own.

```
/*
 * CardDeckTest
 * Tests the CardDeck class.
 */
public class CardDeckTest {
    public static void main(String args[]) {
        //#1
```

```
   //Call the default constructor
   CardDeck deckOfCards = new CardDeck();

   System.out.println("\n Deck Listing:");
   //Traverse the deck and show the cards in it
   deckOfCards.list();
   //Show the current index
//#2
   System.out.println("\n\n Top index of the deck array: "
                              + deckOfCards.getTopIndex());
   //Get one card from the deck of cards -- deal
   Card dealtCard = deckOfCards.deal();
   //show the dealtCard
   System.out.println(" Card dealt " + dealtCard);
   //Get another card from the deck
   dealtCard = deckOfCards.deal();
   //Show the card
   System.out.println(" Card dealt " + dealtCard);
//#3
   //Show the current index
   System.out.println(" Top index: " + deckOfCards.getTopIndex());
   deckOfCards.reset();
   System.out.println("\n Reset deck...Top index now... "
                       + deckOfCards.getTopIndex());
   //Get one card from the deck -- deal
     dealtCard = deckOfCards.deal();
     //show the dealtCard
   System.out.println("\n Dealt " + dealtCard);
//#4
   //Show the number of cards
   System.out.println("\n Number of cards " + deckOfCards.getNumCards() );
   System.out.println("\n The last dealtCard is " +
                   deckOfCards.getCard(deckOfCards.getNumCards() - 1));
   }
 }
```

At comment #1 of the CardDeckTest class, you create an instance of the CardDeck class, which you assign to the deckOfCards identifier. You then proceed to call the list() method, which generates the four-tier set of cards Figure 5.11 illustrates.

You then proceed at comment #2 to call the getTopIndex() method, which reveals that the top attribute of the CardDeck class has been set to 0. Given this starting point, you call the deal() method and assign the Card object returned to the dealtCard variable. You then call the println() method to display the face value of the card. After repeating this operation with the next two statements, at comment #3 you again call the getTopIndex() method. As Figure 5.11 illustrates, the index value is now at 2, having been incremented after the last deal.

To test the reset() method, you call it following the deal of the cards. You then call the getTopIndex() method. When you print the value retrieved, as Figure 5.11 reveals, it has been reset to 0. You then call the deal() method and assign the returned Card object to dealtCard. The value of the Card object associated with the 0 index remains the same as before.

To close out the testing, at comment #4 you call the getNumCards() method to show that the deck contains 52 cards. With a second call to the getNumCards() method, you supply this value to the getCard() method. The card returned is AS (Ace of spades), which corresponds to the last card shown in the rows the list() method generated previously.

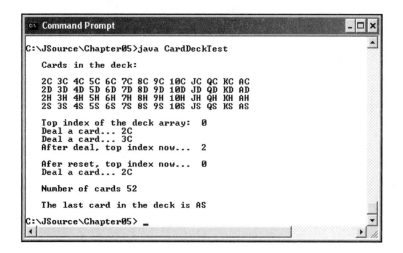

FIGURE 5.11

Calling the methods of the CardDeck class in a selective way allows you to verify the performance of the basic interface features.

Trump

The Trump class provides a context in which to explore the possibilities of creating a game using the Card and CardDeck classes. As Figure 5.12 illustrates, the game involves generation of two-card sets. One card of the set is associated with a dealer. The other card of the set is associated with the player. According to an arbitrary system of rating the cards based on their values, the player and dealer compete on an iterative basis.

```java
/*
  Trump.java
*/
import java.io.*;
import java.util.Random;

public class Trump{
    public static void main(String args[]){
        BufferedReader reader;
        Random rand = new Random();
        int firstCard = 0,
            secondCard = 0;
//#1
        CardDeck deckOfCards = new CardDeck();
        String choice = "";
        reader = new BufferedReader(new InputStreamReader(System.in));
            int n = 236;
            char c = (char )n;
            String line = "\n ";
            for (int ctr = 1; ctr <= 40; ctr++) {
                line += c;
            }
            line += "\n";

            System.out.println("\n Play Trump -- High Card Wins.");
            System.out.println(line);
            while(true){
//#2
                firstCard = rand.nextInt(deckOfCards.getNumCards() );
                secondCard = rand.nextInt(deckOfCards.getNumCards());
                System.out.println("\n Your card: "
                                    + deckOfCards.getCard(firstCard));
                System.out.println(line);
                System.out.println("\n Dealer's card: "
```

```
                                            + deckOfCards.getCard(secondCard));
                System.out.println(line);
//#3

                if(firstCard > secondCard){
                    System.out.println("\n You trump the dealer. ");
                }else if (secondCard > firstCard){
                    System.out.println("\n The dealer trumps you. ");
                }else{
                    System.out.println("\n You and the dealer tied. ");
                }
//#4

                //------------------------------------------------------------
                //Check user preference
                    try{
                        System.out.print("\n Another? Y | Quit Q >>");
                        choice= reader.readLine();
                        System.out.println("\n Play Trump -- High Card Wins.");
                        System.out.print("\n\n");
                    }
                    catch (IOException ioe) {
                        System.out.println("I O Exception Occurred");
                    }//end catch

                    if( choice.equalsIgnoreCase("Q") ){
                            //exits program
                                break;
                    }
            }//end while
                //------------------------------------------------------------
            } //end main
}//end class
```

In the lines associated with comment #1, you create BufferedReader and Random objects. You also declare variables of the int type to allow you to work with card face values and random numbers. You also call the CardDeck constructor and assign the resulting CardDeck object to the deckOfCards identifier. In addition, you create some character graphics by using a cast operation and concatenating the resulting character into a string. You define the choice variable to support the user's interaction.

In the lines accompanying comment #2, you create a while repetition block. As a control for the while statement, you use the true token, which creates an infinite cycle. After the opening brace of the while block, you call the Random::nextInt() method and supply it with an argument you retrieve with the Cards::getNumCards() method. This method returns the number of cards contained in the deckOfCards object. The values that result lie in the range from 0 up to 52.

Through two calls of the nextInt() method, you generate random values for the firstCard and secondCard variables. Given the assignment of values to these variables, you then use them in calls to the CardDeck::getCard() method, which returns Card objects associated with the indexes the random numbers identify. When you concatenate the returned values with introductory text, you see the cards shown in Figure 5.12.

To determine wins, losses, and ties, in the lines trailing comment #3, you implement an if...else if...else structure that evaluates the random numbers assigned to firstCard and secondCard. If the value of firstCard exceeds the value of secondCard, then the dealer wins. If the value of secondCard exceeds the value of firstCard, then the player wins. If the values are equal, then the flow of the program defaults to the else block, and you report a tie.

At comment #4, to control the while block, you use the reader object to call the readLine() method. You retrieve values of Y or Q. You set up a try...catch block to accommodate tie IO operations. You employ the String::equalsIgnoreCase() method to evaluate the player input. To exit the while block, if the user types Q, then the flow of the program enters the if selection block and encounters the break statement. With this, the while block terminates and the program ends.

FIGURE 5.12

Using the CardDeck and Card classes, you create a game that involves comparing card values.

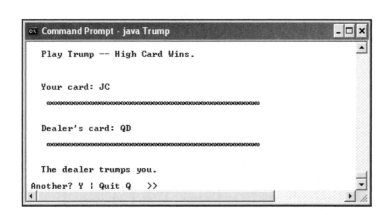

SUMMARY

In this chapter, you have explored a multitude of concepts, practices, and principles related to object-oriented programming. Among other topics, you investigated how classes embody the states and behaviors of real-world entities. To create classes, you examined how to define attributes and methods to reflect states and behaviors. You likewise examined how encapsulation constitutes one of the main features of object-oriented programming. One application of encapsulation is data hiding, which involves barring users of classes from directly accessing the attributes classes contain. Toward this end, you explored the use of keywords associated with definitions of scope and the creation of static, public, private, and protected attributes and methods. In addition, you investigated how UML diagrams can be used to illustrate classes and how classes are often associated on the basis of composition. In the next chapter, you extend your investigations to include inheritance, polymorphism, and the fundamentals of the Java graphical user interface (GUI).

CHALLENGES

1. Using the Car class as a guide, create a class that contains three attributes. Use a common item, such as a tree, a building, or food. Make the class attributes private. Create public accessor and mutator methods for the class. Before you code anything, draw a UML diagram of the class (see Figure 5.2). Indicate what is public and what is private.

2. Develop a constructor that sets the values automatically (a default constructor) and one that requires you to set all the values yourself.

3. Write a main function and create a few instances of the class. Test all of the methods. Test to confirm that the attributes are private. (Try to call them directly with calls such as Car.kphSpeed.) Create output using the println() method.

4. Create a method that combines two of the mutator methods. For example, with reference to the Car class, setSpeed() and setFuel() can be called within the definition of another method called setSpeedAndFuel(float sp, float fl). After you have defined an initial version of this method, define an overloaded version. For example, setSpeedAndFuel(String s). With this method, if the user provides the word "empty," the two class attributes it mutates are set to 0.

CHAPTER 6

BUILDING A
CLASS HIERARCHY

I n this chapter, you further pursue the discussion of object-oriented programming. In Chapter 5, "Object-Oriented Programming," you learned
that a class is a pattern for objects and that objects encapsulate attributes
and methods that address responsibilities you identify through abstraction to
characterize the class. Your work with object-oriented programming practices led
to the development of a system of peer classes. These classes were associated with
each other on the basis of composition. In this chapter, you push the themes relating to object-oriented programming into the areas of inheritance and polymorphism. Encapsulation, inheritance, and polymorphism constitute the three
fundamental practices encompassed by the object-oriented programming
paradigm. Among topics covered in this chapter are the following:

- Exploring inheritance and hierarchies
- Generalization and specialization
- Working with constructors
- Overriding methods
- Using final methods
- How classes are polymorphic

SOFTWARE REUSABILITY

One of the most important benefits of object-oriented programming is that it allows you to reuse software. In Chapter 5, you explored the use of composition as a tool of software reuse. There, you developed the Card and CardDeck classes and then reused them in other classes. After creating instances of the Card and CardDeck classes in the CardDeckTest class, for example, you then created an instance of the CardDeck class in the Trump class. That was an example of software reuse based on composition among a group of peer classes.

While composition provides a way to reuse peer classes, inheritance provides a way to reuse classes through derivation. When you derive one class from another, you directly draw the features from one class into another.

Figure 6.1 uses a UML class diagram to illustrate a generic case of derivation. The arrow points to a class (ClassA) from which two other classes (ClassB and ClassC) are derived.

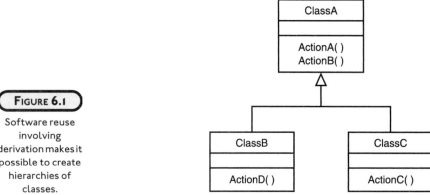

FIGURE 6.1

Software reuse involving derivation makes it possible to create hierarchies of classes.

The two derived classes shown in Figure 6.1, ClassB and ClassC, can use the methods that ClassA provides. An object of the type ClassB, then, can call the ActionA() and ActionB() methods in addition to the ActionD() method. On the other hand, an object of the ClassC class can call the ActionC() method in addition to the ActionA() and ActionB() methods. If you derived a class from the ClassC class, then you would have access to the three methods available to ClassC objects along with those specific to the newly created class.

ClassA is a *base* class. ClassB and ClassC are *derived* classes. The derived classes can access the methods in the base class, but the base class cannot access the methods in the derived classes. Likewise, an object of the ClassB type cannot call the ClassC::ActionC() method unless you create an instance of the ClassC class within the ClassB object (as you created an instance of the `CardDeck` class in the `Trump` class in Chapter 5). `ClassB` and `ClassC` are peer classes. They cannot access each other's methods and attributes through derivation.

SPECIALIZATION AND GENERALIZATION

Inheritance is the term used to designate the general reuse of programs through derivation. Inheritance implies either that you develop a derived class from a base class or, conversely, that you examine a number of different classes and decide to combine their features into a single base class. When you use a base class and derive a specialized class from it, the process is known as *specialization*. This type of activity characterizes most of your work with the Java class hierarchy. As Figure 6.2 illustrates, you draw from the class hierarchy those classes that you require to implement the functionality of your applications.

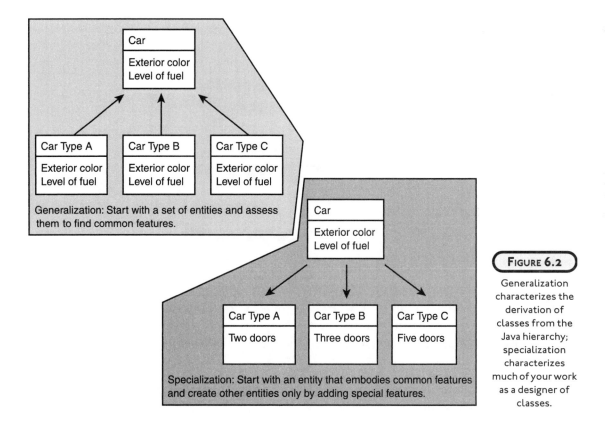

FIGURE 6.2

Generalization characterizes the derivation of classes from the Java hierarchy; specialization characterizes much of your work as a designer of classes.

On the other hand, when you design a set of classes, you often work in the opposite direction. You begin with a set of prospective classes. You examine these classes and decide that it might be best to combine most of their features into a common base class. Then, when you implement your application, you derive specialized classes from the base class and implement only methods and attributes that address specific features of your application. This approach is known as *generalization*. It characterizes more the activities you perform when you design classes than the activities you perform when you use the features of Java to derive one class from another.

Referring to Figure 6.3, you can put yourself in a situation involving generalization and specialization of classes if you consider what happens when you try to create a system of classes that accounts for the differences between cars. Imagine that you are working on a computer game such as *Grand Theft Auto* (Rockstar Games) and that you want to control three types of automobiles. The controls involve the doors and other features of the cars.

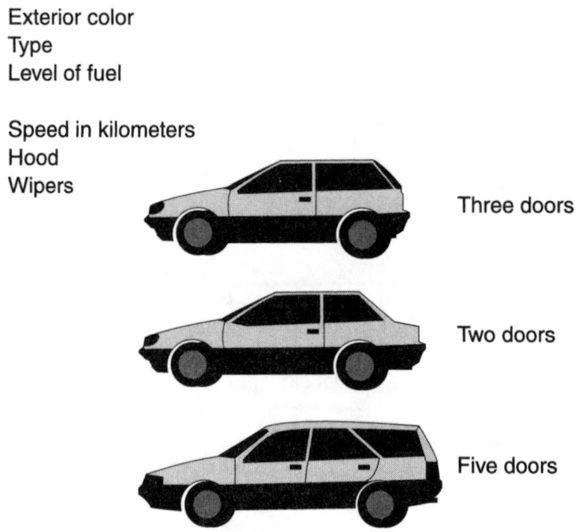

Exterior color
Type
Level of fuel

Speed in kilometers
Hood
Wipers

Three doors

Two doors

FIGURE 6.3

Car types differ
based on the
number of doors.

Five doors

As the players of the game race the cars along the streets featured in the game, the doors of the cars can fly open or remain shut. Likewise, whenever characters in the game climb in or out of a car, one or another door must open. Given certain weather conditions, the wipers can come on. As the cars move along, they consume fuel, so after a time, a car can run out of gasoline and stop.

To review the attributes Figure 6.3 displays, consider the following items that might be used to define general car entities:

- **Exterior color**. All cars have exterior colors.
- **Level of fuel**. All cars have a level of fuel. If the fuel level falls to empty, then the car loses speed and coasts to a stop.

- **Type.** Cars are of a type. Among the types are economy, sedan, and station wagon.
- **Speed.** Cars have maximum speeds. All cars likewise move at a given rate. You can measure speed in terms of kilometers or miles.
- **Hood.** All cars have hoods. Hoods can be open or closed.
- **Trunk door.** The trunk can be open or closed. Not all cars have trunks.
- **Wipers.** All cars have wipers. Wipers can be on or off. They can also go slow or fast.
- **Driver door.** All cars have driver doors. The door can be open or closed.
- **Front passenger door.** All cars have a front passenger door. The door can be open or closed.
- **Left back passenger door.** Not all cars have a left back passenger door. When they have such doors, however, they can be open or closed.
- **Right back passenger door.** Not all cars have a right back passenger door. Again, when they are present, such doors can be open or closed.
- **Rear door.** Not all cars have a rear door. Still, when the are present, they can be open or closed.

After analyzing the candidate attributes, it becomes evident that you can design a comprehensive class. You can call this class Car. Figure 6.4 illustrates this situation.

Car
-exteriorColor:String -levelOfFuel:float -carType:String -kphSpeedHood:float -wiperSpeed:int -driverDoorStatus:boolean -frontPassengerDoorStatus:boolean -leftBackPassengerDoorStatus:boolean -rightBackPassengerDoor:boolean -rearDoorStatus:boolean -truckDoor:boolean

FIGURE 6.4

You can generalize from a set of candidate attributes and form a comprehensive Car class.

Development of attributes proves fairly straightforward. You can account for the exterior color using a String value. For the level of fuel, you can use a float data type. To identify the car type, you can use a String value (Sedan, Wagon, Economy). For the hood and trunk door, you can use a boolean value of true to designate that they are normal (closed) and false to designate an abnormal state (open). You can account for the status of the wipers using an int value. A value of 1 might be low, a value of 2 medium, and a value of 3 high. For all of the doors, as with the hood, you can employ a boolean token of true to designate a normal state (closed) and false to designate an abnormal state (open).

Defining attributes for the generic Car class soon leads to a situation in which you need to develop accessor and mutator methods for the attributes. When you do this, the tasks involved remain elementary. At the same time, the class ends up being fairly large.

The result that proves most troubling is that when you use such a generalized class, some of the objects you create do not conform to the state and behavior of the general class model. For example, consider what happens when you create an object that represents a two-door economy car. As Figure 6.5 illustrates, you end up not being able to use some of the attributes and methods. Economy cars have no rear passenger doors. Rather than a trunk, the type shown has a rear door with a window.

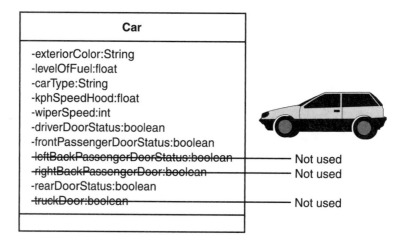

FIGURE 6.5

Generalized classes can lead to situations in which some of the objects you create cannot use all the attributes of the generalized class.

CREATING A CLASS HIERARCHY

If you create a generalized Car class, some of the objects you derive from it do not or cannot use some of its methods or attributes the generalized class provides. To remedy this situation, you can refine the generalized class. To do so, you limit its attributes and methods to an essential group. You then create specialized classes to add details as needed. As Figure 6.6 illustrates, the result is that you end up with a class hierarchy that allows you to create specialized classes that provide methods and attributes that precisely model the state and behavior of the objects they support.

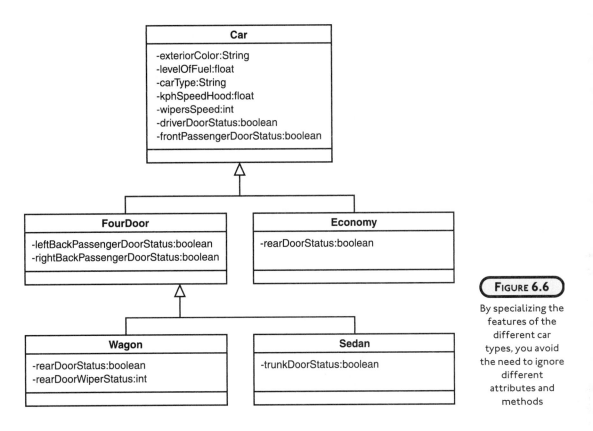

FIGURE 6.6

By specializing the features of the different car types, you avoid the need to ignore different attributes and methods

Figure 6.6 illustrates a class hierarchy for the different types of car a game might feature. Within this hierarchy, all of the classes share a core set of features, but at the same time, specialization allows you to refine each class so that it contains no features that are not used.

To make it so that the two car types that possess four doors do not necessitate the development of redundant methods and attributes, you create an intermediary class. This is the FourDoor class. While derived from the Car class, the intermediary class provides a base class for the Wagon and Sedan classes. With it, you create a set of four accessor and mutator methods. Without it, you create a set of eight such methods. While doubling the number of methods from four to eight might seem trivial, in other situations, which involve dozens of methods, the use of an intermediary class becomes much more critical.

The class hierarchy Figure 6.6 illustrates consists of three tiers of classes. At the first tier is the base class, Car. At the second tier are the Economy and FourDoor classes. These are *peer* classes to each other relative to the Car class hierarchy. They are *subclasses* to the Car class. You can also refer to them as *derived* or *child* classes. They are *parent, base,* or *super* classes to the third-tier classes. At the third tier are the Sedan and Wagon classes. These classes are also peer classes with each other, again relative to the Car class hierarchy. They are subclasses of the FourDoor class.

To save space and simplify the presentation, the Car class hierarchy diagram does not include specifications for methods. The sections that follow in which you implement these classes provide UML diagrams that show these specifications. The objective in this chapter is to illustrate general practices, so the methods you specify and implement are limited largely to mutators and accessors.

CONCRETE CLASSES

One of the most fundamental activities you perform when you create your own class hierarchies involves deriving one concrete class from another concrete class. Every class you have developed so far in this book has been a concrete class. When a class is concrete, you can call its constructor to create an instance of it. As an example of using a concrete class, consider the following statement:

```
ConcreteClass concreteObject = new ConcreteClass();
```

The new keyword allows you to create an object of a given type that you can assign to an identifier (concreteObject, for example). This activity makes the ConcreteClass object concrete. As you discover later on, Java provides other forms of classes (known as abstract classes and interfaces) that do not allow you to create instances of them.

The fact that you derive classes from the base class influences how you implement the attributes and methods of the class. If you desire the derived classes to have access to the attributes of the base class, then you must consider the *scope* or *access permissions* you set for the base class attributes and methods. Recall from Chapter 5 that Java provides you with a set of three keywords that regulate access to methods and attributes: public, private, and protected. Table 6.1 provides discussion of these terms relative to the development of a class hierarchy.

Item	Discussion
TABLE 6.1	**CLASS HIERARCHY SCOPE CONSIDERATIONS**
public	To enforce data hiding, when you implement attributes, you restrict the use of the `public` keyword to finalized (or constant) attributes. On the other hand, the use of interface methods (such as accessors and mutators) should be `public` because you want them to be readily available for controlling the objects you create using the class. Other methods that are part of the interface must also be `public`.
private	When you create peer classes, you can make the attributes of the classes `private` and run into no problems. However, with class hierarchies the situation changes. If you create a derived class and want to access the methods or attributes of the base class, you cannot make the methods and attributes of the base class `private`. If you make them `private`, they cannot be accessed by the derived class. If a method contains functionality that you do not want users to modify in a derived class, then you should define the method as `private`. Imagine a method, for example, that contains complex math formulas. Such methods should be left alone.
protected	To create derived classes that can access the methods and attributes of a base class, you make the methods and attributes of the base class either `protected` or `public`. If the attributes or methods are `protected`, then you cannot use them in a public way. However, you can still access them in the derived class. The `protected` keyword, then, allows you to observe the practice of data hiding when you implement a class hierarchy. If you think you are going to use a class within a hierarchy, then you should consider using `protected` where you usually use `private`.

A Concrete Base Class

To create a concrete class, you proceed along the lines you followed in Chapter 5 when developing systems of peer classes. A concrete base class serves a dual role. First, you can create an instance of such a class, so it can stand on its own. On the other hand, a concrete base class provides the foundation for classes that you can derive from it. Figure 6.7 offers a UML class diagram that depicts the attributes and methods of the Car class.

Implementation of the Car class requires you to define the attributes and afterward develop mutator and accessor methods for the attributes. You define the attributes as `private`. You define the mutator and accessor methods as `public`. You also create constructors. In addition to a default constructor, you implement an overloaded constructor that takes one argument, the unique identifier for the Car object.

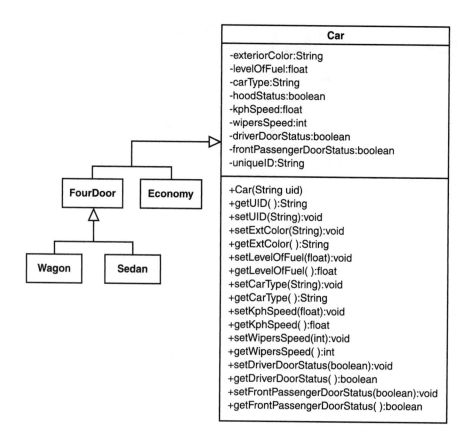

FIGURE 6.7

Implementation
of the base class
involves a fairly
extensive set of
methods.

```
/*
    Car.java
*/
public class Car{
    private String exteriorColor;
    private float levelOfFuel;
    private String carType;
    private boolean hoodStatus;
    private float kphSpeed;
    private int wipersSpeed;
    private boolean driverDoorStatus;
    private boolean frontPassengerDoorStatus;
    private String uniqueID;

    public Car(){
```

```java
      uniqueID = "0000AA";
   }
   public Car(String uid){
      uniqueID = uid;
   }
   public String getUID(){
      return uniqueID;
   }
   public void setUID(String uid){
      uniqueID = uid;
   }
   public void setExtColor(String ec){
      exteriorColor = ec;
   }
   public String getExtColor(){
      return exteriorColor;
   }
   public void setLevelOfFuel(float fl){
      levelOfFuel = fl;
   }
   public float getLevelOfFuel(){
      return levelOfFuel;
   }
   public void setCarType(String ct){
      carType = ct;
   }
   public String getCarType(){
      return carType;
   }
   public void setKphSpeed(float ks){
      kphSpeed = ks;
   }
   public float getKphSpeed(){
      return kphSpeed;
   }
   public void setWipersSpeed(int ws){
      wipersSpeed = ws;
   }
```

```
   public int getWipersSpeed(){
      return wipersSpeed;
   }
   public void setDriverDoorStatus(boolean dds){
      driverDoorStatus = dds;
   }
   public boolean getDriverDoorStatus(){
      return driverDoorStatus;
   }
   public void setFrontPassengerDoorStatus(boolean fpds){
      frontPassengerDoorStatus = fpds;
   }
   public boolean getFrontPassengerDoorStatus(){
      return frontPassengerDoorStatus;
   }
   public void setHoodStatus(boolean hs){
      hoodStatus = hs;
   }
   public boolean getHoodStatus(){
      return hoodStatus;
   }
}//end class
```

To create the `Car` class, you perform tasks you have performed before. You define the class as `public`. In this context, you cannot define it as `private`. You use the `class` keyword to indicate that you are defining a class. For each of the attributes the class offers, all of which are `private`, you create `public` accessor and mutator methods.

Testing the Base Car Class

To test a class, at a minimum you can perform a *verification* test. A verification test involves calling each method in the class to confirm that it has been implemented. Given the list of methods the UML class diagram offers, you can confirm through the test run of the `Car` class that you have implemented all the methods the diagram lists. This verifies that the implementation of the class *complies* with its *specification*. In essence, the UML diagrams serve to designate what should be included in the class. In this respect, they provide a specification.

```
/*
    CarTest.java
*/
```

```
class CarTest{
    public static void main(String Args[]){
//#1 Create two instances of the class using both constructors
        Car carObjectA = new Car();
        Car carObjectB = new Car("0000AC");
//#2 Call all the mutator methods in succession
        carObjectB.setUID("0000AB");
        carObjectB.setExtColor("Red");
        carObjectB.setLevelOfFuel(15.0F);
        carObjectB.setCarType("Sedan");
        carObjectB.setKphSpeed(67.4);
        carObjectB.setWipersSpeed(1);
        carObjectB.setDriverDoorStatus(true);
        carObjectB.setFrontPassengerDoorStatus(true);
        carObjectB.setHoodStatus(true);

//#3 Call all the access methods
        System.out.println(
            "\n   Color:\t\t"          + carObjectB.getExtColor()
          + "\n    Unique ID A:\t\t"   + carObjectA.getUID()
          + "\n    Unique ID B:\t\t"   + carObjectB.getUID()
          + "\n    Fuel Level:\t\t"    + carObjectB.getLevelOfFuel()
          + "\n    Car Type:\t\t"      + carObjectB.getCarType()
          + "\n    K/ph Speed:\t\t"    + carObjectB.getKphSpeed()
          + "\n    Wiper Speed:\t\t"   + carObjectB.getWipersSpeed()
          + "\n    Driver Door:\t\t"   + carObjectB.getDriverDoorStatus()
          + "\n    F P Door:\t\t"      + carObjectB.getFrontPassengerDoorStatus()
          + "\n    Hood Status:\t\t"   + carObjectB.getHoodStatus()
        );
    }//end main

}//end class
```

At comment #1 in the CarTest class, you create two instances of the Car class and assign them to carObjectA and carObjectB. For the carObjectA identifier, you use the default Car constructor, which assigns a value of 0000AA to the uniqueID class attribute. For the carObjectB identifier, you employ the overloaded constructor. As an argument for the constructor, you use a value of 0000AC. Having constructed two objects of the Car class, at comment #2 you begin calling the mutator methods of the Car class. The first call involves the carObjectB object and the setUID() method. Using this method, you reset the uniqueID to 0000AB.

For the methods that feature arguments of the boolean type, you use the true token. For methods that take float values, it is good practice to use the F flag to signal a float. (In this instance, however, for purposes of demonstration, the definition provides a number of the float value without a flag.) To populate attributes of the String type, you provide literal strings.

To display the values you assign to the Car attributes, you employ the println() method and use the concatenation operator along with repeated calls to the accessor methods. Using newline and tab escape sequences, you create a single string that Figure 6.8 displays as a table.

FIGURE 6.8

Calls to the mutator and accessor methods of the Car class allow you to create a table.

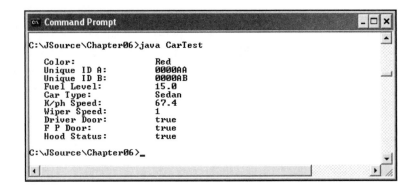

```
C:\JSource\Chapter06>java CarTest

        Color:              Red
        Unique ID A:        0000AA
        Unique ID B:        0000AB
        Fuel Level:         15.0
        Car Type:           Sedan
        K/ph Speed:         67.4
        Wiper Speed:        1
        Driver Door:        true
        F P Door:           true
        Hood Status:        true

C:\JSource\Chapter06>_
```

Second-Tier Classes

Figure 6.9 features a UML class diagram that depicts the attributes and methods of the second tier of classes in the Car hierarchy. Implementation of the Economy class involves creating two methods and one attribute. The methods you implement enable you to set and report the status of the back door of the economy vehicle. Implementing the FourDoor class proves slightly more involved. The FourDoor class includes right and left rear passenger doors.

The same approach to refinement that applied to the Car class now applies to the FourDoor class because the goal lies in restricting implementation activities to those features of the class that users always find useful. Since the FourDoor class serves as an intermediary class, it is not necessary to implement methods to control trunk and back door activities. A vehicle is not likely to have both a truck and a back door, so supporting methods for these features at this point blurs the focus of the class.

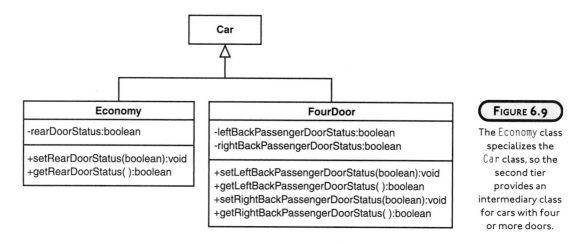

FIGURE 6.9

The Economy class specializes the Car class, so the second tier provides an intermediary class for cars with four or more doors.

The Economy Class and Using extend and super

To implement the Economy class, you employ the extends keyword. When you use the extends keyword to associate the Economy class with the Car class, you make available to the Economy class all the public and protected methods and attributes of the Car class. You can then use the Economy class object to call these methods just as if they were defined within the scope of the Economy class.

```
/*
    Economy.java
*/
 public class Economy extends Car{
   //Add one attribute
   private boolean rearDoorStatus;

//#1 Constructor calls to the parent
   public Economy(){
       super();
   }
//#2 Constructor calls to the parent
   public Economy(String uid){
       super(uid);
   }

//#3 Add new methods
   public void setRearDoorStatus(boolean rds){
      rearDoorStatus = rds;
```

```
    }
    public boolean getRearDoorStatus(){
        return rearDoorStatus;
    }
}//end class
```

Aside from the use of the extends keyword and the definition of the mutator and accessor methods for the Economy class, the most significant feature of the definition of the class involves the use of the super keyword. The super keyword, followed by parentheses, serves to call a constructor in the base (or super) class. The number of arguments within the parentheses that follow the super keyword establishes the identity of the base class constructor.

At comment #1, when you use the super keyword followed by empty parentheses, your action calls the default constructor of the base class. When you call the default constructor of the base class, that constructor sets the value of the Car::uniqueID attribute.

When you use the super keyword, you do not directly access the base class attributes. Were you to attempt this, the definition of the default Economy class constructor would take the following form:

```
    public Economy(){          //Direct access like this is
        uniqueID = 0000AA;     //not permitted in the Economy class
    }                          //uniqueID is private in Car
```

Any such attempt to access the Car class attributes fails. Because all the Car class attributes are defined using the private keyword, the Economy class can access them only through the interface the Car class provides.

In the constructor definition following comment #2, a set of parentheses containing one argument follows the super keyword. The effect of this operation is to call the overloaded version of the Car constructor. The overloaded version of the Car constructor requires one argument. This argument allows the user of the class to set the uniqueID attribute of the Car class. The Economy class constructor passes the euid argument to the overloaded Car constructor.

When you include a statement involving the super keyword in a constructor, you must use the super keyword first. In other words, you cannot include any statements prior to it. The reason for this becomes clearer in the next section, which discusses the constructor call sequence within a class hierarchy.

To use the super keyword to access a constructor of a parent class, you match the number of arguments in the parentheses following the keyword with those used by the constructor in the parent class.

At comment #3, you define the two additional methods you want to add to those that the base class provides. These are the getRearDoorStatus() and setRearDoorStatus() methods. These two methods access the rearDoorStatus attribute of the Economy class.

While you cannot access private attributes in a base class, for different reasons, you cannot create a base class object and then access its attributes from a derived class. The attributes in a base class are not visible to derived classes. In other words, you cannot create a getRearDoorStatus() method in the Car class to access the rearDoorStatus attribute in the Economy class.

Were the class hierarchies to allow for base classes to access the attributes of derived classes, then the notions encompassed by encapsulation and inheritance would be contradicted. Derived classes provide a way to refine the general capabilities base classes provide.

Testing the Economy Class and the Order of Construction

Testing of the Economy class shows that you are able to access all of the methods in the base class interface. The interface methods are defined with public access. The methods of the interface allow you to access the class attributes, which are defined to have private access.

```
/*
    EconomyTest.java
*/
 public class EconomyTest{
    public static void main(String Args[]){
        //#1 Calls the constructors of the parent
        //class
        Economy carObjectA = new Economy();
        Economy carObjectB = new Economy("0000AC");

        carObjectB.setUID("0000AB");
        carObjectB.setExtColor("Geeen");
        carObjectB.setLevelOfFuel(15.0F);
        carObjectB.setCarType("Economy");
        carObjectB.setKphSpeed(67.4F);
        carObjectB.setWipersSpeed(1);
```

```
carObjectB.setDriverDoorStatus(true);
carObjectB.setFrontPassengerDoorStatus(true);
carObjectB.setHoodStatus(true);

//#2 The setting for the rear door of the
//Economy car
carObjectB.setRearDoorStatus(true);


System.out.println(
    "\n   Color:\t\t"           +  carObjectB.getExtColor()
  + "\n   Unique ID A:\t\t"     +  carObjectA.getUID()
  + "\n   Unique ID B:\t\t"     +  carObjectB.getUID()
  + "\n   Fuel Level:\t\t"      +  carObjectB.getLevelOfFuel()
  + "\n   Car Type:\t\t"        +  carObjectB.getCarType()
  + "\n   K/ph Speed:\t\t"      +  carObjectB.getKphSpeed()
  + "\n   Wiper Speed:\t\t"     +  carObjectB.getWipersSpeed()
  + "\n   Driver Door:\t\t"     +  carObjectB.getDriverDoorStatus()
  + "\n   F P Door:\t\t"        +  carObjectB.getFrontPassengerDoorStatus()
  + "\n   Hood Status:\t\t"     +  carObjectB.getHoodStatus()
//#3
  + "\n   Rear Door:\t\t"       +  carObjectB.getRearDoorStatus()
    );
  }//end main
}//end class
```

Following comment #1 in the EconomyTest class, in the implementation of the default Economy class constructors, you use an empty set of parentheses following the super keyword. This action calls the explicit default constructor from the Car class. When you call this constructor, the value of the Car::uniqueID attribute is set to 0000AA. This identifier then becomes the default identifier for the Economy class object.

As is elaborated in the commentary on the WagonTest class, you can insert println() statements in the Economy and Car constructors. These statements allow you to see the following output during the test process (see Figure 6.14 for a screenshot):

```
Car constructing ...
Economy constructing ...
```

These messages show the constructor *call sequence* for the classes in the hierarchy. As you investigate in detail in the discussion of Figure 6.13, construction starts at the base class level. It then proceeds through the hierarchy toward the class that is lowest in the hierarchy (in this case, the Economy class). For this reason, to create an object of the Economy class, you must call the constructor for the Car class. The Car class constructor attends to creating instances of its methods and attributes for use by the Economy class. The methods and attributes of the Economy class are then added to those of the Car class.

At comment #2, you call the setRearDoorStatus() method of the Economy class. You furnish this method with a single argument, a true token of the boolean type. This method sets the rearDoorStatus attribute of the Economy class.

You call the setRearDoorStatus() method along with all the mutator methods obtained from the Car class. To more readily identify the type of car, you call the setCarType() method and provide it with an argument of Economy. For the setLevelOfFuel() and setKphSpeed() methods, you use the F flag with the decimal numbers to indicate that the literal values you supply are of the float type. If you do not use the flags, the compiler generates an error because it identifies the numbers as double values.

In the lines following comment #3, having called accessor methods for selective attributes, you call the getRearDoorStatus() method. As Figure 6.10 illustrates, this call returns a boolean value of true.

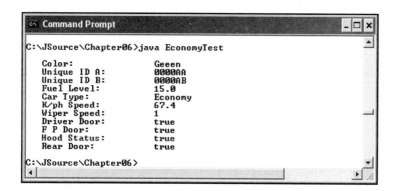

FIGURE 6.10

The Economy class has access to all the classes of the parent (Car) class.

The FourDoor Class

The FourDoor class is a concrete intermediary class. Its purpose is to implement methods that relate to the doors for the backseat passengers of four-door cars. At the same time, it occupies a position within the class hierarchy, so you provide it with constructors that allow you to communicate information to the base class. Even though you do not use this class to create specific objects, you still provide it with constructors so that classes you derive from it can communicate with the Car base class to set the identity value. The FourDoor class adds two attributes to the Car class and for these attributes defines mutator and accessor functions.

```java
/*
  FourDoor.java
*/
public class FourDoor extends Car{
    //#1
    private boolean leftBackPassengerDoorStatus;
    private boolean rightBackPassengerDoorStatus;
    //#2
    public FourDoor(){
    //Calls to the base class default constructor
        super();
    }
    //Overloaded constructor
    public FourDoor(String ufdid){
    //calls too the overloaded base class constructor
        super(ufdid);
    }

    //#3 Accessor and mutator methods for class attributes
    public void setLeftBackPassengerDoorStatus(boolean lbpds){
        leftBackPassengerDoorStatus = lbpds;
    }
    public boolean getLeftBackPassengerDoorStatus(){
        return leftBackPassengerDoorStatus;
    }

    public void setRightBackPassengerDoorStatus(boolean rbpds){
        rightBackPassengerDoorStatus = rbpds;
    }
    public boolean getRightBackPassengerDoorStatus(){
        return rightBackPassengerDoorStatus;
    }
}//end class
```

In the line preceding comment #1, you use the `extends` keyword to derive the `FourDoor` class from the `Car` class. Then, in the lines following comment #1, you declare the `leftBackPassengerDoorStatus` and `rightBackPassengerDoorStatus` attributes of the `FourDoor` class. Both of these attributes you define as `boolean` values.

From there, you proceed in the lines associated with comment #2 to define default and overloaded constructors for the class. Implementation of these constructors follows the same path you pursued in the `Economy` class. The `super` keyword allows you to access the parent class constructors. Using parameter lists in the parentheses that trail the `super` keyword allows you to designate specific constructors in the parent class. In this case, you designate the default and overloaded constructors of the `Car` class.

In the lines trailing comment #3, you implement the accessor and mutator methods for the class. The `setLeftBackPassengerDoorStatus()` method requires one argument, of the `boolean` type. It sets the value of the `leftBackPassengerDoorStatus` attribute. The `setRightBackPassenger DoorStatus()` method also requires one argument, again of the `boolean` type. It sets the value of the `rightBackPassengerDoorStatus` attribute. The two-accessor methods return the `boolean` values the mutator methods allow you to assign to the two class attributes.

Testing the FourDoor Class

Testing the `FourDoor` class involves verifying that the constructors and the four methods you have created perform as specified. To save space, not all of the method calls shown for testing of the `Economy` and `Car` classes appear in the implementation of the `FourDoorTest` class.

```
/*
    FourDoorTest.java
*/
    class FourDoorTest{
        public static void main(String Args[]){
            //#1
            FourDoor carObjectA = new FourDoor();
            FourDoor carObjectB = new FourDoor("0000AC");

            carObjectB.setUID("0000FD");
            carObjectB.setExtColor("Any");
            carObjectB.setCarType("Four Door");
            carObjectB.setDriverDoorStatus(true);
            carObjectB.setFrontPassengerDoorStatus(true);
            //#2
            carObjectB.setLeftBackPassengerDoorStatus(true);
```

```
carObjectB.setRightBackPassengerDoorStatus(true);

System.out.println(
        "\n   Color:\t\t"           + carObjectB.getExtColor()
    + "\n   Unique ID A:\t\t"   + carObjectA.getUID()
    + "\n   Unique ID B:\t\t"   + carObjectB.getUID()
    + "\n   Car Type:\t\t"       + carObjectB.getCarType()
    + "\n   Driver Door:\t\t"
                    + carObjectB.getDriverDoorStatus()
    + "\n   F P Door:\t\t"
                    + carObjectB.getFrontPassengerDoorStatus()
//#3
    + "\n   B P L Door:\t\t"
                    + carObjectB.getLeftBackPassengerDoorStatus()
    + "\n   B P R Door :\t\t"
                    + carObjectB.getRightBackPassengerDoorStatus()
    );
  }//end main
}//end class
```

In the lines associated with comment #1, you create two objects of the FourDoor type. You create these objects with calls to the default and overloaded constructors of the FourDoor class. For the carObjectB identifier, immediately after setting its value to 0000AC in the constructor, you call the setUID() method to change its value to 0000FD. As Figure 6.11 illustrates, the output displayed reflects the change.

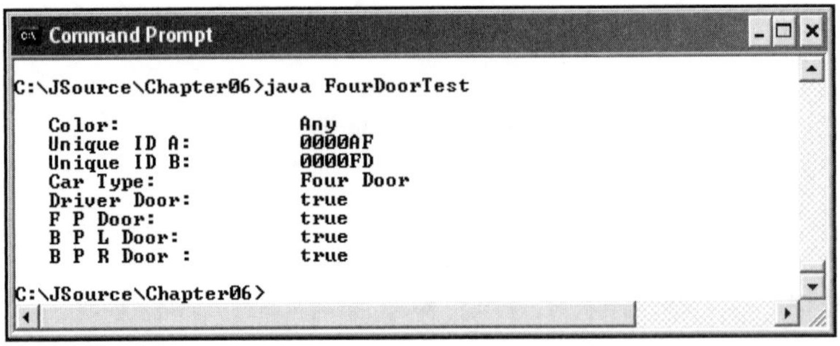

FIGURE 6.11

The test of the FourDoor class verifies intermediate class methods.

```
C:\JSource\Chapter06>java FourDoorTest

   Color:              Any
   Unique ID A:        0000AF
   Unique ID B:        0000FD
   Car Type:           Four Door
   Driver Door:        true
   F P Door:           true
   B P L Door:         true
   B P R Door :        true

C:\JSource\Chapter06>
```

In the lines trailing comment #2, you call the setLeftBackPassengerDoorStatus() and setRightBackPassengerDoorStatus() methods, to which you supply arguments consisting of the boolean true token.

At comment #3, you call accessor methods associated with the Car and FourDoor classes. As Figure 6.11 illustrates, the calls to the Car methods are limited. On the other hand, you call both of the methods you have implemented for the FourDoor class. The getLeftBackPassenger DoorStatus() method takes no arguments and returns a value of true. The getRightBackPassengerDoorStatus() method also takes no argument. It, too, returns a value of true.

Third-Tier Classes

Figure 6.12 offers a UML class diagram that depicts the attributes and methods of the third tier of classes. The FourDoor class is derived from the Car class, and from the FourDoor class you derive the two third-tier classes, Sedan and Wagon. To implement the third-tier classes, you make use of the construction sequence you have created for the FourDoor and Car classes.

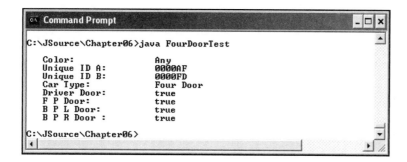

FIGURE 6.12

Specialization of the FourDoor class allows you to create classes that can accommodate backseat passenger doors, rear windows, and trunks.

The Wagon Class

The Wagon class specializes the FourDoor class by adding attributes and methods that address the rear car door. The rear doors of cars almost always have windows, so the class also provides an attribute and methods to accommodate rear window wipers. To sustain the constructor sequence begun with the FourDoor and Car classes, in the Wagon class you also implement default and overloaded constructors. As before, these constructors make use of the super keyword to access the constructors of the parent class.

```java
/*
  Wagon.java
*/
public class Wagon extends FourDoor{
    //#1  Class attributes
    private boolean rearDoorStatus;
    private int rearDoorWiperSpeed;

    //#2 Constructors
```

```
    //Both call to the FourDoor constructors
    //Which invoke the car constructor
    public Wagon(){
        super();
//      System.out.println("\tWagon constructing ...");
    }
    public Wagon(String uwid){
        super(uwid);
//      System.out.println("\tWagon constructing ...");
    }
    //#3 Implementation of accessors and mutators
    public void setRearDoorStatus(boolean rds){
        rearDoorStatus = rds;
    }
    public boolean getRearDoorStatus(){
        return rearDoorStatus;
    }
    public void setRearDoorWiperSpeed(int rws){
        rearDoorWiperSpeed = rws;
    }
    public int getRearDoorWiperSpeed(){
        return rearDoorWiperSpeed;
    }
}
```

In the lines immediately preceding comment #1, you use the class keyword to declare the Wagon class and then employ the extends keyword to derive the Wagon class from the FourDoor class. Trailing comment #1, you declare the rearDoorStatus and rearDoorWiperSpeed attributes of the Wagon class. The first of these attributes is of the boolean type. The second is of the int type.

In the lines following comment #2, you create two constructors. The first is an explicit default constructor. To define it, you use the super keyword. This calls to the constructor of the FourDoor class, and that constructor calls to the constructor of the Car class. The Car class constructor assigns a default value to the Car::uniqueID attribute.

The second constructor is an overloaded constructor. It takes one argument, a String value (uwid) that you pass to the parent constructor by making it an argument in the parentheses following the super keyword.

You define four methods for the Wagon class. As mentioned before, these methods accommodate cars that have rear windows. You define the setRearDoorStatus() method to assign values to the rearDoorStatus attribute. It takes an argument of the boolean type. You define the getRearDoorStatus() to retrieve the value of this attribute. Accordingly, its return type is also boolean. To assign values to the rearDoorWiperSpeed attribute, you define the setRearDoor-WiperSpeed() method. Its argument is of the int type. To retrieve the value of the rearDoor-WiperSpeed attribute, you define the getRearDoorWiperSpeed() method. Its return type is int.

Testing the Wagon Class and the Order of Construction

When you test the Wagon class, you can use a series of println() methods that are in the code samples on the companion website. The messages allow you to witness how the interpreter invokes the class constructors for the three tiers in the order you see in Figure 6.13. The Wagon constructor invokes the FourDoor constructor. The FourDoor constructor invokes the Car constructor. However, the constructors execute from the top of the hierarchy down, so the first phase in the creation of the Wagon object is the creation of the Car object, followed by the FourDoor object, followed by the Wagon object. Generally, the result is an extended Car object—one object. The Wagon object is an extended Car object, and the sequence of constructors expands the object until it includes the functionality included in the base and intermediary class.

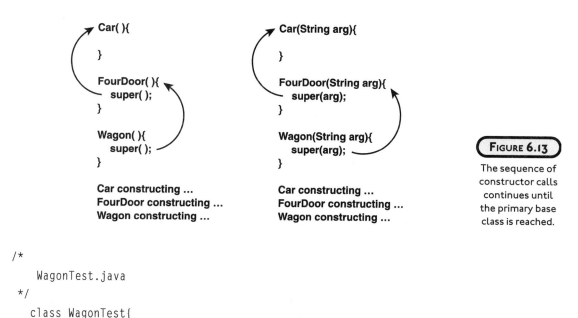

```
Car( ){

}
FourDoor( ){
    super( );
}
Wagon( ){
    super( );
}

Car constructing ...
FourDoor constructing ...
Wagon constructing ...
```

```
Car(String arg){

}
FourDoor(String arg){
    super(arg);
}
Wagon(String arg){
    super(arg);
}

Car constructing ...
FourDoor constructing ...
Wagon constructing ...
```

FIGURE 6.13

The sequence of constructor calls continues until the primary base class is reached.

```
/*
    WagonTest.java
*/
    class WagonTest{
       public static void main(String Args[]){
       //#1
```

```
        Wagon carObjectA = new Wagon();
        Wagon carObjectB = new Wagon("0000WC");

        carObjectB.setUID("0000WC");
        carObjectB.setExtColor("Gray");
        carObjectB.setCarType("Wagon");
        carObjectB.setDriverDoorStatus(true);
        carObjectB.setFrontPassengerDoorStatus(true);
        carObjectB.setLeftBackPassengerDoorStatus(true);
        carObjectB.setRightBackPassengerDoorStatus(true);
    //#2
        carObjectB.setRearDoorStatus(true);
        carObjectB.setRearDoorWiperSpeed(2);

        System.out.println(
            "\n    Color:\t\t"        + carObjectB.getExtColor()
          + "\n    Unique ID A:\t\t"  + carObjectA.getUID()
          + "\n    Unique ID B:\t\t"  + carObjectB.getUID()
          + "\n    Car Type:\t\t"     + carObjectB.getCarType()
          + "\n    Driver Door:\t\t"  + carObjectB.getDriverDoorStatus()
          + "\n    F P Door:\t\t"
                        + carObjectB.getFrontPassengerDoorStatus()
          + "\n    B P L Door:\t\t"
                        + carObjectB.getLeftBackPassengerDoorStatus()
          + "\n    B P R Door :\t\t"
                        + carObjectB.getRightBackPassengerDoorStatus()
    //#3
          + "\n    Rear D Stat:\t\t"
                        + carObjectB.getRearDoorStatus()
          + "\n    R D Wpr Sp :\t\t"
                        + carObjectB.getRearDoorWiperSpeed()
        );
    }//end main
}//end class
```

As in the other test scenarios, you begin at comment #1 of the WagonTest class by creating instances of the Wagon class using the default and overloaded constructor. You assign the class instances to the carObjectA and carObjectB variables.

You can refer generally to classes higher in a hierarchy to a given class as the *super classes* of the class. The upper area of Figure 6.14 illustrates the output of the `println()` statements in the constructors of the super classes and the `Wagon` class. As discussed previously, the first constructor executed is the constructor for the `Car` class. Then comes the constructors for the `FourDoor` and `Wagon` classes. As the construction sequence progresses, the `Car` class is extended to encompass the functionality of the successive derived classes. The messages you see at the top of Figure 6.14 trace the calls to the default and overloaded constructors.

At comment #2, in addition to selective methods from the super classes, you test the mutator and accessor methods you have implemented in the `Wagon` class. To do so, you call the `setRearDoorStatus()` method, supplying it with a `boolean` token value of `true`. You call the `setRearDoorWiperSpeed()` using an integer value of 2.

Trailing comment #3, you call the `getRearDoorStatus()` method, which as Figure 6.14 illustrates returns `true`. Finally, the call to the `getRearDoorWiperSpeed()` method returns a value of 2.

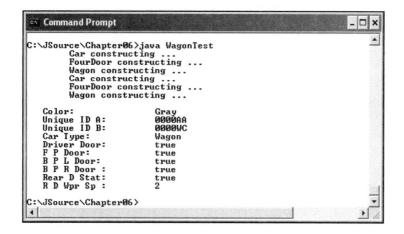

FIGURE 6.14

Messages show the trail of the construction sequence.

METHOD OVERRIDING

The one class not discussed in the `Car` class hierarchy is the `Sedan` class. You implement this class in the same way that you implement the other classes in the hierarchy. The `extends` keyword allows you to derive it from the `FourDoor` class. Use of the `super` keyword allows you to access the constructors for the super classes in the hierarchy.

The `Sedan` class provides an occasion for demonstrating how to *override* methods from super classes. Overriding a method from a super class involves redefining the method in the context of the derived class. An overridden method is not an overloaded method. An overridden method has the same arguments and return type as the method it overrides. This is not true with an overloaded method, which differs from the method it overloads in argument and return types.

As Figure 6.15 illustrates, to override the `setDriverDoorStatus()` and `getDriverDoorStatus()` methods, you alter the target of their activities to involve the `sedanDriverDoorStatus` attribute of the `Sedan` class rather then the `driverDoorStatus` attribute of the `Car` class. The `sedanDriverDoorStatus` attribute is of the `int` type. The `driverDoorStatus` attribute is of the `boolean` type. The overridden methods translate `boolean` values into `int` values.

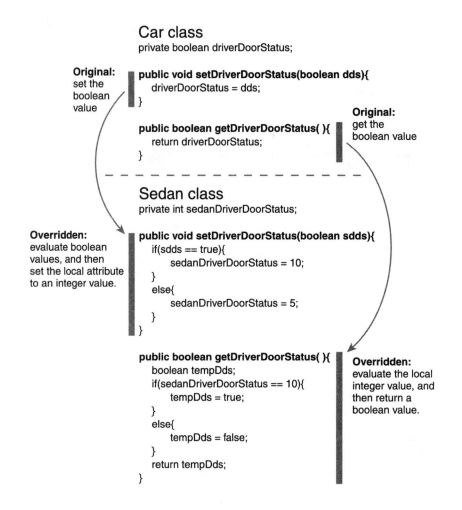

FIGURE 6.15

To override a super class method, you use the same signature line but redefine the method.

The Sedan Class and Overriding

While you derive the Sedan class from the FourDoor class in the same basic manner in which you derived the Wagon class from the FourDoor class, your work with the Sedan class differs slightly. In this instance, in addition to specializing the FourDoor class by adding three new methods to it, you also override two of the methods you inherit from the super classes. These are the Car::setDriverDoorStatus() and Car::getDriverDoorStatus() methods.

As Figure 6.15 (in the previous section) illustrates, the effect of overriding the two methods is that you translate boolean values into an int value that you obtain from and assign to the sedanDriverDoorStatus attribute. Users do not see the numerical value of the attribute as they work with these two overridden methods. The numerical values remain hidden. If they supply a boolean value of true to the mutator method, the method assigns a value of 10 to the sedanDriverDoorStatus attribute. If users supply a boolean value of false to the mutator method, the method assigns a value of 5 to the sedanDriverDoorStatus attribute. The users see only the boolean values.

To provide a way to access the assigned integer value of the sedanDriverDoorStatus attribute, you implement the getSedanDriverDoorStatus() method. This method returns the int value of the attribute.

```
/*
    Sedan.java
*/
public class Sedan extends FourDoor{
//#1
    private boolean trunkDoorStatus;
    private int sedanDriverDoorStatus;
//#2
    //Both call to the FourDoor constructors
    //Which invoke the car constructor
    public Sedan(){
        super();
    }
    public Sedan(String suid){
        super(suid);
    }
//#3-----------------setTrunkDoorStatus---------------------
    public void setTrunkDoorStatus(boolean tds){
        trunkDoorStatus = tds;
```

```
    }
//----------------getTrunkDoorStatus--------------------
    public boolean getTrunkDoorStatus(){
        return trunkDoorStatus;
    }


//#4----------------setDriverDoorStatus--------------------
//overrides super class method
    public  void setDriverDoorStatus(boolean sdds){
        if(sdds == true){
            sedanDriverDoorStatus = 10;
        }
        else{
            sedanDriverDoorStatus = 5;
        }
    }
//#5----------------getDriverDoorStatus--------------------
//overrides super class method
    public boolean getDriverDoorStatus(){
        boolean tempDds;
        if(sedanDriverDoorStatus== 10){
            tempDds = true;
        }
        else{
            tempDds = false;
        }
        return tempDds;
    }
//#6----------------getSedanDriverDoorStatus----------------
    public int getSedanDriverDoorStatus(){
            return sedanDriverDoorStatus;
    }
}
```

In the lines associated with comment #1, you first define the Sedan class as derived from the FourDoor class. You then declare two class attributes, trunkDoorStatus and sedanDriverDoorStatus. The trunkDoorStatus attribute is of the bool type. The sedanDriverDoorStatus attribute is of the int type. The sedanDriverDoorStatus attribute allows you to store a numerical value that you process using overridden versions of parent class methods.

At comment #2, you define the standard constructors for classes in the Car class hierarchy. One of these is an explicit default constructor and uses the super keyword to call the explicit default constructor of the FourDoor class. The second of these is an overloaded constructor. It uses the super keyword to pass its single argument (tds) to the overloaded super class constructor.

In the lines trailing comment #3, you define the setTrunkDoorStatus() and getTrunkDoorStatus() methods. The setTrunkDoorStatus() method takes a boolean value, which it assigns to the trunkDoorStatus attribute. It has a return type of void. The getTrunkDoorStatus() takes no arguments and returns the boolean value assigned to the trunkDoorStatus attribute.

At comment #4, you define the first of the two overridden methods. This is the setDriverDoorStatus() method. To define this method, you use an if…else selection structure to evaluate the boolean argument of the method (sdds). If the value of this argument is true, you assign a value of 10 to the sedanDriverDoorStatus attribute. If the value of this argument is false, you assign a value of 5 to the sedanDriverDoorStatus attribute. In this way, you override the Car:: setDriverDoorStatus() method so that it translates a boolean value into an integer value.

In the method definition associated with comment #5, you work with the getDriverDoorStatus() method. To overload this method, you assess the value assigned to the sedanDriverDoorStatus attribute. To accomplish this task, you create an if…else selection structure. If the value of the sedanDriverDoorStatus attribute equals 10, then you return a boolean value of true. If the value of the sedanDriverDoorStatus does not equal 10, you return a boolean value of false. In this way, you override the Car:: getDriverDoorStatus() method so that it translates an int value into a boolean value.

To ensure that you can access the integer value of the sedanDriverDoorStatus attribute, at comment #6 you define the getSedanDriverDoorStatus() method. This is an accessor method that returns a value of the integer type. It takes no arguments.

Testing the Sedan Class

To test the Sedan class, you employ a minimum number of method calls. The focus of the SedanTest class is to test the overridden methods and the three new mutator and accessor methods.

```
/*
    SedanTest.java
```

```
*/
  class SedanTest{
    public static void main(String Args[]){
    //#1

      Sedan carObjectB = new Sedan("0000SC");

      carObjectB.setExtColor("Gray");
      carObjectB.setCarType("Sedan");
    //#2
      carObjectB.setDriverDoorStatus(true);
      carObjectB.setTrunkDoorStatus(true);
      System.out.println(
          "\n    Color:\t\t"        + carObjectB.getExtColor()
        + "\n    Unique ID B:\t\t"  + carObjectB.getUID()
        + "\n    Car Type:\t\t"     + carObjectB.getCarType()
    //#3
        + "\n    Driver Door:\t\t"  + carObjectB.getDriverDoorStatus()
        + "\n    T D Status :\t\t"
                                    + carObjectB.getTrunkDoorStatus()
        + "\n    S D D Status :\t"
                                    + carObjectB.getSedanDriverDoorStatus()
        );
    }//end main
  }//end class
```

In the lines trailing comment #1, you create a single instance of the Sedan class, carObjectB. To accomplish this, you call the overloaded form of the Sedan constructor and provide it with a character string argument of 0000SC. To define a few of the attributes of the object, you call the setExtColor() method to set the color of the Sedan object to gray. You call the setCarType() method to set the type to Sedan. Both of these methods you derive from the Car class through the FourDoor class.

At comment #2, you call the setDriverDoorStatus() method and provide it with boolean true as an argument. This is the overridden version of the Car:: setDriverDoorStatus() method. Behind the scenes, your call of this function assigns an integer value of 10 to the sedanDriverDoorStatus class attribute. On the visible stage, however, you see only boolean values.

You follow with a call to the setTrunkDoorStatus() method. This you also furnish with an argument of boolean true. Following these method calls, as Figure 6.16 reveals, you call the println() method in conjunction with the getExtColor(), getUID(), and getCarType() methods to display attribute values you ultimately retrieve from attributes defined in the Car class.

In the lines associated with comment #3, you call the getDriverDoorStatus() method, which is the overridden version of the Car::getDriverDoorStatus() method. As the D D bool val item in Figure 6.16 shows, the returned value is a boolean true. This method converts the value of the sedanDriverDoorStatus attribute from an integer to a boolean value. You next call the getTrunkDoorStatus() method, which returns a boolean value of true.

When you call the getSedanDriverDoorStatus() method, you retrieve the numerical value of the sedanDriverDoorStatus attribute. As Figure 6.16 reveals, the value assigned to it is 10, reflecting the value of the boolean true.

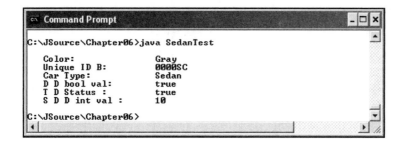

FIGURE 6.16

Defining classes with overridden methods can help you focus their responsibilities more precisely.

FINALIZATION

You have already dealt with the final keyword. In Chapter 5, you used the final keyword to create constant class attributes. You can also use it to create a type of method that you cannot override. To demonstrate the use of the final keyword in relation to methods, consider again the Wagon class. Suppose that you want to prevent users of the Wagon class from overriding the getRearDoorStatus(), setRearDoorWiperSpeed(), and getRearDoorWiperSpeed() methods when they derive classes from the Wagon class. To accomplish this task, you use the following approach:

```
public final boolean getRearDoorStatus(){
    return rearDoorStatus;
}


public final void setRearDoorWiperSpeed(int rws){
    rearDoorWiperSpeed = rws;
}
```

```java
public final int getRearDoorWiperSpeed(){
    return rearDoorWiperSpeed;
}
```

For each method definition, you follow the `public` keyword with the `final` keyword. In every other respect, the definitions of the methods remain the same as before. Use of the `final` keyword does not affect calls you make using objects of the `Wagon` class, nor are calls to the methods of derived class objects affected. The only difference is that users of the `Wagon` class cannot override methods defined using the `final` keyword.

POLYMORPHISM

Polymorphism constitutes the third of the three primary activities you engage in when you perform object-oriented programming. Polymorphism is derived from the ancient Greek terms for "many" and "form." In object-oriented applications, the term communicates the fact that you can use the derived objects of a given super class in any context in which you can use the super class object.

To explore polymorphic operations, in this section and the sections that follow you develop a set of three classes you derive from the `Economy` class. Figure 6.17 provides a UML diagram that illustrates these classes. The classes include the `ChildCart`, `GasElectric`, and `DieselElectric` classes. In each of these classes you override the `getExtColor()` and `setExtColor()` methods, which you initially define in the `Car` class. In each class, to override the `setExtColor()` method you create an extended selection statement that translates a general color, such as blue, green, red, or yellow, into substitute expressions unique to the class.

For the `ChildCart` objects, for example, if you assign `blue` to an object, the `setExtColor()` method translates `blue` into `Sky`. For the `DieselElectric` objects, if you assign a `blue` object, the `setExtColor()` method translates the color into `0000FF-Be`, a combination of a hexadecimal value for a shade of blue and the first and last letter of the word `blue`. For `GasElectric` objects, the `setExtColor()` method translates `blue` to `Sky Blue`.

In each case, you assign the resulting color designation to a class attribute. As Figure 6.17 shows, for the `ChildCart` class, you define the `cCartColor` attribute. For the `GasElectric` class, you define the `gasEleColor` attribute. For the `DieselElectric` class, you define the `diesEleColor` attribute. Each of these is of the `String` type. To retrieve the values you assign to these attributes, you override the `getExtColor()` method.

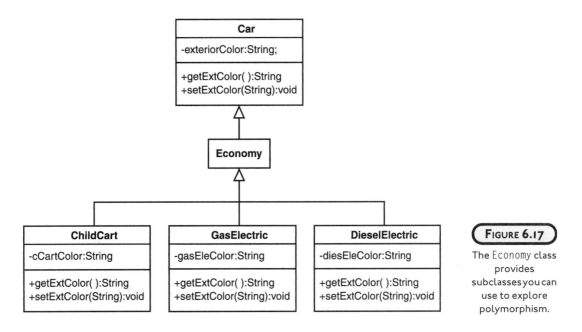

FIGURE 6.17

The Economy class provides subclasses you can use to explore polymorphism.

After you override the getExtColor() and setExtColor() methods in the ChildCart, GasElectric, and DieselElectric classes, you are then in a position to explore how polymorphism works. The explorations take the following forms:

- **Method argument definitions**. In this situation, you can use a base class data type, Economy, to define the argument of a method. Having defined the argument of a method, you can then pass arguments of the ChildCart, GasElectric, and DieselElectric data types to the method.

- **Method return value definitions**. Just as you can use a base class data type, Economy, to define the argument of a method, so you can use a base class data type to define the return value of a method. When you define a method in this way, the method can return an object of any data type that is derived from the base class.

- **Array and container definitions**. If you define an array using the Economy base class type, then you can use the array to store objects of the ChildCart, GasElectric, and DieselElectric data types. The subclasses possess overridden forms of the getExtColor() and setExtColor() methods. Given this situation, using only two statements, one for each method, you can use a dot operator in combination with the array index operator of the array to call these methods for all the objects in the array even though they differ in their data types.

- **Method calls in which you have defined methods differently for different derived classes**. You can create a method in which you define the argument using the base data type, Economy. You can then pass any object-derived data type to the method. Within the method, you can use calls to the methods you have defined for the base class to achieve specific processing goals. In the case of the classes that are derived from the Economy class, for example, you can use the type identifier to retrieve the color assigned to the object. Even though of different types, all classes have a getUID() method defined in the Car class.

The next few sections provide discussion of how you define the three derived classes. The focus in each effort centers on overriding the getExtColor() and setExtColor() methods and creating a unique class attribute to store the color values users assign to objects.

ChildCart

The ChildCart class addresses objects that children use. Colors for these objects assume the form of metaphors. In this respect, blue becomes Sky, and red becomes Ribbon. By overriding the setExtColor() method, you make it possible to translate a general color designation into one that is specific to the objects of the ChildCart class. As is depicted in the UML diagram Figure 6.17 furnishes, the ChildCart class includes an attribute, cCartColor, that allows you to store the color designation for each object. The getExtColor() method allows you to retrieve the color.

```
/*
   ChildCart.java
*/
public class ChildCart extends Economy{
    //#1
    private String cCartColor;
    //#2 Constructor calls to the parent
    public ChildCart(String ccid){
         super(ccid);
    }
    public ChildCart(){
         super();
    }
    //#3
    public void setExtColor(String ec){
            if(ec.equalsIgnoreCase("blue")){
                cCartColor = "Sky";
            }
            else if(ec.equalsIgnoreCase("red")){
```

```
            cCartColor = "Ribbon";
        }
        else if(ec.equalsIgnoreCase("green")){
            cCartColor = "Spring";
        }
        else if(ec.equalsIgnoreCase("yellow")){
            cCartColor = "Home";
        }
        else if(ec.equalsIgnoreCase("white")){
            cCartColor = "Day";
        }
        else if(ec.equalsIgnoreCase("black")){
            cCartColor = "Night";
        }
        else{
            cCartColor = "Day";
        }
    }
    //#4
    public String getExtColor(){
      return cCartColor;
    }
}
```

In the signature line, you employ the extends keyword to derive the ChildCart class from the Economy class. Then, in the lines associated with comment #1, you define the single attribute of the class. This is the cCartColor attribute, which is of the String type. You define it in the private scope, as you have done universally for other classes in the Car class hierarchy.

At comment #2, you define two constructors for the class. Definition of these constructors involves the same activities you have performed when developing constructors for other classes in the Car class hierarchy. You employ the super keyword to access the constructor for the Economy class. As previous discussion has emphasized, the call to the constructor of the immediate super class leads to a succession of calls, so the construction process eventually reaches the Car class.

In the lines associated with comment #3, you attend to a key activity involved in defining the class. This activity involves overriding the setExtColor() method. The signature line of the method remains the same as it is for the super class. It takes an argument of the String type and returns nothing. To override the definition, you evaluate the argument the user provides and translate it into a color specific to the class.

To evaluate the color argument the user provides, you create an extended if…else if…else structure. In this way, you can use the String argument (ec) to call the String::equalsIgnore-Case() method to evaluate the method's argument. The equalsIgnoreCase() returns a boolean value, so the flow of the program enters each block of the selection structure according to whether the color the user provides, regardless of case, matches one of the six color terms included in the structure. Given a match, you assign the translated color to the cCartColor attribute. If the color the user provides does not match any color in the primary set, then the default else block sets the color to Day.

At comment #4, you override the getExtColor() method. Overriding this method involves returning the value of cCartColor rather than the value of the exteriorColor attribute defined in the Car class.

DieselElectric

The DieselElectric class uses color designations that are more codes than expressions that possess the metaphorical values of the ChildCart class. For example, blue becomes 0000FF-Be, and red becomes FF0033-Rd. As with the ChildCart class, you overload the setExtColor() method to translate the general color terms into those specific to the class object. As the UML diagram in Figure 6.17 shows, the DieselElectric class includes the diesEleColor attribute. This attribute allows you to store the color designations of objects of the DieselElectric class, which you retrieve with an overridden version of the getExtColor() method.

```
/*
    DieselElectric.java
*/
public class DieselElectric extends Economy{
    //#1
    private String diesEleColor;
    //#2 Constructor calls to the parent
    public DieselElectric(String deid){
        super(deid);
    }
    public DieselElectric(){
        super();
    }
    //#3
```

```java
    public void setExtColor(String ec){
            if(ec.equalsIgnoreCase("blue")){
                diesEleColor = "0000FF-Be";
            }
            else if(ec.equalsIgnoreCase("red")){
                diesEleColor = "FF0033-Rd";
            }
            else if(ec.equalsIgnoreCase("green")){
                diesEleColor = "00FF00-Gn";
            }
            else if(ec.equalsIgnoreCase("yellow")){
                diesEleColor = "FFFF00-Yw";
            }
            else if(ec.equalsIgnoreCase("white")){
                diesEleColor = "FFFFFF-We";
            }
            else if(ec.equalsIgnoreCase("black")){
                diesEleColor = "000000-Bk";
            }
            else{
                diesEleColor = "FFFFFF-We";
            }
    }
    //#4
    public String getExtColor(){
        return diesEleColor;
    }
}
```

Following use of the extends keyword to make the DieselElectric class a subclass of the Economy class, at comment #1 you declare the diesEleColor attribute. The attribute is of the String type, and you designate it as private. From defining the one attribute of the class, you proceed to define its constructors. As in the other class definitions in the Car class hierarchy, you define a default and an overloaded constructor.

In the lines associated with comment #3, you override the setExtColor() method. To override the method, you evaluate six general colors. You use calls to the String::equalsIgnore-Case() method within an extended selection structure to perform the evaluation. Given a true evaluation for a given color argument, you assign the translated value to the diesEleColor attribute. If the color the user provides lies outside the named set, you translate it to a default value of FFFFFF-We (white).

In the lines accompanying comment #4, you override the getExtColor() method. To accomplish this, you return the value assigned to the diesEleColor attribute. As with the setExtColor() method, the definition of the getExtColor() method retains the same signature line as the one defined in the base Car class.

GasElectric

The GasElectric class translates colors in a direct way. For example, blue becomes Sky Blue, and red remains Red. Still, the translations involve a few changes, so it remains necessary to override the setExtColor() method to translate the color terms for the class object. To translate the colors, as the UML diagram in Figure 6.17 reveals, you define a single class attribute, gasEleColor. To access the values you assign to this attribute, you override the getExtColor() method.

```
/*
    GasElectric.java
*/
public class GasElectric extends Economy{
    //#1
    private String gasEleColor;

    //#2 Constructor calls to the parent
    public GasElectric(String geid){
        super(geid);
    }
    public GasElectric(){
        super();
    }
    //#3
    public void setExtColor(String ec){
            if(ec.equalsIgnoreCase("blue")){
                gasEleColor = "Sky Blue";
            }
            else if(ec.equalsIgnoreCase("red")){
                gasEleColor = "Red";
            }
            else if(ec.equalsIgnoreCase("green")){
```

```
            gasEleColor = "Lime Green";
        }
        else if(ec.equalsIgnoreCase("yellow")){
            gasEleColor = "Yellow";
        }
        else if(ec.equalsIgnoreCase("white")){
            gasEleColor = "White";
        }
        else if(ec.equalsIgnoreCase("black")){
            gasEleColor = "Black";
        }
        else{
            gasEleColor = "While";
        }
    }
    //#4
    public String getExtColor(){
        return gasEleColor;
    }
}//end class
```

In the class signature line, you use the extends keyword to make GasElectric a subclass of the Economy class. Then, at comment #1 you declare the gasEleColor attribute, which is private and of the String type. After defining this attribute, you define two constructors. As with the other two subclasses of the Economy class, you define a default and an overloaded constructor.

In the lines trailing comment #3, you override the setExtColor() method so that it evaluates six general colors. As in previous implementations, you call the String::equalsIgnore-Case() method to perform evaluations. You use an extended selection structure to accommodate the terms evaluated. You assign the results of the evaluation to the gasEleColor attribute. If the color the user provides lies outside the named set, you assign a default value of White to the gasEleColor attribute.

At comment #4, you override the getExtColor() method and have it return the value assigned to the gasEleColor attribute. As with the work you have performed with the other subclasses, you do not change the signature line of either the setExtColor() or getExtColor() method.

Using Polymorphic Options

The PolyTest class provides you with a context in which to explore the polymorphic operations discussed earlier in this section. You first define an array of the Economy type. You then create instances of the three classes you have derived from the Economy class and assign them to the array. This demonstrates how polymorphism allows you to use an array of a base class to accommodate objects of derived classes.

You then use a for repetition block to traverse the array and use it to call the two methods you have overloaded in the three derived classes. When you call the methods, the results differ even though you call the same two methods. This shows how polymorphism allows you to "bind" objects and method calls as your program executes.

As a third endeavor, you define the argument of a method using the Economy class type. Given this definition, you can then pass objects of all the base class types as arguments and process them using commonly shared methods derived from super classes.

As a final exploration, you create a method in which you define the return type using the Economy class. This method takes as an argument a String value that allows you to traverse the array to find the ID of a given object that can be of any of the three types you derive from the Economy class. When you find the object, regardless of its subtype, you can return it.

```java
/*
   PolyTest.java
*/
public class PolyTest{
   //#1 Array of base class type
      static Economy[] ecoCars = new Economy[3];
      static String[] ecoColors = {"Blue",    "Red",    "Green",
                                   "Yellow",  "White",  "Black"};
//-------------------------------main---------------------------------
      public static void main(String Args[]){
   //#2  Declare and assign to array
         ChildCart ccObject = new ChildCart("CC0001");
         DieselElectric deObject = new DieselElectric("DE0001");
         GasElectric geObject = new GasElectric("GE0001");

         ecoCars[0] = ccObject;
         ecoCars[1] = deObject;
         ecoCars[2] = geObject;
```

```
//#3  Polymorphic calls to the setExtColor() method
      System.out.print("\n\n  A. Polymorphic array: \n");
      for(int octrl = 0; octrl < ecoCars.length; octrl++){
          System.out.print("\n  ");
          for(int ictrl = 0; ictrl < ecoColors.length; ictrl++){
             ecoCars[octrl].setExtColor(ecoColors[ictrl]);
             System.out.print(ecoCars[octrl].getExtColor()
                                          + "  ");

          }//end inner for
      }//end outer for


//#4  Polymorphic argument definition for printCar()
      System.out.print("\n\n  B. Polymorphic arguments:  \n");
      printCar(ccObject);
      printCar(deObject);
      printCar(geObject);


//#5  Polymorphic return type for findCar
      System.out.print("\n\n  C. Polymorphic return values  \n");
      ccObject.setExtColor("Black");
      System.out.println("  Find CC0001 color :\t "
                          + findCar("CC0001").getExtColor() );
      geObject.setExtColor("Green");
      System.out.println("  Find GE0001 color :\t "
                          + findCar("GE0001").getExtColor() );
      deObject.setExtColor("Red");
      System.out.println("  Find DE0001 color :\t "
                          + findCar("DE0001").getExtColor() );
        }//end main
//4.1-----------------------printCar-----------------------------
//Takes as an argument any object of a class derived from the Economy class
      public static void printCar(Economy ecoOb){
          System.out.print("\n    "
          +   ecoOb.toString() + "     \t"
          +   ecoOb.getUID() + "     \t"
          +   ecoOb.getExtColor()
          );
      }
```

```
//5.1----------------------findCar--------------------------------
//Returns any object of a class derived from the Economy class
      public static Economy findCar(String carUID){
          Economy tempCar = new Economy();
          for(int octrl = 0; octrl < ecoCars.length; octrl++){
              if(carUID.equalsIgnoreCase( ecoCars[octrl].getUID()) ){
                  tempCar = ecoCars[octrl];
                  break;
              }
          }
          return tempCar;
      }
}//end class
```

In the lines associated with comment #1 in the PolyTest class, you define two arrays. Both are static, so you can make use of them in other static methods. You define the first array (ecoCars) so that it is of the Economy type. This is the base class of the hierarchy you have created to experiment with polymorphic operations. The ecoCars array has three elements to accommodate each of the subclasses. The second array (ecoColors) is of the String type, and it stores the general color words the setExtColor() methods of the subclasses all recognize.

In the lines trailing comment #2, you define objects of the ChildCart, DieselElectric, and GasElectric types (ccObject, deObject, and geObject). You then assign the three objects to the ecoCars array. You can assign the objects of the three types to the array without problems because you have defined the array using the Economy class type. An array of a base class type can accommodate objects of the classes derived from the base class.

At comment #3, you create embedded for blocks. The outer block traverses the three items in the ecoCars array. The inner block traverses the six items in the ecoColors array. In the inner block, you use the ecoCars array to call the setExtColor() method. In each of the definitions of the three derived classes, you have overridden this method. With each call of the setExtColor() method, you use as an argument to the method one of the colors from the ecoColors array.

Since you use the array length attribute to govern the iterations of the inner block, for each item in the ecoCars array the cycles of the block call the setExtColor() six times, assigning the six successive colors to the object you have stored in the ecoCars array. Immediately after assigning a color to the object in the ecoColors array, you move on to the next statement, which uses the ecoCars array to call the getExtColor() method. As item A in Figure 6.18

shows, the result is that you see the values you have assigned to the ecoColors array translated into the values that are specific to the class objects stored in the ecoCars array.

In the lines following comment #4, you make three successive calls to the printCar() method. At comment #4.1 you initiate the definition of the printCar() method. You define the method using static so that it can be called by the main() method without the need to create an object of the PolyTest type. The method is public and possesses a return type of void.

The argument of the printCar() method is of the Economy type. When you define the argument in this way, you make it so that the method can process objects of types derived from the Economy class. Given this definition of the argument (ecoOb), you can then use the argument to call methods supported by the Economy class. Two such methods are the getUID() method and the overridden getExtColor() method. In addition, you can call the toString() method, which all Java objects possess. This method identifies the type of the object with which you call it. As you see at item B of Figure 6.18, polymorphic operations allow you to retrieve the identifier of each of the three types of object along with the color that you have assigned to the object. (The identifier differs for different computes and different executions of the program because it is based on the position of the object in memory.) In the lines associated with comment #5, you make calls to the setExtColor(), findCar(), and getExtColor() methods. You call the setExtColor() method to explicitly set the colors of objects. In this way, you can more readily recognize the objects in subsequent operations. After setting color values, you then call the findCar() method.

You define the findCar() method in the lines trailing comment #5.1. As with the printCar() method, you define the findCar() method as public and static. Its return type, however, is of the Economy type, which means that it can return any object of a type derived from the Economy class.

To define the argument of the findCar() method (carUID), you use the String type. The carUID argument designates the identifier you assign to objects through construction or by calling the setUID() method. To process the argument, you create a local instance of the Economy class (tempCar). You then create a for repetition statement that traverses the ecoCars array.

As the repetition statement traverses the array, you use an if selection statement in conjunction with a call by the carUID argument to the equalsIgnoreCase() method to retrieve and evaluate the identifier of each object assigned to the ecoCars array. When you locate the object in the array that corresponds to the identifier, you assign the object to the tempCar object. The tempCar object can accommodate all three subclasses because it is of the base class (Economy) type. You then break from the repetition block and use the return keyword to return the value assigned to `tempCar`. No problem arises during the return operations because the return type is `Economy`, which like the `tempCar` object handles objects of any of the `Economy` subclasses.

In the lines trailing comment #5, you use a dot operator to append calls to the `getExtColor()` method to each call of the `findCar()` method. Since you have defined the `getExtColor()` for all classes, you are able to use it on a polymorphic basis. The object the `findCar()` method returns is the object you identify in the argument to the `findCar()` method. The color values the `getExtColor()` method returns appear after item C of Figure 6.18.

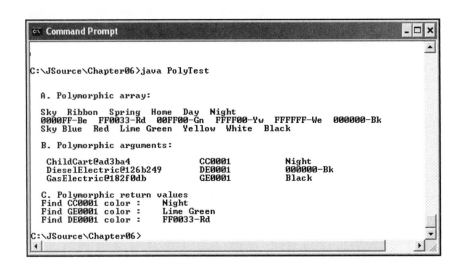

SUMMARY

In this chapter, you have explored inheritance and polymorphism. Together with encapsulation, the practices constitute the core activities of object-oriented programming. In your explorations of inheritance and polymorphism, you created a class hierarchy that descends from the `Car` class. As you developed this hierarchy, you worked with the `extends` and `super` keywords. The `extends` keyword allowed you to derive one class from another. The `super` keyword allowed you to create constructors in derived classes that could access the constructors in parent classes. In addition to working with constructors, you also worked with overridden and finalized methods. Overridden methods enabled you to experiment with four fundamental aspects of polymorphism. The next chapter involves you in a few more aspects of polymorphism. After that, you are ready to proceed into the Java class hierarchy to explore its GUI offerings.

CHALLENGES

1. Refer to Figure 6.6. Given this configuration, derive a class from the FourDoor class that allows you to address the needs of cars for handicapped drivers. When you model the class, assume they are vans set up for people in wheelchairs. The wheelchairs have a side door elevator ramp. Add a method to indicate whether the ramp door is open or closed. Add a method to indicate whether the elevator is lowered or raised.

2. Implement the class you designed in Challenge 1.

3. Write a test driver for the class. Base your work on the WagonTest class. Test each of the methods you have added and others as you think necessary.

4. Refer to the class diagram in Figure 6.17. Create a class for three-wheel fully electric cars that can have two passengers. The type of car has two doors that open upward, one on each side. It also opens from the back.

5. Implement the test you designed in Challenge 4. Overload the setExtColor() and getExtColor() methods and establish your own color scheme, such as "ElectricBlue," "ElectricRed," and so on.

6. Write a test driver for the class. Add a reference to this class to the PolyTest class. Identify the car as FE0001 in the output.

ABSTRACT CLASSES AND INTERFACES

This chapter takes you into what might be viewed as a few advanced topics of object-oriented programming. You investigate abstract classes, interfaces, and inner classes. Along with these topics, you explore the use of `final` classes and a few extended dimensions of polymorphism. In addition to these topics, you begin working with one of the `Collection` classes that Java offers and then move on to exploring the use of the Java graphical user interface (classes). The `JFrame` class allows you to create a basic window. The `JTextArea` class allows you to create a customer client array to which to write your output. Derivation and implementation of classes allow you access to classes. Still other classes allow you to create a scrollbar. Such activities provide a foundation for extensive exploration of the Java class hierarchy. The chapter addresses the following topics, among others:

- Exploring the `abstract` keyword abstract classes
- Defining abstract methods in abstract classes
- Defining abstract methods in concrete classes
- Use of abstract classes for references in polymorphic contexts
- Using interfaces and the `implements` keyword
- Developing inner classes

- Developing a class for handling events
- Inner classes and `final` classes

ABSTRACT CLASSES

You can view an abstract class as the opposite of a concrete object. As the discussion in Chapter 6 emphasizes, you can use a constructor to create an instance of a concrete class. With the `Car` class hierarchy, for example, you created the `Car` class and then derived `FourDoor` and `Economy` from it. The super class and subclasses are concrete, as you demonstrate when you create instances of them for testing purposes. The statements you employ in the testing program to create instances of these classes take the following form:

```
Car carObject = new Car()
Economy ecoObject = new Economy()
```

Abstract classes differ from concrete classes because you cannot create instances of them. You cannot create instances of them because they contain one or more abstract methods. An abstract method, as the next section discusses, is a method that you do not fully define. You can make use of abstract classes only if you derive classes from them and in the derived classes define the abstract methods the abstract classes contain. If in the subclass you do not complete the definition of the abstract methods in the super class, then the subclass itself becomes abstract. Figure 7.1 summarizes this situation.

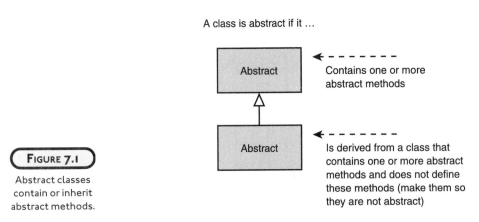

A class is abstract if it ...

Abstract — Contains one or more abstract methods

Abstract — Is derived from a class that contains one or more abstract methods and does not define these methods (make them so they are not abstract)

FIGURE 7.1

Abstract classes contain or inherit abstract methods.

To create an abstract class, you proceed just as you do when creating a concrete class. However, you add a term to the signature line of the class. This is the `abstract` keyword. The Java compiler does not recognize an abstract class as properly defined unless you include this keyword in the signature. Any class with which you use it becomes abstract. Here is an example of how you can declare the `Car` class as an abstract class:

```
public abstract Car {      //use of abstract to define the class
    // body left out
}
```

If you derive a class from an abstract super class, you must define the derived class as abstract unless you define the abstract methods you inherit from the super class in the context of your derived class.

If you do not define the inherited abstract methods, then you need to make only one change to the normal routine you use to create a derived class. You add the abstract keyword to the signature line of the derived class. Here's an example of the signature line of a class that inherits abstract methods from a super class:

```
public abstract Economy extends Car{
```

As you know from prior discussions, the extends keyword allows the Economy class to have access to all the public methods the Car class contains. If the Economy class is not to remain abstract, then you must define all the abstract methods from the Car class within the Economy class. (Subsequent sections discuss this activity in greater detail.)

An abstract class is not often *purely* abstract. A purely abstract class contains only abstract methods. In Java, the term *interface* is applied to such classes. A later section of this chapter discusses such classes in detail.

Abstract classes usually consist of a mixture of abstract and non-abstract methods. An abstract method is a method that forms part of the interface of a class but that you do not implement. To define an abstract method, you employ, as you do with the class, the abstract keyword.

The Car class (see the next section) is an example of such a class. It usually consists largely of non-abstract methods, but it contains a few abstract methods that force the user of the class hierarchy to define subclasses so that they specialize specific tasks. The next section discusses abstract methods in greater detail.

Abstract Methods

An abstract class usually contains at least one abstract method. In fact, the formal definition of an abstract class is that it is a class that contains an abstract method. While this definition retains its validity in the context of Java, it remains important to realize that you do not always see the methods that make the class abstract presented explicitly within the class. The methods that make the class abstract can be inherited from a super class.

When you define a method as abstract, you always do so using the abstract keyword as part of the signature line of the method. In the Car class, to make the getExtColor() method abstract, you use the following approach:

```
//An abstract method is not defined
public abstract void getExtColor(boolean dds);
```

When you define a method as abstract, you employ the abstract keyword after the scope keyword and prior to the return type. You terminate the declaration of the method with a semicolon following the closing parentheses of the argument definition. You do not use opening and closing braces to define the body of the method.

To make it so that this method is no longer abstract, you must define it. To define a method, you add a body to it. To add a body, you employ opening and closing parentheses. Here is an example of how to define the getExtColor() method so that it is no longer abstract:

```
//Minimally defined method - no longer abstract
public abstract void getExtColor(boolean dds){
        //You do not have to include statements
}
```

To define a method, you can at a bare minimum add only the opening and closing curly braces to the signature line of the method. This is known as an *empty* method definition. In many instances, you create empty definitions when the super class you are working with contains several abstract methods but you want to work with only one of them. You fully define (or implement) the method you need to use. You provide the other methods with empty definitions so that you can satisfy the conditions for making your class concrete.

Picturing Abstract Classes and Methods

To picture abstract classes and methods, you can employ a version of the UML class diagram. If you show the Car, FourDoor, and Economy classes (refer to Chapter 6) as abstract classes, the UML representation takes the form shown in Figure 7.2. To show that a class is abstract, you use a combination of italics and appended notations. The names of the classes appear in italics, and beneath the name of the class, within the curly braces, you see that explicit identification of the classes as abstract (*{abstract}*).

In addition to identifying classes as abstract, you can also identify methods as abstract. To accomplish this, you append curly braces enclosing the term *abstract* to the end of the method in the UML diagram. In Figure 7.2, the Car class contains two abstract methods, setExtColor() and getExtColor().

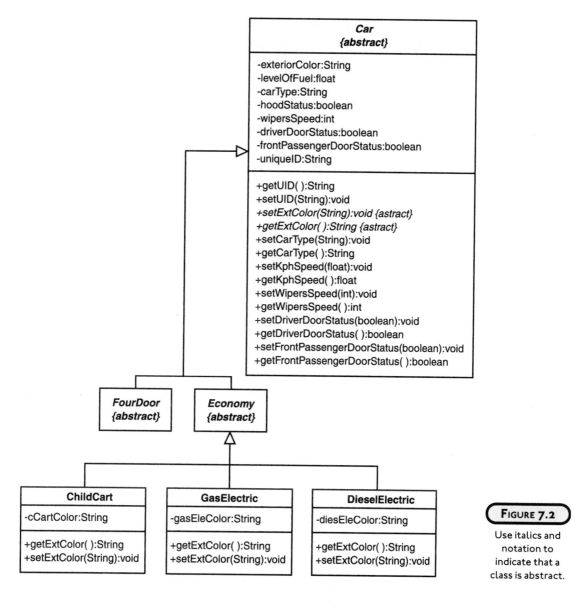

FIGURE 7.2

Use italics and notation to indicate that a class is abstract.

Approaches software developers use to indicate abstraction vary. Methods often lack the appended notation (*{abstract}*). Instead, you see only the name of the method in italics:

```
setExtColor(String):void
```

The FourDoor and Economy classes are abstract. They are abstract because they do not implement the abstract methods of the Car class. As mentioned previously, when you derive classes from a super class, the derived classes are also abstract unless you implement the abstract methods you have derived from the super class. If you do not implement the abstract methods you derive from the superclass, the compiler enforces the abstraction rule. When it enforces this rule, it generates errors until you either implement the inherited methods or declare the derived classes explicitly abstract.

Figure 7.3 illustrates how this works. The Car hierarchy in this chapter is the same as the hierarchy you worked with in Chapter 6, with the difference now that you use abstraction to define the classes in the top two tiers of the hierarchy. To make things easier to illustrate, Figure 7.3 does not show the methods you see in Figure 7.2. Likewise, you do not see the methods of the Economy class (see Chapter 6, Figure 6.9).

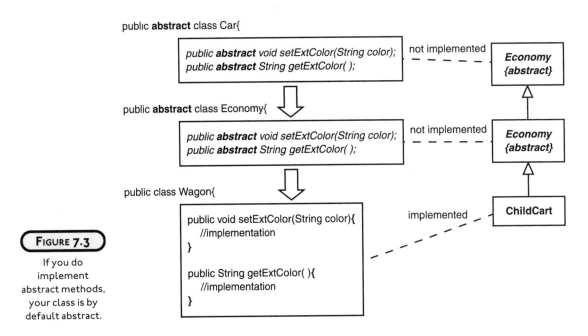

FIGURE 7.3

If you do implement abstract methods, your class is by default abstract.

The methods you worked with in Chapter 6 remain within the classes in the revised Car hierarchy, but you can no longer create Car, FourDoor, or Economy class objects, which form the first two tiers of the Car class hierarchy. You cannot create these class objects because these three classes contain abstract methods. They are abstract classes. On the other hand, it remains that you can define objects of the classes on the third tier. On the third tier, the classes (ChildCart, GasElectric, and DieselElectric) contain no abstract methods. These classes are concrete.

At the top of the hierarchy, the Car class provides two abstract methods, setExtColor() and getExtColor(). The presence of these two methods in the Car class makes the Car class abstract.

When you derive the `Economy` class from the `Car` class, you again refrain from implementing the `setExtColor()` and `getExtColor()` methods. These methods remain abstract. Because they are abstract, you must declare the `Economy` class as abstract. As with the `Car` class, you cannot create an instance of the `Economy` class. The same applies to the `FourDoor` class.

Things change at the third tier. When you create the `ChildCart`, `GasElectric`, and `DieselElectric` classes, you define the `setExtColor()` and `getExtColor()` methods. The definitions you provide in this case are the same as those you provided in Chapter 6. In Chapter 6, however, you were overriding the methods you inherited from the super class. In this case, you are defining the methods for the first time.

Defining these two inherited methods allows the classes in which they are defined to be concrete. Given a concrete definition of a class, you can create an instance of it.

Using Abstraction in the Car Hierarchy

When you create abstract classes, you pressure the users of your class hierarchy to employ it in specific ways. In the case of the `Car` hierarchy, when you make the `Car` and `Economy` classes abstract, you make it so that users must derive a concrete class from the abstract classes before they can create an instance of a class that represents a car. To create a concrete class, they must define the `setExtColor()` and `getExtColor()` methods. These methods force them to customize the way they set colors for the cars.

In the definition of the `Car` class, you designate both of these methods as abstract. In the `Economy` class you leave these methods undefined, so the `Economy` class remains abstract. Within the `Economy` class, you define the `getRearDoorStatus()` and `setRearDoorStatus()` methods, along with the `rearDoorStatus` attribute. Nothing in this activity makes the class abstract. What makes the class abstract is that you have not implemented the abstract methods derived from the `Car` class.

As the definitions of the `Car` and `Economy` classes show, an abstract class can consist of implemented and abstract methods. It can include attributes. It can also include default and overloaded constructors. The work of the constructors involves the same construction sequences you saw at work in Chapter 6. The construction sequences initialize attributes of the super classes. The only restriction is that you cannot use the `new` keyword (or operator) to create an instance of the class.

The Car Class as an Abstract Class

To be able to implement a new version of the `PolyTest` class that incorporates abstract classes, you begin with the classes you developed in Chapter 6. There, you defined the `Car` class as concrete. In this chapter, you define it as abstract. Declaration of the class as abstract involves using the abstract keyword in the signature line of the Car class declaration and creating the setExtColor() and getExtColor() methods as abstract.

One other change pertains, also. You change the definition of the exteriorColor attribute. You change its scope definition from private to protected. Since you define the mutator and accessor methods for this attribute as abstract, you must make the attribute available to subclasses if you want to be able to access it. The protected status makes it available in this way.

```java
/*
    Car.java
*/
public abstract class Car{
    //#1 Changed to protected
    protected String exteriorColor;
    private float levelOfFuel;
    private String carType;
    private boolean hoodStatus;
    private float kphSpeed;
    private int wipersSpeed;
    private boolean driverDoorStatus;
    private boolean frontPassengerDoorStatus;
    private String uniqueID;

    //#2 You leave the constructors in because
    // They can still be accessed by the
    //construction sequence when you
    //create a concrete class
    public Car(){
        uniqueID = "0000AA";
    // System.out.println("\tCar constructing ...");
    }
    public Car(String uid){
        uniqueID = uid;
    // System.out.println("\tCar constructing ...");
    }
    public String getUID(){
        return uniqueID;
    }
```

```
public void setUID(String uid){
    uniqueID = uid;
}


//#3 Defined as abstract
public abstract void setExtColor(String ec);
public abstract String getExtColor();

public void setLevelOfFuel(float fl){
    levelOfFuel = fl;
}
public float getLevelOfFuel(){
    return levelOfFuel;
}
public void setCarType(String ct){
    carType = ct;
}
public String getCarType(){
    return carType;
}
public void setKphSpeed(float ks){
    kphSpeed = ks;
}
public float getKphSpeed(){
    return kphSpeed;
}
public void setWipersSpeed(int ws){
    wipersSpeed = ws;
}
public int getWipersSpeed(){
    return wipersSpeed;
}
public void setDriverDoorStatus(boolean dds){
    driverDoorStatus = dds;
}
public boolean getDriverDoorStatus(){
    return driverDoorStatus;
}
```

```
    public void setFrontPassengerDoorStatus(boolean fpds){
        frontPassengerDoorStatus = fpds;
    }
    public boolean getFrontPassengerDoorStatus(){
        return frontPassengerDoorStatus;
    }
    public void setHoodStatus(boolean hs){
        hoodStatus = hs;
    }
    public boolean getHoodStatus(){
        return hoodStatus;
    }
}//end class
```

Preceding comment #1 of the updated version of the Car class, you employ the abstract keyword in the signature line of the class to make the class abstract. Immediately after comment #1, you define the exteriorColor attribute. You define the scope of the attribute so that it is protected.

In the lines trailing comment #2, you define default and overloaded constructors for the Car class. These constructors do not differ from those you implemented for the Chapter 6 version of the Car class. Even though the current version of the Car class is abstract, the constructors are still called as a part of the construction sequence for concrete classes derived from the Car class.

In the lines associated with comment #3, you declare two abstract methods. (They are in bold typeface.) These are the setExtColor() and getExtColor() methods. To declare these methods, you use the abstract keyword in their signature lines. You leave them without definitions by terminating their signature lines with semicolons rather that providing open and close curly braces to define their bodies.

For both of the methods, you provide complete signature definitions. The setExtColor() method returns void. Its argument (ec) is of the String type. The getExtColor() method has a return type of String and takes no arguments.

> After you name an argument in the signature line of an abstract method, when you implement the method in a concrete class, it is not necessary to precisely repeat the name of the argument. For example, you can rename String ec to String cce.

Given the lack of definitions and the use of the `abstract` keyword in their signature lines, the `setExtColor()` and `getExtColor()` methods are abstract. The inclusion of these methods in the `Car` class makes the `Car` class abstract. Any classes you derive from the `Car` class are also abstract unless you define these methods.

The Economy Class as an Abstract Class

As the UML diagram in Figure 7.2 illustrates, you derive the `Economy` class from the `Car` class. When you derive the `Economy` class from the `Car` class, your objective is to specialize the `Car` class so that it can accommodate cars that have back doors. Accommodating cars with back doors involves adding two methods and an attribute to the class. At the same time, you seek to prevent users from creating objects of the `Economy` class, so you allow the `Economy` class to remain abstract. Toward this end, you declare it using the `extends` and `abstract` keywords as you derive it from the `Car` class, and you do not define the `setExtColor()` and `getExtColor()` methods, which you derive from the `Car` class.

```
/*
    Economy.java
*/
//#1
public abstract class Economy extends Car{
    private boolean rearDoorStatus;

//#2 Constructors call to the super class
    public Economy(String euid){
       super(euid);
    }
    public Economy(){
       super();
    }
//#3 Add new methods
    public void setRearDoorStatus(boolean rds){
       rearDoorStatus = rds;
    }
    public boolean getRearDoorStatus(){
       return rearDoorStatus;
    }
 }//end class
```

In the lines accompanying comment #1 of the Economy class definition, you provide the signature of the class. Definition of the signature involves using the abstract keyword to designate the class as abstract (the word is in bold). You also use the extends keyword to derive the contents of the class from the Car class. When you derive the Economy class from the Car class, you must either define the abstract methods the Car class contains or allow the Economy class to become abstract. In this case, you allow it to become abstract.

Immediately following comment #1, you create a class attribute, rearDoorStatus, which is of the boolean type. You use the private access modifier to prevent other classes from accessing it. This attribute tracks the status of the back door of the vehicle. If the back door is closed, the attribute is assigned a value of true. If it is open, the attribute is assigned a value of false.

Even if it is abstract, the Economy class still serves in an intermediary position because classes you derive from the Economy class must still communicate with the Car class. To make this possible, you define two constructors. The constructors serve to populate the uniqueID attribute of the Car class with an initial value. You use the super keyword to communicate with the constructor. In the first of the two constructors, you employ the super keyword to call the overloaded constructor of the Car class, which takes one argument. In the second of the two constructors, you call the default constructor of the Car class. Classes you derive from the Economy class can then call these constructors to communicate with the Car class.

At comment #3, you create two new methods, setRearDoorStatus() and setRearDoorStatus(). These methods allow you change the state of the back door of an economy car. Although you fully implement these methods, they are still part of an abstract class, so you cannot access them unless you derive a class from the Economy class. Since they are not abstract, you do not need to define them. To make it convenient to access them, you define them as public.

Creating a Concrete Class

In Figure 7.2, you see the same set of third-tier classes you worked with in Chapter 6. In Chapter 6, when you created the ChildCart, GasElectric, and DieselElectric classes, the focus of your work was on *overriding* the setExtColor() and getExtColor() methods. What constituted overriding in the hierarchy in Chapter 6 now becomes method definition. You can override a method only if it has been defined. In this case, no such method exits. Only signature lines exist in the super classes.

Definition of the setExtColor() and getExtColor() methods involves precisely the same efforts you expended when overriding them, however. To define a method that you inherit from an abstract class, you perform the same actions involved in overriding the method.

```
/*
     ChildCart.java
*/
public class ChildCart extends Economy{
     //#1
     private String cCartColor;
     //#2 Constructor calls to the parent
     public ChildCart(String ccid){
          super(ccid);
     }
     public ChildCart(){
          super();
     }
     //#3
     public void setExtColor(String ec){
               if(ec.equalsIgnoreCase("blue")){
                    cCartColor = "Sky";
               }
               else if(ec.equalsIgnoreCase("red")){
                    cCartColor = "Ribbon";
               }
               else if(ec.equalsIgnoreCase("green")){
                    cCartColor = "Spring";
               }
               else if(ec.equalsIgnoreCase("yellow")){
                    cCartColor = "Home";
               }
               else if(ec.equalsIgnoreCase("white")){
                    cCartColor = "Day";
               }
               else if(ec.equalsIgnoreCase("black")){
                    cCartColor = "Night";
               }
               else{
                    cCartColor = "Day";
               }
     }
     //#4
```

```
    public String getExtColor(){
        return cCartColor;
    }
}
```

Prior to comment #1 in the `ChildCart` class definition, you create a signature line for the `ChildCart` class. You do not use the `abstract` keyword as you did in the second-tier class definition. You use the `extends` keyword to derive the class from the `Economy` class. Following the opening of the class, you declare a class attribute, `cCartColor`. As in Chapter 6, this attribute is `private` and of the `String` type.

At comment #2, you define default and overloaded constructors for the class. You use the `super` keyword to call the constructors in the `Economy` class. Recall from the discussion in Chapter 6 that the construction sequence then calls the constructors from the `Car` class.

In the lines following comment #3, you implement the `setExtColor()` method. Implementation of this method proceeds in the same manner described in Chapter 6. You use an if…else if…else structure to process the argument of the method (ec). The `String:: equalsIgnoreCase()` method allows you to test the values supplied to the ec argument. For each selection test, you assign a distinct value to the `cCartColor` attribute.

At comment #4, you define the `getExtColor()` method. This method returns the current value of the `cCartColor` attribute. Given the definition of the `getExtColor()` and `setExtColor()` methods, the `ChildCart` class is concrete, so you can create instances of it.

Other Concrete and Abstract Classes

To reduce the size of the chapter, you see the implementation of only the `Car`, `Economy`, and `ChildCart` classes. The implemented forms of the classes are included on the companion website. For review, the shaded class symbols in Figure 7.4 represent the classes shown in this chapter.

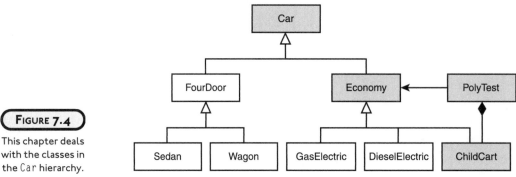

FIGURE 7.4

This chapter deals with the classes in the `Car` hierarchy.

To review the definitions of the second-tier classes, you need to make no changes to the definition of the FourDoor class other than to change the signature line. The change to the FourDoor class is as follows:

```
public abstract class FourDoor extends Car{
```

You add only the abstract keyword to the class signature. You leave the abstract methods in the super class (Car) undefined.

For the two third-tier classes derived from the FourDoor class, you can make them concrete. To make them concrete, you add empty definitions of the two abstract methods inherited from the super classes. In both classes, you follow the same approach. Here is how you implement the Wagon class:

```
/*
 Wagon.java
*/
public class Wagon extends FourDoor{
    //#1
    //lines left out. . .
    //#2 Empty definitions of the inherited methods
    public void setExtColor(String ec){
    }
    public String getExtColor(){
        return new String();
    }
}
```

Preceding comment #1, as in Chapter 6, you define the signature line so that the class extends the FourDoor class. Trailing comment #2, you define the setExtColor() method by adding open and closing curly braces. No other additions to this method are needed. To define the getExtColor() method, you must return a String value. To return the value, you can use the new keyword in conjunction with the String constructor. This enables the method to return an empty String object. The definition of the Sedan class as a concrete class involved precisely the same activities.

For the GasElectric and DieselElectric classes, you proceed along the same lines you follow as you define the ChildCart class. Each implements a different set of color values. Each has a distinct color attribute.

Polymorphic Uses of Abstract Data Types

The PolyTest class provides you with a context in which you can explore how working with abstract classes differs from working with concrete classes. In this context, the differences tend to be fairly minor. One of the main tasks you face when you use abstract classes is that you must avoid trying to create instances of the abstract classes.

In the version of the PolyTest class you developed in Chapter 6, you were able to create an array instance of the Economy class. That is no longer possible in an implementation of the Car hierarchy that includes an abstract version of the Economy class.

References and Identifiers

While you cannot create an instance of an abstract class, you can create an identifier using the type the class defines. An identifier is a word to which you have applied the class type. Here is an example of declaring an identifier of the Economy type:

```
Economy carReference;
```

Because the Economy class is abstract, you cannot use the new keyword to fully define the carReference identifier as an object of the Economy class, but you can still make use of it. You can make use of it to store instances of concrete classes you derive from the Economy class. You can do this because such an identifier allocates memory for an object of the class with which you define it. Every class you derive from the Economy class is of the Economy class type. As Figure 7.5 illustrates, the ChildCart class is derived from the Economy class, so if you create a reference to the Economy class, you can assign an object of the ChildCart class to it. A reference, then, is an identifier of a given type. At the same time, you do not define a reference. You use it to store an object you have defined.

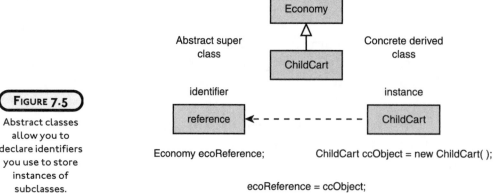

FIGURE 7.5

Abstract classes allow you to declare identifiers you use to store instances of subclasses.

In the `PolyTest` class you see an example of this when you create identifiers for the `Economy` class. The `Economy` class is abstract, but you can still use the `Economy` identifiers to store instances of the `ChildCart`, `GasElectric`, and `DieselElectric` classes.

References and Collections

In the revised version of `PolyTest` class, when you assign instances of concrete classes to an identifier of an abstract super class type, you are using polymorphism in a different manner than you used it in the version of the `PolyTest` class you developed in Chapter 6. You no longer create an array of the type `Economy` in which to store the objects of the types you derive from the `Economy` class. You cannot do this because to create an array, you must be able to invoke the `new` keyword and construct an instance of an `Economy` object. Abstract classes prevent you from constructing instances of them. For the revised version, you accommodate the abstract status of the `Economy` class by using a *collections container*.

Collections containers receive extensive discussion in the next and following chapters. For now, the important thing to remember is that while a container resembles an array, it is much more complex. The container you use in the `PolyTest` class is of the `Vector` class. The Java class hierarchy provides you with the `Vector` class along with several other container classes you explore later on in this chapter. You do not have to define a `Vector` object using the `Economy` class, as you do arrays. An object of the `Vector` class can store objects derived from the `Object` class. The `Object` class lies at the base of the entire Java class hierarchy. You implicitly derive all classes you create in Java from the `Object` class.

In the revised version of the `PolyTest` class, you replace the array you used in Chapter 6 with a `Vector` container. After that, all of the polymorphic features of the `PolyTest` class work as they did in the previous version of the class. The abstract class objects provide references that you can use for polymorphic operations. The `Vector` container provides you a way to store a set of objects of classes you derive from the `Economy` class. Here is the implementation of the `PolyTest` class:

```
/*
 PolyTest.java
*/
import java.util.*;
public class PolyTest{
//#1
// You can no longer create an instance of the Economy class
// static Economy ecoCars[3] = new Economy[3];
// A container that can store references
```

```
    static Vector<Economy> ecoCars = new Vector<Economy>();
    static String[] ecoColors = {"Blue",    "Red",    "Green",
                                 "Yellow",  "White",  "Black"};
//---------------------------main---------------------------
    public static void main(String Args[]){
    //#2  Create instances of the concrete classes
        ChildCart ccObject = new ChildCart("CC0001");
        DieselElectric deObject = new DieselElectric("DE0001");
        GasElectric geObject = new GasElectric("GE0001");

        //Assign colors to the three concrete objects
        ccObject.setExtColor(ecoColors[0]);
        deObject.setExtColor(ecoColors[1]);
        geObject.setExtColor(ecoColors[2]);

    //#3 Create a reference to the abstract Economy class
        Economy ref;
        //#Add the concrete objects to the Vector container
        ecoCars.add(ccObject);
        ecoCars.add(deObject);
        ecoCars.add(geObject);

    //#4  Polymorphic calls to the getColor() method
        System.out.print("\n\n  A. Polymorphic presentation:  \n");
        for(int octrl = 0; octrl < ecoCars.size(); octrl++){
            //Cast the objects to the Abstract super class type
            //and store them in a reference to Economy
                ref = (Economy)ecoCars.get(octrl);
            //Use the reference to call a method
                System.out.print("\n  " + ref.getExtColor() );
            }//end outer for

    //#5  Polymorphic argument definition for printCar()
        System.out.print("\n\n  B. Polymorphic arguments:  \n");
        printCar(ccObject);
        printCar(deObject);
        printCar(geObject);
```

```
//#6  Polymorphic return type for findCar
    System.out.print("\n\n  C. Polymorphic return values  \n");
    ccObject.setExtColor("Black");
    System.out.println("  Find CC0001 color :\t "
                    + findCar("CC0001").getExtColor() );
    geObject.setExtColor("Green");
    System.out.println("  Find GE0001 color :\t "
                    + findCar("GE0001").getExtColor() );
    deObject.setExtColor("Red");
    System.out.println("  Find DE0001 color :\t "
                    + findCar("DE0001").getExtColor() );


}//end main

//5.1----------------------printCar-----------------------------
//Takes as an argument any object of a class derived
//from the Economy class
    public static void printCar(Economy ecoOb){
        System.out.print("\n    "
        +   ecoOb.toString() + "      \t"
        +   ecoOb.getUID() + "         \t"
        +   ecoOb.getExtColor()
        );
    }

//6.1----------------------findCar-----------------------------
//Returns any object of a class derived from the Economy class
        public static Economy findCar(String carUID){
        //Use a reference and cast it
        Economy tempCar = null;
        for(int octrl = 0; octrl < ecoCars.size(); octrl++){
            //Cast it after you retrieve it from the container
            //And put it in the Vector
            tempCar = (Economy)ecoCars.get(octrl);
            if(carUID.equalsIgnoreCase( tempCar.getUID()) ){
                tempCar = (Economy)ecoCars.get(octrl);
                break;
            }
```

```
        }
        return tempCar;
    }
}//end class
```

> When you compile the PolyTest class, you must first copy the classes on which it depends into
> your working directory and compile them. These classes are as follows: Car, FourDoor, Wagon,
> Sedan, Economy, ChildCart, StandardColors, DieselElectric, and GasElectric.

In the lines associated with comment #1 of the PolyTest class, you comment out the approach used to create an array you used in Chapter 6. Since the Economy class is now abstract, instead of creating an array, you now create a Vector object (ecoCars). As mentioned previously, a Vector object provides a container that can accommodate any object you want to assign to it that is derived from the Object class. All the Java classes you create fall into this category. In addition to the Vector object, as in Chapter 6, you create an array of the string type, ecoColors. To this array you assign a set of standard colors. To use the Vector class, you must import the java.util package.

In the lies trailing comment #2, you create instances of the three concrete classes. In this chapter, you have reviewed only the creation of the ChildCart class. In Chapter 6, you explored the creation the GasElectric and DieselElectric classes. You use the overloaded constructors for each of the objects of these classes. In this way you can explicitly define the identification numbers you assign to them.

Having created the three objects from the concrete classes, you call the setExtColor() method to assign standard colors to the objects. The action of this method is polymorphic. Representing methods that have been uniquely defined for the three classes, the method translates the standard colors into color terms specific to each class.

At comment #3, you create an identifier (ref) of the Economy type and then proceed to call the add() method of the Vector class to add the subclass objects of the Economy class to the ecoCars container. The three assignments prove successful due to the polymorphic relationships that pertain between the container and the objects of the subclasses.

In the lines associated with comment #4, you create a for repetition statement. To govern the action of the statement, you call the Vector::size() method, which returns the number of objects in the Vector container. You supply the incremented octrl control variable as an argument to the Vector::get() method. This method returns a copy of each object stored in the ecoCars container, which you must cast to the Economy type before assigning it to the ref identifier.

As the output associated with item A in Figure 7.6 illustrates, to show the colors of the three objects, you call the print() method and use the ref identifier to call the getExtColor() method. Again, the polymorphic definition of the getExtColor() method allows it to retrieve the different values you have assigned to the objects that call it.

In the lines affiliated with comment #5, you call the printCar() method. This method you define in the lines trailing comment #5.1. To define the method, you use the static keyword so that you can call it in the static main() method without having to create an object of the PolyTest class. To define the argument of the method, you use the abstract Economy array type. The array type allows you to pass any arguments to the method that represents objects of classes that are subclasses of the Economy class. That the Economy class is abstract does not prevent you from using it to define method arguments.

Within the definition of the printCar() method, you call the toString() method, which is a method defined for all Java objects. This returns the class name of the object along with its address. You also call the getUID() method, which is defined in the Car class. The action of the constructors passes the object identifier information to the Car class. As a last action, you call the getExtColor() method. As a polymorphic method, it returns the unique color value of each object. The lines trailing item B in Figure 7.6 illustrate the output of the printCar() method.

At comment #6, you use each of the subclass objects to call the setExtColor() method. The calls to the method reset the color values of the objects. You then call the findCar() method and supply it with literal character strings that identify the objects stored in the ecoCars container.

You implement the findCar() method in the lines associated with comment #6.1. To implement this method, you provide it with a return type of Economy. In this way, it can return any object defined using a subclass of Economy. After defining the String argument of the method (carUID), you then declare a reference identifier (tempCar) of the Economy type. You then create a for repetition statement to traverse the ecoCars container. As before, the Vector::size() method allows you to control the number of iterations of the for block. As the flow of the program traverses the items in the ecoCars container, you call the Vector::get() method to retrieve copies of them and assign them to the tempCar reference. Prior to assigning them to the tempCar reference, you cast them as Economy objects.

You then create an if selection statement and use the carUID String argument to call the equalsIgnoreCase() method. As an argument for the equalsIgnoreCase() method, you provide the value returned by a call to the getUID() method. When the selection expression evaluates to true, you call the Vector::get() method to retrieve the object in the ecoCars container that the octrl control variable identifies. After casting this object to the Economy type, you assign it to the tempCar identifier. Given this assignment, the flow of the program encounters the break keyword and exits the for block. The last action of the findCar() methods returns the value of tempCar.

As the output accompanying item C in Figure 7.6 illustrates, using CC0001, GE0001, and DE0001 as arguments to the findCar() method results in the return of the three objects of the three concrete subclasses.

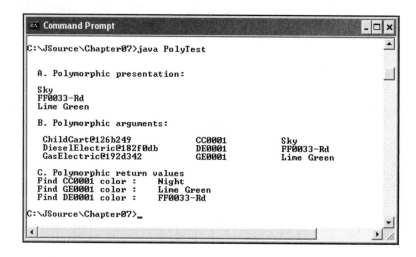

FIGURE 7.6

Polymorphism allows you to make use of abstract and concrete classes.

INTERFACES

You use the keyword interface in a way that is similar to the way you use the class keyword. The results differ, however. When you use the interface keyword, you define a class that must consist entirely of abstract methods. Likewise, when you employ this keyword to define a class, the class can have only constants as attributes. You define the attributes using public, static, and final.

A class you define using the interface keyword is known as an *interface*. The StandardColors interface provides a set of constant definitions of colors you can use in the implementation of the third-tier classes in the Car hierarchy. To define this interface, you can use the following approach:

```
/*
    StandardColors.java
*/

public interface StandardColors{
    public static final String BLU = "blue";
    public static final String RED = "red";
    public static final String GRN = "green";
    public static final String YLW = "yellow";
    public static final String WHT = "white";
    public static final String BLK = "black";
}
```

The StandardColors interface provides you with constant definitions for the concrete classes you derive from the Economy class. The subclasses of the Economy class inherit the interface in the same way that they inherit an abstract class. An interface is still a class. It is a purely virtual (or abstract) class.

To derive a class from an interface, you use the implements keyword instead of the extends keyword. Here's an example of how to define the DEInterfaceTest class so that you derive it from the StandardColors interface:

```
public class DEInterfaceTest implements StandardColors{
```

In this class signature, you *implement* the StandardColors interface. Given this definition, you can develop a test class that uses colors you obtain from the StandardColors interface rather than repeatedly using literal string values. Here is the implementation of the DEInterfaceTest class:

```
/*
    DEInterfaceTest.java
*/

    public class DEInterfaceTest implements StandardColors{

        public static void main(String Args[]){
        //#1  Create instances of the DieselElectric class
            DieselElectric deObjectB = new DieselElectric("DE0001");
            DieselElectric deObjectR = new DieselElectric("DE0002");
            DieselElectric deObjectG = new DieselElectric("DE0003");
            DieselElectric deObjectY = new DieselElectric("DE0004");
            DieselElectric deObjectW = new DieselElectric("DE0005");
```

```java
        DieselElectric deObjectK = new DieselElectric("DE0006");

//#3  //Assign interface colors to the three concrete objects
        deObjectB.setExtColor(StandardColors.BLU);
        deObjectR.setExtColor(StandardColors.RED);
        deObjectG.setExtColor(StandardColors.GRN);
        deObjectY.setExtColor(StandardColors.YLW);
        deObjectW.setExtColor(StandardColors.WHT);
        deObjectK.setExtColor(StandardColors.BLK);


//#3  Access the interface colors
        System.out.print("\n\n  A. Interface colors  \n");
        System.out.println("  StandardColors.BLU :\t "
                    + StandardColors.BLU  + "\t"
                    + deObjectB.getExtColor() );
      System.out.print("\n  B.  \n");
      System.out.println("  StandardColors.RED :\t "
                    + StandardColors.RED  + "\t"
                    + deObjectR.getExtColor() );
      System.out.print("\n  C.  \n");
      System.out.println("  StandardColors.GRN :\t "
                    + StandardColors.GRN  + "\t"
                    + deObjectG.getExtColor() );
      System.out.print("\n  D. \n");
      System.out.println("  StandardColors.YLW :\t "
                    + StandardColors.YLW  + "\t"
                    + deObjectY.getExtColor() );

      System.out.print("\n  E.  \n");
      System.out.println("  StandardColors.WHT:\t "
                    + StandardColors.WHT  + "\t"
                    + deObjectW.getExtColor() );
      System.out.print("\n  F. \n");
      System.out.println("  StandardColors.BLK :\t "
                    + StandardColors.BLK  + "\t"
                    + deObjectK.getExtColor() );
    }//end main
}//end class
```

In the signature line of the class definition (preceding comment #1), you use the implements keyword to derive the DEInterfaceTest class from the StandardColors interface. Following comment #1, you then define six DieselElectric objects using an overloaded constructor, which allows you to assign a sequence of identifications to them.

At comment #2, you employ the DieselElectric object to call the setExtColor() method. As arguments for the method calls, you access the color definitions you have created in the StandardColors interface. To access the StandardColors attribute corresponding to blue, you employ StandardColors.BLU. For green, you employ StandardColors.GRN. Each of these attributes is of the String type.

To show the StandardColors values as they appear when accessed from the StandardColors interface and as translated by the setExtColor() method of the DieselElectric class, you call the DieselElectric::getExtColor() method. The result is the sets of values Figure 7.7 displays.

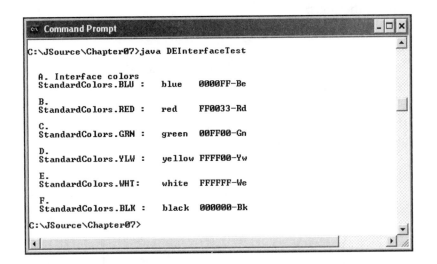

FIGURE 7.7

Using an interface allows you to create standard color values.

MULTIPLE INHERITANCE AND THE USE OF INTERFACES

Java prevents you from using the extends keyword to derive a class from two or more super classes. Such derivation is known as *multiple inheritance*. Java does not allow multiple inheritance. However, it does allow implementation of multiple interfaces.

To implement multiple interfaces, you define your class in the same way that you have defined classes in this and previous chapters. To this basic definition, you add the implements keyword and the name or names of the interface classes you want to implement. Here's an example of using multiple interfaces with the PolyTestView class:

```
public class PolyTestView extends JFrame implements StandardColors,
                                                     ActionListener{
```

The PolyTestView class constitutes a concrete class that you use for testing. It inherits methods from a Java swing class named JFrame, which allows you to create an application window. Since you can use the extends keyword only once, you must turn to the implements keyword if you wish to derive additional functionality from super classes.

You created the StandardColors interface to provide a set of constants representing colors. The ActionListener interface is an interface that you obtain from the java.awt.event package. It allows you to process graphical user interface (GUI) events such as those generated by buttons.

An interface completely lacks definition, and for this reason, it differs from an abstract class, which might consist of methods and attributes that you have defined. Recall that you define an abstract class as a class that contains at least one abstract method. An interface consists wholly of abstract, undefined methods.

Picturing Interfaces

To depict an interface, you can use a UML diagram. The diagram includes a "stereotype" above the interface that indicates that the class is an interface. Figure 7.8 illustrates a rudimentary UML diagram in which the PolyTestView class implements the StandardColors interface. A dashed arrow replaces the solid arrows you use when you extend abstract or concrete classes. The angled characters always enclose the interface stereotype.

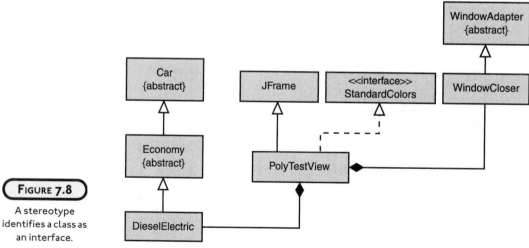

FIGURE 7.8

A stereotype identifies a class as an interface.

To review, Figure 7.8 illustrates how DieselElectric inherits the functionality of the Economy and Car classes. Within the DieselElectric class, when you define the abstract methods inherited from the two super classes, you make the DieselElectric class concrete. You can then create multiple instances of the DieselElectric class on a composition basis in the PolyTestView class.

As you discover in the next section (see Figure 7.12), the PolyTestView class allows you to create a graphical user interface (GUI). To create the interface, you derive the PolyTest class from the JFrame class, which you obtain from the Java class hierarchy. You also define the PolyTestView class so that it implements the StandardColors interface. In addition, you create a class called WindowCloser that extends the Java WindowAdapter class. The WindowCloser class allows you to set up cleanup operations for your application. As the darkened diamonds indicate, the PolyTestView class is composed of instances of the DieselElectric and WindowCloser classes.

Creating a Test Application

The system of classes Figure 7.8 depicts provides a way to make use of a few of the classes from the Car hierarchy along with other classes from the Java class hierarchy to create the application that Figure 7.12 illustrates. This is the most elementary type of windowed application you can create. It consists of a frame, a text area, a scrollbar, and a few other components. In this respect, Figure 7.8 provides only a partial view of the classes involved in the development of the application.

To develop the application, you work on two classes. The first is the PolyTestView class. It contains several methods and allows you to explore the fundamentals of creating a Windows application in Java. The second is a class that allows you to properly exit from your application at the end of a user session (WindowCloser).

Implementing a GUI Application

The PolyTestView class allows you to explore a combination of the composition, inheritance, and implementation activities you have worked with in the last two chapters. To develop the class, you work with items drawn from the Swing, awt, and event packages of Java. The Swing package provides you with classes such as JFrame and JTextArea. These classes allow you to define elements of a window application. In addition, your application is composed of a class derived from the WindowAdapter class, which receives extended discussion later in this chapter. This class processes a message (or event) that is generated when you click the control button in the corner of your window. This event causes the window to close.

```java
/*
PolyTestView.java
*/

import javax.swing.*;
import java.awt.*;
import java.awt.event.*;

public class PolyTestView extends JFrame implements StandardColors{
    //#1 Class attributes for GUI
    JTextArea frameTextArea;
    Container frameContainer;

//------------------------PolyTestView----------------------------
    //#2 Default constructor
    public PolyTestView() {
        super("PolyTestView Application");
        //call the primary function of the application
        init();
    }
//------------------------------init------------------------------
    public void init(){
        //#3 JFrame method to close the window
        addWindowListener(new WindowCloser());

        //#4 Define GUI components
        frameContainer = getContentPane();
        frameTextArea = new JTextArea("\tDieselElectric Test Class.", 50, 50);

        frameTextArea.setEditable(true);
        frameTextArea.setLineWrap(true);
        //Add the text area to container
        frameContainer.add(frameTextArea);
        //#5 Set window size and make the window visible
        setSize(520, 300);
        setVisible(true);

        //#6 Call the testing function
```

```
        runGeneralTest();
}
//------------------------runGeneralTest------------------------
public void runGeneralTest(){
    //#7
        DieselElectric deObjectB = new DieselElectric("DE0001");
        DieselElectric deObjectR = new DieselElectric("DE0002");
        DieselElectric deObjectG = new DieselElectric("DE0003");
        DieselElectric deObjectY = new DieselElectric("DE0004");
        DieselElectric deObjectW = new DieselElectric("DE0005");
        DieselElectric deObjectK = new DieselElectric("DE0006");

        deObjectB.setExtColor(StandardColors.BLU);
        deObjectR.setExtColor(StandardColors.RED);
        deObjectG.setExtColor(StandardColors.GRN);
        deObjectY.setExtColor(StandardColors.YLW);
        deObjectW.setExtColor(StandardColors.WHT);
        deObjectK.setExtColor(StandardColors.BLK);

    //#8  call the JTextArea::append() method
            frameTextArea.append("\n\n  A. Interface colors  \n");
            frameTextArea.append("  StandardColors.BLU :\t "
                        + StandardColors.BLU  +  "\t"
                        + deObjectB.getExtColor() );
            frameTextArea.append("\n  B.  \n");
            frameTextArea.append("  StandardColors.RED :\t "
                        + StandardColors.RED  +  "\t"
                        + deObjectR.getExtColor() );
            frameTextArea.append("\n  C.  \n");
            frameTextArea.append("  StandardColors.GRN :\t "
                        + StandardColors.GRN  +  "\t"
                        + deObjectG.getExtColor() );
            frameTextArea.append("\n  D.  \n");
            frameTextArea.append("  StandardColors.YLW :\t "
                        + StandardColors.YLW  +  "\t"
                        + deObjectY.getExtColor() );

            frameTextArea.append("\n  E.  \n");
```

```
        frameTextArea.append(" StandardColors.WHT:\t "
                        + StandardColors.WHT  + "\t"
                        + deObjectW.getExtColor() );
        frameTextArea.append("\n  F. \n");
        frameTextArea.append(" StandardColors.BLK :\t "
                        + StandardColors.BLK  + "\t"
                        + deObjectK.getExtColor() );
    }//end main

//-----------------------main------------------------
    //#9
    public static void main(String args[])
    {
        new PolyTestView();
        }
    }
```

Before you compile the `PolyTestView` **class, first compile the** `WindowCloser` **class.**

To create a GUI for your test program, prior to comment #1 you define a signature for the `PolyTestView` class that extends the `JFrame` class. The `JFrame` class allows you to access the primary functionality that creates a window. You also implement the `StandardColors` interface. Implementation of this interface allows you to access the color attributes used in calls to the `DieselElectric` and other classes derived from the `Economy` class.

Following comment #1, you declare GUI components common to Java windows applications. In Figure 7.12 you see the result of the use of the `JTextArea` class in the white "client" area of the window. The `Container` class provides a framework in which to place components you want to include in your window. Its use becomes one of the most involved aspects of developing GUI applications. A `Container` object can be viewed as a layer of a frame. A frame has three basic layers.

So that you can place a `JTextArea` in your `JFrame` object, you call the `getContentPane()` method, which returns the content pane of the `JFrame` object. The content pane complements the root pane. Figure 7.9 provides a simplified view of how a Java Swing frame is laid out. The story is more complex that this, but it is important at this point to recognize that when you add a component (such as a JTextArea object) to a JFrame, the component is not made a direct part of the frame. This notion is at the heart of the Swing component group of Java.

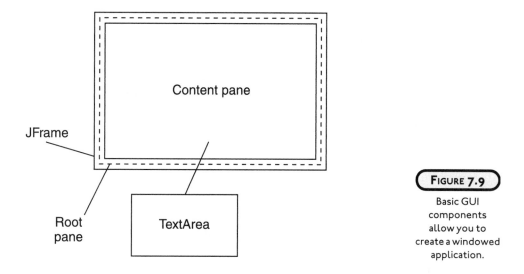

FIGURE 7.9

Basic GUI components allow you to create a windowed application.

At comment #2 of the PolyTestView class definition, you implement a default constructor for the class. To implement the constructor, you use the super keyword, which calls an overloaded constructor of the JFrame class. As Figure 7.12 reveals, the argument for this constructor sets the title of the window ("PolyTestView Application").

In the lines trailing comment #3, you define the init() method. The name of this method is short for initialization. In other contexts, such as those provided by applet creation, the init() method possesses special significance because you use it to override an inherited method. In this context, it constitutes an arbitrarily defined method that takes care of setting up basic features of the window.

In the definition of the init() method, you begin by calling the addWindowListener() method, which is a method that the JFrame class inherits from a super class in the Java class hierarchy (Window). The addWindowListener() method allows you to audit events that relate to the application window. As an argument for the addWindowListener() method, you provide an instance of the WindowCloser class. You create this class later on in this chapter.

The WindowCloser class processes an event that relates to the closing of your window. An event is a message, a signal. When you click the "x" control on the title bar, you invoke a *window event*. You use a method to process this event. In this instance, you process the event so that you can close your application window. The discussion relating to Figures 7.10 and 7.11 examines this operation in greater detail.

To create an instance of a `Container` object, you call a special method, `getContentPane()`. This method is defined in a super class of the `JFrame` class called `RootPaneContainer`. From it you can obtain a reference to a content pane object. As mentioned previously, the content pane allows you to place items in a frame.

You assign the reference to the content pane to the `frameContainer` attribute. You then define an instance of the `JTextArea` class. The `JTextArea` constructor requires three arguments. The first argument is of the `String` type. It consists of an expression you want to display in a text area. The second argument, of the `int` type, designates the number of rows of text you want to appear in the text area when it first appears. The third argument, again of the `int` type, designates the number of columns. The text area, then, accommodates 50 columns and 50 rows.

After you create an instance of the `JTextArea` object, you call the `JTextArea::setEditable()` method. This method requires an argument of the `boolean` type. If set to `true`, it allows you to modify the text that appears in the text area. Next, you call the `JTextArea::setLineWrap()` method. This method requires an argument of the `boolean` type. The method makes it so that when the cursor reaches the right margin of the text area (50 columns), it automatically returns to the left margin of the text area. Having defined the `JTextArea` object, you call the `Container::add()` method to add the `JTextArea` object to the content pane.

In the lines trailing comment #5, you are ready to display the window. To display the window, you first call the `setSize()` method. A frame by default in Java has dimensions of 0 height and 0 width, so if you do not set its size, you do not see your window. The first argument designates the width of the frame. The second argument designates the height. Both arguments are of the `int` type. The `JFrame` class inherits this method from the `Container` class.

After establishing the size of the window, you then call the `setVisible()` method. This method makes your window visible. It requires one argument, of the `boolean` type. If you set the argument to `true`, you see the window. If you set it to `false`, even if the window has been instantiated, you do not see it.

At comment #6, you call the `runGeneralTest()` method. The call to this method closes the actions you perform as a part of the `init()` method. In the lines associated with comment #7, you define the `runGeneralTest()` method. Most of the code in this method is the same as the code you see in the `DEInterfaceTest` class, developed earlier in the chapter. In this respect, refer to the discussion of the `DEInterfaceTest` class for details concerning the use of the constructors and calls to methods defined in the `DieselElectric` class.

In the current context, the most important task you perform when you develop the `runGeneralTest()` method involves repeated calls to the `JTextFrame::append()` method. The append() method works in a way that closely resembles the print() or println() method, with the significant difference that it writes to a text area rather than the prompt line shown in a DOS window. As Figure 7.12 shows, by default the font you see in the client area is of a sans serif font type. This font is not of a fixed-width type, as you have seen in the DOS applications developed in previous exercises. Controlling the appearance of the font constitutes but one of many activities you perform when you use objects of the JTextArea class.

At comment #9, you create a main() method. As usual, the main() method is static. It takes the standard String argument and returns void. It contains one statement. The statement involves using the new keyword (or operator) to create an instance of the PolyTestView class. To perform this work, you call the default constructor for the class.

Accommodating Window Closing Events

When you create a window, you start a process. To make it so that your system knows to close down the widow and terminate the process relating to it, you must accommodate the window event the red control "x" (at the upper right up your window) generates. To accomplish this, you implement a method that invokes the System::exit() method. This method forces your system to end the process relating to your window.

Figure 7.10 illustrates the situation that arises when you use the DOS window to invoke the PolyTestView application. When you create an instance of the PolyTestView class, the operating system spawns a process. This process continues to execute until you tell it to stop.

As it stands, unless you specifically tell the process to terminate, it continues to run indefinitely. This situation can create a problem because even after you click the "x" of the PolyTestView Application window bar, you do not automatically terminate the process.

> To replicate the activities shown in Figure 7.10, you must comment out the line immediately following comment #3 of the PolyTestView class.

As Figure 7.10 illustrates, in the Windows Task Manger, you see the java.exe item active when the PolyTestView window is open, and you see the java PolyTestView command displayed in the background DOS window. (To access the Task Manager Process tab, press Alt + Control + Delete and then click the Process tab.) When you click the red control button on the application window to close the window, even though the PolyTest Application vanishes, you still see the java command you have issued in the DOS window, indicating that the process has not ended. It does not terminate until you select it and click the End Process button.

When it terminates, the prompt in the DOS window refreshes, so you see only
C:\JSource\Chapter07>.

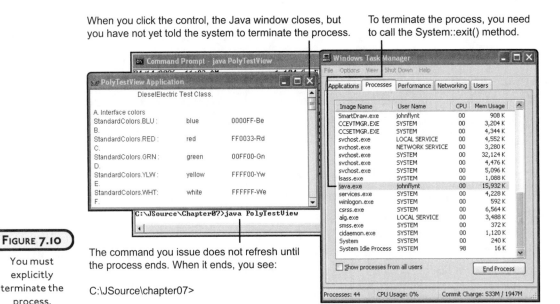

When you click the control, the Java window closes, but
you have not yet told the system to terminate the process.

To terminate the process, you need
to call the System::exit() method.

FIGURE 7.10

You must
explicitly
terminate the
process.

The command you issue does not refresh until
the process ends. When it ends, you see:

C:\JSource\chapter07>

As Figure 7.11 illustrates, to terminate the application process when you click the "x" control, you call the WindowAdapter::windowClosing() method. This method processes the message from the control by invoking the System::exit() method, which has the same effect as clicking the End Process button in the Task Manager.

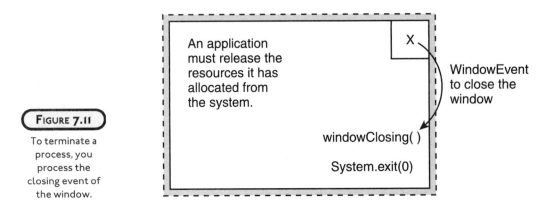

FIGURE 7.11

To terminate a
process, you
process the
closing event of
the window.

You must compose and compile the `WindowCloser` class before you compile your `PolyTestView` class. To create the `WindowCloser` class, you extend the `WindowAdapter` class, which is an abstract class in the Java class hierarchy that provides you with the `windowClosing()` method. The `windowClosing()` method takes one argument, which is of the `WindowEvent` type. When you click the "x" control, the window generates a message of this type.

```
/*
  WindowCloser.java
 */
import java.awt.event.*;

public class WindowCloser extends WindowAdapter{
  //Default constructor
  public WindowCloser(){}
  //Define the WindowAdapter method
  public void windowClosing(WindowEvent wE){
      //Call to the system to exit the application
      System.exit(0);
  }//end
}
```

In the implementation of the `windowClosing()` method, you call the `System.exit()` method. You provide the `exit()` method with an argument of the `int` type. An argument of 0 indicates that the application terminates with normal status. After you implement this method, you can then call it in the `init()` method of the `PolyTestView` class. To call it, you create an instance of the `WindowCloser` class. When you call the constructor, you also call the `windowClosing()` method.

PolyTestView Application	_ □ ✕

DieselElectric Test Class.

```
A. Interface colors
StandardColors.BLU :       blue        0000FF-Be
B.
StandardColors.RED :       red         FF0033-Rd
C.
StandardColors.GRN :       green       00FF00-Gn
D.
StandardColors.YLW :       yellow      FFFF00-Yw
E.
StandardColors.WHT:        white       FFFFFF-We
F.
StandardColors.BLK :       black       000000-Bk
```

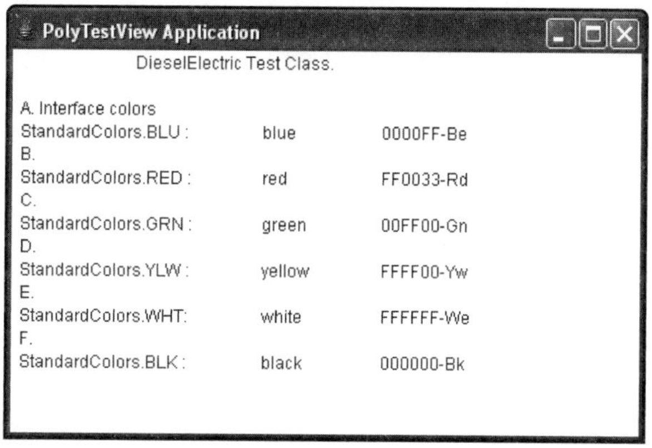

FIGURE 7.12

Together, the `PolyTestView` and `WindowCloser` classes allow you to create an application window that you can terminate without problems.

INNER CLASSES

An inner class is a class you define inside another class. Inner classes allow you to encapsulate functionality you require in the containing (or outer) class. You implement an inner class in the same way you implement any other class. Usually, you declare inner classes as private. In this way, its functionally addresses only the needs of the class that contains it.

The inner class has access to the attributes and methods of the class that contains it. To access the attributes and methods, you call them directly. No object of the outer class is needed. In this respect, an inner class resembles a class method.

You can also implement an inner class within the scope of a method the outer class contains. If you create an inner class within the scope of a method, you can still access the attributes of the containing class. You cannot, however, access variables you create within the scope of the method unless you define them as constants (by using the final keyword).

Explicitly Named Inner Classes

An explicitly named inner class is a class that you define within another class just as you define any other class. You provide it with a name, a constructor, and other class features. Then, in the definition of the outer class, you create a class attribute or a variable using the inner class.

The InnerClassTest class provides you with a setting in which to explore the definition of an explicit inner class. InnerClassTest serves as an outer class. The name of the inner class is InnerClass. Within the inner class you define a public method, showInner(). To use the inner class, you create a constructor for the class that defines a class attribute of the outer class. After creating an instance of the inner class in the outer class, you use the inner class object to access the inner class attribute. The use of the inner class method (showInner()) reveals that you can automatically access the outer class attributes from within the inner class.

```
/*
  InnerClassTest.java
*/
    public class InnerClassTest implements StandardColors{

//#1
    DieselElectric deObjectB;
    DieselElectric deObjectR;
    InnerClass innerObj;

//-------------------InnerClass-------------------------
```

```
        InnerClassTest(){
        //#2 Create instances of the DieselElectric class
            deObjectB = new DieselElectric("DE0001");
            deObjectR = new DieselElectric("DE0002");



        //#3 Create an instance of the inner class
            innerObj = new InnerClass();
            //call the inner class method
            //Call outer method
            showOuter();
            //Call inner method
            innerObj.showInner();
        }
//-----------------showOuter----------------------------
    //#4
        public void showOuter(){
            deObjectB.setExtColor(StandardColors.BLU);
            deObjectR.setExtColor(StandardColors.RED);

            System.out.print("\n\n  A. Outer class  \n");
            System.out.println(" StandardColors.BLU :\t "
                                + deObjectB.getUID() +  "\t"
                                + deObjectB.getExtColor() );
            System.out.print("\n");
            System.out.println(" StandardColors.RED :\t "
                                + deObjectR.getUID() +  "\t"
                                + deObjectR.getExtColor() );

            //Access the attribute in the inner class
            System.out.print("\n\n  B. Call from Outer to Inner \n");
            System.out.println(" StandardColors.RED :\t "
                + innerObj.deObjectW.getUID() +  "\t"
                + innerObj.deObjectW.getExtColor() );
        }
//-----------------main----------------------------
    // #5
    public static void main(String Args[]){
```

```
                new InnerClassTest();
        }//end main
//==================InnerClass======================
        //#6
        private class InnerClass implements StandardColors{
            public DieselElectric deObjectW;

            //Constructor
            InnerClass(){
                deObjectW = new DieselElectric("IC0001");
                deObjectW.setExtColor(StandardColors.WHT);
            }


//------------------ showInner ----------------------------\
        //#7
        public void showInner(){
            //Access the attributes of the outer class
            System.out.print("\n\n  C. Inner Access to Outer \n");
            System.out.println("  StandardColors.BLU :\t "
                            + deObjectB.getUID() +  "\t"
                            + deObjectB.getExtColor() );
            System.out.print("\n");
            System.out.println("  StandardColors.RED :\t "
                            + deObjectR.getUID() +  "\t"
                            + deObjectR.getExtColor() );
            System.out.print("\n\n  D. Inner Access to Inner  \n");
            System.out.print("\n");
            System.out.println("  StandardColors.WHT :\t "
                            + deObjectW.getUID() +  "\t"
                            + deObjectW.getExtColor() );

        }

    }//end InnerClass
//========================================================
}//end outer class
```

In the lines associated with comment #1, you declare three attributes: two of the DieselElectric type (deObjectB and deObjectR) and one of the InnerClass type (innerObj). The InnerClass type receives definition in the InnerClassTest class.

At comment #2, you create the default constructor for the InnerClassTest class. To implement the constructor, you create two instances of the DieselElectric class using the overloaded constructor, which allows you to designate unique identifiers for the objects (DE0001 and DE0002). You assign the instances of the DieselElectric class to the deObjectB and deObjectR attributes.

After creating the instances of the inner and outer class objects, at comment #3 you then call the InnerClassTest::showOuter() method. Following that, you employ the innerObj class attribute to call the InnerClass::showInner() method.

In the lines associated with comment #4, you define the InnerClassTest::showOuter() method. Definition of this method involves calling the getUID() and getExtColor() methods of the DieselElectric class. As Figure 7.13 shows, when you invoke these methods, you see the unique identifiers and color codes for the two InnerClassTest attributes.

The third set of calls within the showOuter() method proves the most important in this context because you use the InnerClassTest::innerObj attribute to call the deObjectW class attribute of the InnerClass class. As discussion of the implementation of the class notes, you declare this attribute as public. You can then directly access the attribute of the inner class by using an object of the inner class type to identify the attribute. Given access to the attribute, you can then call the methods (such as getUID()) that its class provides:

```
innerObj.deObjectW.getUID() //access inner class attributes
```

Following the definition of the showOuter() method, you define the main() method for the InnerClassTest class. To create an instance of the class when you execute the class, you create a statement that involves the use of the new operator and the default class constructor. The effect of this statement is to create the instance of the class that you see displayed at the monitor.

In the lines accompanying comment #6, you define the inner class (InnerClass). To define the inner class, you employ the implements keyword to access the color values defined in the StandardColors interface. You then declare a class attribute (deObjectW) of the DieselElectric type. Following the declaration of the attribute, you create the InnerClass default constructor. In the body of the constructor, you initialize the deObjectW attribute and then call the setExtColor() method to set its color. As an argument to the setExtColor() method, you employ the StandardColors.WHT attribute, which you obtain from the StandardColors interface.

In the lines trailing comment #7, you define the showInner() method. When you define this method, you use some of the same method calls you used in the showOuter() method. Specifically, you call the getUID() and getExtColor() methods of the DieselElectric class. You also directly access the deObjectW attribute from the inner class, as expected. However, you also directly access the deObjectB and deObjectR attributes from the outer class. From within the inner class, you can directly access the private attributes of the outer class.

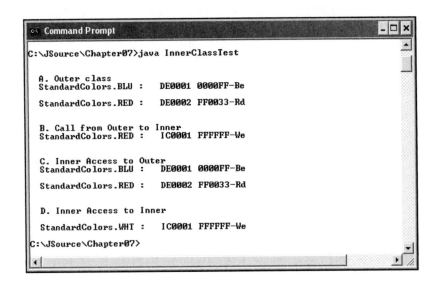

FIGURE 7.13

The inner class can access attributes of the outer class.

When you compile a class that contains an inner class, you see the usual *.class file in your directory, but you also see another *.class file that contains the byte code for the inner class. You see the following files:

```
InnerClassTest$InnerClass.class
InnerClassTest.class
```

A dollar sign indicates that the inner class (InnerClass) is compiled as a part of the outer (InnerClassTest) class. Both class files remain necessary.

As you see in the next section, if you use an anonymous inner class, then you see a dollar sign followed by a number:

```
PolyTestViewIAC$1.class
```

Inner Anonymous and Final Classes

As has already been discussed, when you exit a window, you must call the System.exit() method to perform cleanup. When you click the close control on a Java window, a WindowEvent message is issued. In the earlier example, you implemented a WindowCloser class to process this message.

Another approach—one that does not involve creating a separate class—allows you to create an inner anonymous class. You can create such a class within the scope of the main() method. In the PolyTestViewIAC class, to implement an inner anonymous class, you work wholly within the main() method. You create an instance of the PolyTestViewIAC class and then use the resulting object to call the addWindowListener() method.

As an argument to this method (see comment #2 in the PolyTestViewIAC class), you define the WindowAdapter class. To define the class, you define its default constructor. Definition of the constructor involves defining, in turn, the windowClosing() method so that it invokes the System.exit() method.

Another feature of the PolyTestViewIAC class is that it is a final class. This feature is added purely for the sake of demonstration. However, such classes can prove of importance in contexts in which you want to prevent users of a class system from extending a class. The final keyword applied to a class definition prevents the class from being extended through derivation.

```java
/*
  PolyTestViewIAC.java
 */
import javax.swing.*;
import java.awt.*;
import java.awt.event.*;
//#1
public final class PolyTestViewIAC extends JFrame
                                    implements StandardColors{
// Class attributes for GUI
   JTextArea frameTextArea;
   Container frameContainer;
//----------------------PolyTestView----------------------------
// Default constructor
   public PolyTestViewIAC() {
      super("Using an Inner Anonymous Class ");
      //Call the primary method of the application
```

```
      init();
    }
//------------------------------init------------------------------
    public void init(){
      // JFrame method to close the window
      // Define GUI components
      frameContainer = getContentPane();
      frameTextArea = new JTextArea("\tDieselElectric Objects.", 100, 10);
      frameTextArea.setEditable(true);
      frameTextArea.setLineWrap(true);
      frameContainer.add(frameContainer);
      //Set window size and make the window visible
      setSize(520, 300);
      setVisible(true);
      // Call the testing method
      runGeneralTest();
    }
//------------------------runGeneralTest----------------------
    public void runGeneralTest(){
      DieselElectric deObjectB = new DieselElectric("DE0001");
      DieselElectric deObjectR = new DieselElectric("DE0002");
      deObjectB.setExtColor(StandardColors.BLU);
      deObjectR.setExtColor(StandardColors.RED);
      frameTextArea.append("\n\n   A. Interface colors  \n");
      frameTextArea.append("  StandardColors.BLU :\t "
                      + StandardColors.BLU  +  "\t"
                      + deObjectB.getExtColor() );
      frameTextArea.append("\n  B.  \n");
      frameTextArea.append("  StandardColors.RED :\t "
                      + StandardColors.RED  +  "\t"
                      + deObjectR.getExtColor() );
    }
//------------------------main------------------------
    public static void main(String args[])
    {
//#2 Create an instance of the class
      PolyTestViewIAC ptView = new PolyTestViewIAC();
      //#3 Use class instance to call the window listener
```

```
    ptView.addWindowListener(
        new WindowAdapter(){
            public void windowClosing(WindowEvent e){
                System.exit(0);
            }//end windowClosing method definition
        }//end WindowAdapter class definition
    ); // end of call to addWindowListener
  }//end main
}//end class
```

At comment #1, at the beginning of the class definition, you use the `final` keyword to prevent the `PolyTestView` class from being extended. In this context, use of the term has no implications. The keyword is used only to demonstrate its use.

All of the important work you perform in relation to the `PolyTestViewIAC` class occurs within the scope of the `main()` method beginning at comment #2. There, you create an instance of the `PolyTestViewIAC` class using a call to the default constructor of the class. You assign this instance of the class to the `ptView` variable. Then, at comment #3, you use this variable to call the `addWindowListener()` method.

As an argument to the `addWindowListener()` method, you create an inner anonymous class. As explained previously, to create the class, you call the constructor for the `WindowAdapter` class and in effect overload it to define the `windowClosing()` method so that it calls to the `System.exit()` method. Figure 7.14 illustrates the application as it executes. Clicking the close control invokes the window event handler and allows the application to terminate correctly.

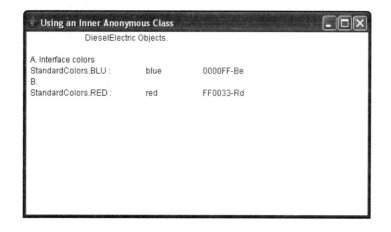

FIGURE 7.14

The `windowClosing()` method terminates the process.

SUMMARY

In this chapter, you have explored abstract classes and interfaces. The use of abstract classes allows you to control access to the classes in a class hierarchy. Using abstract classes, for example, you can guide users to implement specific methods. You can also control how users access classes within a given hierarchy, ensuring that the classes higher in the hierarchy remain unmodified. An interface is a class that contains only abstract methods or consists of a set of constants. The `implements` keyword allows you to add to the functionality of your classes after you have used the `extends` keyword to access primary functionality from an abstract class. The `extends` keyword allows you to access only one class. The `implements` keyword allows you to access multiple classes. Using the `extends` keyword in conjunction with the `implements` keyword allows you to make use of the GUI classes in the Java class hierarchy. The next chapter offers much more on this topic.

CHALLENGES

1. In the definition of the `Economy` class given in this chapter, implement the `StandardColors` class so that you do not have to use literal string values in the definition of the `ChildCare::setExtColor()` method. In the end, then, you can use `StandardColors.BLU` in place of "blue" in the `equalsIgnoreCase()` method. Revise the `setExtColor()` method for all the colors.

2. Revise the `setExtColor()` methods in the `DieselElectric` and `GasElectric` classes to incorporate the `StandardColors` interface values. Run the test driver to test your changes.

3. In the `InnerClassTest` class, for `InnerClass`, add an additional attribute of the `GasElectric` type. Set the value of this attribute in the `InnerClass` constructor. Then create an access method, `getInnerValues(string ct)`, in which you return the information on the car and its color based on whether the user enters `ge` or `de` as an argument. Call this method in the outer class.

4. Skip ahead to Chapter 9. View Figure 9.2. The circle with a plus sign in it represents an inner class. Draw a rough diagram to show that `InnerClass` is an inner class in `InnerTestClass`.

GRAPHICAL USER
INTERFACE ACTIVITIES

This chapter allows you to move forward from the work you began in Chapter 7 and explore a number of new graphical user interface (GUI) classes. When referring to the classes you employ to develop GUI features, Java programmers often use the term *component*. A label, a frame, or a text field, for example, are GUI components. To explore how to work with GUI components, you can begin in the context of a complete application and then work into details from there. What this implies in practical terms is that you work from the JFrame class you developed in the last chapter and then add details to it, such as a menu, a status bar, and various dialogs. In short, you develop the features of an application that resemble those of almost any Windows application. Among the topics you investigate are the following:

- Sizing and positioning a window
- Creating a menu for a window and adding items to the menu
- Processing menu events
- Implementing labels and dialogs
- Setting the look-and-feel of your application
- Positioning your window on the desktop

SETTING UP A WINDOW

In this chapter, you work with the LabView class through several iterations. To identify the different versions, a directory designation precedes each of the class names. The first iteration, for example, is named LabViewA.Labview. The directory designation possesses no significance other than as a way to help you identify the classes in this book. In the folders that contain the classes, the classes all have the same name. To compile and run each file, access the directory that contains it and issue the standard javac and java commands (javac LabView.java and java LabView). If the classes require supplementary classes, then you must compile the supplementary classes first.

For each iteration, you access the file from a different folder, and the folder names differ only by one letter each. The first iteration of the LabView class file appears in the LabViewA folder. The second appears in the LabViewB folder. Figure 8.1 illustrates the window that you create when you implement the LabViewA.LabView class.

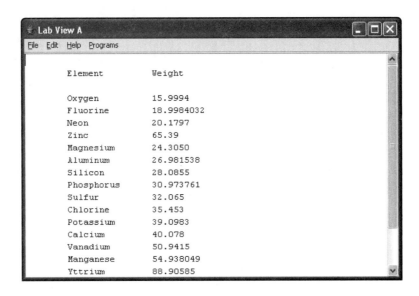

FIGURE 8.1

Several primary activities combine to create a window for a Windows XP system.

LAB VIEW A

This chapter provides two versions of the LabView application. The first is in the LabViewA folder in the source code. The second is in the LabViewB folder in the source code. Figure 8.1 illustrates the first version after you have completely implemented its functionality. Sections that follow provide detailed discussions of the activities you engage in as you implement this functionality. As you go, you encounter the following topics:

- **Specializing the** `JFrame` **class**. Toward this end, you create a `Container` object to store a reference to the content pane of the frame. The content pane allows you to place GUI components in the frame. To accommodate a component for a text area, you create a `JScrollPane` and assign a `JTextArea` object to it. When you use a `JScrollPane` object to hold a `JTextArea` object, as Figure 8.1 illustrates, you automatically generate a scrollbar that allows you to scroll the text area.

- **Using a layout manager**. Java makes several types of layout managers available to you. In this instance, you use a `BorderLayout` object as a layout manager. To use the `BorderLayout` layout manager, you use one of the constant attributes defined in the `BorderLayout` class (`CENTER`). The value of this attribute allows you to assign the `JScrollPane` and `JTextArea` objects to the center of the frame. Likewise, when you resize the frame, the text area and scrollbar automatically resize along with the frame.

- **Creating a main menu for your application**. You do not yet add event processing capabilities to the menu, but the menu is still operational so that you can see the menu items. To add a menu, you use three types of GUI components. The first is a menu bar (`JMenuBar`), the second is a menu (`JMenu`), and the third is a menu item (`JMenuItem`). You supplement these menu features with mnemonic shortcuts. As a result, when you press the Alt key in combination with the mnemonics, you can navigate to a menu item and invoke the action you associate with it.

- **Implementing pluggable look-and-feel**. The `UIManager` class allows you to detect the platform on which your application executes and automatically change its appearance so that it conforms to user interface features that characterize the platform. If you flip to the previous chapter and compare Figure 7.14 with Figure 8.1, you can see how the `UIManager` accommodates the Windows XP platform. The window in Figure 7.14 possesses no `UIManager`. It uses default user interface features. Such features include rounded corners. In Figure 8.1, the window is defined using the `UIManager` class definitions for Windows. As a result, you see sharper corners and a less metallic look. These are characteristic of the look-and-feel of Windows. Below is the listing for the implementation of the `LabViewA.LabView` class. Subsequent sections discuss specific aspects of the implementation.

- **Working with character data**. You examine the use of the Java Patterns package to create regular expressions.

```
/*
package Chapter08.LabViewA.LabView;
*/
import javax.swing.*;
import java.awt.*;
```

```java
import java.awt.event.*;
import java.util.*;

public class LabView extends JFrame{

    //#1
    private JTextArea frameTextArea;          //create a text area
    private Container frameContainer;         //for the content pane
    private JScrollPane scrollForTextArea;    //scrollbar
    private BorderLayout frameLayout;         //default
    final int width = 640, height = 480;      //Standard size


    //#2
    private JMenuBar bar;
    private JMenu fileMenu, editMenu, helpMenu, programMenu;
    private JMenuItem saveText, closeApp, clearText,
                      aboutThisApp,
                      programA,
                      programB,
                      programC;

    //#3
    public LabView(String title){
        //Call to JFrame constructor
        super(title);
        //Call initialization
        init();
    }

    public void init(){
    //#4
        //Use the WindowCloser Class
        addWindowListener(new WindowCloser());
    //#5
        //Set up the Window for the operating system
        setLookAndFeel();
```

```
//#6
    //Get the content pane
    frameContainer = getContentPane();
    //Create an instance of a JTextArea
    frameTextArea = new JTextArea("\n\tElement\t\tWeight\n",
                                  18, 70);
    //Configure the JTextArea
    frameTextArea.setEditable(false);
    frameTextArea.setLineWrap(true);

    //Set the text area in the scroll pane
    scrollForTextArea = new JScrollPane(frameTextArea);

//#7
    //Create an instance of a border layout
    frameLayout = new BorderLayout();
    frameContainer.setLayout(frameLayout);

    //Add the scroll pane to the center of the layout
    frameContainer.add(scrollForTextArea, BorderLayout.CENTER);

    //Size the JFrame and set it to visible
    setVisible(true);
    setSize(height, width);

//#8 Add a menu
    makeMenu();

//#9
    //This will provide both
    //If the lineWrap() method is false
    pack();
    showElements();
}


//-----------------------setLookAndFeel()---------------------
    //#5.1
    public void setLookAndFeel(){
```

```java
    try{
        String lookAndFeel = UIManager.getSystemLookAndFeelClassName();
        UIManager.setLookAndFeel(lookAndFeel);
    }
    catch(Exception lFE){
      //process exception
    }
  }

//8.1------------------------makeMenu()-----------------------
  public void makeMenu(){
      //Create a menu bar
      bar = new JMenuBar();

      //create File menu
      fileMenu = new JMenu("File");
      fileMenu.setMnemonic('F');
        //With menu items
        saveText = new JMenuItem("Save");
        saveText.setMnemonic('S');

        closeApp = new JMenuItem("Close");
        closeApp.setMnemonic('C');

        //Add the File items to File menu
        fileMenu.add(saveText);
        fileMenu.add(closeApp);

      //create Edit menu
      editMenu = new JMenu("Edit");
      editMenu.setMnemonic('E');
        //With menu items
        clearText = new JMenuItem("Clear Text");
        clearText.setMnemonic('X');
        //Add the Edit items to the Edit menu
          editMenu.add(clearText);
```

```
        //create Help menu
        helpMenu = new JMenu("Help");
        helpMenu.setMnemonic('H');
            //With menu items
            aboutThisApp = new JMenuItem("About...");
            aboutThisApp.setMnemonic('A');
            //Add the Help items to the Help menu
            helpMenu.add(aboutThisApp);

        //create Programs menu
        programMenu = new JMenu("Programs");
        programMenu.setMnemonic('P');

            //With menu items
            programA = new JMenuItem("Program A");
            programB = new JMenuItem("Program B");
            programC = new JMenuItem("Program C");

            //Add the Programs menu items to Programs menu
            programMenu.add(programA);
            programMenu.add(programB);
            programMenu.add(programC);

        //Add File, Edit, Help, and Programs to bar
        bar.add(fileMenu);
        bar.add(editMenu);
        bar.add(helpMenu);
        bar.add(programMenu);

        //Add the menu bar to the content pane
        setJMenuBar(bar);
    }//end makeMenu

//#9.1--------------------showElements()------------------
    public void showElements(){
        //Create a string
        String elementsAtomicMass =
                    "Oxygen    , 15.9994 , Fluorine  , 18.9984032, " +
```

```
                "Neon      , 20.1797 , Zinc       , 65.39      , " +
                "Magnesium, 24.3050 , Aluminum   , 26.981538 , " +
                "Silicon   , 28.0855 , Phosphorus, 30.973761 , " +
                "Sulfur    , 32.065  , Chlorine   , 35.453     , " +
                "Potassium, 39.0983 , Calcium    , 40.078     , " +
                "Vanadium , 50.9415 , Manganese , 54.938049 , " +
                "Yttrium   , 88.90585, Germanium , 72.64      , " +
                "Barium    , 137.327 , Bismuth    , 208.98038 , " +
                "Calcium   , 40.078  , ";
      //Split the string into array elements
      String elementsAndMass[]  = elementsAtomicMass.split(",\\s");


      //Increment by 2s to see both columns
      //Subtract 1 to allow counting by 2s
      for(int cntr = 0; cntr < elementsAndMass.length - 1; cntr += 2){
         frameTextArea.append("\n\t");
         frameTextArea.append(elementsAndMass[cntr]
                          + "\t"
                          + elementsAndMass[cntr+1]
                          );
      }
   }


//#3.1-----------------------main()--------------------------------
   public static void main(String args[]){
      new LabView("Lab View A");
   }
}
```

The sections that follow examine specific features of the implementation of the LabViewA version of the LabView class. The discussion unfolds according to the topic discussed rather than the order in which you encounter features as you read the code.

Layout Management

Following comment #1, you create a Container class object, frameContainer. In addition, you create an attribute of the BorderLayout and JScrollPane types (frameLayout and scrollForTextArea). In conjunction with the JTextArea object (frameTextArea), these objects allow you to provide your window with a text area and position the text area in the center of the window. The significance of this activity becomes evident if you click the corner or edge of the window and resize it as illustrated in Figure 8.2.

Equal distribution of the text area

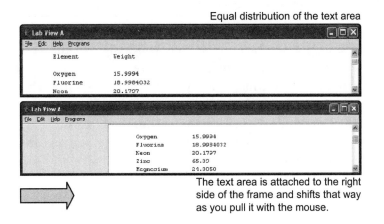

The text area is attached to the right side of the frame and shifts that way as you pull it with the mouse.

FIGURE 8.2

Layout management allows you to determine what happens when you resize your frame.

As Figure 8.2 illustrates, you can use the layout manager to restrict the movement of the text area and scroll pane so that they draw to the right when you pull your window to the right. The top window is defined using the CENTER attribute of the BorderLayout class, so that as you resize the frame, the text area expands proportionally. The lower window is defined using the EAST attribute of the BorderLayout class, and as a result, the text area remains attached to the right (EAST) side of the frame as you resize the window.

When you use the CENTER attribute, regardless of how you resize the frame, the text area and scroll pane resize with it. The combination of the layout manager, the scroll pane, and the text area creates this behavior.

If you want to re-create the changes shown in Figure 8.2, find the following line in the LabView class.

```
//Add the scroll pane to the center of the layout
frameContainer.add(scrollForTextArea, BorderLayout.CENTER);
```

Then change the line as follows:

```
//Add the scroll pane to the center of the layout
frameContainer.add(scrollForTextArea, BorderLayout.EAST);
```

After recompiling the program, pull the window to the right, as shown.

The code you use to implement this functionality begins at comment #6 of the LabViewA.LabView class. There, you call the getContentPane() method to retrieve a reference to the content pane for your frame. You assign this reference to the frameContainer attribute, which is of the Content type.

You then create an instance of the JTextArea class that you assign to the frameTextArea attribute. To format the heading for the data you see in Figure 8.1, you create a string that incorporates newline and tab characters, which allow you to set up two column headings for a selection of chemical elements and their masses. You also call the JTextArea::setEditable() and JTextArea::setLineWriap() methods. The setEditable() method takes one argument. If set to the boolean true, you can change data in the edit area. If set to false, you cannot. In this case, to render the data for display only, you set the argument to false.

To attach your text area to a scroll pane, you use the JScrollPane constructor. As an argument to the constructor, you provide the frameTextArea attribute. In this way, the scroll pane becomes a wrapper component for the JTextArea component. You assign the result to the scrollForTextArea attribute, which is of the JScrollPane type.

In the lines trailing comment #7, you create an instance of the BorderLayout class. The BorderLayout class manages the area in the content pane so that it is divided into five sections, as Figure 8.3 illustrates.

To associate the BorderLayout object with the Container object, you call the setLayout() method. This method takes a layout manager as an argument. It then applies the designated layout manager to the Container object. As an argument for the setLayout() method, you submit the frameLayout attribute.

After associating the layout manager with the content pane, you then call the Container::add() method. Java offers several overloaded versions of the Container::add() method. For this version of the add() method, you use two arguments. The first designates an object of the Container type. You use the scrollForTextArea attribute.

The second argument of this version of the add() method is of the Object type and can be any of a number of layout management values. In this case, you use the BorderLayout.CENTER constraint, which forces the layout manager to position the scroll pane in the center of the content pane area.

As shown in Figure 8.3, the BorderLayout constraint values available to you consist of NORTH, SOUTH, EAST, WEST, and CENTER. The lower frame of Figure 8.3 shows the results of using the BorderLayout.EAST constraint, which attaches the scroll pane to the right border of the frame. To experiment with the layout manager, change the values and resize the window after recompiling. Except for the CENTER constraint, in each instance, the scroll pane and its associated text area adhere to one or another border of the frame.

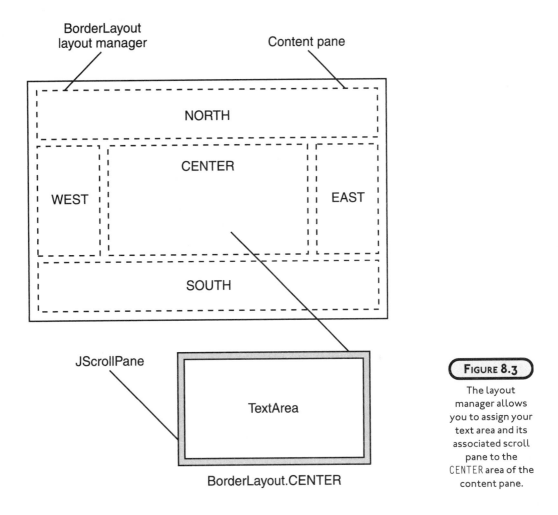

FIGURE 8.3

The layout manager allows you to assign your text area and its associated scroll pane to the CENTER area of the content pane.

As the discussion in Chapter 7 detailed, you call the setVisible() method to make the entire frame visible. You likewise call the setSize() method to establish the height and width of the frame. At comment #9, you call the Window::pack() method, which has the effect of pulling the text area, container, and JFrame object together so that they appear as a snug unit.

Other Layout Managers

The BorderLayout class is one of several layout manager classes that Java provides. Table 8.1 discusses a few of the layout managers. As examples in this and subsequent chapters

TABLE 8.1   LAYOUT MANAGERS

Manager Name	Discussion
CardLayout	Allows you to set up components as cards of equal sizes. You can stack the cards as you do a deck of cards and then flip through them. You see one card at a time.
GridBagLayout	Allows you to set up components according to the cells of a grid. You define the dimensions of the grid. The components line up in the grid, but you can define the layout so that a given item can occupy more than one cell.
GridLayout	In some ways, this layout manager provides features that resemble those of the GridBagLayout manager. However, the uses you can make of it are much more restricted. This layout manager allows you to assign components to grid cells of equal size. One component appears in each cell, and when you resize the container, the cell and the component are also resized.
BoxLayout	Allows you to arrange components (buttons or fields, for example) either horizontally or vertically. The manager proves valuable when used with other managers. Since it constrains all the components in it so that they are the same size, you can use it to uniformly define sets of fields or buttons.
FlowLayout	Allows you to arrange components so that as you add them to a container, they appear left-to-right and top-to-bottom, just as if you were typing characters into a text area.

show, you often use the layout managers in combinations (or layers). For example, you can use the BoxLayout manager inside the BorderLayout manager to create five areas in which you stack fields or buttons (covered in subsequent sections) on top of each other. To accomplish such tasks, you make use of the JPanel class, which is derived from the Container class.

Layout managers are not visible to you. They serve to organize the items you place in your frames. They regulate the proximity and size of components. To use them, you add them to a Container (or JPanel) object, but at the same time, they allow you to place such objects inside of each other. By layering objects in this way, you are able to construct complex interfaces.

Table 8.1 provides a summary of the primary layout manager classes. Each class possesses associated attributes and methods, and in some cases, as with the GridBagLayout class, setting up the manager requires extensive work. In addition, as mentioned before, you often use them in association with each other, in which case incorporating panels into your work becomes necessary.

Pluggable Look-and-Feel

At comment #5 in the `LabViewA.LabView` class definition, you call the `setLookAndFeel()` method, which you define in the lines trailing comment #5.1. To set the look-and-feel of the `LabView` application, you call the `UIManager::getSystemLookAndFeelClassName()` method. This method returns a string value that identifies the platform on which your application executes. You assign this value the `lookAndFeel` variable you define within the scope of the `setLookAndFeel()` method. You then supply the `lookAndFeel` variable as an argument to the `setLookAndFeel()` method, which is defined so that it automatically adjusts the components of your application so that they incorporate the appropriate platform features.

Java developers refer to the fact that you can change the appearance of your application to accord with the platform on which it executes as a pluggable look-and-feel GUI feature. The two main platforms addressed are those based on Microsoft Windows and UNIX/LINUX Motif. The `LookAndFeelTest` class offers a way that you can retrieve the current platforms supported by Java. Figure 8.4 shows you the output.

```
/*
    LookAndFeelTest.java
*/
import javax.swing.*;
import java.awt.*;
import java.awt.event.*;

public class LookAndFeelTest{
    public static void main(String Args[]){
            UIManager.LookAndFeelInfo[] platform =
                UIManager.getInstalledLookAndFeels();
        for(int cntrl = 0; cntrl < platform.length; cntrl++){
            System.out.println("\n    " + platform[cntrl].getClassName());
        }
    }//end main
}
```

You can use the strings Figure 8.4 provides to set your application to have a specific appearance regardless of the platform on which it is running. You can use the entire string or just the last item.

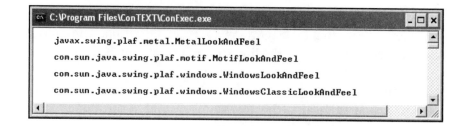

FIGURE 8.4

You can view and
specifically
implement any of
the default look-
and-feel values.

As an example, you can use `MetalLookAndFeel` to set your window as follows:

```
UIManager.setLookAndFeel("MetalLookAndFeel");
```

When you change platforms, your application performs in slightly different ways, reflecting the differences of platform. It remains, however, that Sun guarantees that the primary functionality remains portable.

Adding Menu Features

The content pane of your `JFrame` object can automatically accommodate a menu. When you add the menu, it locks to the top of the content pane. Formatting elements that you introduce in addition to the menu do not obscure the menu. As Figure 8.5 illustrates, to create a menu, you begin with a `JMenuBar` object. To the `JMenuBar`, you add `JMenu` objects. You then add `JMenuItem` objects to each of the `JMenu` objects.

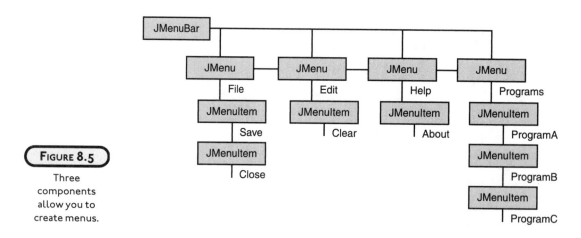

FIGURE 8.5

Three
components
allow you to
create menus.

At comment #8 of the `LabViewA.Labview` class, you call the `makeMenu()` method, which you define in lines trailing comment #8.1. The first menu component you define is the `JMenuBar` object. You call the default `JMenuBar` constructor and assign the object to the `bar` attribute.

Having created the JMenuBar object, you add JMenu objects to it, but before you can add the JMenu objects, you must fully implement them. To fully implement them, you must add JMenuItem components to them, fully defining them.

To create the first of four main menu items, the File menu, you call the JMenu constructor. This constructor takes one argument, of the String type. You provide a literal string, "File". You assign the resulting object to the fileMenu attribute.

Immediately following the creation of the fileMenu object, you call the setMnemonic() method and provide it with an argument of the char type. You place the letter in single quotes ('F') to define it as an argument of the char type.

When they create mnemonics for menus, programmers usually employ a standard set of letters. Among these standard letters are "F," which designates "File," "S," which designates "Save," and "E," which designates "Edit."

When you designate a mnemonic for menus or a menu item, Java automatically underlines the letter you have designated. You can use the same letter for both the menu and the menu item. If you employ the same letters for two menus, then a conflict occurs.

To create menu items to add to the fileMenu attribute, you call the JMenuItem constructor. For the File menu, you create Save and Close menu items. To create the Save option, you provide the literal string "Save" to the JMenuItem constructor and assign the instance of JMenuItem that results to the saveText attribute. To create the Close option, you provide the literal string "Close" to the JMenuItem constructor and assign the resulting instance to the closeApp attribute.

As with the File menu object, you call the setMnemonic() method to automate access to the menu items through the Alt key. For the Save menu item, you supply the character "S." For the Exit menu item, you provide the character "C."

To add JMenuItem objects to JMenu objects, you call the JMenu::add() method. For the File menu, you employ the fileMenu attribute to call the add() method. The add() method requires one argument, of a Component type. All the menu components are derived from the Component class, so for the File menu you provide the saveText and closeApp attributes as arguments. The Save and Close menu items in this way become affiliated with the File menu.

You use the same approach to creating the Edit, Help, and Programs menus (refer to Figure 8.5). To each you assign one or more JMenuItem objects. When you have completely configured all the menus, you can then call the JMenuBar::add() method to add them to the menu bar. You perform these operations in the lines just preceding the closing parentheses of the makeMenu() method. Having added each menu to the bar, you then call the

`JFrame::setJMenuBar()` method, which adds the menu bar to the container for your frame. Here are the lines:

```
//Add File, Edit, Help, and Programs to bar
bar.add(fileMenu);
bar.add(editMenu);
bar.add(helpMenu);
bar.add(programMenu);

//Add the menu bar to the content pane
setJMenuBar(bar);
```

THE MAIN MENU AND SDI

The `LabView` window provides an example of a *single document interface* (SDI). The main menu of an SDI application allows you to close the application. It also allows you to work only one general task at a time. Windows Notepad provides an example of an SDI application. As Figure 8.6 illustrates, you work within a client area with one document at a time. You open or create a document in this area. When you finish working with the document, you close the document you are working with. You can then open another document and begin working with that. The focus of the application consists of one document only.

Microsoft Word provides an example of a *multiple document interface* (MDI). The main menu of an MDI application allows you to close the application, as with an SDI application. However, it also allows you to work with many tasks at one time. In this respect, when you use Microsoft Word, you can open several documents at once and have them visible in the client area. Each document you make active becomes active relative to the main menu of the application. The menu still defines the tasks that the application allows you to perform, but as you work, you are not restricted to one target document at a time.

Developing an MDI application lies beyond the scope of this book, but it remains that a substantial number of applications fall into this category. On the other hand, a substantial number of applications are also of the SDI type. The `JFrame` object can serve as the basis of an SDI application. The `LabView` application is such an application because all its actions either allow you to invoke dialogs (a topic introduced later in this chapter) or invoke methods that relate primarily to a single focus activity.

Whether you work with an MDI or SDI application, the `JMenu` class provides one of the primary interface components.

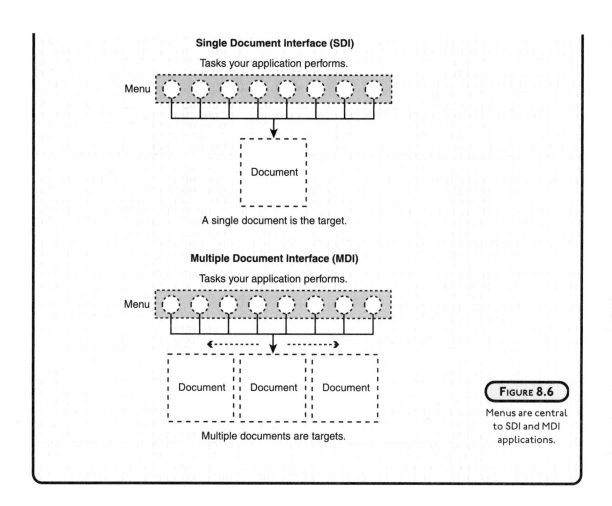

Single Document Interface (SDI)

Tasks your application performs.

Menu

Document

A single document is the target.

Multiple Document Interface (MDI)

Tasks your application performs.

Menu

Document Document Document

Multiple documents are targets.

FIGURE 8.6

Menus are central to SDI and MDI applications.

Arrays and Patterns

At comment #9, following a call to the Window::pack() method, you call the showElements() method. You define this method in the lines accompanying comment #9.1. Definition of the method involves creating a String variable (elementsAtomicMass) that contains a series of chemical elements and their atomic masses. You employ a comma followed by a space to separate each element or weight in the string from the next element or weight. After creating the string variable, you then use the String::split() method to divide the items the string contains into the elements of an array.

The String class provides overloaded versions of the split() method. For the argument of the split() method as shown in the lines trailing comment #9.1, you employ a *regular expression*. A regular expression creates a pattern. In this case, you create a pattern that consists of a comma followed by a white space. The double slashes (\\) preceding the "s" allow you to create an escape sequence. The escape sequence is \s and tells the compiler to look for any white space character. To get the compiler to recognize that you are employing an escape sequence, you must precede the slash that marks the escape sequence with a slash.

Regular expressions for Java are provided by the `java.util.regex.Pattern` package. Another overloaded version of the `split()` method allows you to use a string expression alone. The equivalent of the regular expression is a comma followed by a literal white space (", "). Another method that uses regular expressions is the `String::matches()` method.

The spaces you see in the string you assign to the `elementsAtomicMass` variable enable you to create array elements of uniform length. The `split()` method searches only for a pattern that consists of a comma and a white space. For this reason, it allows any number of white spaces to be included in the strings that it stores in the array. Here is how you set up the items to place in the array:

```
"Oxygen    , 15.9994 , Fluorine  , 18.9984032, " +
"Neon      , 20.1797 , Zinc      , 65.39      , " +
"Magnesium, 24.3050 , Aluminum   , 26.981538 , " +
```

In each case, the `split()` function preserves the number of characters that exist between the comma-space dividers.

You employ a `for` repetition statement to set up a block in which you iterate through the `elementsAndMass` array in increments of 2. To control the repetition block, you use the `length` attribute of the `elementsAndMass` array to retrieve the number of items in the array. You then subtract 1 from the length of the array to prevent the control from exceeding the length of the array.

Incrementing by 2 allows you to retrieve each element name and element mass from the `elementsAndMass` array and display them in rows of a table. To achieve the aligned columns you see in Figure 8.1, you employ tabs. Since the lengths of the `String` elements you retrieve from the array are uniform, the columns are even.

LAB VIEW B

In the second version of the `LabView` class (`LabViewB.LabView`), you add many features. Among these features are the following:

- **Event handling**. You create event handlers by implementing the `ActionListener` interface, which requires you to define the `ActionListener::actionPerformed()` method.

- **Built-in dialog boxes**. You use three versions of the `JOptionPane` dialogs. These allow you to check whether the user wants to exit the application, provide information on the application, or interact.

- **Java `Toolkit` functionality**. By accessing information on your monitor, you can center the Lab View window on your desktop.

- **Method invocation through menus**. You develop a method that allows you to invoke a selected type of functionality from among a set of functionalities. Among these is a display of the data from the Periodic Table of Elements.

- **Review of `String` and `Number` objects**. One method allows you to enter information in a dialog and see the processing output in the client area.

- **Use of a `JLabel` object**. You use the `JLabel` object as a status bar. You assign it to the `SOUTH` area the `BorderLayout` layout manager furnishes. The status bar then displays information about the menu items as you invoke them.

The sections that follow deal with each of these topics. Due to the complexity of the code, it is necessary, as in previous sections, to jump to different areas of the class to view the features relevant to each topic. Figure 8.7 provides a view of the Lab View B application after you have involved the Add Numbers menu item of the Programs menu. This option allows you to enter numbers in a dialog and see them repeatedly summed and rendered to the client area.

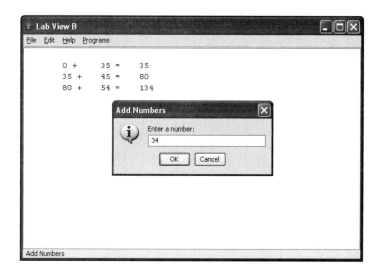

FIGURE 8.7

Lab View B
provides active
menus and many
other features.

The numbering in this version of the `LabViewB.LabView` class definition differs from the previous version. Only features dealt with in the sections have numbers assigned to them. For information on the features not identified with numbers, see the sections under the discussion provided for Lab View A. Here is the code for LabViewB:

```java
/*
 Chapter08.LabViewB.LabView;
*/

import javax.swing.*;
import java.awt.*;
import java.awt.event.*;
import java.util.*;

//#1 Implement event processing
public class LabView extends JFrame implements ActionListener{
    private JTextArea frameTextArea;          //create a text area
    private Container frameContainer;          //for the content pane
    private JScrollPane scrollForTextArea;     //scroll bar
    private BorderLayout frameLayout;          //default
    final int width = 640, height = 480;       //Standard size

//#2 New attributes for data processing
    // and status bar
    private JLabel statusBar;
    private int addedNumber;

    private JMenuBar bar;
    private JMenu fileMenu, editMenu, helpMenu, programMenu;
    private JMenuItem saveText, closeApp, clearText,
                      aboutThisApp,
                      programA,
                      programB,
                      programC;
    // Constructor
    public LabView(String title){
        //Call to JFrame constructor
        super(title);
        //Call initialization
        init();
```

```
    }

  public void init(){
    //Use the WindowCloser Class
    addWindowListener(new WindowCloser(this));
    //Set up the Window for the operating system
    setLookAndFeel();

    //Get the content pane
    frameContainer = getContentPane();
    //Create an instance ofa JTextArea
    frameTextArea = new JTextArea("",
                                  18, 70);
    frameTextArea.setEditable(true);
    frameTextArea.setLineWrap(true);
    //Set the text area in the scroll pane
    scrollForTextArea = new JScrollPane(frameTextArea);

    //Create an instance of a border layout
    frameLayout = new BorderLayout();
    frameContainer.setLayout(frameLayout);

//#3 Add the status bar (JLabel)
    frameContainer.add(scrollForTextArea, BorderLayout.CENTER);
    //create a label to use as a status bar
    statusBar = new JLabel(" ");
    frameContainer.add(statusBar, BorderLayout.SOUTH);

    setSize(height, width);
    makeMenu();
//#4 Position the window in the center of the desktop
    positionWindow();
    pack();
    setVisible(true);
  }


//--------------------------setLookAndFeel()---------------------
  //Set the look and feel for the application
```

```java
public void setLookAndFeel(){
   try{
      String lookAndFeel = UIManager.getSystemLookAndFeelClassName();
      UIManager.setLookAndFeel(lookAndFeel);
   }
   catch(Exception lFE){
     //process exception
   }
 }


//3.1
//--------------------setStatus()--------------------------
 private void setStatus(String msg){
    statusBar.setText("  " + msg);
 }


//#4.1 Position the Frame
 private void positionWindow(){
    Dimension sizeOfScreen = Toolkit.getDefaultToolkit().getScreenSize();
    Dimension sizeOfFrame = this.getSize();
    if(sizeOfFrame.height > sizeOfScreen.height){
       sizeOfFrame.height = sizeOfScreen.height;
    }
    if(sizeOfFrame.width > sizeOfScreen.width){
       sizeOfFrame.width = sizeOfScreen.width;
    }
    this.setLocation( (sizeOfScreen.width - sizeOfFrame.width) /2 ,
               (sizeOfScreen.height - sizeOfFrame.height) /2 );
 }


//--------------------------makeMenu()--------------------------
  private void makeMenu(){
       //Create a menu bar
     bar = new JMenuBar();

     //create File menu
     fileMenu = new JMenu("File");
     fileMenu.setMnemonic('F');
```

```
        //With menu items
        saveText = new JMenuItem("Save");
        saveText.setMnemonic('S');
//#5  //generate events and add handlers
        saveText.addActionListener(this);

        closeApp = new JMenuItem("Close");
        closeApp.setMnemonic('C');
        closeApp.addActionListener(this);

        //Add the File items to File menu
        fileMenu.add(saveText);
        fileMenu.add(closeApp);

    //create Edit menu
    editMenu = new JMenu("Edit");
    editMenu.setMnemonic('E');

      //With menu items
      clearText = new JMenuItem("Clear Text");
      clearText.setMnemonic('X');
      //Add the Edit items to Edit menu
      editMenu.add(clearText);
      clearText.addActionListener(this);

    //create Help menu
    helpMenu = new JMenu("Help");
    helpMenu.setMnemonic('H');
       //With menu items
       aboutThisApp = new JMenuItem("About...");
       aboutThisApp.setMnemonic('A');
       aboutThisApp.addActionListener(this);
       //Add the Help items to Help menu
       helpMenu.add(aboutThisApp);

    //create Programs menu
    programMenu = new JMenu("Programs");
```

```java
        programMenu.setMnemonic('P');

        //With menu items
        programA = new JMenuItem("Show Element Array ");
        programA.setMnemonic('E');
        programA.addActionListener(this);

        programB = new JMenuItem("Add Numbers");
        programB.addActionListener(this);
         programB.setMnemonic('N');

        programC = new JMenuItem("Program C");
        programC.addActionListener(this);
        programC.setMnemonic('C');

        //Add the Programs menu items to Programs menu
        programMenu.add(programA);
        programMenu.add(programB);
        programMenu.add(programC);

        //Add File, Edit, Help, and Programs to bar
        bar.add(fileMenu);
        bar.add(editMenu);
        bar.add(helpMenu);
        bar.add(programMenu);

        //Add the menu bar to the content pane
        setJMenuBar(bar);
    }//end makeMenu

//#6 Handle the events the menu generates
//----------------------actionPerformed()----------------------
//#6.1 Use message dialog
 public void actionPerformed(ActionEvent actionEv){
    if(actionEv.getSource() == closeApp){
      this.setStatus("Close");
       int flag = JOptionPane.showConfirmDialog(
                        this, "Quit Lab View?",
```

```
                            "Exit Lab View",
                            JOptionPane.YES_NO_OPTION,
                            JOptionPane.WARNING_MESSAGE );
          if(flag == JOptionPane.YES_OPTION){
              System.exit(0);
          }
      }
    else if(actionEv.getSource() == clearText){
      setStatus("Cleared and number reset");
      clearClientArea();
    }
    else if(actionEv.getSource() == aboutThisApp){
      setStatus("About Lab View");
//#6.2 Use message dialog
      JOptionPane.showMessageDialog(this, "Lab View B",
                                "About Lab View B",
                                JOptionPane.INFORMATION_MESSAGE);
    }
    else if(actionEv.getSource() == programA){
      setStatus("Elements");
      clearClientArea();
      showElements();
    }
    else if(actionEv.getSource() == programB){
      setStatus("Add Numbers");
//#6.2 Use input dialog
      addNumbers();
    }
    else if(actionEv.getSource() == programC){
      setStatus("Program C");
      clearClientArea();
      frameTextArea.append("Program C");
      showTestDialog("Program C");
    }
   }//end actionPerformed


//------------------------ clearClientArea ()--------------------------
  private void clearClientArea(){
```

```
        frameTextArea.setText("");
        resetNumber();
}


//#6.2.1
//------------------------addNumbers()-------------------------
private void addNumbers(){
    try{
    String dialogValue =
                JOptionPane.showInputDialog(this, "Enter a number:",
                            "Add Numbers",
                            JOptionPane.INFORMATION_MESSAGE);
    int tempValue =+ Integer.parseInt(dialogValue);
    frameTextArea.append("\n \t" + String.valueOf(addedNumber)  +
                        " + \t" + String.valueOf(tempValue)    +
                        " = \t" + String.valueOf(
                                    addedNumber += tempValue));
    }catch(Exception jEx){
        showTestDialog("No value entered.\nEnter integer values.");
    }
}


//#6.2.2
//-----------------------showTestDialog()---------------------
private void showTestDialog(String testItem){
     JOptionPane.showMessageDialog(this, testItem);
}


//#6.2.3
//-----------------------resetNumber()---------------------
private void resetNumber(){
    addedNumber = 0;
}

//#7.1-------------------showElements()---------------------
  private void showElements(){
     //Create a string
     String elementsAtomicMass =
```

```
                         "Oxygen     , 15.9994 , Fluorine  , 18.9984032, " +
                         "Neon       , 20.1797 , Zinc      , 65.39      , " +
                         "Magnesium, 24.3050 , Aluminum  , 26.981538 , " +
                         "Silicon   , 28.0855 , Phosphorus, 30.973761 , " +
                         "Sulfur    , 32.065  , Chlorine  , 35.453     , " +
                         "Potassium, 39.0983 , Calcium    , 40.078     , " +
                         "Vanadium , 50.9415 , Manganese , 54.938049 , " +
                         "Yttrium  , 88.90585, Germanium , 72.64      , " +
                         "Barium    , 137.327 , Bismuth   , 208.98038 , " +
                         "Calcium  , 40.078  , ";
       //Split the string into array elements
       String elementsAndMass[]  = elementsAtomicMass.split(",\\s");


       //Increment by 2s to see both columns
       //Subtract 1 to allow counting by 2s
       frameTextArea.append("\n\tElement\t\tWeight\n");
       for(int cntr = 0; cntr < elementsAndMass.length - 1; cntr += 2){
          frameTextArea.append("\n\t");
          frameTextArea.append(elementsAndMass[cntr]
                            + "\t"
                            + elementsAndMass[cntr+1]
                            );
       }
    }


//#3.1--------------------------main()---------------------------------
   public static void main(String args[]){
      new LabView("Lab View B");
   }//end main
}//end class
```

Event Handling

In the work on LabViewA.LabView class, you created a menu for the application. You could use the mouse to access menu items. Alternatively, you could use the Alt key in combination with mnemonics to access these items. Your work with the menus did not allow you to perform actions with them, however, because you did not associate events and event handlers with them.

As a review, recall from the discussion of the implementation of the WindowCloser class in Chapter 6 that a window can generate an event. You extend the WindowAdapter class to access a method called windowClosing() (defined in the WindowCloser class) that allows you to process (or handle) this event.

The same general relationship pertains between the menu features you created for the LabView class in the previous sections of this chapter. In each case, when you navigate to a menu item and press the Enter key or click on the menu item name, you invoke a menu event. The event generates a message. To be able to respond to the message, you must implement a message handler. As you obtained a method that allowed you to handle window events from the WindowAdapter class, so you can obtain a method that allows you to process menu events from the ActionListener interface. The ActionListener interface provides one method that you must define when you derive your class from it. This is the ActionListener::actionPerformed() method.

> When you use the WindowCloser class in the LabView class, first compile the WindowCloser class. Otherwise, the compiler generates an error.

The Handler

The handler for messages your menu issues is the actionPerformed() method. To access this method, you implement the ActionListener interface. In the class signature line directly following comment #1 of the LabViewB.LabView class definition, you use the implements keyword to access the ActionListener interface. At the same time, as before, you use the extends keyword to derive LabView from the JFrame class.

As soon as you implement the ActionListener interface, you must then define the actionPerformed() method. If you do not define this method, then your class becomes abstract. At comment #6, you define the method by declaring it as public, with a return type of void. You provide the method with one argument, of the ActionEvent type. The ActionEvent data type characterizes all messages you generate from the menu. Your definition of the signature line for the actionPerformed() method must be the same as the signature line the ActionListener interface provides. You cannot define the method as private, for example, and you cannot alter its return type.

You obtain the ActionListener interface from the Java util package. It is derived from the EventListener class. It has only one method, the actionPerformed() method. The data type of the actionPerformed() method, ActionEvent, is derived from the EventObject and AWTEvent classes. It is provided by the `java.awt.event` package. Each time you evoke a menu event, a message of the type `ActionEvent` is issued.

For now, put aside attending to the specifics of how to process events. Consider instead that you must implement the `actionPerformed()` method at least as an empty definition before you can proceed with anything else. The empty definition is as follows:

```
private void actionPerformed(EventObject actionEv){
}
```

What you name the argument (`actionEv`) is up to you, of course. As for the rest, you must conform to the pattern the `ActionListener` interface provides.

Associating Events with Menu Items

Having implemented an empty version of the `actionPerformed()` method, you can then start defining your menu items so that they generate messages the handler can process. To define a menu item so that it can generate messages, at comment #5 of the `LabViewB.LabView` class definition, you use the `JMenuItem saveText` attribute to call the `addActionListener()` method. As is evident in the lines that follow, you add an action listener to every `JMenuItem` object. Among these are the `saveText`, `closeApp`, `clearText`, `aboutThisApp`, and `programA` attributes. Here is the statement that adds the listener for the `closeApp` attribute:

```
closeApp.addActionListener(this);
```

The `addActionListener()` method activates the `JMenuItem` object so that it can generate messages of the `ActionEvent` type. The action it listens for is the action the user takes toward the object. If you click on a menu item, for example, this counts as an action. An object that can listen for an action can generate an event.

The `this` keyword serves to identify the message that the object issues as belonging to the current class, `LabView`. Given that the message is identified with the current class, you can always retrieve it using the name of the object that generates it. For the `closeApp` menu event, for example, the menu event is of the type `ActionEvent`, but its name is `closeApp`.

Identifying and Processing Messages

After you call the `addActionListener()` method to define the `JMenuItem closeApp` attribute as an event generator, when you click the words in the menu associated with the `closeApp` attribute, an event of the `ActionEvent` type is generated. The event name is `closeApp`. The `actionPerformed()` method captures any event of the `ActionEvent` type; however, it does not distinguish the names of such events. To distinguish such events, you must define a selection structure.

To define a selection structure for the closeApp menu item, you create an if…else if selection statement as in the lines trailing comment #6.1. If you implement a cascading selection structure for the closeApp and other menu items defined in your menu, the structure takes the following form:

```
if(actionEv.getSource() == closeApp){
}
else if(actionEv.getSource() == clearText){
}
else if(actionEv.getSource() == aboutThisApp){
}
else if(actionEv.getSource() == programA){
}
else if(actionEv.getSource() == programB){
}
if(actionEv.getSource() == programC){
}//end actionPerformed
```

In each instance, as Figure 8.8 illustrates, you use the name of the event (which is also the name of the object that generates the event) and test it against a value that you retrieve from the ActionEvent argument of the actionPerformed() method. The ActionEvent data type features a method that allows you to retrieve the names of objects that generate events. This is the ActionEvent::getSource() method. The getSource() method returns a reference to the object that generates the event, and you can then use the standard equal operator to implement a test.

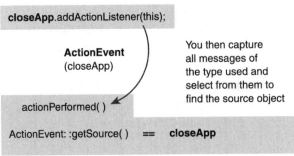

You define a menu item to generate a message…

closeApp.addActionListener(this);

ActionEvent
(closeApp)

You then capture all messages of the type used and select from them to find the source object

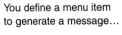

actionPerformed( )

ActionEvent: :getSource( ) == **closeApp**

FIGURE 8.8

After you assign an action listener to an object, you can retrieve messages the object generates.

As the flow of the program progresses from the start of the `actionPerformed()` method, the value of the `actionEv` argument is tested against each object you name in the selection structure. When a test proves true for a given object, then the flow of the program enters the block associated with the test. You can then define actions within the block you want to have invoked.

JOptionPane Dialogs

Figure 8.9 illustrates a typical modal dialog. A modal dialog halts interactions with your application until you respond to it. You implement the modal dialog featured in Figure 8.9 to prompt the user of your application to confirm the closure of the application. Modal dialogs serve to allow you to ensure that users do not take actions that can lead to dissatisfying results. When you close most applications, if you have not saved your work, a modal dialog prompts you to save your work before closing.

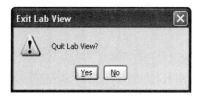

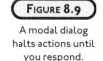

FIGURE 8.9

A modal dialog halts actions until you respond.

Modal dialogs constitute a common feature of almost any window application, and for this reason the developers of Java provide a class that allows you to easily create such dialogs. This is the `JOptionPane` class.

To use the `JOptionPane` constructor, you call one of several constructor functions. Each constructor function creates a different type of dialog. Some dialogs allow you to solicit information through a text file. Others only display information and allow users to close them after viewing the information. Here are the primary constructors:

```
JOptionPane.showInputDialog()
JOptionPane.showMessageDialog()
JOptionPane.showOptionDialog()
```

All have the same general order of arguments. You use a combination of predefined and customized argument values. At minimum, you can use only two arguments, one to identify the frame that hosts the dialog, the other a message for the dialog. In the lines associated with comment #6.1.2, for example, you employ the following constructor:

```
JOptionPane.showMessageDialog(this, testItem);
```

In this case, the `this` keyword identifies the parent frame, and the `testItem` argument provides a string to display in the text area of the dialog, as Figure 8.10 shows:

As an example of a fuller set of possibilities for using `JOptionPane` objects, here is the code you use to define the `JOptionPane` that you invoke in the test statement for the `closeApp` object (see comment #6.1):

```
int flag = JOptionPane.showConfirmDialog(
                this,
                "Quit Lab View?",
                "Exit Lab View",
                JOptionPane.YES_NO_OPTION,
                JOptionPane.WARNING_MESSAGE );
```

For the `showConfirmDialog()` constructor, the first argument (`this`) designates the parent frame. The parent frame of the Lab View application is the `LabView` class itself, which you derive from the `JFrame` class. The dialog cannot exist separately from its parent frame. The second argument consists of text or information that appears within the body of the dialog. The third argument provides the text that appears in the title bar of the dialog. The second to the last argument allows you to designate user options for the dialog. In this case, you stipulate Yes and No buttons only. The last argument designates the icon you want to use with your dialog box. The `WARNING_MESSAGE` icon consists of the yellow warning sign displayed in Figure 8.9.

In addition to allowing you to define values for text, buttons, and icons, the `JOptionPane` can return a value. The `JOptionPane` class defines the return values. In the lines associated with comment #6.1, for example, you use a selection statement to determine whether the user wants to close the application:

```
if(flag == JOptionPane.YES_OPTION){
    System.exit(0);
}
```

The user generates the value you test against the JOptionPane.YES_OPTION by clicking the Yes button in the dialog. This value is of the int type, so you can process it by assigning it to a temporary local value (flag) and testing it through selection.

Table 8.2 provides a summary of the three types of defined values you use with objects of the JOptionPane class. The values in the top block of the table allow you to designate the buttons that appear. The values in the second block of the table allow you to designate the type of default icon you see in the dialog. The bottom block of the table identifies the defined values the table returns. These are integer values. As the example of the closeApp message response reveals, you can identify a local variable of the int type and then use a selection statement to test the returned value. These values are all defined with public scope, and you call them by using JOptionPane as a prefix.

TABLE 8.2	DEFINED VALUES FOR JOPTIONPANE OBJECTS
Button Designations	**Discussion**
DEFAULT_OPTION	Default options vary for the different types of JOptionPane constructors. You can see one, two, or three buttons, depending on the purpose of the dialog.
YES_NO_OPTION	This provides Yes and No buttons.
YES_NO_CANCEL_OPTION	This provides Yes, No, and Cancel buttons.
OK_CANCEL_OPTION	This provides Yes and Cancel buttons.
Icon Designations	**Discussion**
ERROR_MESSAGE	You see an "X" inside a red circle.
INFORMATION_MESSAGE	You see an "i" in a lightly shaded circle.
WARNING_MESSAGE	You see an exclamation mark in a yellow background.
QUESTION_MESSAGE	You see a question mark.
PLAIN_MESSAGE	No icon appears.
Returned Values	**Discussion**
YES_OPTION	Corresponds to the Yes button.
NO_OPTION	Corresponds to the No button.
CANCEL_OPTION	Corresponds to the Cancel button.
OK_OPTION	Corresponds to the OK button.
CLOSED_OPTION	Corresponds to the control close button.

Dialog Input Processing

In addition to returning defined values, JOptionPane objects can return values from input fields. In the lines associated with comment #6.2.1, you implement an input dialog using the JOptionPane.showInputDialog() constructor. This flow of the program invokes the constructor when the user selects the Add Numbers option from the Programs menu. Here is the definition of the addNumbers() method, which the menu selection invokes:

```
//#6.2.1
try{
    String dialogValue =
            JOptionPane.showInputDialog(this, "Enter a number:",
                            "Add Numbers",
                            JOptionPane.INFORMATION_MESSAGE);
    int tempValue =+ Integer.parseInt(dialogValue);
    frameTextArea.append("\n \t" + String.valueOf(addedNumber)  +
                    " + \t" + String.valueOf(tempValue)       +
                    " = \t" + String.valueOf(
                                addedNumber += tempValue));
}catch(Exception jEx){
    showTestDialog("No value entered.");
}
}
```

The Programs > Add Numbers option (Alt P, N) allows the user to sum a set of numbers on a continuing basis. Figure 8.11 provides an example of a use session. The dialog provides a field in which the user can enter a value. During a normal use session, the user enters a value and clicks OK. When the dialog closes, as you see in the preceding code example, the dialog returns a value of the String type, which you assign to the dialogValue variable. To process the value, you then call the parseInt() method of the Integer class to convert the value to an int value. You assign this value to a locally defined int variable, tempValue. You can then employ the tempValue variable in conjunction with the class attribute addedNumber to sum the successive values the user enters.

To display the numbers in the text area of the frame, you call the JFrame::append() method and create a string that shows addition processes. You call the String::valueOf() method to convert the numbers to String values so that they can be displayed in the text area.

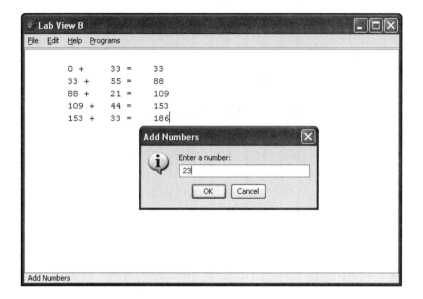

FIGURE 8.11

An input dialog
allows you to
create a sum that
you display in the
text area.

Processing Dialog Exceptions

In the definition of the JOptionPane.showInputDialog object shown in Figure 8.12, you place the use of the dialog within a try…catch block. As you see in the lines affiliated with comment #6.2.1, when you process the input from the dialog, the user can follow one of two problem paths:

- Enter values that have decimal points or that are letters or words.
- Enter no values and click on Cancel.

FIGURE 8.12

Processing
exceptions
generally and
using a generic
dialog
accommodates
irregular patterns
of use.

The two forms of use generate two types of exception. One involves no input—which is an acceptable if exceptional course of action. The other involves a problem number or a word, which is likely to be intended. To process the errors, you can implement a single catch block that you define with the general Exception type. Within the block, you can call the showTestDialog() method, which you supply with a message of No value entered. Enter integer values. as Figure 8.12 illustrates.

Window Location Using the Java Toolkit

When you create an instance of a JFrame, the window that you see appears by default in the upper-left corner of your monitor. The dimensions of a monitor are measured by pixel values or values peculiar to the manufacturer of your monitor. In most cases, however, you can identify the upper-right corner of your monitor as the coordinate position (0,0). The two zero values designate the x and y coordinates of your monitor. The x coordinate extends horizontally to the right. The y coordinate extends vertically downward. Both extend in positive directions from the upper left.

The window you create with the JFrame class is defined in similar fashion. When you designate the size of the frame as your JFrame object (640 by 480 pixels, for instance), the dimensions of your frame extend from the upper-right corner of your window. Figure 8.13 illustrates the situation.

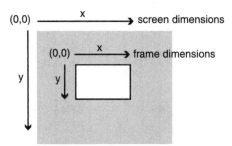

For the upper left position of your JFrame window

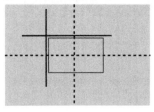

FIGURE 8.13

You work with screen and window dimensions to center your application.

find the middle x screen coordinate and subtract half the width of the window

find the middle y screen coordinate and subtract half the height of the window

To be able to position a JFrame object, as the lines associated with comment #4.1 reveal, you call the setLoction() method. This sets the location of the upper-left corner of your window relative to the upper-left corner of your screen. To determine the position of the upper-left corner, you must perform a standard set of calculations. Here's the calculation as implemented in the positionWindow() method:

```
Dimension sizeOfScreen = Toolkit.getDefaultToolkit().getScreenSize();
Dimension sizeOfFrame = this.getSize();
//lines left out...
this.setLocation( (sizeOfScreen.width - sizeOfFrame.width) /2 ,
          (sizeOfScreen.height - sizeOfFrame.height) /2 );
```

To calculate the x value that allows you to position your window in the center of your monitor screen, as Figure 8.13 illustrates, you can begin with the x dimensions of the screen and the frame. The sizeOfScreen.width and sizeOfFrame.width variables designate the dimensions relating to x values. To obtain the x coordinate for the upper-left corner of your window, you subtract the width of your window from the width of your screen and then divide the difference by 2.

You then calculate the y coordinate to use to position your window. The sizeOfScreen.height and sizeOfFrame.height variables designate the dimensions relating to y values. To obtain the y coordinate for the upper-left corner of your window, you subtract the height of your window from the height of your screen and then divide the difference by 2.

You employ the Dimension data type to perform this calculation. The Dimension data type provides two attributes, width and height. To obtain the size of your monitor area, you call the Toolkit.getDefaultToolkit().getScreenSize() method. The getScreenSize() method returns a value of the Dimension type. For the size of your window (or JFrame object), you call the JFrame::getSize() method. The return type of this method is also Dimension.

The Java Toolkit class is an abstract class that you access through the getDefaultToolkit() method. One distinctive feature about the Toolkit class is that it allows you to interact with your native operating system. It proves useful as a way to obtain system information. It also provides you a way to obtain information about your desktop.

In the lines trailing comment #4, you call the positionWindow() method just before you call the pack() and setVisible() methods. If you do not position your window prior to making it visible, you can see a flash as it moves from the upper left of your monitor area. Likewise, if you have not invoked the pack() method, it is possible that you might see a similar but far less pronounced movement.

Use of a JLabel Object for a Status Bar

The JLabel class provides one of the most fundamental components of the Java GUI. A label consists of a rectangular pane to which, among other things, you can write text. In later exercises, you see much more of this component. For now, you use it to provide an elongated field at the bottom of your window in which you can display basic information about menu choices. Figure 8.14 provides a superimposed set of screenshots that show a few of the changes that occur as you select different menu options. In each case, the JLabel object you station at the bottom of the window displays the expression that the setStatus() method provides to it.

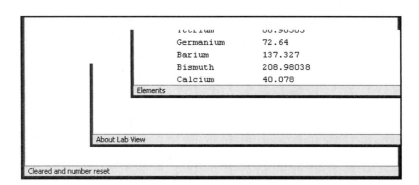

Germanium	72.64
Barium	137.327
Bismuth	208.98038
Calcium	40.078

Elements

About Lab View

Cleared and number reset

FIGURE 8.14

You display messages for each menu action.

Implementation of the setStatus() method begins with the JLabel attribute you define in the lines accompanying comment #1. There, you declare the statusBar attribute. Then, in the lines trailing comment #3, you create an instance of the JLabel class and assign it to the statusBar attribute. Immediately after that, you call the Container::add() method to add the statusBar object to the frameContainer object:

```
statusBar = new JLabel(" ");
frameContainer.add(statusBar, BorderLayout.SOUTH)
```

The second argument to the add() method consists of a BorderLayout attribute, SOUTH. As Figure 8.2 illustrates, this attribute designates that your label is to be placed in the SOUTH region as defined by the BorderLayout manager. The height of the region is controlled by the size of the JLabel you place in it.

To set the text value for the label, in the setStatus() method (refer to comment #3.1), you call the JLabel::setText() method:

```
statusBar.setText("  " + msg);
```

This method requires an argument of the String type.

For each menu invocation, you call the setStatus() method and provide it with a text message that accords with the action of the menu. Here are the lines associated with the clearText menu item:

```
else if(actionEv.getSource() == clearText){
    setStatus("Cleared and number reset");
    clearClientArea();
```

SUMMARY

In this chapter, you have taken advantage of your work with class hierarchies, derivation, and implementation to access a number of the Swing classes from the Java class hierarchy. You have used these classes to develop an SDI application with a menu. This application allows you to use a single application to perform a number of tasks. To supplement your efforts, you incorporated instances of the JOptionPane, which allows you to display messages and solicit input from the user of your application. You also explored techniques for setting the look-and-feel of your application and positioning it in your monitor screen. The next chapter carries these efforts forward, allowing you to implement dialogs that you design yourself and to use some of the powers afforded to you by the Collections classes of java.

CHALLENGES

1. Add another catch block to the code associated with the addNumbers() method (see comment #6.2.1) to catch the number exception separately. Provide a separate generic JOptionPane to guide the user to the right type of input.

2. Add an attribute and a method to the LabView class that allows you to automatically clear the application text area when you invoke the Programs > Add Numbers menu item for the first time. To accomplish this, monitor the value of statusBar. If it is set to the string that characterizes the Add Numbers menu options, do not clear the text area when you invoke the Add Numbers option. On the other hand, if you invoke the Add Numbers option and find statusBar set to another value, then clear the field.

3. Add another menu option in the Programs list. Call it Program D. Take one of the programs you developed in Chapters 2 through 4 and rewrite it so that it is a function in the LabView class. Replace calls to the println() or print() methods with calls to append() method.

4. Locate the JOptionPane for the Help > About menu option and change the wording so that it specifically identifies version 1.0 of Test Lab.

5. Open the WindowCloser class and study how the class can be altered so that it invokes the dialog you see when you click the red "x" control. Go to the LabView class (Lab View B) and find the call to the WindowCloser class constructor. How does this constructor differ from the WindowCloser in the Lab View A version of the class?

REFACTORING AND DATA CONTAINERS

This chapter continues the work of Chapter 8 by allowing you to apply the practices encompassed by inheritance, association, and the creation of windows, menus, and dialogs to explore how you can refactor some of the code in the LabView class. When you refactor the code, you are in a position to implement software patterns that allow you to make effective use of the GUI components. Toward this end, you explore how to refactor the LabView class using the Model-View-Controller and Façade patterns. One result of this work is the creation of the Elements class, which contains an interclass called PairedData. As you develop these classes, you employ such classes as Hashtable, Enumeration, String-Tokenizer, StringBuffer, and ArrayList. These classes acquaint you with the extensive set of data container (or Collection) classes that Java provides. The topics explored in this chapter include the following:

- Moving toward customized dialogs with LabView
- Familiarizing yourself with formalized refactoring
- Exploring the MVC and Façade patterns
- Using a Hashtable container
- Using the StringTokenizer and Enumeration classes
- Exploring the StringBuffer class

CUSTOM DIALOGS AND THE LAB VIEW APPLICATION

As Chapter 8 discussed, you use the JOptionPane dialogs to create functionality that accommodates a number of user interactions. Dialogs of the JOptionPane type provide easy ways to present information involving or to request acknowledgments. For more involved interactions, you create customized dialogs. When you create customized dialogs, you can include any GUI component Java provides. Among these are text fields, buttons, and drawing panels.

The use of JDialog objects introduces you to several new GUI classes, but at the same time, it allows you to see how the functionality of the LabView class can be organized so that you can use it on a *componential* basis. In other words, you separate the actions that compose the Lab View application into a diversity of classes that provide supplemental services. Some of these classes process data. Others serve largely to demonstrate features of the Java GUI classes.

> In this chapter, unlike Chapter 8, you do not see all the code for the LabView class. To view the complete LabView code, see the folder for the Chapter 9 code. The Chapter 9 version of the LabView class differs from the versions you worked with in Chapter 8. The discussion you find in this chapter focuses on changes you make to the code shown in Chapter 8. In this respect, to review those portions of the code not discussed, see Chapter 8.

Refactoring and Software Patterns

As you implement new components of the LabView class in this chapter, you explore two additional notions associated with object-oriented programming. The first is that of *refactoring*. Refactoring involves refining your code after you have initially developed it. It encompasses activities that allow you to make the classes and methods you have implemented simpler to understand and maintain. Toward this end, software engineers have developed a body of approximately 30 key practices for refactoring.

Table 9.1 provides a selective summary of some of the activities that characterize refactoring. Some of these approaches to refactoring lie beyond the scope of this chapter. Others do not. The items in the table allow you to see the range of options that refactoring covers. While some of the practices related to refactoring depend on a sense of what looks right or wrong in a given body of code, all ultimately imply the use of a *patterned* approach to solving problems. The table footnote reference for Table 9.1 identifies a standard work on a patterned approach to refactoring.

TABLE 9.1	OCCASIONS FOR REFACTORING

Reasons to Refactor	Description
Duplicate code	The same lines appear in several places in your class. You can create a method that contains this code.
Long methods	Your class contains methods that are extremely long and complex. You can take parts of these methods and create shorter utility methods. Sometimes you can even create separate classes.
Large classes	A class contains so many methods that you must organize them into subgroups. In this case, you can probably find reason to develop classes that provide a focus for these methods.
Long parameter lists	A constructor or a method contains a large number of parameters, some of which you do not need. You might be trying to do too much with the class. You can create a simpler, more focused class.
Shotgun surgery	Classes can sometimes be implemented so that when you make a change in a given method, you must visit one or more other methods to attend to compiler errors that your changes generate. This can extend to other classes as well. When this happens, you can work on refining the interfaces of your classes so that they provide services in more generic ways.
Feature envy	Sometimes one class or method relies so heavily on another class or method that you begin wondering why they are separate. This might be a good reason for merging them.
Data clumps	Sometimes you use data from a set of classes to create a given entity. If you find that this happens often, instead of making the same set of method calls over and over again, you can create a single method or single class that provides all the data with a single call or in a convenient object.
Temporary fields	If you find a large number of temporary fields in your methods, it is likely that you can find ways to eliminate some of them.
Message chains	One object requires an object from another class, which requires an object from yet another class. Long lines of cascaded method calls sometimes justify the creation of classes or methods that provide the required services through a single object or a simple method call.
Data class	Sometimes you find that you create classes that are just sets of data, without methods. In this case, you might consider how widely the data is used. It might be better to make such a class an inner class.

Source: Martin Fowler, Kent Beck, John Bryant, William Opdyke, and Don Roberts, *Refactoring: Improving the Design of Existing Code* (Addison-Wesley: Boston, 1999).

A software pattern consists of a commonly recognized way to solve a problem. A pattern might suggest a way to design a set of classes. At other times, it might establish a procedure for structuring the methods in a class. A pattern does not tell you exactly what to do. It is a general way to solve a problem. Part of its purpose, in fact, is to help you perceive the types of problems that characterize most software development efforts.

In previous chapters, you dealt with class hierarchies and systems of peer classes. You created these on a custom basis. When you designed abstract classes that encapsulated general characteristics of cars and then began developing derived classes that defined specific cars, you followed a pattern.

Models and Views

Using patterns involves organizing your classes and some of the methods within the classes so that they provide services in standardized ways. Software developers apply names to patterns so that they can easily identify the services they address. One such pattern is called the Model-View or Model-View-Controller (MVC) pattern. This pattern guides you in the development of applications that resemble Lab View.

As you discover in the sections that follow, such an application can be characterized by two general types of classes. One type consists of classes (dialogs) that display data. Another type of classes processes data to be displayed. Although in many respects the Lab View application continues to merge these two activities, the Model-View-Controller pattern allows you to assert the principle that you should keep the two activities separated.

Figure 9.1 provides a general view of how you can apply the Model-View-Controller pattern to the Lab View application. In Chapter 7, recall that when you invoked the menu item that displayed tabular data on chemical elements, the code that furnished the table, along with its data, was contained within the LabView class. You placed part of the code in the section of the class involved with processing menu events. You placed another part of the code in a utility method within LabView.

To implement the MVC pattern, when you refactor the LabView code, you extract the portions of the code that attend to the processing of the chemical data and place it in a separate class. This separate class is the Elements class. The LabView class then becomes a *client* of the Elements class.

As Figure 9.1 shows, the Elements class provides the LabView class with a service. The service consists of processing data. Given successful implementation of the MVC pattern, it becomes possible for the Elements class to work in many contexts involving different sets of data. At the same time, you do not encumber the LabView class with code that does not relate to its primary responsibility, which is to guide users to different dialog options.

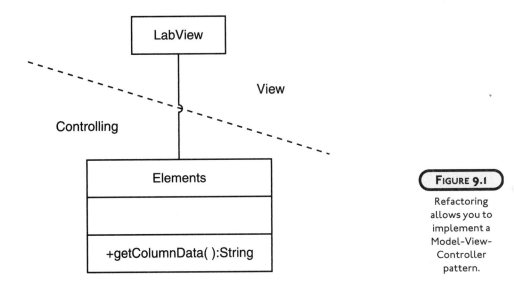

FIGURE 9.1

Refactoring allows you to implement a Model-View-Controller pattern.

REFACTORING THE SHOWELEMENTS() METHOD

To refactor the code in the LabView class, you begin with the lines in the menu processing section and the showElements() method you created in Chapter 8. You remove the data processing activities from the showElements() method. You place this code in a separate class, Elements. To show the difference refactoring makes, consider the version of the LabView class you worked with in Chapter 8. Here is the showElements() method as implemented in the LabViewB version of the LabView class:

```
//Version LabView::showElements() from LabViewB (see Chapter 8)
//#7.1---------------------showElements()-----------------------
  private void showElements(){
    //Create a string
    String elementsAtomicMass =
            "Oxygen   , 15.9994 , Fluorine  , 18.9984032, " +
            "Neon     , 20.1797 , Zinc      , 65.39      , " +
            "Magnesium, 24.3050 , Aluminum  , 26.981538 , " +
            "Silicon  , 28.0855 , Phosphorus, 30.973761 , " +
            "Sulfur   , 32.065  , Chlorine  , 35.453     , " +
            "Potassium, 39.0983 , Calcium   , 40.078     , " +
            "Vanadium , 50.9415 , Manganese , 54.938049 , " +
            "Yttrium  , 88.90585, Germanium , 72.64      , " +
            "Barium   , 137.327 , Bismuth   , 208.98038 , " +
            "Calcium  , 40.078  , ";
```

```
//Split the string into array elements
String elementsAndMass[]  = elementsAtomicMass.split(",\\s");

//Increment by 2s to see both columns
//Subtract 1 to allow counting by 2s
frameTextArea.append("\n\tElement\t\tWeight\n");
for(int cntr = 0; cntr < elementsAndMass.length • 1; cntr += 2){
  frameTextArea.append("\n\t");
  frameTextArea.append(elementsAndMass[cntr]
                    + "\t"
                    + elementsAndMass[cntr+1]
                    );
  }
}
```

The LabViewB version of the showElements() method processes the data that goes into the table. It proves to be a difficult, cumbersome method to work with for a variety of reasons. Consider a few:

- It sets up a complex string of element names and weights.
- You must carefully format each element in the string to make the table display correctly.
- You implement a great deal of code that attends to such things as splitting an array and then outputting data to the text client area of the Lab View application.
- This method proves to be one of the largest in the LabView class.

If you consider the occasions for refactoring that Table 9.1 lists, it becomes evident that justification exists for refactoring the showElements() method. For example, the method loads data and then formats the data. These activities result in a long, involved method. To change the appearance of the table, you must change the data and the code that prints the data. Since the method includes so much code, it becomes easy to create compiler errors as you make the changes.

As implemented in Chapter 8, the showElements() method encumbers the LabView class with activities that make the LabView class hard to maintain and violates the separation of responsibilities that the MVC pattern recommends. In the version of the method you implement in this chapter, you take steps to remedy this situation. To begin with, here is the version of the showElements() method you find at comment #4.1 in the Chapter 9 version of LabView:

```
//Current Chapter version of the LabView::showElements()
//------------------------- showElements()--------------------------
```

```
//#4.1
private void showElements(){
    //set the appearance of the font
    frameTextArea.setFont(new Font("Courier", Font.TYPE1_FONT, 12));
    clearClientArea();
    try{
  //Create an instance of the Elements class to call
  //data processing services
        Elements ele = new Elements();
        writeToTextArea( ele.getColumnData("Elements   Weights",
                                                5, 20) );
        writeToTextArea( ele.getColumnData("--------   -------",
                                                5, 20) );

        writeToTextArea( ele.getColumnData(ele.getData(),
                                                5, 20) );

    }
    catch(NoClassDefFoundError ncf){
        JOptionPane.showMessageDialog(this, ncf.toString(),
                            "Not found",
                            JOptionPane.WARNING_MESSAGE);

      }
  }
```

In the Chapter 9 version of the showElements() method, most of the activity involves calls to two methods from the Element class and one method from the LabView class. Toward this end, you create an instance of the Element class (ele). You use the LabView::writeToTextArea() method to convey data to the text area of the application. You call the Element::getColumnData() method to obtain data for the table and to format the table heading. Arguments you supply to the getColumnData() method allow you to set the width of the columns and how far the table is indented from the left side of the text area. To obtain data for the table, you call the Element::getData() method. This method provides data as defined in the Element class. You no longer encumber the method with primary code relating to specific operations involving data processing.

IMPLEMENTING THE ELEMENTS CLASS

As the discussion in the previous section reveals, refactoring involves assessing code to discover whether you can simplify it. When you refactor the showElements() method, you remove most of the primary implementation code from the method and place it in methods in the Elements class.

Implementing the Elements class involves focusing on the responsibilities of a class that organizes and manipulates data and has no concern with displaying the data or invoking dialogs. Further, if you remove the primary processing activity from the LabView class and delegate it to the Elements class, you place yourself in a position to implement a large number of refinements that improve the services you can provide the LabView class.

Given this advantage, the Elements class provides an opportunity to explore a few of the data containers that Java provides. When you draw on the capabilities these containers provide, you can create complex functionality that you can make available to LabView and other classes through a simple interface. When you wrap complex functionality that one set of classes provides in another class that enables you to use the functionality without being exposed to its complexity, the pattern that governs your work is known as the Façade pattern. As Figure 9.2 illustrates, the Elements class implements a version of the Façade pattern.

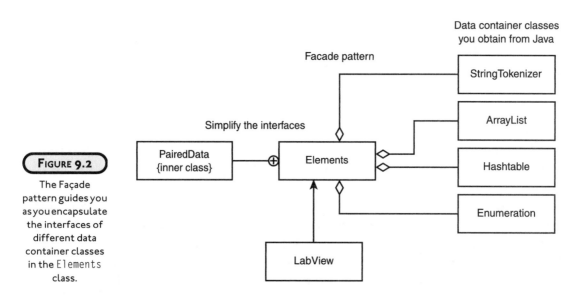

FIGURE 9.2

The Façade pattern guides you as you encapsulate the interfaces of different data container classes in the Elements class.

As Figure 9.2 illustrates, the Façade pattern you employ as you work with the Elements class involves using some of the data container (or collection) classes that Java provides. This set of classes is extensive and in itself easily becomes the topic of a complete book. In the context this book furnishes, it is possible to examine the Hashtable, ArrayList, Enumeration, and StringTokenizer classes. In addition to these classes, it's useful to consider the StringBuffer class, which supplements the work you perform using data containers.

In addition to implementing a Façade pattern to refine the interfaces of the four data container classes, you also implement an inner class, PairedData, which enables you to more easily accommodate data elements that consist of two parts, as is the case with chemical elements and their weights. In the UML diagram Figure 9.2 provides, the symbol you use to show that the Elements class contains the inner PairedData class consists of a line capped with a circle that encloses a plus sign. The capped portion of the line is nestled against the outer class. Here is the code for the Elements and PairedData classes. Subsequent sections discuss its features in detail.

```java
/*
Elements.java
*/
import javax.swing.*;
import java.awt.*;
import java.awt.event.*;
import java.util.*;

public class Elements{
    private String elementData;
//#1  Create a Hashtable and other attributes
    private Hashtable <String, String> parseTable;
    private int rowNumber;
    private int tokenNumber;
//-------------------getColumnData--------------------------
// Default constructor
    Elements(){
      setData();
    }
//#2
    //-------------------getColumnData--------------------------
    public void setData(){

            elementData =
                "Oxygen    , 15.9994 , Oxygen     , 18.9984032, " +
                "Oxygen    , 20.1797 , Zinc       , 65.39     , " +
                "Magnesium, 24.3050 , Aluminum   , 26.981538 , " +
                "Silicon   , 28.0855 , Phosphorus, 30.973761 , " +
                "Sulfur    , 32.065  , Chlorine   , 35.453    , " +
```

```
                    "Potassium, 39.0983 , Calcium    , 40.078    , " +
                    "Vanadium , 50.9415 , Manganese , 54.938049 , " +
                    "Yttrium  , 88.90585, Germanium , 72.64      , " +
                    "Barium   , 137.327 , Bismuth   , 208.98038 , " +
                    "Calcium  , 40.078  , ";
    }//end setData
//#3
 //------------------getColumnData-----------------------------
    public void setData(String data){
        elementData = data;
    }
//#4
 //------------------getColumnData-----------------------------
    public String getData(){
        return elementData;
     }//end method
//#5
 //------------------getColumnData-----------------------------
public String getColumnData(String data,
                            int leftMarg, int colWidth){
    //New instance of the hash table
    parseTable = new Hashtable<String, String>();
    //Alternative approach
    //parseTable.clear();
    String returnString = new String();

//#6
    //Clean up the data and then create tokens
    String tempData = removePunctuation(data);
    StringTokenizer tokens = new StringTokenizer(tempData);
    //Retrieve the number of tokens for the class attribute
    tokenNumber = tokens.countTokens();

//#7
    //Put them in a hashtable
     while(tokens.hasMoreTokens()){
         parseTable.put(tokens.nextToken(),
                     tokens.nextToken() );
```

```
    }//end while

//ArrayList (rather than a Vector)
//Use the internal class
//#8
    ArrayList<PairedData> displayTable
                            = new ArrayList<PairedData>();


//#9
    //Retrieve an enumeration from the Hashtable
    //hasMoreElements() controls the rep statement
    Enumeration<String> aknum = parseTable.keys();
    for(Enumeration<String> aenum = parseTable.elements();
                            aenum.hasMoreElements() ; ){
       //Create a new item with each repetition
       PairedData newItem = new PairedData(
                    aknum.nextElement().toString(),
                    aenum.nextElement().toString()
                    );
       //Add item to the ArrayList
       displayTable.add(newItem);
    }//end for


//#10
    //Retrieve the number of rows in the attribute
    rowNumber = displayTable.size();
    //Display the sorted words

//#11 Use StringBuffer to set uniform columns
    for(int itr = 0; itr < displayTable.size(); itr++){
       StringBuffer mbuf = new StringBuffer(leftMarg);
       returnString += "\n";
       mbuf.setLength(leftMarg);
       returnString += mbuf.toString();

       StringBuffer wbuf
```

```
                  = new StringBuffer(displayTable.get(itr).
                                                  getWord());


        String tabStr = new String("\t");
  //11.1
        if(displayTable.get(itr).getWord().length()
                                          <= wbuf.length() - 1){
            tabStr += "\t";
        }

          wbuf.setLength(colWidth);
          returnString +=  wbuf.toString();

          StringBuffer sbuf
            = new StringBuffer(displayTable.get(itr).
                                              getStat());

          sbuf.setLength(colWidth);
  //-----
          returnString += tabStr;

          returnString +=  sbuf.toString();
      }
//11.2
      return fixGlyph(returnString);
  }//end method

//#11.3
//-----------------fixGlyph()-----------------------------
  String fixGlyph(String str){
     StringBuffer strb = new StringBuffer(str);

     for(int ctr = 0; ctr < strb.length(); ctr++){
        if(strb.charAt(ctr) == (char)0){
            strb.replace (ctr, ctr + 1, " ");
        }
```

```
//     System.out.print(strb.charAt(ctr));
    }
  return strb.toString();
}


//--------------------- getNumberOfTokens ----------------------
//#6.2
    public int getNumberOfTokens(){
          return tokenNumber;
  }


//--------------------- getNumberOfRows ----------------------
//#10.1
  public int getNumberOfRows(){
          return rowNumber;
  }
//----------------- removePunctuation--------------------
//#6.1
//Use a string buffer and create a string
//Traverse a string and remove punctuation. Periods not deleted.
  public String removePunctuation(String punctStr){
        String tempString = new String();
        StringBuffer buf = new StringBuffer();
        tempString = punctStr;
        String testChar;
        for(int ctr = 0; ctr < tempString.length(); ctr++){
           testChar = String.valueOf(tempString.charAt( ctr ));
           if(testChar.equals( "," )||
             testChar.equals( "!" )||
             testChar.equals( ";" )||
     //    testChar.equals( "." )||
             testChar.equals( "(" )||
             testChar.equals( ")" )||
             testChar.equals("--")){
     //    System.out.println("\n--Removed: " + testChar);
             testChar = "";
           }
           buf.append(testChar);
```

```
        }
        //Convert buffer to a string
        tempString = buf.toString();
        return tempString;
    }


//================= class PairedData===================
  //#8.1
//Data class only, so set as an inner class
protected class PairedData{
    String wordItem;
    String statItem;

    public PairedData(String word, String stat) {
        wordItem = word;
        statItem = stat;
    }
    public PairedData() {
        wordItem = " - ";
        statItem = " - ";
    }
    public String getWord(){
        return wordItem;
    }
    public String getStat(){
        return statItem;
    }
    public void finalize(){}
}

//=======end inner class ===========================

    //Test code
    public static void main(String args[]){
        Elements ele = new Elements();
        System.out.print(
                ele.getColumnData("Elements    Weights", 5, 20) );
        System.out.print(
```

```
                    ele.getColumnData("--------    -------", 5, 20) );
        System.out.print(
                    ele.getColumnData(ele.getData(), 5, 20));
        System.out.print(
                    ele.getColumnData("Tokens " +
                                    ele.getNumberOfTokens() , 5, 20) );
    }
}//end class
```

The next few sections explore the features of the `Elements` class. Figure 9.3 provides an example of the results you achieve after you use the Programs > Show Element Table menu item to create an instance of the `Elements` class and call its interface methods. The data appears in formatted columns. You set the width of the columns using arguments to the `getColoumnData()` method. In addition, you can use this method to generate the column headings and formatting bars.

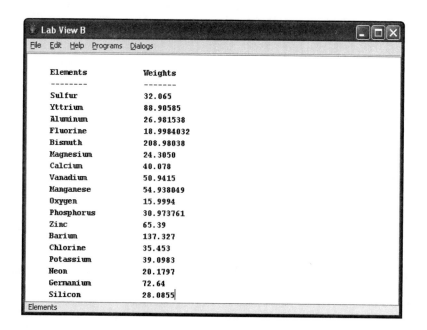

FIGURE 9.3

The `Elements::get-ColumnData()` data method allows you to format data for display.

Hashtable

At comment #1 of the `Elements` class, you declare a `Hashtable` data container. The `Hashtable` class provides a data container that stores elements that consist of two parts. One part is a *key*. The other part is a *value*. For this reason, programmers usually refer to `Hashtable` items as *key-value* pairs.

You identify the key-value pairs in a `Hashtable` data container according to the values of the keys. Consider a key as a "look-up" item for each key-value pair. Each key must be unique. All keys must be of the same data type. You establish the type of the keys, along with that of the values, when you declare the `Hashtable` data container object.

Like the key items, the value items in a hash must all be of the same type. However, when you create key-value pairs, it is not necessary to assign data to the value items. If you do not assign data to the value items, then the compiler automatically assigns `null` to them. Also, the data you assign to the value item does not have to be unique. As Figure 9.4 illustrates, you might assign the value associated with `Oxygen` to another element.

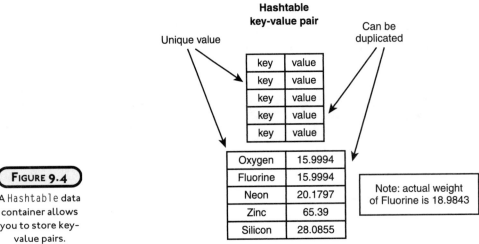

FIGURE 9.4

A `Hashtable` data container allows you to store key-value pairs.

When you assign data to a `Hashtable` object, the order the data assumes depends on the operation of the algorithm the `Hashtable` class encapsulates. The `Hashtable` class is one of the many Java implementations of what is generally known as a *map* or a *set*. Such data containers make it possible for you to quickly search a collection of data. To make this possible, when you insert an item as a key, the container provides a built-in algorithm that transforms and orders it so that it facilitates rapid searches.

How the data container organizes the data depends on the operation of the algorithm. As Figure 9.5 illustrates, at the top of the figure, you see the raw data string you create in the `Elements::setData()` method (see comment #2 of the `Elements` class definition). `Oxygen` occurs as the first item, `Calcium` last. To construct a `Hashtable` object, you create key-value pairs using element names and their associated atomic weights. You then assign these pairs to the `Hashtable` object.

The lower part of Figure 9.5 shows the sequential output of the `Hashtable` of the `Elements` class. The order of the items retrieved from the container does not match that of the string you use to create the `Hashtable` object. The reason this occurs rests on the work of the algorithm that the `Hashtable` object encapsulates.

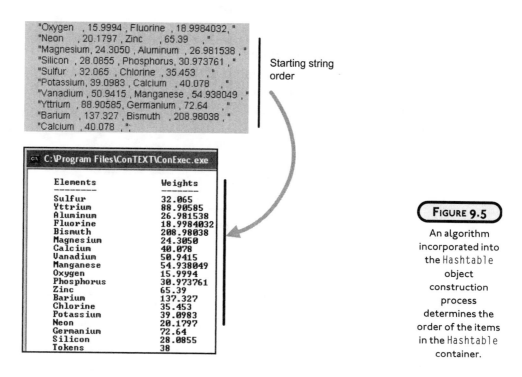

Starting string order

FIGURE 9.5

An algorithm incorporated into the `Hashtable` object construction process determines the order of the items in the `Hashtable` container.

Hashtable Construction Activities

As used in the implementation of the `getColumnData()` method, the `Hashtable` object allows you to work with the items you obtain from a string and turn them into data items of the `PairedData` type. In this context, the `Hashtable` data container serves in an intermediary role. To understand its role, consider the following activities you attend to in the `getColumnData()` method:

- Accept a string that consists of paired data values such as those you see in Figure 9.5.
- Convert the string into a `StringTokenizer` object.
- Fetch the data from the `StringTokenizer` object and place it in a `Hashtable` data container.
- Retrieve keys from the `Hashtable` data container to create an `Enumeration` container.

- Use the Enumeration data container to extract keys and values from the Hashtable data container and place them in an ArrayList data container you define using the PairedData data type.
- Extract the items from the ArrayList container and employ String and StringBuffer objects to format and concatenate it so that it can be provided to client classes as a single return value.

Figure 9.6 furnishes a UML diagram to illustrate the flow of activity in the getColumnData() method. The darkened circle indicates the start of the activity. The circle with the dot within it indicates the end of the process. The rectangles with rounded corners indicate the changed states of the data within the method. To effect these changes of state, you employ Java data container classes and the StringBuffer class.

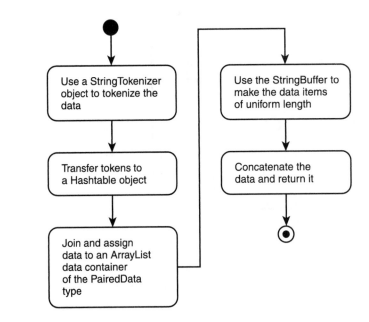

FIGURE 9.6

Implementation of the getColumnData() method involves using several data containers.

The path to implementing the getColoumnData() method begins with the construction of the Hashtable attribute you declare in association with comment #1 of the Elements class definition. To access the Hashtable and other data container data types, you employ the following import statement:

```
import java.util.*;
```

To declare a Hashtable object, you explicitly designate the types of data you intend the Hashtable object to store. Trailing comment #1, you see the following declaration statement for the parseTable identifier:

```
private Hashtable<String, String> parseTable;
```

In the lines associated with comment #5, you call the default Hashtable constructor to create an instance the Hashtable class that you assign to the parseTable identifier:

```
parseTable = new Hashtable<String, String>();
```

In the Elements class, the need to clear the Hashtable object with each invocation of the getColumnData() method justifies separating the declaration of the Hashtable identifier from creation of the Hashtable object. If you both declare and define an instance of a Hashtable object using the default Hashtable constructor, here is the form your statement assumes:

```
private Hashtable<String, String> parseTable
                    = new Hashtable<String, String>();
```

In this instance, you define a data container that consists of keys and values of the String type. This type of construction sequence differs from those of other Java objects. The angle braces provide places for you to define the data types of the keys and values. On the other hand, you still see the opening and closing parentheses of the typical class constructor. For the default constructor, the parentheses remain empty. (As Table 9.1 shows, the Hashtable and other data container classes also furnish overloaded constructors.)

You must specifically designate data types in the definition statement because a Hashtable can store objects of almost any reference type. When you designate the types, you ensure that as you assign references to the container, you do not lose their definitions. In the background, the Java compiler and interpreter use the type information to safely manage the objects you store in the container.

The data types of the key and the value items do not have to be the same. For example, you might employ the following approach to defining a Hashtable container that stores keys of the Integer type and values of a customized data type called Customer:

```
private Hashtable<Integer, Customer> parseTable
                    = new Hashtable<Integer, Customer>;
```

As Figure 9.7 illustrates, when you designate the key data type as Integer and the value data type as Customer, you follow a possible scenario in which the container key designates a unique personal identifier number and the container value stores a reference to a data class with many attributes.

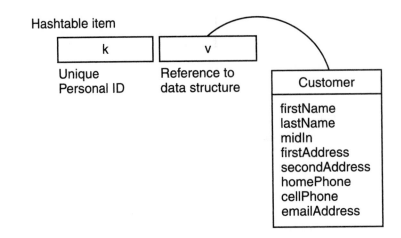

FIGURE 9.7

Use Hashtable
objects to pair
identifiers with
reference to
classes that store
sets of data.

When you assign data types to Java data containers, you can use only reference data types. You cannot use primitive data types, such as int, float, char, or double. Here is an example of a declaration that generates an error:

```
public Hashtable<int, String> parseTable;   //generates error
```

The error results from the use of the primitive data type int to define the type of the key. Instead of int, you must use Integer. To correct the situation, then, you use the following form:

```
public Hashtable<Integer, String> parseTable;
```

To accommodate int data items, you cast values of the int to the Integer type prior to assigning them to the data container. You can use similar approaches for all the other primitive data types.

The data containers you have access to when you work with Java are far too numerous to be comprehensively discussed in this book. However, the developers of Java have designed the data containers so that their interfaces conform to a standard abstract class model. While differences exist, you find some interfaces almost completely the same. This is the case with the Hashtable, the HashMap, and to a lesser extent, the HashSet classes. Table 9.2 provides a selection of the methods associated with the Hashtable class.

TABLE 9.2   SELECTIVE METHODS OF THE HASHTABLE INTERFACE

Item	Discussion
`void clear()`	Returns `void`. This method deletes all the keys (and) values in a hashtable.
`containsKey()`	Takes a key of the appropriate type as an argument. Returns the `boolean` `true` token if it locates the key. Example of use (`String` type): `parseTable.containsKey("Warm")`.
`containsValue()`	Takes a value of the appropriate type as an argument. Returns the `boolean` `true` token if it locates the value. Example of use (`String` type): `parseTable.containsKey("Phoenix")`.
`elements()`	Returns a set of enumerators for the hashtable, which you assign to an `Enumeration` container. An `Enumeration` container consists of a set of pointers to the items in the hash. You can use the `Enumeration` object to traverse the key-value pairs in a `Hashtable` data container. You must specify the type when you declare the `Enumeration` object. Example of use (`String` type): `Enumeration<String> enu = parseTable.elements();`
`isEmpty()`	This method returns the `boolean` `true` token if the `Hashtable` data container contains no keys. If the container is not empty, then the method returns the `boolean` `false` token.
`keys()`	The method returns a set of enumerators for the keys in a hashtable. Example of use (`String` type): `Enumeration<String> enu = parseTable.keys();`
`put(key, value)`	This method allows you to insert (or map) a key-value pair into a `Hashtable` data container. The types of the key and value must correspond to those you have defined for the container.
`remove(key)`	Deletes the key and its corresponding value from this `Hashtable` container.
`size()`	This method provides the number of keys in this hashtable. The return type is `int`.

The expression *data container* characterizes an object that programmers design to control and manage a collection of data. The Java developers elected to call data containers `Collections`. In this chapter and elsewhere in this book, the discussion incorporates the expressions *data container*, *collection*, or *container* in reference to objects designed to hold and manage collections of objects. Along the same lines, it remains important to keep in mind that a GUI container is a class designed to organize and manage GUI components. It is not a data container of the type dealt with in this chapter.

In the lines associated with comment #5 of the Elements class, you create an instance of the Hashtable class (parseTable). To accomplish this, you call the default Hashtable constructor (Hashtable<><>()) and define it with arguments of the String type. Your use of the constructor corresponds precisely to the declaration of the parseTable identifier following comment #1.

You are then ready to populate the parseTable object. To populate the parseTable object, in the lines accompanying comment #7, you call the Hashtable::put() method. As Table 9.1 discusses, the put() method takes two arguments. The first argument designates a key. The second argument designates a value. The arguments must be of the type or types you have used to define the Hashtable object. In this case, you use arguments of the String type. To obtain values to serve as arguments for the put() method, you employ a StringTokenizer, which the next section discusses in detail.

Tokenizing a String

After constructing a Hashtable object, in the lines accompanying comment #7, you use an object of a StringTokenizer type (tokens) to populate the Hashtable object. You perform this activity in the context of the getColumnData() method. In the lines trailing comment #5, you define this method so that it takes three arguments. The first argument (data) is of the String type and consists of a string bearing the data you want to put into tabular form. Its second argument provides the number of characters you want to use for the left margin of the table. This argument is of the int type. The third argument provides the character width of the columns in the table.

To process the first argument of the getColumnData() method, you employ a StringTokenizer to break the string into tokens and place them in the Hashtable data container. A token is letter, a word, or an expression. The StringTokenizer data container provides you with methods that you use to manipulate the tokens. As Figure 9.8 illustrates, among these are the hasMoreTokens(), countTokens(), and nextToken() methods.

By default, when the StringTokenizer constructor tokenizes a string, it uses white spaces to determine the points at which it separates items into tokens. As the definition of the setData() method reveals (see comment #2), the body of data you supply to the StringTokenizer() constructor assumes the following form:

```
"Oxygen    , 15.9994 , Fluorine  , 18.9984032, " +
"Neon      , 20.1797 , Zinc      , 65.39      , " +
"Magnesium, 24.3050 , Aluminum  , 26.981538 , " +
```

Starting string

Oxygen 15.9994 Fluorine 18.9984032 Neon 20.1797 Zinc 65.39

Tokenizer

Oxygen 15.9994 Fluorine 18.9984032 Neon 20.1797 Zinc 65.39	**StringTokenizer container** **hasMoreTokens( )** **nextToken( )** **countTokens( )**

FIGURE 9.8

A StringTokenizer constructor transforms a string into a collection of tokens.

You create a method (removePunctuationAction()) that removes punctuation from the string, but even when the string possesses punctuation, the default StringTokenizer constructor ignores it. It divides items according to the white space that follows the commas. If you want to change this situation, as Table 9.3 reveals, the developers of Java have created an overloaded StringTokenizer constructor. This constructor allows you to designate a delimiter.

You construct the StringTokenizer object in the lines following comment #6. There, you supply the default StringTokenizer() constructor with an argument of the String type (tempData). This argument represents the string returned by the Elements::removePunctuationAction() method. This method accepts an argument of the String type. In this instance, you provide the data parameter of the getColumnData() argument list. The constructor makes each item in the string into a separate token. You assign the tokens to the StringTokenizer tokens object.

At comment #7, you create a while repetition statement. As the control expression for this statement, you employ the StringTokenizer::hasMoreTokens() method. As Figure 9.9 illustrates, as the repetition block repeats, this method tests whether the object continues to contain tokens. With each iteration of the block, the number of tokens decreases by two, because within the block you call the nextToken() method twice. The nextToken() method extracts a token from the container. When you call the Hashtable::put() method, you use the tokens you obtain in this way to create key-value pairs that you assign to the Hashtable data container (parseTable).

Table 9.3 reviews the constructors and methods that constitute the interface of the StringTokenizer class. As mentioned previously, an overloaded constructor allows you to customize your approach to parsing a string into tokens.

TABLE 9.3 STRINGTOKENIZER CONSTRUCTORS AND METHODS

Method	Discussion
StringTokenizer(String)	Accepts an argument of the String type and divides the string according to the default tokenizer (white space).
StringTokenizer(String, String)	Constructs a string tokenizer for the specified string.
countTokens()	Returns a value of the int type that designates the number of items the StringTokenizer has defined.
boolean hasMoreElements()	Returns a value of the boolean type. Determines whether a tokenizer contains elements.
boolean hasMoreTokens()	Returns a value of the boolean type. Determines whether a tokenizer contains tokens.
nextElement()	Returns Object references to the tokens in the tokenizer. With each call to this method, you advance one token.
nextToken()	Returns String references to the tokens in the tokenizer. With each call to this method, you advance one token.
nextToken(String)	This method allows you to iterate through the tokenizer by using the delimited. It takes a single argument of the String type. The argument designates the delimiter. It advances the tokenizer each time it is called. It returns String references to the tokens in the tokenizer.

StringTokenizer action

while(tokens.hasMoreTokens){

nextToken( ) ← Oxygen
nextToken( ) ← 15.9994
Fluorine
18.9984032
Neon
20.1797
Zinc
65.39

parseTable.put(key   value)

Hashtable action

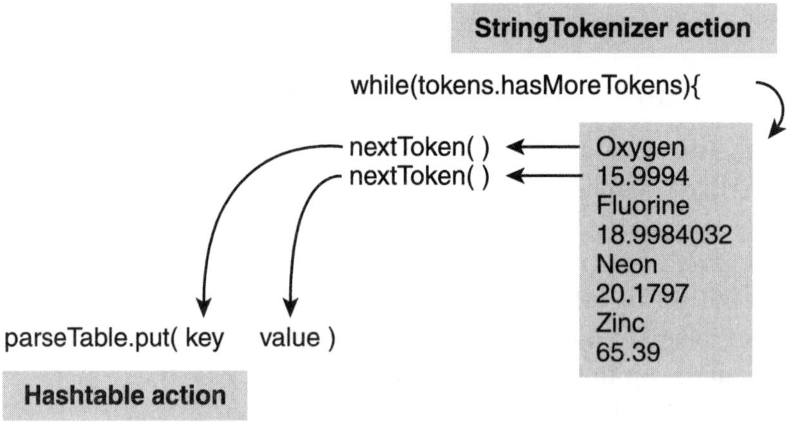

FIGURE 9.9

Using the StringTokenizer object, you transform a string into a collection of tokens that you can then place in a Hashtable data container.

In addition to employing the nextToken() method, in the lines associated with comment #6, you call the getNumberOfTokens() method. This method returns an int value. You assign the returned value to an attribute of the Elements class, tokenNumber. To retrieve the count, in the

lines associated with comment #6.2, you define an accessor method, getNumberOfTokens().
This method returns the value of tokenNumber. In the main method at the end of the
Elements class definition, when you call the getNumberOfTokens() method, you see that the
tokens container contains 38 items, each a chemical name or weight. (See Figure 9.5, which
shows the output of the test main() method of the Elements class.)

ENUMERATION

In the lines associated with comment #9, you use the parseTable object to call the
Hashtable::keys() method. The keys() method returns a set of enumerators to key-value pairs
in the parseTable data container. You assign these to the aknum identifier, which is of the
Enumeration data type. To define the aknum identifier, you use the following statement:

```
Enumeration<String> aknum = parseTable.keys();
```

This statement declares the aknum identifier using the same approach you use for the
Hashtable identifier. You enclose the type of the Enumeration container in angle brackets. The
type in this instance is String.

An Enumeration object stores enumerators. An enumerator is also known as a *pointer* or *itera-
tor*. Such language tends to be fairly general, however. An enumerator points to an item in a
Hashtable data container. Figure 9.10 illustrates this situation. The enumerators are more or
less the addresses of the elements in memory (which is how programmers sometimes define
pointers and iterators). Because an Enumeration object consists of such addresses, the interpreter can traverse them very quickly.

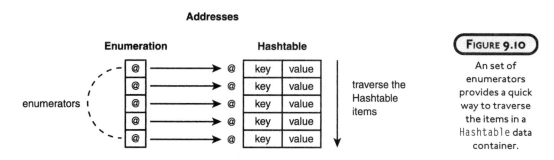

Addresses

FIGURE 9.10

An set of enumerators provides a quick way to traverse the items in a Hashtable data container.

In addition to creating the Enumeration object (aknum) to hold enumerators for the
parseTable key items, you also create the Enumerator object named aenum to hold enumerators
for the parseTable value items. To assign values to the aenum object, you call the
Hashtable::elements() method, which returns values you have assigned to key-value pairs.

The aenum object serves to control a for repetition statement that you create to traverse the key-value pairs in the parseTable object. At this point, all the values have been stored sequentially in the two Enumeration objects, so if you traverse these objects in tandem, you can retrieve the key-value pairs and assign them together to single strings.

To control the repetition block, you set up the control expression of for statement so that you first assign the values to the aenum object using the Hashtable::elements() method. In the second part of the control expression, you call the Enumeration::hasMoreElements() method. This is one of only two methods that comprise the interface for Enumeration class. The method returns true as long as the Enumeration object contains enumerators to a given data set.

To increment the for statement, you call the nextElement() method, the second of the two Enumeration class methods. This method returns an item from the Enumeration object each time you call it. During each cycle of the for block, you call this method twice. You call it the first time using the aknum object, which stores enumerators that point to keys. For the second call, you employ the aenum object, which stores enumerators that point to values. The two calls work in tandem. The first retrieves the name of a chemical element. The second retrieves the weight of the chemical element.

In both cases, you supplement the calls to the nextElement() method with a call to the Hashtable::toString() method, which ensures that the key and value data are both returned as String objects. You make the returned objects arguments in the constructor for the PairedData class constructor. This constructor you define in the inner class definition of PairedData (discussed further on). Here is the code:

```
PairedData newItem = new PairedData(
                        aknum.nextElement().toString(),
                        aenum.nextElement().toString()  );
```

For each iteration of the block, you construct a new PairedData object. You can then store the paired data object in an ArrayList data container. The next section discusses the ArrayList class in greater detail.

ArrayList

As with hashes, maps, and sets, the developers of Java have created a group of classes that attend to activities you commonly associate with arrays. Among these classes are the ArrayList and Vector classes. In Chapter 7, in the PolyTest class, you made use of the Vector class that you defined using an abstract data type.

The Vector class resembles the ArrayList class because both types of data containers can expand or contract with use. In this respect, they differ from primitive arrays, which as exercises in Chapter 3 showed must remain the same size for the duration of the program in which you declare them. `Vector` and `ArrayList` objects allow you to add items to them or remove items from them with convenient method calls. Their interfaces include several other useful methods. Table 9.4 provides discussion of a few of these methods.

| TABLE 9.4 | SELECTED METHODS OF THE ARRAYLIST CLASS |

Method	Discussion
`boolean add(I)`	Thus method takes an argument of the type of the `ArrayList` container. It appends the item (`I`) you identify with the argument to the end of the list.
`add(int, I)`	This method takes two arguments. Its return type is `void`. The first designates a position in the `ArrayList` container. The second identifies an item you want to insert at this position.
`addAll(AL)`	The method allows you to append a list of the `ArrayList` (AL) type to another. The method takes one argument, the list that you want to append. Example of use: `displayTableB.addAll(displayTableA)`
`addAll(int, AL)`	The method allows you to insert one list of the `ArrayList` (AL) type to another. The method takes two arguments. The first identifies the position in the target list at which you want to insert the second list. The second argument names the list that you want to insert. Example of use: `displayTableB.addAll(8, displayTableA)`
`clear()`	This method removes all the elements from the `ArrayList` container.
`contains(I)`	This method allows you to identify whether an `ArrayList` container contains a given item. The item (`I`) you test for must be of the same type as the items the container stores. It returns true if it locates the item. It returns false otherwise.
`ensureCapacity(int)`	This method possesses a return type of `void`. As an argument it takes a number that you supply to set the size of the container.
`get(int)`	This method retrieves an item from an `ArrayList` container. It takes one argument, of the `int` type. The argument identifies the position of the item in the container.
`indexOf(I)`	This method possesses a return type of `int`. As an argument it takes an item (`I`) of the same type as the container. It returns the position of the first occurrence of the item in the container. If you want to completely traverse a container and find all items, as soon as you find the first item, you increment the returned value by one and continue the traversal.
`isEmpty()`	This method returns a Boolean value. If the container is empty of items, it returns true.

`lastIndexOf(I)`	This method works as the obverse of the `IndexOf()` method. It finds the position of the last occurrence of a given item (I) in a container. Its return type is `int`.
`remove(int)`	This method removes and retrieves an item from a container. Its return type is the type of the container. It takes as an argument the `int` value designating the position of the item you want to remove.
`remove(O)`	This method possesses a return type of `boolean`. As its argument, you provide an object (O) representing the item you want to remove. If it finds and removes the item, the method returns true.
`removeRange(int, int)`	This method allows you to remove a range of items from a container. Its return type is `void`. It takes as its arguments the value of the `int` type. One designates the start of the range. The second designates the end of the range. The items the values specifically identify are not included among those removed.
`E set(int, I)`	This method allows you to replace an item in a container with another item (I). Its return type is the type of the container you use it with. The first argument is of the `int` type. This argument designates the position of the item you want to replace. The type of the second argument is the same type as the container. For this argument, you provide an object or value you want to use as a replacement. The method returns the replaced item.
`size()`	This method returns the number of items in the container. Its return value is of the `int` type.
`trimToSize()`	This method reduces the size of the container so that it corresponds exactly with the number of items the container contains. Its return type is `void`.

In the lines associated with comment #8, you declare and define an `ArrayList` container of the `PairedData` type (`displayTable`). To construct this container, you employ the same approach you used when dealing with `Enumeration` and `Hashtable` objects. You employ the angle brackets to identify the type of the items you want to assign to the container. Here is the definition statement:

```
ArrayList<PairedData> displayTable
                = new ArrayList<PairedData>();
```

You employ the `PairedData` data type to define the data type of the `ArrayList` container. You designate the data type when you declare the identifier and when you call the constructor. In this case you call the default constructor.

At this point, in the lines trailing comment #9, the `displayTable` container contains no `PairedData` objects. To assign objects to it, you call the `ArrayList::add()` method. As discussed previously, to call the `add()` method, you implement a `for` repetition statement that you control using `Enumeration` objects. You call the `Enumeration::nextElement()` method to retrieve the names of chemical elements and their associated atomic weights. You assign these to an object of the `PairedData` type, `newItem`. With each iteration of the `for` block, you call the `add()` method to assign a new `PairedData` object to the `displayTable` container.

At comment #10, you call the `ArrayList::size()` method to obtain the number of items in the `ArrayList` container. You assign this value to the `rowNumber` attribute. To make this number available through the class interface, in the lines associated with comment #10.1, you define the `getNumberOfRows()` method. Given a two-column table, the value this method returns equals half the value the `getNumberOfTokens()` method returns.

STRING AND STRINGBUFFER

In the lines associated with comment #11, you create a `for` repetition block that you control by employing the `ArrayList displayTable` container to call the `size()` method. As Figure 9.11 illustrates, the purpose of this block is to create a string of uniform length that you can employ to construct the columns of a table. Without this block, you must carefully format the data as you do in the lines accompanying comment #2. To render this unnecessary, you make use of the `StringBuffer` class.

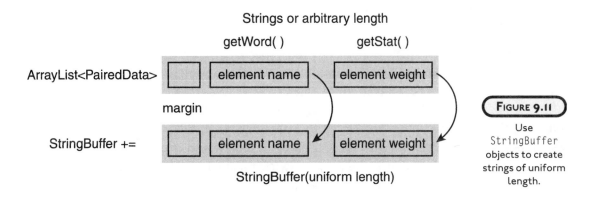

FIGURE 9.11

Use `StringBuffer` objects to create strings of uniform length.

The `StringBuffer` class allows you to resize strings. Your first use of the `StringBuffer` class involves creating a `StringBuffer` object, `mbuf`, which contains white spaces that establish the left margin of the table. To set the exact length of the `mbuf` variable, you employ the `leftMarg` argument from the argument list of the `getColumnData()` method (see comment #5). This argument is of the `int` type. You call the `StringBuffer::setLength()` method to set the exact length in characters of the mbuf variable. Having set the mbuf variable to the length the leftMarg argument establishes, you then use the StringBuffer::toString() argument to convert the StringBuffer variable into a string that you can concatenate with the returnString variable, which is of the String type. (You declare the returnString variable in the lines associated with comment #5.)

Following your work with the mbuf variable, you turn to the wbuf and sbuf variables. To populate the wbuf variable, you call the PairedData::getWord() method to retrieve the name of a chemical element from the displayTable container. To retrieve specific PairedData objects from the displayTable container, you call the ArrayList::get() method. This method takes an int value as an argument. As an argument you supply the itr control variable, which the for statement augments as it traverses the ArrayList container.

You then use the wbuf variable to call the setLength() method, to which you assign the colWidth argument of the getColumnData() method (again, see comment #5). Having set the length of the StringBuffer variable, you call the toString() method to convert the StringBuffer variable into a String object. As before, you concatenate the String object with the returnString variable.

For the sbuf variable, you perform the same actions you performed with the wbuf variable. The only difference is that you call the PairedData::getStat() method. This method returns the weight associated with a chemical element name. You assign the value to the StringBuffer sbuf variable, call the setLength() method to convert the value to a String object, and then concatenate the String object with the returnString variable.

After the flow of the program exits the repetition block, you use the return keyword to return a string that represents a table that is indented a specific number of spaces and provides data in columns of uniform width. See Figure 9.3 for the appearance of the resulting table as displayed in the Lab View application text area.

Glyph Problems

The graphical object that represents a character on your monitor is called a *glyph*. Numbers identify glyphs. When a computer cannot identify the glyph for a character, you see hollow or darkened boxes rather than characters. Such boxes often appear when your computer cannot find a glyph appropriate for representing a white space. When this happens, you can eliminate the problem by traversing the string you are trying to print and finding the unidentified glyph for a white space (which has a value of 0). You replace the unidentified glyph with a glyph your computer can recognize.

In the lines associated with comments #11.2 and #11.3, you define and call the fixGlyph() method. This method filters white space glyphs for the ElementsDialog class. It takes a single argument of the String type. You use the argument of the method to create an object of the StringBuffer type. You then construct a for repletion block and traverse the characters in the StringBuffer. As you go, you call the charAt() and replace() methods of the StringBuffer class to locate and replace glyphs identified by 0. You then use the String class constructor to convert the StringBuffer to a String and return the result.

Tabs

In the lines associated with comments #11.1 and #11.2, you insert tabs between the table elements. For all elements, by default, you insert a tab between the name of the element and in the first column the data corresponding to it in the second column. For elements with short names, such as "Zinc," you insert two tabs. To decide whether to insert a second tab, you create a selection structure:

```
//11.1
 String tabStr = new String("\t");
 if(displayTable.get(itr).getWord().length()
                       <= wbuf.length()){
      tabStr += "\t";
 }
```

If the length of the element name is less than or equal to the length of the left margin, then you concatenate a second tab with the tabStr variable.

Cleaning Up Data

In the lines associated with comment #6, you call the removePunctuation() method. You define this method in the lines associated with comment #6.1. The purpose of the method is to remove punctuation from a string. The method takes one argument, punctStr, which is of the String type. To process the string, you begin by declaring a temporary String variable, tempString, and a temporary StringBuffer variable, buf. You then assign the value of the punctStr argument to the tempString variable. In addition, you declare a String variable named testChar.

After declaring testChar, you create a for repetition block. To control the block, you call the String::length() attribute, which returns a value equal to the character length of a String object. You increment the counter (ctr) to that and use it as an argument to the String::charAt() method. The charAt() method returns a value of the char type. It traverses the characters of the string one at a time and returns characters to the testChar variable. Because the return type of the charAt() method is the char type, you call the String::valueOf() method to convert the char value to a String value.

During each iteration of the `for` block, you can examine a single character in the string. To examine the character, you create an `if` selection statement. For the test expression of this statement, you set up a series of calls to the `String::equals()` method. You use the OR (`||`) operator to join these into a compounded logical expression. In the course of the expression, you test for punctuation items you want to remove. If the expression identifies an unwanted punctuation character, you eliminate the character by assigning an empty string (`""`) to the `testChar` variable.

With each repetition of the `for` block, when the flow of the program exits the selection block, you call the `append()` method to add the value of the `testChar` variable to the `buf` variable. If the selection test does not find that the value of `testChar` corresponds to the items of unwanted punctuation, then the value of `testChar` is appended to the `StringBuffer` object.

When the flow of the program exits the repetition block, you call the `StringBuffer::toString()` method and convert the `StringBuffer` object to a `String` object. You assign this object to the `tempString` variable. You then use the `return` keyword to return the value of `tempString`.

The Inner Class and the finalize Method

In the lines associated with comment #8, you define an `ArrayList` container, `displayTable`. To designate the data type of the container, you employ the `PairedData` data type. In the lines trailing comment #8.1, you define the `PairedData` class. To define the `PairedData` class, you declare it as `protected`. One reason for declaring it as `protected` is that you can access it in the event that you derive a class from the `Elements` class. No methods exist to provide access to the inner class if you declare it as `private`.

The `PairedData` class serves to structure data for a two-column table. To define the constructors for the class, you first create an overloaded constructor that allows you to assign a key term to the `wordItem` attribute and a value term to the `statItem` attribute. Both attributes are of the `String` type. For the default constructor, you define the attributes using strings that contain a dash.

In addition to the accessor and mutator methods, the `PairedData` class contains a `finalize()` method. This method is a default method of every class you create using Java. The developers of Java define it in the `Object` class. Using the `finalize()` method is a matter of policy. It allows you to place statements in your code that are performed when all objects of the class in which you define it reach the end of their lives.

The interpreter invokes the default (super class) version of this method if you do not define a method in your own class. Invocation of the method helps with what is known as *garbage collection*. Garbage collection involves ensuring that the resources of your computer are not burdened with unwanted, unused objects while your program is running.

Since all classes in a hierarchy implicitly possess `finalize()` methods, you should resist making a `finalize()` method `private`. If you derive a class from a class in which the `finalize()` method is `private`, your chain of destruction can be adversely affected.

Extensive discussion of garbage cleanup lies beyond the scope of this chapter, but it remains a crucial feature of the Java programming language.

Mutator and Accessor Methods of the Elements Class

In the lines accompanying comments #2, #3, and #4, you define the accessor and mutator methods for the `Elements` class. The `getData()` method returns the value of the `elementData` attribute. You set the value of this attribute using two methods. If you use the overloaded version of the `setData()` method, you provide an argument of the `String` type. For the default version of the `setData()` method, you provide no argument. The method automatically populates the `elementData` attribute with the data introduced in Chapter 8. Such an approach to providing the `Elements` class with data is at best provisional. The purpose is to allow for easy testing of the class.

EXCEPTIONS

In the refactored implementation of the `LabView` class, you call the constructor for the `Elements` class. You invoke the construction of an `Elements` object with a selection statement. To ensure that the `LabView` class can handle a situation in which it does not find the `Elements` class or in which something goes wrong during the construction process, you set up a try…catch block that processes `Exception` messages for missing classes. For convenience, here is a truncated version of the `showElements()` method, which contains the try…catch block:

```java
private void showElements(){
    // lines left out
    clearClientArea();
    try{
        // lines left out
        Elements ele = new Elements();
        // lines left out
    }
    catch(NoClassDefFoundError ncf){
        JOptionPane.showMessageDialog(this, ncf.toString(),
                                    "Not found",
                                    JOptionPane.WARNING_MESSAGE);
        }
    }
```

In this situation you employ the NoClassDefFoundError class to designate the argument for the catch expression. This Exception type is defined along with many other Exception types in the java.lang package. If the Elements class is not visible to the Lab View application or the construction process is in some way flawed, then the system generates the NoClassDefFoundError exception.

Exception classes provide a toString() method. If you submit the returned value of the toString() method as the second argument to the JOptionPane constructor, you generate text for display in the text field of the dialog. Figure 9.12 illustrates what happens if you delete the byte code (class) file for the Exception class and then try to construct an instance of the class using the Show Elements Table menu item.

FIGURE 9.12

You can process
error messages
that occur if
composed classes
are missing.

SUMMARY

In this chapter, you have explored the use of refactoring and the application of patterns. By refactoring a method in the LabView class, you have been able reduce the size of the class. Given the implementation of a new class, Elements, you have been able to reduce the complexity of the code that remains in the LabView class. From an extensive body of code that involves primary development of the functionality that allows you to format and display a table, you have changed over to calling two methods that allow you to format and then display data.

In the development of the Elements class, you explored a few of the data containers Java offers. These included the Hashtable, StringTokenizer, ArrayList, and Enumeration classes. These classes provide powerful, convenient interfaces for managing large collections of data.

In addition, you made use of the StringBuffer class, which differs from the String class because it is defined to accommodate strings that change in length. Using the setLength() method, you were able to create functionality that automatically formats a body of data for display in columns of equal width.

The activities in this chapter prepare you to move to more extensive challenges in the next chapter. What applies to the development of the Elements class also applies to the development of classes that provide additional GUI features.

For more information on patterns, refactoring, and data structures, consult the following books:

Horstmann, Cay. *Object-Oriented Design and Patterns*. Hoboken, NJ: John Wiley & Sons, 2002.

Main, Michael. *Data Structures and Other Objects Using Java (3rd Edition)*. Reading, MA: Addison-Wesley Publishing Company, 2005.

CHALLENGES

1. LabView:: showElements() method (comment #4.1) contains a statement that allows you to format the font for the table. Does this provide an opportunity for refactoring? Consider the writeToTextArea() method. Create an overloaded version of the method that allows you to provide arguments for font display and remove the statement that implements font parameters from the showElements() method. The argument types are String, Font, and int.

2. Inspect the code at comments #10 and #10.1 of the Elements class definition. Add a test line to the code in the main() method to determine whether the number of rows equals half the number of tokens.

3. At comment #11, you write code that establishes uniform column widths for the data you work with in the getColumnData() method. Refactor the code so that you create a separate method, setColumns(). This method should have three arguments of String, int, and int types.

4. In the code associated with comment #6.1, the number of temporary String variables you declare within the method seems excessive. Can you refactor the method so that it contains fewer temporary variables?

EXTENDING
APPLICATIONS

This chapter continues the work of Chapter 9. It invites you to explore the practices encompassed by patterns and refactoring and leads into work with customized dialogs, threads, input-output activities, and the use of the Java `Graphics` class. Learning how to program with Java involves years of exploration and testing. This book provides only a beginning. As you move from this book into further explorations, the extent to which this book provides only a beginning is likely to become much clearer. Of the approximately 2,500 classes you find in the Java class hierarchy, you have touched on only a few dozen in the course of this book. This chapter closes out the beginning this book provides. To continue on with your work with Java, it is likely that your path will lead to study of the documentation provided with the JDK. Keep in mind that the JDK contains many tutorials. Likewise, the number of Internet sites that provide introductory lessons on Java have proliferated over the years. Among the topics this chapter covers are the following:

- Understanding associations between classes
- Working with child and parent windows
- Creating an abstract dialog class
- Deriving dialog classes

- Exploring mouse actions and drawing
- Using some of the Java input-output classes

> As in Chapter 9, in this chapter you do not see all the code for the LabView class. To view the code for the LabView class, see the folder for the Chapter 10 code. The version of the LabView class that appears in this chapter differs in some ways from the version you use in Chapter 9.

USING DIALOGS TO EXTEND THE APPLICATION

In Chapter 9, you explored the Model-View-Controller pattern to create association relations between the LabView and the Elements classes. Now you can employ the same pattern to extend your work to encompass other classes. In Chapter 9, you implemented the Elements class so that it provided a background service to the LabView class. It generated data for a table. You can now refactor the LabView class once again so that you explore how to move the calls to the Elements class to a customized dialog class.

You create customized dialog classes using the JDialog class. The JDialog class is a peer of the JFrame class. They are both derived from the Window class. Likewise, the relationship between the JDialog and JFrame objects is characterized by *association*, which establishes that one class can be aware of another and yet never require the creation of an instance of it.

In Figure 10.1 the open arrows illustrate associations. In this respect, the LabView class is aware of such classes as MousePlay and ElementsDialog. When you create an instance of the LabView class, you do not also automatically create instances of the MousePlay or ElementsDialog classes. This is association. On the other hand, when you create an instance of the ElementsDialog class (as you see in the sections that follow), you always also create an instance of the Elements class. This is composition.

In this chapter, the work you perform involves developing a number of dialogs that encapsulate components that the Java Swing classes provide. Figure 10.1 lists the dialogs you develop. Here is a summary of the dialogs:

- ElementsDialog. Introduces you to the JDialog class and a few associated classes. Allows you to make use of the Elements class on a basis of composition.
- PrimaryDialog. Furnishes an abstract JDialog class. You can use this class to define functionality common to all of the dialogs you develop. This is an abstract class.

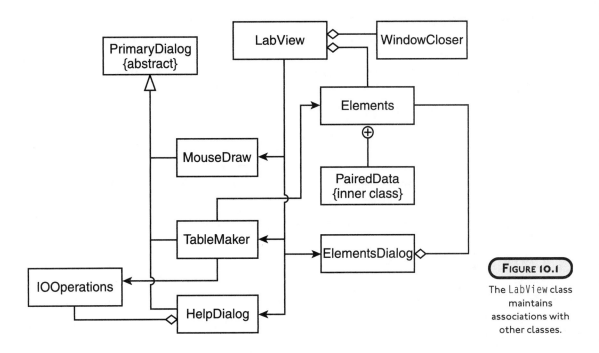

FIGURE 10.1

The LabView class maintains associations with other classes.

- MouseDraw. Provides you with the chance to explore events related to using a mouse and pressing keys. You can also work with the Graphics class.

- TableMaker. Allows you to work with the Box and BorderLayout layout managers and such GUI classes as JTextArea, JTextField, JButton, JLabel, and JPanel. You read data from a file and write it to a file.

- StartAndStop. Explores the use of the Runnable interface for the implementation of the Thread class.

- UserID. Allows you to use the JButton and JTextField classes in conjunction with file input-output operations.

- HelpDialog. Allows you to read from a file and display it in a text area.

In addition to implementing dialogs, you develop another background data processing class. This is the IOOperations class. When you develop this class, you explore classes that handle input-output operations. Among the classes that support such operations are FileInputStream, InputStreamWriter, and BufferedWriter. Having developed the IOOperations class, you can make use of it in the UserID and HelpDialog classes, and it provides an occasion for refactoring the ElementsDialog class.

Activities in this chapter constitute basic explorations of the Java classes. Needless to say, such explorations furnish only a beginning. In light of this, it remains important, as you go, to extend your knowledge of the Java classes by exploring the documentation that the JDK provides or that you can view online. As shown earlier in this book, here is one of the Sun URLs at which you can find the Java 5 documentation:

http://java.sun.com/j2se/1.5.0/docs/api/index.html

Again, as mentioned previously, the Java 5 class hierarchy provides roughly 2,500 classes, each of which provides an interface consisting of from a few to a few dozen methods. Exploring all the options is clearly a project that involves years of effort.

Child Windows

Referring once again to Figure 10.1, the `ElementsDialog` class provides an example of a `JDialog` class. Objects of the `JDialog` type closely resemble those of the `JFrame` class, with the exception that you almost always use objects (windows) of the `JDialog` type in positions that are subordinate to `JFrame` objects (or windows). For this reason, the dialogs you create using the `JDialog` class are called *child* windows. They are children of a `JFrame`, or *parent* window.

As mentioned before, `JDialog` windows are not children in the sense of being derived from `JFrame` windows. As the development of the `Elements` class anticipates, the relationship between a child and a parent window is characterized by a service that the dialog provides. The service centers on the delivery of information or provision of a context of interaction.

As Figure 10.2 illustrates, when you select a menu item in the menu of a `JFrame` window, you create an instance of a `JDialog` window in the same way that you create an instance of the `Elements` class when you select the Programs > Show Element Table menu option. Both are services. As with the services you receive from the `Elements` class, the `JDialog` window remains in existence for only as long as the `JFrame` object exists, and you access it through the `JFrame` object. Also, when you close the parent object, then you also close the child window.

In Chapter 9, you refactored the code in the `LabView` class so that you transferred the code that processes data relating to chemical elements to the `Elements` class. The interface you developed for the `Elements` class reduced the amount of code in the `LabView::actionPerformed()` and `LabView::showElements()` methods to a minimum. These changes helped shape the class so that its responsibilities align with the Model-View-Controller (MVC) pattern.

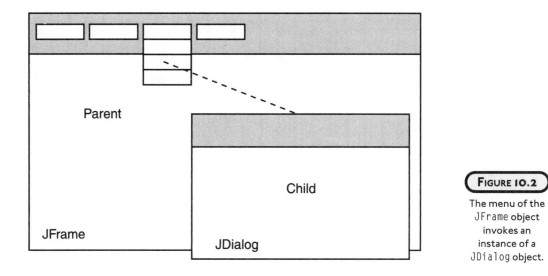

Given this beginning, you can take another step toward shaping the Lab View application so that it separates display from processing activities. Use of a JDialog class object constitutes part of this step. When you refactor the LabView class this time, you move the call to the Elements::getColumnData() method to the ElementsDialog class.

The JDialog Window

The ElementsDialog class provides a context in which to experiment with refactoring by making it so that you can call a dialog from the Lab View application that displays chemical elements in a dialog rather than in the main client area. Figure 10.3 provides a view of the Lab View application after you have implemented the ElementsDialog class and called it from the Programs menu. The chemical data now appears in the text area of the dialog. The text area of the main window remains empty.

Figure 10.4 isolates a few of the details of Figure 10.1. As the figure shows, the ElementsDialog class is composed of an instance of the Elements class. It is not merely associated with the Elements class. When you invoke the construction of the ElementsDialog object, you cause the loadData() method to execute. The loadData() method automatically creates an instance of the Elements class. And instance of the ElementsDialog class always brings with it an instance of the Elements class. It remains, however, that the ElementsDialog class is associated with the LabView class because whether you create an instance of the ElementsDialog call after you have created an instance of the LabView class depends on whether you select the appropriate menu item.

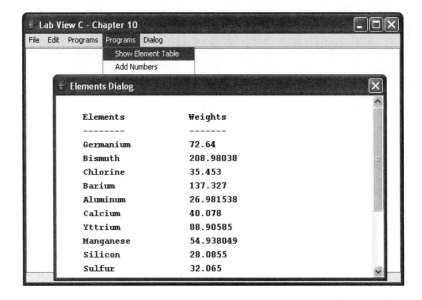

FIGURE 10.3

The
ElementsDialog
class allows you to
remove calls to
the Elements
class from the
LabView class.

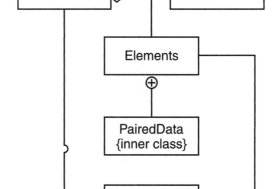

FIGURE 10.4

The
ElementsDialog
class is associated
with the LabView
class and
composed of an
instance of the
Elements class.

To implement the ElementsDialog class, you extend the JDialog class. To make the ElementsDialog window a child window of the LabView window, you define the ElementsDialog constructor so that it can receive an argument (parent) from the LabView class (see comment #2). The data type of this attribute is JDialog, and when you call the ElementsDialog constructor in the LabView class, you provide the this keyword as the argument. In the ElementsDialog constructor, you pass this argument to the argument list associated with the super keyword. The result is that you subordinate the ElementsDialog class to the LabView class. As mentioned previously, one is not derived from the other. Rather, one is subordinated to the other through a parent-child windowing relationship. Here is the code for the ElementsDialog class. The sections that follow discuss its features in detail.

```java
/*
  ElementsDialog.java
*/
import java.awt.*;
import javax.swing.*;

public class ElementsDialog extends JDialog{
    private String displayText;
    private JTextArea dialogDisplay;
    private JScrollPane areaScroll;
//#1
    private Box frameBox;
    private Container frameContainer;
//------------------------ElementsDialog------------------------
    //Constructor
    public ElementsDialog(JFrame parent, String title){
//#2
        super(parent, title);
    //Redundant, but you can still use this
        this.setTitle(title);
        setModal(true);
        init();
    }
//------------------------init----------------------------------
    private void init(){
//#3  //Add the default window closing operation
        setDefaultCloseOperation(DISPOSE_ON_CLOSE);
        setLookAndFeel();

//#4  Intialize the class attribute with the data
        displayText = new String("");
        loadData();



//#5  //A box layout manager
        frameContainer = getContentPane();
```

```
        //set up the TextArea component
        dialogDisplay = new JTextArea(displayText, 20, 20);
        dialogDisplay.setEditable(false);
//#5.1
        dialogDisplay.setFont(new Font("Courier", Font.TYPE1_FONT, 12));
        areaScroll = new JScrollPane(dialogDisplay);
        //designate a layout manager
        frameBox = Box.createHorizontalBox();
        frameBox.add(areaScroll);
        frameContainer.add(frameBox);

        setSize(500,300);
        positionWindow();
        setVisible(true);

    }//end init
  //#6
//----------------------positionWindow------------------------
    public void positionWindow(){
      Window local;

      Dimension sizeOfScreen = Toolkit.
                            getDefaultToolkit().getScreenSize();
      Dimension sizeOfFrame = this.getSize();
      if(sizeOfFrame.height > sizeOfScreen.height){
         sizeOfFrame.height = sizeOfScreen.height;
      }
      if(sizeOfFrame.width > sizeOfScreen.width){
         sizeOfFrame.width = sizeOfScreen.width;
      }
      this.setLocation( (sizeOfScreen.width - sizeOfFrame.width) /2 ,
                 (sizeOfScreen.height - sizeOfFrame.height) /2 );
    }
//----------------------setLookAndFeel------------------------
    //Set the look and feel for the application
    public void setLookAndFeel(){
      try{
        String lookAndFeel = UIManager.
                          getSystemLookAndFeelClassName();
```

```
          UIManager.setLookAndFeel(lookAndFeel);
        }
     catch(Exception lFE){
        //process exception
        }
  }

//#7
  //-------------------------- loadData()---------------------------
  private void loadData(){
     try{
    //Create an instance of the Elements class to call
    //data processing services
        StringBuffer tempString = new StringBuffer();
        Elements ele = new Elements();
        tempString.append(ele.getColumnData("Elements   Weights",  5, 20));
        tempString.append( ele.getColumnData("--------    -------", 5, 20) );
        tempString.append( ele.getColumnData(ele.getData(), 5, 20) );
        setDisplayText(tempString.toString());
     }
     catch(NoClassDefFoundError ncf){
        JOptionPane.showMessageDialog(this, ncf.toString(),
                                   "Not found",
                                   JOptionPane.WARNING_MESSAGE);
         }
  }

//-----------------writeToTextArea()-----------------------------
 public void writeToTextArea(String txt){
    dialogDisplay.setText(txt);
 }

//#7.1
//-----------------setDisplayText()------------------------------
 public void setDisplayText(String txt){
    displayText = txt;
 }
//-----------------getDisplayText()------------------------------
 public String getDisplayText(){
```

```
    return displayText;
  }
//------------------------main-----------------------------------
    public static void main(String Args[]){
            new ElementsDialog(null, "Elements");
    }
}//end class
```

In the lines preceding comment #1 of the ElementsDialog class definition, you use the extends keyword to derive the ElementsDialog class from the JDialog class. In the lines trailing comment #1, after declaring the String (displayText), JTextArea (dialogDisplay), and JScrollPane (areaScroll) attributes, you also declare a Box layout manager as an attribute. A Box layout manager allows you to organize the contents of your window as a vertical or horizontal column, one component either beside or below the next. In this case, you have only one component: the text area with its JScrollPane housing, but the layout manager still serves a useful purpose by allowing you to center and size this component.

When you compile the code for this chapter, the order of dependencies is along the following lines:

```
PrimaryDialog
Elements
ElementsDialog
IOOperations
HelpDialog
MouseDraw
TableMaker
WindowCloser
LabView
```

Place these files in your working folder. On a pragmatic basis, you compile classes at random and then follow the prompts the error messages provide. You can also simply work through the directory for Chapter 10 and compile each of the files in succession. In addition to the *.java files, you also require the text files, which are as follows:

elementData.txt
elementTable.txt
helpText.txt

JDialog Construction

At comment #2, you define an overloaded constructor for the class. The constructor takes two arguments. The first argument is of the JFrame type. It allows you to identify the parent window. When you identify the parent window, you identify the window from which you intend to create an instance of the ElementsDialog class. In the current context, this is the LabView class, but you design the constructor so that it can work with any class. The call using the super keyword performs the work of establishing the child-parent relationship.

In this instance, unlike previous instances involving the JFrame class, the super keyword by default involves two parameters. The first is the identity of the parent class. When you call the constructor in the parent class, the value you supply for this argument is the this keyword. Given a call using the super keyword, the life of the ElementsDialog is subordinate to the life of the parent class, LabView. The second argument is of the String type. It allows you to set the title of the dialog. The call to the super keyword enables you to establish the identity of the parent frame and to set the title of the dialog. In this respect, the call to the setTitle() method is not needed. It is left in purely to illustrate its use.

Disposal and Initialization

After defining the constructor for the ElementsDialog class, you call the init() method, which contains the code that attends to most of the activities performed during the life of the ElementsDialog object. Within the init() method, just after comment #3, you call the setDefaultCloseOperation() method. This method allows you to close a dialog window. The arguments you provide to it allow you to follow a number of courses. The most common is to destroy the dialog when you click the close control button. To designate this course of action, you use the DISPOSE_ON_CLOSE constant. Next, you call the setLookAndFeel() method, which remains the same as the method you defined in Chapters 8 and 9.

In the lines accompanying comment #4, you create an instance of a String object and assign it to the displayText attribute. Initializing the attribute in this way prevents the actions of the class from inserting a null token at the start of the string when you load data into it. To load data into it, you call the loadData() method.

In the lines trailing #7, you define the loadData() method. This method takes no arguments and returns void. Its primary responsibility is to create an instance of the Elements class and to populate the displayText attribute. To create an instance of the Elements class, you enclose a call to the constructor in a try…catch block. You create an instance of the StringBuffer class (tempString), and then using calls to the Elements::getColumnData() and the StringBuffer::append() methods, you build the table of elements.

The first call to getColumnData() method allows you set up the column headings. The second call to the getColumnData() method allows you to create divider lines at the top of the columns. The final call allows you to create the data columns for the table. After you have appended all the components of the table to the tempString variable, you call the StringBuffer::toString() method to convert the StringBuffer object into a String object. You call the ElementsDialog::setDisplayText() method to assign the string bearing the heading and data for the table to the displayText attribute.

The Box Layout Manager

At comment #5 in the definition of the ElementsDialog class, after loading the data for the table the dialog displays, you call the getContentPane() method to create an instance of the Container class, which you assign to the frameContainer attribute. A Container (content pane) object allows you to place items in a frame or dialog. The getContentPane() method encapsulates a construction routine for the Container object. Given the creation of this object, you can then proceed to define a layout for it and add components to it.

After defining the container, you create an instance of the JTextArea class you use as the main display area of the dialog. You assign this to the dialogDisplay attribute. When you create an instance of the JTextArea, you provide the displayText attribute as the first argument to the JTextArea constructor. The displayText attribute is of the String type and stores the headings and text of the table. Using the attribute as an argument to the JTextArea constructor has the effect of immediately populating the text area with the table you have created with the call to the loadData() method. For the second and third arguments of the constructor, you assign values for the number of rows and the number of columns you want to use in the initial definition of the JTextArea object.

After its construction, you use the JTextArea object to call the setEditable() method. This method takes one argument, of the boolean type. You set it to false, making it so that the user cannot alter the text in the area. You then associate the JTextArea object to the JScrollPane object by making the dialogDisplay attribute an argument of the JScrollPane constructor.

After defining the text area and its scroll pane, you move on to create a layout manager. Toward this end, you define an instance of the Box layout manager (frameBox). To set the orientation of the Box layout manager, you call the createHorizontalBox() method, which designates a container that holds a succession of objects positioned one after the other in horizontal succession. Using the frameBox identifier, you then call the Box::add() method to position the JScrollPane object (which houses the JTextArea object) in the frameBox layout. Finally, you associate the frameBox layout with the frameContainer object.

As a final bit of work in the `init()` method, you call `JDialog::setSize()`, `ElementsDialog::positionWindow()`, and `JDialog::setVisible()` methods. These method work in the same way they worked with the `JFrame` class. The `setSize()` method sets the horizontal and vertical dimensions of the frame. The `setVisible()` method sets the frame to visible. (When you create an abstract `JDialog` object, you set this method to `false`.) For the definition of the `positionWindow()` method, which commences at comment #6, you use the same approach that you used for the `JFrame` widows.

Fonts

At comment #5.1, you call the `TextArea.setFont()` method to alter the typeface of the font that the `JTextArea` object displays. This is largely a contingency measure to compensate for the fact that the columns of the table become slightly out of line if left with the default display values. Figure 10.5 provides a composite view of screenshots that reveal the difference that the font face can make in the display.

The top view shows the default text, which becomes slightly out of line in certain areas because the `JTextArea` object requires that you provide it with information concerning the definitions of the fonts you use. The two lower views show different uses of monospaced fonts. When you define the font using a monospaced font (such as Courier), even when you use bold and italic in your definition, the text lines up well.

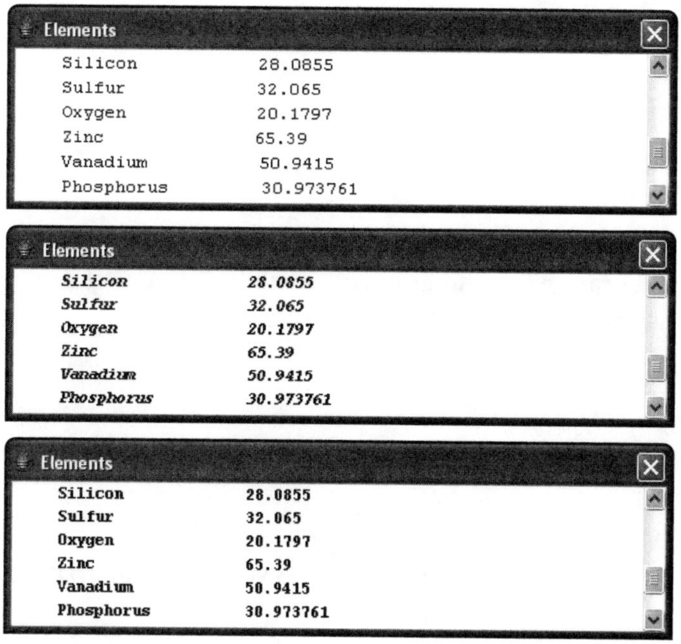

FIGURE 10.5

You can define the Font attributes for the JTextArea object.

Here is the statement that renders the font face you see in the lower two windows shown in Figure 10.5:

```
dialogDisplay.setFont(new Font("Verdana", Font.BOLD + Font.ITALIC, 12));
dialogDisplay.setFont(new Font("monospaced", Font.BOLD, 12));
```

The constructor for Font objects takes three arguments. The first argument names a font. Typical names are serif, sansserif, and monospaced. You can also try any font that you have loaded on your system. When you select a font for a table or a formatted display, achieving desirable results requires use of different methods of the Font class that allow you to designate specific control values, such as those that pertain to leading and height.

The second argument designates the style of the font. Among common styles are Font.PLAIN, Font.BOLD, and Font.ITALIC. As you see in the previous example, you combine styles using a plus sign. The final argument designates the point size of the font.

The developers of Java have included the setFont() method in the interfaces of almost all components that display fonts (JLabel, JButton, JTextField). You can also use the setFont() method objects of the Graphics type.

Lab View Menu Considerations

See the sidebar on "Refactoring and Menu Construction" for a discussion of how to understand the current version the LabView::makeMenu() method. To accommodate the dialogs in this chapter, you add new menu items. The complete list of new JMenuItem objects is as follows:

```
private JMenuItem saveText,    closeApp, clearText,
                  aboutThisApp, helpInfo,
                  programA,    programB,
                  programD,    programE;
```

To activate the menu so that you can create an instance of the ElementsDialog, you use the existing menu configuration for the programA attribute. Here is the code from the LabView:: actionPerformed() method that pertains to this item:

```
else if(actionEv.getSource() == programA){
   //Refactored code
     setStatus("Elements");
     showElements();
 }
```

The definition of the LabView::showElements() method involves only a call to the constructor of the ElementsDialog class. Here is the refactored method:

```
private void showElements(){
    setStatus("Elements Dialog");
    clearClientArea();
    try{
        new ElementsDialog(this, "Elements Dialog");
    }
    catch(NoClassDefFoundError ncf){
        JOptionPane.showMessageDialog(this, ncf.toString(),
                                "Not found",
                                JOptionPane.WARNING_MESSAGE);
        }
}
```

Refactoring allows you to reduce the method so that you no longer perform primary processing in the LabView class. Processing now takes place in the background. The ElementsDialog object assembles a string containing the table. The Elements class takes care of primary processing. The LabView object draws on both classes through a relationship characterized by association. It is a client of the classes that provide services.

REFACTORING AND MENU CONSTRUCTION

In the version of the LabView class for this chapter, you optimize the code involved with creating the menu. According to Table 9.1, duplicate code justifies refactoring. When you first develop a menu, repeating the same code can ensure that you sustain your development effort at a clear, understandable level. Given success with the primary implementation, however, you can assess what you have done and determine if the redundancy remains justified. If you find that you can eliminate redundancy without making the code difficult to understand, then refactoring becomes a reasonable course of action.

To refactor the code in the makeMenu() method of the LabView class, consider first the approach you have used in previous chapters to create a menu and a menu item. Here is a sampling from the code in Chapter 9:

```
//Create File menu - Chapter 9 version
fileMenu = new JMenu("File");
    fileMenu.setMnemonic('F');
        saveText = new JMenuItem("Save");
```

```
            saveText.setMnemonic('S');
            saveText.addActionListener(this);

            closeApp = new JMenuItem("Close");
            closeApp.setMnemonic('C');
            closeApp.addActionListener(this);
```

For the creation of the JMenu and JMenuItem objects, you employ several lines of code. The purpose of the lines remains clear due to the redundancy, and in this respect you can justify repeating the lines. On the other hand, the makeMenu() method requires nearly 100 lines due to the repeated lines.

To remedy this situation, you assess which lines are repeated. The repeated lines fall into two groups. You create an instance of the JMenu object, add a mnemonic, and add an event listener. The same process is necessary for the JMenuItem object. You use these two sets of lines over and over. Given this starting point, it becomes evident that you can refactor the code to create two methods that encapsulate these steps. Each method requires only two arguments. Here are the methods that result:

```
//--------------------makeMenu----------------------
public JMenu makeMenu(String name, char mnem){
    JMenu menu;
    menu = new JMenu(name);
    menu.setMnemonic(mnem);
    return menu;
}
//--------------------makeMenuItem----------------------
public JMenuItem makeMenuItem(String name, char mnem){
    JMenuItem mItem;
    mItem = new JMenuItem(name);
    mItem.addActionListener(this);
    mItem.setMnemonic(mnem);
    return mItem;
}
```

After you have created these two methods, you can then create the JMenu and JMenuItem objects with three lines. Here is the result:

```
    //Create File menu - Chapter 10 version
```

```
        fileMenu = makeMenu("File", 'F');
          saveText = makeMenuItem("Save", 'S');
          closeApp = makeMenuItem("Close", 'C');
```

You reduce the lines necessary to create the menu and menu items from 8 to 3 (excluding the comments). The length of the makeMenu() method drops to around 50 lines (comments included). With the addition of the two new methods, the number of lines for the three methods is around 60. Refactoring allows you to reduce the line count by roughly a third and make the creation of menus and menu items much easier to negotiate.

AN ABSTRACT PRIMARY DIALOG

Figure 10.1 depicts an abstract class, PrimaryDialog, which you derive from the JDialog class. When you implement this class, you bring forward much of the work you have put in place in the concrete ElementsDialog and allow other classes to make use of it. Here is the code for the PrimaryDialog class:

```
/*
   PrimaryDialog
*/
import java.awt.*;
import java.awt.event.*;
import javax.swing.*;

//Remove "abstract" for testing
//#1
public abstract class PrimaryDialog extends JDialog{

//----------------------PrimaryDialog----------------------
    public PrimaryDialog(JFrame parent, String title) {
        super(parent, title);
        setTitle(title);
        //Set position relative to the parent
        setLookAndFeel();
        positionWindow();
//#2
        this.setModal(true);
        setDefaultCloseOperation(DISPOSE_ON_CLOSE);
```

```
        //Do not make it visible
          this.setSize(300, 300);
         //Remove comments for testing
         // this.setVisible(true);
     }//end constructor
//#3
//-------------------------setLookAndFeel------------------------
   //Set the look and feel for the application
   public void setLookAndFeel(){
      try{
         String lookAndFeel = UIManager.
                                getSystemLookAndFeelClassName();
         UIManager.setLookAndFeel(lookAndFeel);
      }
      catch(Exception lFE){
        //process exception
      }
   }
//#4
//----------------------positionWindow-----------------------
    public void positionWindow(){
       Dimension sizeOfScreen = Toolkit.
                                getDefaultToolkit().getScreenSize();
       Dimension sizeOfFrame = this.getSize();
       if(sizeOfFrame.height > sizeOfScreen.height){
          sizeOfFrame.height = sizeOfScreen.height;
       }
       if(sizeOfFrame.width > sizeOfScreen.width){
          sizeOfFrame.width = sizeOfScreen.width;
       }
       this.setLocation( (sizeOfScreen.width - sizeOfFrame.width) /2 ,
                  (sizeOfScreen.height - sizeOfFrame.height) /2 );
    }
//#5 Remove comments for testing (see #1 for removal of abstract)
//   public static void main(String Args[]){
//        new PrimaryDialog(null, "Test Primary");
//   }
}//end of class
```

To define the `PrimaryDialog` class, in the lines trailing comment #1, you use the abstract keyword to define the class. You employ the extends keyword to derive the class from the `JDialog` class. From there, you move on to define the constructor for the class. To define the constructor, you call the super keyword to designate the parent class and to provide the dialog with a title. After that, you call the `setModal()` method to ensure that the dialog retains the focus while it is active. The `setModal()` method take a single argument, of the boolean type. You provide it the true token to create a modal dialog.

In more sophisticated settings, you can define a desktop window that allows you to create dialogs that remain active while you create instances of other dialogs. To keep things simple, in this context the goal is to create one dialog at a time. For this reason, you assign true to the `setModal()` method.

In addition to the `setModal()` method, you include calls to the `setSize()` and `setVisible()` methods. The `setVisible()` method is defined in the `Component` class. It takes a boolean value as it argument. You set it to false because you do not want the abstract dialog to appear when you create an instance of dialog you derive from it. To set the dialogs to visible, you can override this method in derived classes. This also applies to the `setSize()` method.

At comments #3 and #4, you define the `setLookAndFeel()` and `positionWindow()` methods. Since you define them as public, you can access them in classes that you derive from the `PrimaryDialog` class.

Figure 10.6 provides a view of an instance of the `PrimaryDialog` class that you arrive at if you change the default setting of the `setVisible()` method from false to true and remove the abstract keyword from the signature line. To test the class, remove the comments from the `main()` method.

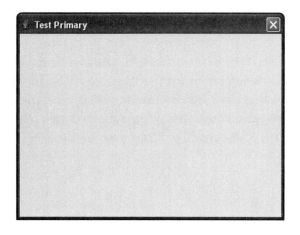

FIGURE 10.6

For testing, remove the abstract keyword, set the frame to visible, and uncomment the main() method.

MOUSE DRAWING AND GRAPHICS

When you derive a class from the PrimaryDialog class, the code you require to set up a basic frame proves to be minimal. When you develop the MouseDraw class, you take advantage of this situation to explore the MouseListener, MouseMotionListener, and KeyListener interfaces. In addition, you explore some of the methods of the Graphics class.

To explore the methods of the Graphics class, you implement the paint() method, which is defined in the Container class. The paint() method allows your frame to be redrawn. When it is redrawn, you can use the Graphics argument of the paint() method to create a wide variety of graphical effects. Figure 10.7 shows you the results of a session with the MouseDraw class.

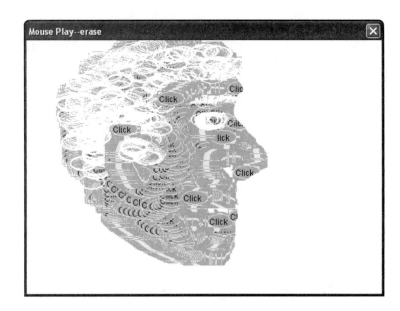

FIGURE 10.7

The MouseDraw class allows you to use mouse and key events to invoke the paint() method in selective ways.

To customize how and when you call the paint() method, you can wrap calls to it in other methods. This strategy guides the development of the MouseDraw class in which you create the drawArea() and eraseArea() methods. Both of these methods take an argument of the Graphics type, so you can call them from within the paint() method on a selective basis. Here is the code for the MouseDraw class. Subsequent sections provide detailed discussion of its features.

```
/*
   MouseDraw.java
*/
```

```
import java.awt.*;
import java.awt.event.*;
import javax.swing.*;
import java.util.*;


//#1
public class MouseDraw extends PrimaryDialog
                        implements MouseListener,
                                   MouseMotionListener,
                                   KeyListener{
  private String msgString, keyCode,
                 keyAction, mouseAction,
                 title, area;
  private int xPos, yPos = -10;
  final Color baseColor;
//-------------------------Constructor--------------------------
  public MouseDraw(JFrame parent, String tle) {
    super(parent, tle);
    title = tle;
    keyAction = "draw";
//#1
    baseColor = Color.WHITE;
    setLookAndFeel();
    setBackground(Color.WHITE);
//#2 Process mouse messages
    addMouseListener(this);
    addMouseMotionListener(this);
//#3 Process keyboard messages
    addKeyListener(this);
    this.setSize(540, 400);
    positionWindow();
    setResizable(false);
    setVisible(true);
  }


//--------------------------paint-------------------------------
//#4
  public void paint(Graphics g){
```

```java
        if(keyAction.equalsIgnoreCase("draw")){
            drawArea(g);
        }
        if(keyAction.equalsIgnoreCase("erase")){
            eraseArea(g);
        }
    }
//=====================Utility Methods===r=====================
//#5
//------------------------drawArea--------------------------
    public void drawArea(Graphics g){
        g.setColor(Color.cyan);
        g.draw3DRect(5,6,7,8,true);

        g.setColor(Color.green);
        g.drawRect(xPos - 3, yPos - 16, 40, 20);
        g.fillRoundRect(xPos - 3, yPos - 16, 40, 20, 30,30);

        g.setColor(Color.yellow);
        g.drawOval(xPos - 3, yPos - 16, 40, 20);

        g.setColor(Color.blue);
        g.drawString("Click", xPos, yPos);
    }
//------------------------eraseArea--------------------------
    public void eraseArea(Graphics g){
        g.setColor(Color.WHITE);
        g.drawOval(xPos - 3, yPos - 16,40,20);
    }

//------------------------setValues--------------------------
//#6
    public void setValues(String event, int x, int y){
        msgString = event;
        yPos = y;
        xPos = x;
        repaint();
    }
```

```java
//--------------------------showMA--------------------------
  public void showMA(String mo){
    setTitle(title + "--" + keyAction + "  " + mo);
  }
//-----------------------setKeyAction-----------------------
  public void setKeyAction(String ka){
     keyAction = ka;
  }


//====================MouseMotionListener====================
//--------------------------mouseDragged---------------------
//#2.1
  public void mouseDragged(MouseEvent mE){
    setValues("Drag", mE.getX(), mE.getY());
    showMA("Dragging");
  }


//--------------------------mouseMoved----------------------
  public void mouseMoved(MouseEvent mE){
     showMA("Moving");
  }


//====================MouseListener====================
//--------------------------mouseClicked--------------------
//#2.2
  public void mouseClicked( MouseEvent mE){
    setValues(")))", mE.getX(), mE.getY());
    showMA("Clicked");
  }
//--------------------------mousePressed--------------------
//#7
  public void mousePressed( MouseEvent mE){
    setValues(")))", mE.getX(), mE.getY());
    showMA("Pressed");

  }
//--------------------------mouseReleased-------------------
  public void mouseReleased( MouseEvent mE){
```

```
     showMA("Moving");

  }
//-----------------------mouseEntered--------------------
  public void mouseEntered(MouseEvent mE){
     showMA("Entered");
  }

//-----------------------mouseExited--------------------
  public void mouseExited(MouseEvent mE){
     showMA("Exiting");
  }


 //=====================KeyListener====================
//#3.1
//-----------------------keyPressed--------------------
  public void keyPressed(KeyEvent kE){
       keyCode = kE.getKeyText(kE.getKeyCode());

       if(keyCode.equalsIgnoreCase("e")){
          System.out.println("Erase");
          setKeyAction("erase");
          setTitle(title + "--" + keyAction);
       }
       if(keyCode.equalsIgnoreCase("d")){
          System.out.println("Draw");
          setKeyAction("draw");
          setTitle(title + "--" + keyAction);
       }
   }
//-----------------------keyReleased--------------------
  public void keyReleased(KeyEvent kE){

     setTitle(title + "--" + keyAction);
  }
//-----------------------keyTyped--------------------
  public void keyTyped(KeyEvent kE){}
```

```
//------------------------------main----------------------------
  public static void main(String args[]){
    new MouseDraw(null, "Mouse Play");
  }
}
```

The MouseDraw class consists largely of a list of methods you must define when you implement the MouseListener, MouseMotionListener, and KeyListener interfaces. At comment #2.1, you define the methods associated with the MouseMotionListener interface. These are the mouseDragged() and mouseMoved() methods. Along the same lines, at comment #2.2, you define the five methods associated with the MouseListener interface. These methods are the mouseClicked(), mousePressed(), mouseReleased(), mouseEntered(), and mouseExited() methods.

These MouseMotionListener and MouseListener methods process the events their names imply. For example, when you click a mouse, you do not hold the key down. Instead, you tap it. When you press a mouse button, however, you hold the key down for a moment. Use the MouseDraw application to explore these activities if they remain unfamiliar to you.

To define the event context for the MouseDraw dialog, in the lines associated with comments #2 and #3, you call the addMouseListener(), addMouseMotionListener(), and addKeyListener() methods. These methods associate the entire dialog pane with the mouse and key listeners. In each case, it is as though you are using the this keyword to indicate that any action in the dialog can generate an event.

The functionality of the MouseDraw class centers on the paint() method. As mentioned previously, the dialog invokes the paint() method whenever it registers a change. When you call the addMouseListener() and its associated methods to make the entire dialog the source of event generation, then you create a situation in which any movement of the mouse can trigger the paint() method.

The argument to the paint() method is of the Graphics type. The Graphics class furnishes a powerful interface that allows you to draw characters and geometric and freeform shapes. It also allows you to apply color definitions to the background and foreground of the dialog pane.

To experiment with a few Graphics interface features, in the lines trailing comment #1, you call the setBackground() method to change the pane so that it is white. As Figure 10.7 illustrates, setting the background to white makes the images you draw stand out more clearly.

To draw on the pane, in the lines associated with comment #5 you create the drawArea() method. This method takes an argument of the Graphics type, so you can call it from within the paint() method.

> The MouseDraw class is derived from the PrimaryDialog class. When you work with the MouseDraw class, if you see a gray dialog that does not respond to mouse actions, it is likely that you have not replaced the abstract keyword in the signature line of the PrimaryDialog class. The PrimaryDialog signature line reads as follows:
>
> ```
> public abstract class PrimaryDialog extends JDialog{
> ```

In the definition of the drawArea() method, you call a number of Graphic methods. The setColor() method allows you to apply different colors to a succession of objects. For example, you call the setColor() method prior to the draw3Direct() method and provide it with an argument of Color.cyan. The rectangle that results assumes the color of cyan. You then call the setColor() method again, providing it with an argument of Color.green. The rectangle you draw in the next statement—which involves the drawRect() method— appears as green.

In addition to the drawArea() method, you define the eraseArea() method. This method uses calls to methods in the Graphics interface to allow you to paint the dialog surface white. Painting it in this way erases images.

The setValues() method allows you to set the xPos and yPos attributes, which are used in calculations that determine the placement of Graphics images on the dialog pane.

In the paint() method, you set up selection statements that test for draw and erase. To set these values, you define the keyPressed() method (see comment #3.1). When you type a key, you press it. In light of this, by pressing the "e" or "d" key, you issue KeyEvent messages associated with the letters "e" and "d".

The keyPressed() method captures this message, which you use the getKeyCode() method to retrieve. By calling the getkeyText() method, you convert the message into a String value. You then call the equalsIgnoreCase() method to compare the message (which identifies the key) with a literal key value. In this way, you can test for any key value generated by the keyboard.

When you detect a press of the "e" key, you set the keyAction attribute to "erase." When you detect a press of the "d" key, you set the keyAction attribute to "draw." These two values determine, then, the outcome of the selection actions in the paint() method. If you press the "d" key, the mouse paints ovals and other graphical images using cyan, yellow, and other colors. If you press the "e" key, the mouse paints only white.

To add the MouseDraw dialog to the LabView application, add the programD JMenuItem object. Here is the code in the LabView class that you add:

```
//#5 Add new dialogs
   else if(actionEv.getSource() == programD){
     setStatus("Mouse and Graphics");
     clearClientArea();
     new MouseDraw(this, "Mouse and Graphics");
```

INPUT-OUTPUT OPERATIONS

The IOOperations class provides you with a way to read from and write to text files. The operations involve what are known as *data streams*. You can view a data stream as a long series of characters that your computer can read from or write to a device. Among a multitude of other items, a device can be a printer, an Internet connection, a disc, or a monitor.

It allows you to work with Unicode files, which are files that you typically create when you use Notepad, WordPad, or Microsoft Word. Unicode file formatting reflects a worldwide standard for text. It is comparable to the American National Standard Institute format, but it has been adopted on a much wider basis.

The IOOperations class draws on some basic components of the Java IO library. To access this library, you import the java.io.* package. The classes you incorporate in the IOOperations class include a fairly standard set of classes you combine to allow you to process the text file. Figure 10.8 illustrates the sequence of classes you use to develop the IOOperations class.

Table 10.1 summarizes a few details concerning the classes and methods employed in the IOOperations class.

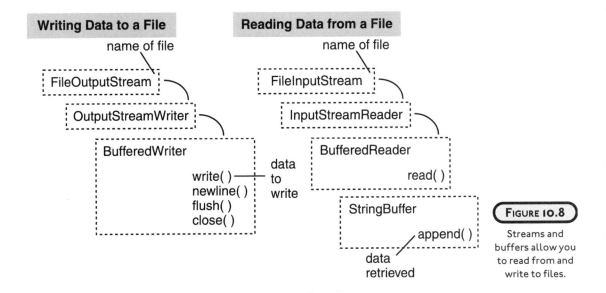

FIGURE 10.8

Streams and buffers allow you to read from and write to files.

TABLE 10.1   INPUT-OUTPUT CLASSES AND METHODS

Item	Discussion
`FileOutputStream`	A stream that is for output. It allows you to write data to a file. It is meant for writing raw streams, such as bytes, but it is suitable for characters.
`OutputStreamWriter`	This class provides a bridge between character streams and byte streams. This class allows you to specify a character set.
`BufferedWriter`	Allows you to write to a character-output stream. The buffer is more or less a space reserved for placing data into a system. The class makes it possible for you to write single characters and arrays without running out of space. You can specify the buffer size, but if you do not, then a default works for most purposes.
`write(ch)`	A `BufferedWriter` method that allows you to write a single character at a time.
`write(String, int, int)`	A `BufferedWriter` method that allows you to write several characters at a time. The first argument is the string you want to write. The second argument designates the character in the string at which you want to begin writing. The last argument designates how many characters you want to write from the starting point.
`newLine()`	This method is a `BufferedWriter` method that allows you to create a newline character (\n). Some systems do not accept the escape sequence.
`close()`	This method closes the stream. When you close a stream, you make it so that it can accept no more data.
`flush()`	This method flushes the stream. When you flush a stream, you write its contents completely.
`FileInputStream`	A `FileInputStream` allows you to obtain input bytes from a file. The class allows you to process streams of raw bytes.
`InputStreamWriter`	This class provides a bridge from byte streams to character streams. You must decode the bytes as you read them according to a character set designation.
`read()`	This method reads one or more bytes from a byte stream.
`BufferedReader`	This class allows you to read data in the form of characters. It provides a space, or buffer, to ensure that as you read data, the process moves along in an efficient way. You can specify the size of the buffer.
`StringBuffer`	The `append()` and `insert()` methods of the `StringBuffer` class are overloaded so that they accept data of any type. These methods convert data to a string and insert or append the string into a buffer.

> Java also provides a basic class that enables you to process only character data. This class requires that you create only one object and then call the write() and close() methods. Here is an example of its use:
>
> ```
> FileWriter output = new FileWriter(fileName);
> output.write(whatToWrite);
> output.write("\n");
> output.close();
> ```
>
> A corresponding operation is the ReadFile. Use of this class takes the following form:
>
> ```
> StringBuffer buf = new StringBuffer();
> FileReader fileReader = new FileReader(nameOfFile);
> BufferedReader in = new BufferedReader(fileReader);
> String str;
> while ((str = in.readLine()) != null) {
>     buf.append(str);
> }
> in.close();
> ```

The approach used to implement the IOperations class involves the OutputStreamWriter and InputStreamReader. When you employ an OutputStreamWriter, you designate the character set you want to use. In this case, the character set is Unicode. In the context involving such applications as Notepad, Microsoft Word, and WordPad, you might also use UTF-8, which is another generally used character set. Here is the code for the IOperations class:

```
/*
  IOperations.java
*/

import java.io.*;
import java.awt.*;
import java.awt.event.*;

public class IOperations {
  private String fileName, workingString;
```

```
//#1
   private FileOutputStream outStream;
   private OutputStreamWriter outWriter;
   private BufferedWriter out;
   private FileInputStream inStream;
   private InputStreamReader inSReader;
   private BufferedReader reader;

//------------------IOOperations----------------------
//#2
   //default constructor, no file or string preset.
   public IOOperations() {
     workingString = new String("No message assigned.");
     fileName = new String("default.txt");
  }
//--------------------IOOperations--------------------
   //Constructor with file name
   public IOOperations(String fName){
     fileName = new String(fName);
  }
//--------------------IOOperations--------------------
   //Constructor: text and file to be written to
   public IOOperations(String textToWrite, String fName){
      workingString = new String(textToWrite);
      fileName = new String(fName);
  }
//--------------------setFileName----------------------
//Set the file name
   public void setFileName(String fName){
      fileName = fName;
  }
//--------------------getFileName---------------------
 public String getFileName(){
      return fileName;
  }
//--------------------writeToFile---------------------
//#4
//Accepts a String argument and writes it to a file
```

```
//Use in conjunction with setFileName();
  public void writeToFile(String whatToWrite){
     try{
        outStream = new FileOutputStream(fileName);
        outWriter =  new OutputStreamWriter(
                              outStream,"Unicode");
        out = new BufferedWriter(outWriter);
        out.write(whatToWrite);
        out.newLine();
        out.flush();
        out.close();
     }
     catch(IOException iOE){
        System.out.println(iOE.toString());;
     }//end catch
  }//end writeFile
//---------------------writeToFile---------------------
//#5
//name of the file, text to write
   public void writeToFile(String fName, String whatToWrite){
      try{
         FileOutputStream outStream =
                           new FileOutputStream(fName);
         OutputStreamWriter outWriter =
                           new OutputStreamWriter(
                               outStream, "Unicode");
         BufferedWriter out =
                           new BufferedWriter(outWriter);
           out.write(whatToWrite);
           out.newLine();
           out.flush();
           out.close();
          }
      catch(IOException iOE){
          iOE.toString();
      }//end catch
    }//end
//---------------------readFromFile---------------------
```

```
//#6
    public String readFromFile(String nameOfFile){
        try{
            inStream = new FileInputStream(nameOfFile);
            inSReader = new InputStreamReader(inStream);
            reader = new  BufferedReader(inSReader);
            StringBuffer buf = new StringBuffer();
            int ch;
            while((ch = reader.read()) > -1){
                buf.append((char)ch);
            }
            reader.close();
            workingString = new String(buf.toString());

        }
    catch(IOException iOE){
            System.out.println(iOE.toString());
        }//end catch
    return workingString;
    }//end readfile
}//end class
```

In the lines trailing comment #1 of the IOOperations class, you declare class attributes that allow you to work from raw streams to character buffers. Table 10.1 provides discussion of each of these classes.

In the lines associated with comment #2, you define three constructors for the class. The first is a default constructor. In the event that the user does not specify a filename or text to be written, the constructor provides default values. The second constructor accepts a single argument of the String type and allows you to designate a filename. The third constructor allows you to designate both a filename and data to be written. Both arguments are of the String type. Whether you are to write to or read from the file does not matter. The method you call determines the action you take toward the file.

Writing to a File

At comment #3, you define accessor methods for the filenames, and after that, at comment #4, you define the first of two writeToFile() methods. This version of the method takes one argument: the text you want to write. It is of the String type. To define the method, you employ the sequence of classes shown in Figure 10.8. First, you call the constructor for the

FileOutputStream. The FileOutputStream constructor takes one argument, the name of the output file. The type of the argument is String.

The FileOutputStream constructor creates a raw connection to the file you name. In the event the file does not exist, it provides for its creation. You assign the instance of the FileOutputStream class to the outStream attribute. You then use the outStream argument in the constructor for the OutputStreamWriter, which allows you to refine the raw flow of data in the form of a character stream. The constructor for the OutputStreamWriter takes two arguments. The first is of the FileOutputStream type. The second is of a String type and designates a character set. In this instance, you designate the Unicode character set.

You assign the OutputStreamWriter object to the outWriter attribute, and you use the outWriter object as an argument to the BufferedWriter constructor. The BufferedWriter class creates a space in which characters can be read (a buffer). You assign the BufferedWriter object to the out attribute and then use a series of BufferedWriter methods to transfer data to the file. The first call is to the write() method, which transfers the content of the whatToWrite identifier to the file. Next, you call the newLine() method, which appends a newline character to the end of the file.

To clear the stream of all data, you call the flush() method. Calling this method ensures that the stream does not come to an end before all the data in it has been transferred to the file. To terminate the stream, you call the close() method.

At comment #5, you create an overloaded version of the writeToFile() method that allows you to designate the name of a file along with the text to be written to it. Both arguments are of the String type. You define this method in precisely the same way you defined the previous version, with the exception that you use the fName argument from the argument list of the method as the argument to the FileOutputStream constructor.

Reading from a File

At comment #6, you define the readFromFile() method. This method takes one argument, the name of the file from which you want to retrieve data. The argument is of the String type. In the definition of the method, you first create a FileInputStream object and assign it to the inStream identifier. This object serves to establish a raw connection with your file. If a file does not exist, then the constructor generates an exception, and the process comes to an end.

You use the inStream attribute as an argument to the InputStreamReader constructor. The InputStreamReader class translates the raw byte stream into characters. You assign the InputStreamReader reference to the inSReader attribute. Then you use this attribute as the argument for the BufferedReader constructor. The BufferedReader object attends to creating a space for retrieved data (a buffer). You assign the BufferedReader object to the reader attribute.

Using the reader attribute, you create a while repetition statement. To control the while repetition statement, you call the BufferedReader::read() method, which returns characters as long as it finds them in a stream. When it finds no more characters, it returns a negative value and discontinues trying to retrieve characters.

You assign the returned value of the read() method to the ch variable, which in this case is of the int type. Within the block, you cast the ch variable to the char type and then call the StringBuffer::append() method to join it to the end of a growing string.

When the read() method discontinues reading new characters, the flow of the program exits the while block. After the flow of the program exits the block, you call the BufferedReader::close() method to terminate the stream. To assign the string of characters that the buf variable holds to the workingString attribute, you call the StringBuffer::toString() method. As a last action, you return the value of the workingString attribute.

In the next section, you can test the input activities of the IOOperations class. To accomplish this, you implement a help dialog. To test the output capabilities of the IOOperations class, you can use the Table Maker dialog. It is not necessary to make any changes to the LabView class to use the IOOperations class.

READING INFORMATION FOR A HELP DIALOG

Adding a help dialog to the Lab View application provides a way that you can test the IOOperations class. To implement the dialog, you have six class attributes. Four of these are GUI components. One is a String object. The last is of the IOOperations class. You derive the class from the PrimaryDialog class, which provides you with most of the background functionality you require for a dialog. Here is the code for the HelpDialog class:

```java
/*
  HelpDialog.java
*/
import java.awt.*;
import javax.swing.*;

public class HelpDialog extends PrimaryDialog{
//#1
    private IOOperations ioObject;
    private String helpText;
```

```
        private JTextArea helpDisplay;
        private JScrollPane areaScroll;
        private Box frameBox;
        private Container frameContainer;
//-------------------HelpDialog----------------------
        //Constructor
//#2
        public HelpDialog(JFrame parent, String title){
            super(parent, title);
            init();
        }
//-------------------------init-----------------------
        private void init(){
          setLookAndFeel();
          ioObject = new IOOperations("helpText.txt");
          helpText = new String(ioObject.readFromFile("helpText.txt"));
          frameContainer = getContentPane();
          helpDisplay = new JTextArea(helpText, 40, 40);

  //3

          frameBox = Box.createHorizontalBox();
          helpDisplay.setEditable(false);
          areaScroll = new JScrollPane(helpDisplay);
          frameBox.add(areaScroll);
          frameContainer.add(frameBox);
          setSize(540,300);
          positionWindow();
          setVisible(true);
          pack();
        }//end init
//-------------------------main----------------------
        public static void main(String args[]){
            new HelpDialog(null, "Help Dialog");
        }
}//end of class
```

Prior to comment #1, you use the extends keyword in the signature line of the class declaration to derive the class from the PrimaryDialog class. Then you declare a IOOperations object, ioObject, that you can use to read data from a file. For the presentation of the data, you declare three GUI components. One is of the JTextArea class. Another is of the JScrollPane class. You also declare a Box class object to use for layout management and a Container object to associate the manager with your window.

In the lines accompanying comment #2, you define the constructor, which assumes the form of the other overloaded constructors you have created for dialogs you derive from the PrimaryDialog class. You use the super keyword to identify the parent window and the title of the dialog.

Immediately after defining the constructor, you defined the init() method, which the constructor calls. In the init() method, after you call the setLookAndFeel() method from the super class (PrimaryDialog), you call the overloaded IOOperations constructor. This constructor takes an argument of the String type. For the argument you provide the name of a file that provides help information on the Lab View application ("helpText.txt"). You assign the instance of the IOOperations class to the ioObject attribute.

In the next line, you use the ioObject attribute to call the IOOperations::readFromFile() method. This method requires an argument of the String type. You again provide the name of the help information file. After the readFromFile() method retrieves the text from the file, you assign the text to the helpText attribute. You then use the JTextArea constructor to assign the contents of the helpText attribute to the helpDisplay attribute. At this point, then, the text area object is populated with the text from the help file.

In the lines trailing comment #3, you attend to the task of displaying the help text. Your first action involves calling the Box::createHorizontalBox() method to set up the layout of the Box object (frameBox). Next, you attend to the JTextArea attribute. After setting it so that users cannot alter the text, you use the helpDisplay attribute as an argument to the JScrollPane constructor and create the areaScroll attribute. You are in a position to call the Container::add() method to assign the JScrollPane object and its associated JTextArea object to the frameContainer object. With that, the window is set up, ready to display the help information.

You call the setSize() method to make the dialog large enough to accommodate the text. You call the super class positionWindow() method to position your dialog. After calling the setVisible() method to make the dialog visible, you call the setModal() method and supply it with a value of true. The user must now close the window before performing other operations. You also call the setResizable() method. This method takes a boolean argument, and you provide it with an argument of true to prevent users from resizing the dialog.

To make it so that you can create an instance of the HelpDialog class in the LabView class, you add a few statements to the LabView::actionPerformed() method. Here are the lines:

```
else if(actionEv.getSource() == helpInfo){
  setStatus("Help Information");
  new HelpDialog(this, "Help Information");
}
```

To call the HelpDialog constructor, you provide the this keyword as the first argument. The this keyword identifies the LabView class as the parent window class. For the second argument, you supply the name you want to appear in the title of the dialog. This is the same name that you provide to the setStatus() method, which displays a message in the status bar. Figure 10.9 shows you the appearance of the Help Information dialog as invoked from the Lab View application menu.

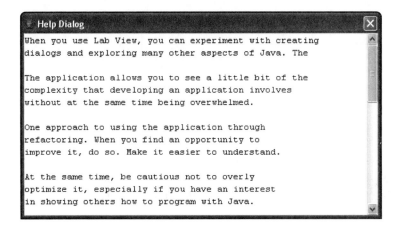

FIGURE 10.9

Reading from a file allows you to write to a dialog text area and provide help information.

THE TABLEMAKER CLASS

The Table Maker dialog pulls together services from the Elements and IOOperations classes to make it possible for you to load a file from your disk, transform it into a table, and then write the resulting table to a separate file. To use the Table Maker dialog, you require a source data file (elementData.txt), which is provided in the Chapter 10 code directory. By default, the Table Maker dialog creates the elementTable.txt file. Figure 10.10 illustrates the elementTable.txt file as viewed in WordPad:

To view the Table Maker output file, use Notepad or WordPad. The best results accompany the use of WordPad. On the other hand, you can also open the file with Word, FrameMaker, or WordPerfect and see the same results you see with WordPad.

As for the source file, the story differs. It is important to retrieve, view, and store the source file as a *.txt file in Unicode, UTF-8, or ANSI format.

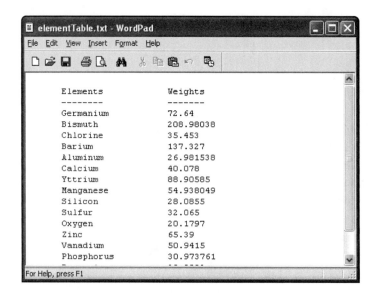

FIGURE 10.10

View the output file in WordPad, Notepad, or Word.

You can compile the Table Maker dialog as a separate executable for testing purposes. However, you derive it from the `PrimaryDialog` class, so before developing the `TableMaker` class, first develop and compile the `PrimaryDialog` class.

Figure 10.11 provides a view of the Table Maker dialog. You open Dialog > Table Maker from the main menu. At this point, the user has opened the dialog and clicked the Load button in the flow part of the dialog to load the contents of the default elementData.txt file. The name of this file appears in the Source File field.

To generate a table, the user then clicks the Format button. The resulting table appears in the lower text area. (See Figure 10.13 to view the table in the lower field.) The Clear button clears both text areas, allowing the user to start over. The Done button closes the application. In addition to clicking buttons, the user can employ shortcut keys for the buttons as indicated. To generate an output file, the user clicks the Save button. The elementTable.txt file appears as the default filename in the Save To field.

Subsequent sections explain the code in detail. Generally, when you create the application, you face the following tasks:

- **Layout of the window.** You must use a set of three layout managers to create the window. You first block it off into top, middle, and lower parts using `Box` and `JPanel`. You then use separate layout managers for each of the top and middle parts.
- **Set up event processing.** You use action listeners for keys and buttons.

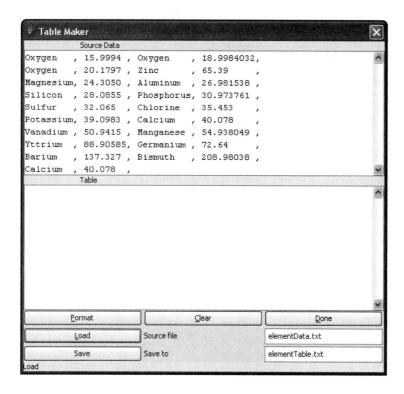

FIGURE 10.11

To load data from
a file, click the
Load button.

- **Process the data.** You use the I0Operations and Elements classes on an associative basis to process data so that you can put it in a tabular form.

Here is the code for the TableMaker class:

```java
/*
  TableMaker.java
*/
import javax.swing.*;
import java.awt.*;
import java.awt.event.*;
import java.util.*;
import java.io.*;

//#1
public class TableMaker extends PrimaryDialog
                    implements ActionListener,
                                    KeyListener{
    private Container       frameContainer;
```

```
   private BorderLayout    frameLayout;
   private JTextArea       topTextArea,    lowerTextArea;
   private JScrollPane     topScrollPane,  lowerScrollPane;
   private JButton  clearButton,
                    formatButton,   closeButton,
                    loadButton,     saveButton;
   private JLabel   sourceLabel,     tableLabel,
                    fileNameLabel,   resultsNameLabel,
                    statusBar;
   private JTextField sourceFileField, resultsFileField;
   private JPanel   lowerPanel;
   private Box      boxForTop;
   private GridLayout tPLayout, bPLayout;
   private String defaultText = new String("");

   private StringBuffer inputString;
//#2
   public TableMaker(JFrame parent, String title) {
      super(parent, title);
      init();
   }

   public void init(){
      frameContainer = getContentPane();
      frameLayout = new BorderLayout();
//#3
      makeUpperPanel();
//#4
      makeLowerPanel();

      this.setResizable(false);
      pack();
      positionWindow();
      setVisible(true);
   }
//#3.1
//--------------------makeUpperPanel--------------------------------
   public void makeUpperPanel(){
```

```
      boxForTop = Box.createVerticalBox();
                                     //10 rows and 66 columns
      topTextArea = new JTextArea(defaultText, 10,65);
      topTextArea.setLineWrap(true);
      topTextArea.setEditable(false);

      lowerTextArea = new JTextArea("", 10,65);
      lowerTextArea.setLineWrap(true);

      topScrollPane = new JScrollPane(topTextArea);
      lowerScrollPane = new JScrollPane(lowerTextArea);
      lowerScrollPane.setVerticalScrollBarPolicy(
                      JScrollPane.VERTICAL_SCROLLBAR_ALWAYS);
      topScrollPane.setVerticalScrollBarPolicy(
                      JScrollPane.VERTICAL_SCROLLBAR_ALWAYS);
      topTextArea.setWrapStyleWord(true);
      lowerTextArea.setWrapStyleWord(true);
      lowerTextArea.setTabSize(20);
      //Labels at the tops of the text areas
      sourceLabel = new JLabel("Source Data");
      tableLabel = new JLabel("Table");
      boxForTop.add(sourceLabel);
      boxForTop.add(topScrollPane);
      boxForTop.add(tableLabel);
      boxForTop.add(lowerScrollPane);
      frameContainer.add(boxForTop, BorderLayout.NORTH);
   }

//#4.1
//-------------------makeLowerPanel--------------------------
   public void makeLowerPanel(){
      lowerPanel = new JPanel();
      bPLayout = new GridLayout(3, 4, 3, 3);
      lowerPanel.setLayout(bPLayout);

      addKeyListener(this);
      formatButton = new JButton("Format");
      formatButton.setMnemonic('F');
      formatButton.addActionListener(this);
```

```
        clearButton = new JButton("Clear");
        clearButton.addActionListener(this);
        clearButton.setMnemonic('C');

        closeButton = new JButton("Done");
        closeButton.addActionListener(this);
        closeButton.setMnemonic('D');

        loadButton = new JButton("Load");
        loadButton.setMnemonic('L');
        loadButton.addActionListener(this);

        saveButton = new JButton("Save");
        saveButton.addActionListener(this);
        saveButton.setMnemonic('L');

        fileNameLabel = new JLabel("Source file");
        resultsNameLabel = new JLabel("Save to");
        sourceFileField = new JTextField("elementData.txt");
        resultsFileField = new JTextField("elementTable.txt");
        statusBar = new JLabel("Initiate operations");

        lowerPanel.add(formatButton);
        lowerPanel.add(clearButton);
        lowerPanel.add(closeButton);
        lowerPanel.add(loadButton);
        lowerPanel.add(fileNameLabel);
        lowerPanel.add(sourceFileField);
        lowerPanel.add(saveButton);
        lowerPanel.add(resultsNameLabel);
        lowerPanel.add(resultsFileField);

        frameContainer.add(lowerPanel,BorderLayout.CENTER);
        frameContainer.add(statusBar, BorderLayout.SOUTH);
    }
//#5
//--------------------keyPressed-------------------------------------
    public void keyPressed(KeyEvent kEvent){

        String keyID = kEvent.getKeyText(kEvent.getKeyCode());
        String temp = kEvent.getKeyModifiersText(kEvent.getModifiers());
```

```
        if(temp.equals("Ctrl") && keyID.equals("F")
                            || keyID.equals("f")){
          formatButton.doClick();
        }
        else if(temp.equals("Ctrl") && keyID.equals("X")
                            || keyID.equals("x")){
          clearButton.doClick();
        }
        else if(temp.equals("Ctrl") && keyID.equals("Q")
                            || keyID.equals("q")){
          closeButton.doClick();
        }
      }//end keyReleased
//--------------------keyTyped----------------------------------
    public void keyTyped(KeyEvent kEvent){
      }
//--------------------keyReleased-------------------------------
    public void keyReleased(KeyEvent kEvent){
      }
//#6
//--------------------actionPerformed---------------------------
    public void actionPerformed(ActionEvent aE){
      if(aE.getSource() == formatButton){
        statusBar.setText("Format");
//#7
        formatData();
      }
      else if(aE.getSource() == clearButton){
        statusBar.setText("Clear");
        clearData();
      }
      else if(aE.getSource() == loadButton){
//#8
        statusBar.setText("Load");
        loadData();
      }
      else if(aE.getSource() == saveButton){
//#9
```

```java
          statusBar.setText("Save");
         saveTable();
        }
       else if(aE.getSource() == closeButton){
//#10
          statusBar.setText("Close");
          closeAction();
        }
  }//end actionPerformed

//#7.1
//--------------------formatData---------------------------------
   public void formatData(){
        try{
      //Create an instance of the Elements class to call
      //data processing services
           StringBuffer tempString = new StringBuffer();
           Elements ele = new Elements();
           tempString.append(ele.getColumnData("Elements    Weights",
                                                   5, 20));
           tempString.append( ele.getColumnData("--------    -------",
                                                   5, 20) );
           tempString.append( ele.getColumnData(getDefaultText(),
                                                   5, 20) );
           setDefaultText(tempString.toString());
           writeLowerTextArea(getDefaultText());
        }
       catch(NoClassDefFoundError ncf){
          JOptionPane.showMessageDialog(this, ncf.toString(),
                                  "Not found",
                                  JOptionPane.WARNING_MESSAGE);
        }
     }//end

//#8.1
   //------------------loadData------------------------------------
   private void loadData(){
      try{
         IOperations ioObject = new IOperations();
```

```
            StringBuffer tempString = new StringBuffer(ioObject.
                        readFromFile(sourceFileField.getText().trim()));
          setDefaultText(tempString.toString());
            //Display retrieved data
          writeTopTextArea(getDefaultText());
        }
        catch(NoClassDefFoundError ncf){
           JOptionPane.showMessageDialog(this, ncf.toString(),
                                   "Not found",
                                   JOptionPane.WARNING_MESSAGE);
        }
   }

//#9.1
 //------------------saveTable----------------------------------
 public void saveTable(){
      IOOperations ioObject = new IOOperations();
      String fileName = new String(resultsFileField.getText().trim());
      String table = new String( lowerTextArea.getText());
      System.out.println("file name: "+ fileName + "\n");
      System.out.println(table);
      ioObject.writeToFile(fileName, table);
 }


//#10
//------------------closeAction---------------------------------
   public void closeAction(){
         this.setVisible( false );
   }
//------------------writeTopTextArea()-------------------------
 public void writeTopTextArea(String txt){
    topTextArea.setText(txt);
 }
//------------------writeLowerTextArea --------------------------
 public void writeLowerTextArea(String txt){
    lowerTextArea.setText(txt);
 }
```

```
//-----------------setDefaultText-----------------------------
 public void setDefaultText(String txt){
    defaultText = txt;
 }
//-----------------getDefaultText-----------------------------
public String getDefaultText(){
    return defaultText;
}
//-------------------clearData---------------------------------
  public void clearData(){
        lowerTextArea.setText("");
        topTextArea.setText("");
   }
//-------------------clearAction------------------------------
   public void clearAction(){
     lowerTextArea.setText("");
   }
//-----------------------------main---------------------------
   public static void main(String args[]){
     new TableMaker(null, "Table Maker");
   }
}
```

In the lines associated with comment #1 of the TableMaker class definition, you use the extends keyword to derive the class from the PrimaryDialog class. You also employ the implements keyword to access the ActionListener and KeyListener interfaces. The ActionListener interface allows you to associate events with JButton objects. The KeyListener interface allows you to implement control key actions, among others.

You define a multitude of attributes for the class. Declaration of the attributes in this way serves in part as a learning exercise. Most of the class objects that compose the class appear in this section of the class definition.

Following the declaration of the attributes, you attend to the definition of the constructor for the class. As with the other constructors for classes derived from the PrimaryDialog class, you provide it with two arguments. The first identifies the parent window. The second names the dialog. In addition to defining the constructor to accord with the super class, you also call the setLookAndFeel() and positionWindow() methods, which the super class provides.

Layout for the Dialog

Implementation of the `TableMaker` class involves using a variety of GUI objects and three types of layout manager. To start things off, in the `init()` method just prior to comment #3, you create a `Container` (content pane). To format the pane, you use a `BorderLayout` manager, which allows you to divide it into upper (`NORTH`), middle (`CENTER`), and lower (`SOUTH`) parts. The `NORTH` and `CENTER` areas prove most important because they each contain several components. The `SOUTH` area contains a `JLabel` object, which serves as a status bar. To attend to the tasks of setting up the `NORTH` and `CENTER` areas of the content pane, at comments #3 and #4, you call the `makeUpperPanel()` and `makeLowerPanel()` methods.

The upper part of the dialog is not actually a panel, but using these method names allows you to view the division of upper sections as symmetrical. You lay out the components in the `NORTH` area of the dialog using a `Box` object. You lay out the lower part of the dialog using a `JPanel` object to which you assign a `GridLayout` layout manager. This you place in the `CEN-TER` area of the content pane.

Layout for the NORTH Area

To define the `makeUpperPanel()` method, in the lines trialing comment #3.1 you call the `Box::createVerticalBox()` method and assign the resulting formatted object to the `boxForTop` object. Given the definition of the `boxForTop` object, you then define the components that are to go in it. These components consist of two `JTextArea` objects and two `JLabel` objects. You use the `Box::add()` method to add these components to the `boxForTop` object. A `JLabel` object appears above each of the `JTextArea` objects.

A significant feature of the definition of the `JTextArea` objects consists of the arguments for the constructors. The first argument is of the `String` type and designates the default text for the `JTextArea` object. You assign an empty string for this argument. The second and third arguments designate the number of rows (10) and the number of columns (65). Given the approach you use to laying out this dialog, the number of columns you assign to the `JTextArea` objects determines the width of the dialog.

To make it so that the text areas can accommodate long text strings, you call the `JTextArea::setLineWrap()` method, which takes a `boolean` value as its argument. You assign the `true` token. To define the `JScrollPane` objects that house the `JTextArea` objects, you call the `JScrollPane::setVerticalScrollBarPolicy()` method. You supply this method with the predefined `VERTICAL_SCROLLBAR_ALWAYS` value to ensure that the scrollbars are always visible. You likewise call the `JTextArea::setWrapStyleWord()` method to prevent words from being broken by line returns. To set the size of the tab, you call the `JTextArea::setTabSize()` method.

After you have added all the components in the top part of the dialog to the boxForTop object, you add the boxForTop object to the frameContainer object. You use the BorderLayout.NORTH value to position it.

Layout for the CENTER Area

You create the layout for the lower panel in the makeLowerPanel() method. To define the method, as Figure 10.12 illustrates, you first create an instance of a JPanel object and assign it to the lowerPanel attribute. To the JPanel object, you apply a GridLayout layout manager. You define the layout manager so that it can accommodate three columns and four rows.

Given this situation, to add components to the JPanel object, you start in the upper-left corner with a JButton object, formatButton. You then add the component you want to appear to its immediate right. This is the clearButton object. You add a third, the closeButton object. It also appears on the right of the clearButton. When you add the next component, the loadButton object, the GridLayout layout manager forces it to the left, so that it is positioned beneath the formatButton. You proceed in this way until you have added all the components to the lowerPanel object. You then add the lowerPanel object to the frameContainer object. To position it, you use the GridLayout.CENTER value.

Positioning of the two sets of components in the GridLayout.NORTH and GridLayout.CENTER areas leaves the GridLayout.SOUTH area still open. To this area you assign the statusBar attribute, which is a JLabel object. It spreads across the bottom of the dialog. When you use the GridLayout layout manager, you do not need to be concerned about the EAST and WEST areas if you have populated the SOUTH, NORTH, and CENTER areas. Those areas collapse and become invisible.

Event Processing

To process events for the TableMaker class, you define the KeyListener::keyPressed() and the ActionListner::actionPerformed() methods. The KeyListener interface requires that you define the keyTyped() and keyReleased() methods, but in both cases you leave the definitions empty.

You define the keyPressed() method in the lines associated with comment #5. To activate components so that they can generate events, in the makeLowerPanel() method you call the addActionListener() method for all of the JButton objects in the dialog. In the keyPressed() method, you set up an a if…else…if structure to process three types of keystrokes, all of which consist of a combination of the control key (Ctrl) and letter keys from the keyboard. Ctrl + F or Ctrl + f invokes the action associated with the JButton formatButton component. You also process key events for the clearButton and closeButton objects.

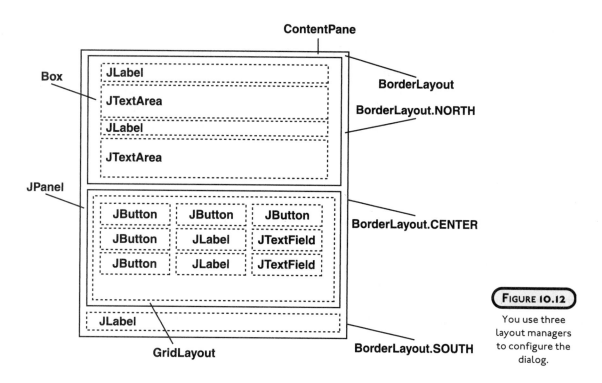

FIGURE 10.12

You use three layout managers to configure the dialog.

To process the events, you call the doClick() method. This method augments ActionListener event processing by allowing you to use the Ctrl key action in addition to regular Alt key actions. (setMnemonic() sets up actions for the Alt keys.)

In addition to processing events you generate using the Ctrl key, you attend to events generated by the ActionListener interface. All the buttons in the application generate such events. You process all such events in the same way. For example, in the lines associated with comment #7, you attend to the action event associated with the formatButton object.

To process the formatButton event, you call the ActionEvent::getSource() method to retrieve the reference identity of the object that generates the event. You then use a selection statement to test the identity against the object identifier. If the expression proves true for the formatButton object, then the flow of the program enters the formatButton block. After writing a message to the status bar to tell users the Format button has been clicked, you call the formatData() method.

You handle processing for each JButton event in a similar fashion. You test the identity of the event against the object identifier, and if the comparison renders true, then you send a message to the status bar and call a method that performs the desired action.

Processing Details

Three methods attend to most of the processing the dialog performs. These are the `loadData()`, `formatData()`, and `saveTable()` methods. The `loadData()` method attends to obtaining data from a file. The `saveTable()` method attends to writing data to a file that you have formatted as a table. The user invokes the `loadData()` method by clicking the Load button. Clicking the Save button causes the `saveTable()` method to execute. As mentioned previously, clicking the Format button invokes the `formatData()` method.

Loading Data

In the lines associated with comment #8.1, you define the `loadData()` method. To define the method, you use the default `IOOperations` constructor to create an instance of the `IOOperations` class that you assign to the `ioObject` variable. You then create a `StringBuffer` object, `tempString`.

For the argument to the constructor of the `StringBuffer` object, you use the `ioObject` identifier to call the `IOOperations::readFromFile()` method. The method takes an argument of the `String` type that names a file to be accessed. To provide the name of a file, you call the `JTextField::getText()` method, which retrieves the name of a file from the `sourceFileField` component. You call the `String::trim()` method to eliminate extra spaces from the filename.

The returned value of the `readFromFile()` method consists of the contents of the named file. You assign this data to the `tempString` identifier. You then use this identifier as an argument to the `TableMaker::setDefaultText()` and `TableMaker::writeTopTextArea()` methods. The effect of the first call is to set the `defaultText` attribute. The second call writes the data to the top text area so the user can inspect it.

Formatting

In the lines associated with comment #7.1, you define the `formatData()` method. Definition of this method involves the same set of actions discussed in relation to the `ElementsDialog` class. You first construct a `StringBuffer` object, `tempString`. Using the `tempString` object, you call the `StringBuffer::append()` method to assemble the components of the table.

To access the header and data for the table, you call the constructor of the `Elements` class. You assign the `Elements` object to the `ele` identifier. Then, in three calls to the `Elements::getColumnData()` method, you provide the `StringBuffer::append()` method with data with which to create a table.

The first two calls to the `getColumnData()` method attend to setting up table headings. The last call provides the data. To obtain this data, you call the `TableMaker` accessor method, getDefaultText(). This method returns a string containing the data you have loaded with the loadData() method.

After appending all the data you need for the table to the StringBuffer object, you then call the StringBuffer::toString() method to make the StringBuffer data the argument of the setDefaultText() method. You can then call the getDefault() method to make the converted string the argument of the writeLowerTextArea() method, which makes the formatted table visible to the user.

Saving Data

To define the saveData() method, you create an instance of the IOOperations class and assign it to the ioObject identifier. You then use the ioObject identifier to call the IOOperations::writeToFile() method. The writeToFile() method requires two arguments, both of the String type. The first argument furnishes the name of the file to which you want to write data. To obtain the name of the file, you use the JTextField::getText() method. In this way, you obtain the filename residing in the resultsFileField object. To eliminate extra spaces, you also call the String::trim() method. For the data to write to the file, you call the JTextArea::getText() method, which provides you with the formatted table from the lowerTextArea object.

Other Concerns

To close the dialog, you define the closeAction() method to use the setVisible() method to render the dialog no longer visible. To clear data from the JTextArea object, you define the clearData() method to call the JTextArea::setText() method for the topTextArea and lowerTextArea attributes. You provide them with empty strings. Since processing of data centers on writing to and reading from these JTextArea objects, you can start new sessions if you click the Clear button.

To invoke an instance of the TableMaker class in the LabView class, you define the programE JMenuItem attribute to display a menu item for the Table Maker dialog. You then implement a selection statement for the programE attribute. Here are the lines from the LabView class as defined for Chapter 10:

```
else if(actionEv.getSource() == programE){
    setStatus("Table Maker");
    clearClientArea();
    new TableMaker(this, "Table Maker");
}
```

Figure 10.13 provides a view of the application after you have loaded and formatted data for a table. At this point, you can click Clear to remove data to start over. Alternatively, you can click Save to write the formatted table to a file. To save the data to a file that is not overwritten during subsequent user sessions, it is necessary to provide a name other than the default name the Save To field furnishes.

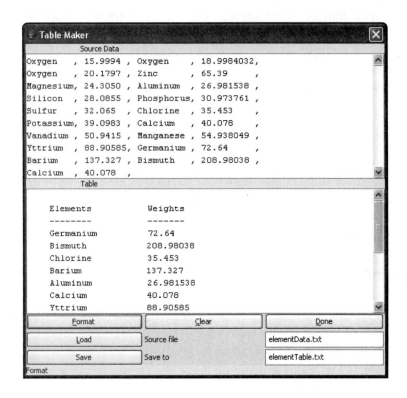

FIGURE 10.13

After clicking the Format button to generate the table, you can click the Save button to save the results to a file.

SUMMARY

In this chapter, the adventure began with an experiment involving the development of a concrete JDialog class. The JDialog object you created behaved in a fashion similar to JFrame objects, but when you associated it with a parent window, its role changed. One significant change involved the modality of the dialog. As defined in this chapter, dialogs remain wholly subordinate to parent windows. When you invoke them, all actions in your application come to focus on theme. When you complete this action, you close them and proceed with other activities.

In addition to other activities, in this chapter you used the Java stream classes to implement the IOperations class. In a way, the IOperations class serves as an example of a Façade class.

It wraps the somewhat involved functionality of the reading and writing methods of Java in a simple interface. Using the interface this class provides, you were able make new uses of the interface the `Elements` class provides.

This chapter brings you to the end of your beginning adventure with Java. Needless to say, much more remains to be explored. What you have gained through the experiments the book provides consists largely of a starting set of concepts and practices you can carry with you as you work with Java. Keep in mind as you go that Java consists of thousands of classes, and each class contains many methods and attributes. Even if at times the tasks you undertake seem daunting, it remains that each step forward provides you with greater opportunities for exploration, learning, and the development of a wide variety of applications.

CHALLENGES

1. In the definition of the `TableMaker` class, the code associated with comment #4.1 contains many redundancies. Refactor the code so that you create a method that allows you to define a `JButton` object. The method should take three arguments. Use calls to this method to replace redundant lines.

2. In the definition of the `TableMaker` class, the `formatData()` method contains a few fixed values. Create an overloaded version of the method that allows you to alter the column indentation and width of the column.

3. If you create an overloaded version of the `formatData()` method, add `JLabel` and `JTextField` objects to the interface so that you can provide these values when you create a table. Add class attributes for the values.

4. At comment #2 of the `Elements` class, redefine the `setData()` method so that instead of a literal string of text, it reads in a string from a file.

5. At comment #5 of the `Elements` class, the definition of the `getColumnData()` method is long enough to justify refactoring. Refactor this method. Place the text in the `for` repetition block following comment #11 in a separate method. Call your new method in the `getColumnData()` method.

ConTEXT for Java

Setting Up an Editor for Java

To set up an editing environment for your Java programs, you have a number of options. One option is to employ a generic editor like Notepad. However, when you employ a basic editing application like Notepad, you find yourself repeatedly performing the same elementary tasks, and your productivity tends to be reduced as a consequence.

To prevent the loss of productivity, you can acquire an editor that makes it easier for you to work with your Java files. ConTEXT is one such editor. It provides easy access to editing operations, color-coding for Java keywords, and a good set of utilities that help you manage files and project folders. ConTEXT is the product of a developer named Eden Kirin and is available to you free as a download (http://www.context.cx/).

> At this point, create a directory named ConTEXT in your Documents and Settings directory or some other directory that is easy to remember and access. Alternatively, use the downloads directory you used to download the JDK. You use this directory as a temporary storage place for the files you download for ConTEXT.

Obtaining ConTEXT

To obtain a copy of ConTEXT, access the following site: http://www.context.cx.

Figure A.1 illustrates the download site. Notice that you can donate to the ConTEXT development effort if you feel inclined. To begin the download, click the Download ConTEXT link.

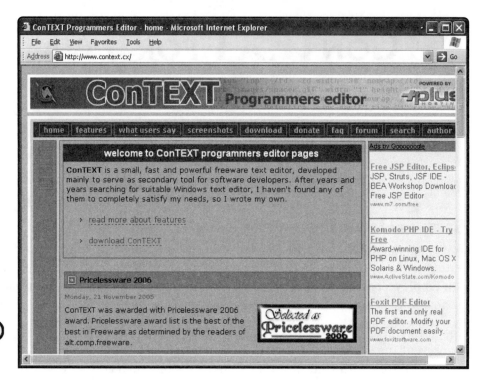

After you click the download link on ConTEXT's front page, you see a page with a box at the top that contains a DOWNLOAD link. (See Figure A.2.) Click the DOWNLOAD link.

After you click the DOWNLOAD link, a dialog box appears that asks you whether you want to run or save the downloaded file. Click Save and store the ConTEXTsetup.exe file on your hard drive. (Use the ConTEXT folder you created above.) (See Figure A.3.) The ConTEXT installation file is relatively small, so the download proceeds quickly. Click Close when the download completes.

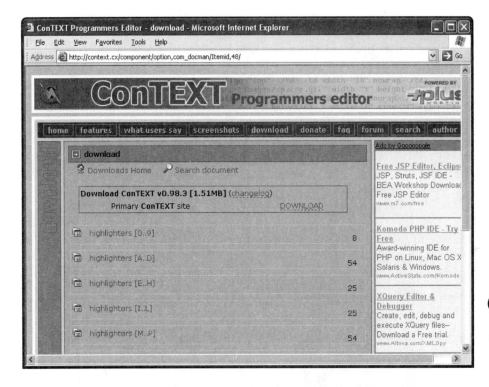

Click the DOWNLOAD link in the box at the top.

FIGURE A.3

Download the ConTEXTsetup executable.

Installing ConTEXT

To use the Windows installation utility to install ConTEXT, begin with the Start menu and select Control Panel. From the Control Panel items, click Add or Remove Programs. In the Add or Remove Programs dialog, click Add New Programs.

In the Add New Programs dialog, click CD or Floppy and Next. Then click Browse. This allows you to navigate to your temporary ConTEXT directory. Click on the ConTEXTsetup.exe file you have obtained from the ConTEXT site. Click Open. In the Run Installation Program dialog, click Finish.

After you click Finish, you see a dialog that provides a security warning. ConTEXT poses no risk. Click Run.

You see the first of the ConTEXT installation dialogs. (See Figure A.4.) Click Next.

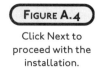

FIGURE A.4

Click Next to proceed with the installation.

You see the dialog that provides you with the default location for the installation of ConTEXT. (See Figure A.5.) Accept the default location by clicking Next.

You see the dialog for installation options. (See Figure A.6.) Leave all of the items selected and click Next.

In the Select Start Menu Folder dialog (see Figure A.7), click Next to accept the default folder.

You see the Additional Tasks dialog. (See Figure A.8.) Uncheck all of the options. Click Next after you have unchecked the options.

You see the Ready to Install dialog. (See Figure A.9.) Click Install.

A progress dialog appears briefly and exits when done. At this point, your version of ConTEXT is installed. To verify the installation, select the ConTEXT item from your Start > All Programs menu. Figure A.10 illustrates the ConTEXT menu offerings.

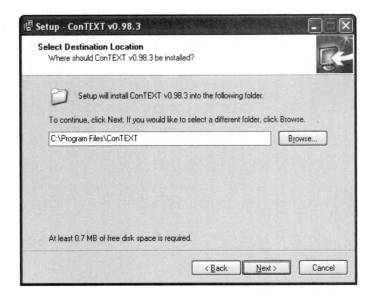

Click Next to accept the default location.

FIGURE A.6

Click Next to accept full installation.

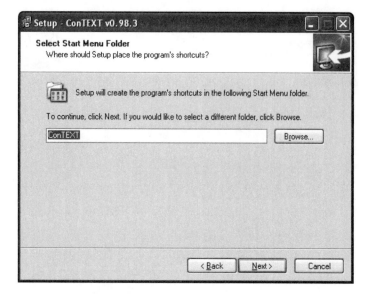

FIGURE A.7

Accept the default
Start Menu folder.

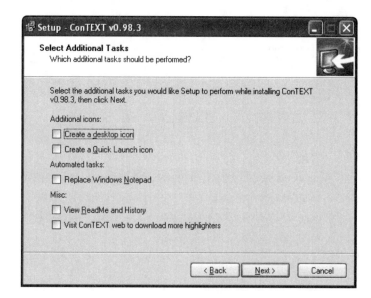

FIGURE A.8

Uncheck all of the
Select Additional
Tasks items.

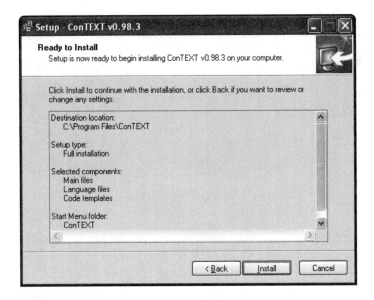

FIGURE A.9

Click Install.

FIGURE A.10

ConTEXT appears
with other
applications in
your All Programs
menu.

SETTING CONTEXT OPTIONS

After you have installed ConTEXT, select All Programs > ConTEXT > ConTEXT. This opens the editor. Figure A.11 illustrates ConTEXT's primary editing environment. It provides a standard set of main menu options.

You can then access your file by selecting File > Open. Alternatively, you can use the File Explorer tab in the File Panel on the left of the ConTEXT window. If you do not see the File Panel, select View > File Panel. The small tree icon on the left allows you to navigate to directories. When you access a given directory, all files in the directory appear in the File Panel. This feature proves essential when you work with projects involving multiple files.

On the right end of the File Panel toolbar you find a drop-down list from which you can select the types (extensions) of the file you want to display in the File Panel. Java files have a *.java extension. Compiled Java files bear a *.class. To see everything, select the *.* option.

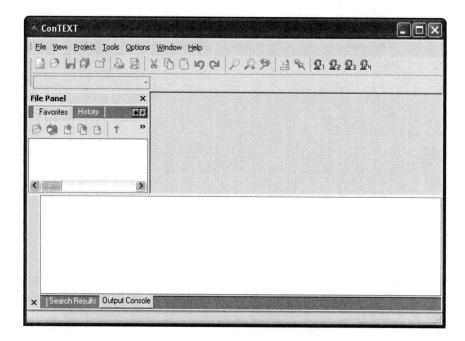

FIGURE A.11

First view of
ConTEXT.

To begin work with ConTEXT, you require little preliminary training. However, before you can work with it to perform Java programming tasks, you must attend to a few configuration tasks.

Accessing Your Java Files

There are two ways to access source files with ConTEXT. Both are easy. Here are your options:

- From the main menu, select File > Open, and use the Open File dialog to navigate to the C:\JSOURCE\CHAPTER01 directory and the HelloWorld.java file.

- After a time, you are likely to end up using the alternative approach. Alternatively, you use the File Explorer tab in the File Panel on the left of the ConTEXT window. If you do not see the File Panel, select View > File Panel. Click the small tree icon on the left of the toolbar. This allows you to navigate to directories. When you access a given directory, all files in the directory appear in the File Panel. This feature proves essential when you work with projects involving multiple files. On the right end of the File Panel toolbar you find a drop-down list from which you can select the types (extensions) of the file you want to display in the File Panel. Java files have a *.java extension. Compiled Java files bear a *.class extension. To see everything, select the *.* option.

Figure A.12 illustrates what you see after you have selected the HelloWorld.java file using the File Panel File Explorer tab.

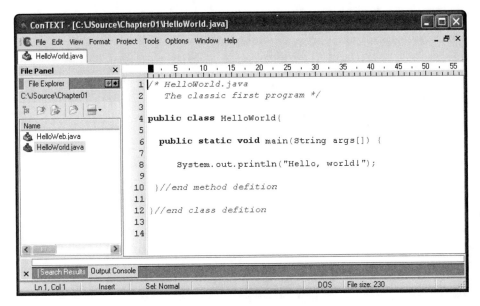

Access the
HelloWorld.java
file using the File
menu or the File
Panel.

Selecting the Highlighter for Java

The highlighter allows you to more clearly read the syntax options of your Java programs as you edit them. By default, ConTEXT provides a Java highlighter, but you must configure ConTEXT to use it. To designate the highlighter for Java, select Tools > Set Highligher and then click the Java option in the list. (See Figure A.13.)

Setting Up the Highlighter

To set up your highlighter, select Options > Environment Options. When the Environment Options window opens, click the Colors tab. (See Figure A.14.)

After selecting the ConTEXT Color tab, you can either leave the default values or spend some time setting up your own color scheme. To set a color for an item, click the item you want to change and then select the Foreground and Background colors. You can also select from Bold, Italic, and Underline options.

Setting Up Associations

You also want to associate ConTEXT with your *.java files when you click on them. To configure ConTEXT so that it can work with these files, select Options > Environment Options. Then click the Associations tab. (See Figure A.15.)

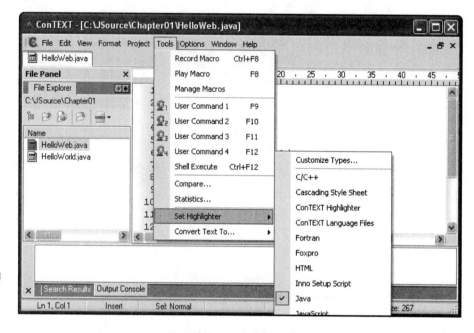

FIGURE A.13

Set the highlighter
for Java.

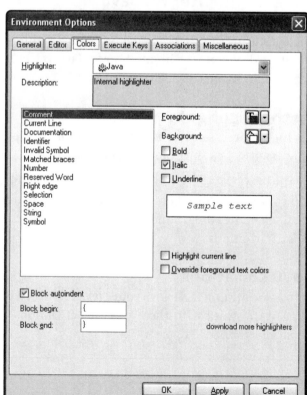

FIGURE A.14

Set colors for your
editor.

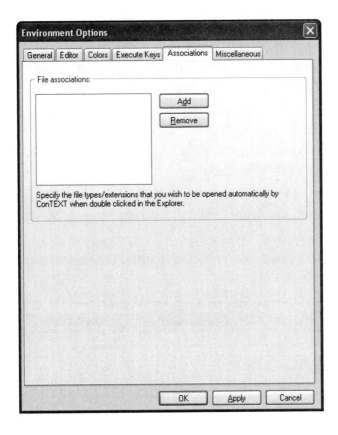

FIGURE A.15

The Associations
tab allows you to
identify file types.

To create an association with your Java source files, click the Add button on the Associations tab. A ConTEXT Associations dialog appears (see Figure A.16). To add an association for Java file types, in the Enter file extension field, type java. You do not have to type a period since ConTEXT adds one. Click OK when you are done.

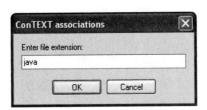

FIGURE A.16

Add an association
for Java source
files.

After you have added an association, click the Apply button in the Associations tab. Then click OK to close the Options window.

Setting the Backup Directory

Before editing the HelloWorld.java file, it is a good idea to create a backup directory. To create a backup directory, use Windows Explorer to navigate to the C:\JSource directory. Create a Directory called Backup.

Then select Options > Environment Options from the ConTEXT main menu. Click the General tab. In the General tab, check to see that the box for Back Up Files on Save is checked. Then click the ellipsis button on the right. Navigate to the C:\JSource\Backup directory you have created. Select this directory and click OK.

While you are in the General tab, you can also set the When Started option. To set this option, select Open Last File/Project from the drop-down list. Click Apply and OK when you finish changing the fields.

Figure A.17 shows the General tab panel after you have changed the backup directory and the open options.

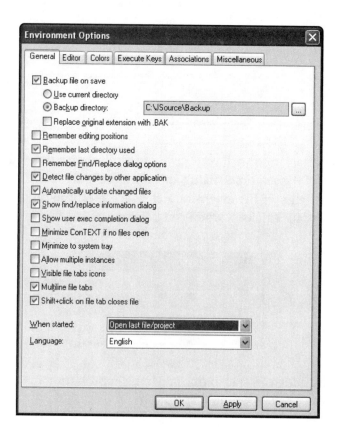

Set the backup directory.

Word Wrap and the Ruler

A final item to attend to involves setting the word wrapping option. When you resize your window, you want the text area to compensate for the changed sized. To turn the Wordwrap on, select View > Wordwrap.

If it so happens that you find the ruler turned on, you can also turn it off by selecting Ruler from the View menu. When the ruler displays, the editing area available to you decreases.

SETTING THE FUNCTION KEYS

ConTEXT makes it so that you can program its function keys to automatically execute the javac and java commands. To program these keys, you associate them with the appropriate commands in the JDK.

Associating F9 with the javac Command

To perform the tasks in this section, you must first have your HelloWorld.java file open in the ConTEXT editor. If you have not opened this file, click on the navigation tree in the File Panel, as shown in Figure A.18, and open the HelloWorld.java file.

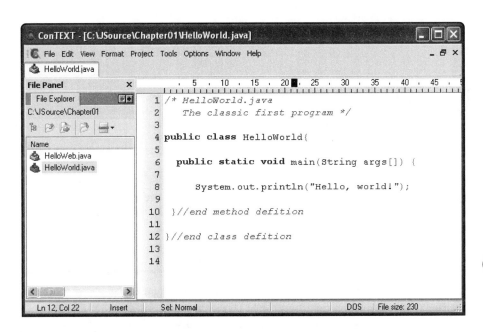

FIGURE A.18

ConTEXT and the HelloWorld.java file.

Click in the editing area to activate the HelloWorld.java file. Then from the top menu of ConTEXT, select Options > Environment Options and click the Execute Keys tab.

If you do not see a Java extension in the User exec panel box, click the Add button at the bottom of the panel. In the Extension edit window, where it says Enter Extensions Separated with Commas, type java. Then click the OK button. At this point, you see a Java extension in the User exec panel and a set of four keys beneath it.

Click the F9 key in the tree under the java extension. This activates the fields for the F9 key. When the fields are active, populate them as shown in Figure A.19.

To populate the Execute files, click the ellipsis button to the right of the field and navigate to the following path and executable:

C:\Program Files\Java\jdk1.5.0_06\bin\javac.exe

The javac.exe file is the program you invoke when you type java at the Command Prompt in a DOS session.

In the Start In field, as shown in Figure A.19, type %p, which designates the directory path of the file currently active in the ConTEXT edit area.

For the Parameters field, type %f, which designates the name of the file currently open in the ConTEXT edit area.

Finally, click the checkbox preceding the Pause After Execution label. When you activate this option, the DOS window that opens when you press F9 stays open so that you can see error messages.

Refer to Figure A.19 to verify your settings. Then click Apply and OK at the bottom of the Execute Keys tab when you finish. This returns you to the ConTEXT editor.

Testing F9

After you configure the F9 key, the next step is to test it. To test the key, begin in the ConTEXT editor with the HelloWorld.java file active in the editing area. Press the F9 key. The program invokes the javac command and your Java file is compiled. As Figure A.20 illustrates, you see the output in a DOS window.

> If your file contains errors, the compile reports errors at this time. You usually see a line number that identifies the location of your error. When you press Return, you can immediately locate the error according to the line number. If you do not see line number, select Options > Environment Options and then the Edit tab. Click the checkbox for the line numbers item.

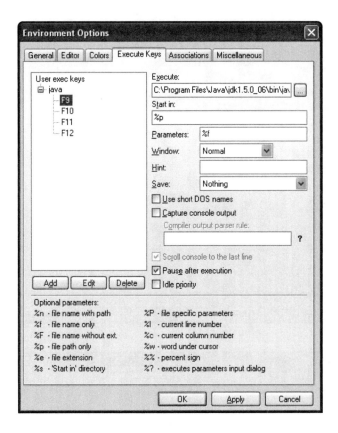

To set the Execute field, navigate to the JDK directory and the javac.exe file.

If your files contain no syntax or other errors, the Finished message indicates that all is well, and you press Enter to continue with your work.

Associating F10 with the java Command

The discussion in this section assumes you have configured the F9 key so that it compiles your Java files. If you have not yet set up the F9 key, then return to the section titled "Associating F9 with the javac Command."

To associate the F10 key with the `java` command, compile your HelloWorld.java file. To accomplish this, open the file in the editor if it is not already open and click once in the edit area to activate the edit area. Before you can run a file, you must first compile it, so at this point use the precaution of pressing the F9 to compile the file. Figure A.21 illustrates the editor after the execution of the `javac` (F9) command. This is where you need to start when you configure the F10 key.

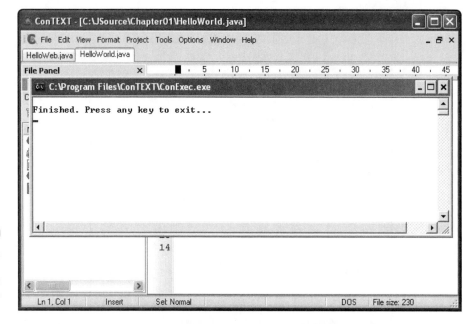

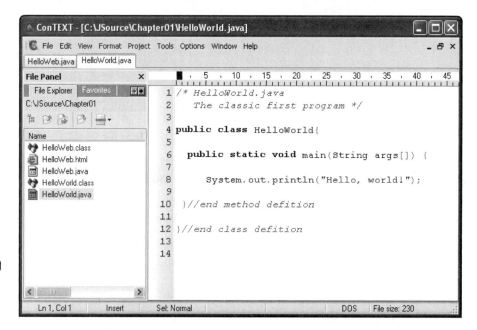

Having executed the `javac` command, from the top menu of ConTEXT, select Options > Environment Options and click the Execute Keys tab.

Click on the F10 key in the tree under the java extension you set previously. This activates the fields for the F10 key. When the fields are active, populate them as shown in Figure A.22.

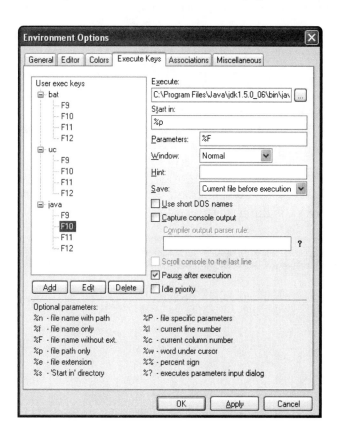

To populate the Execute field, click the ellipsis button to the right of the field and navigate to the following path and executable:

C:\Program Files\Java\jdk1.5.0_06\bin\java.exe

The java.exe file is the program you invoke when you type `java` at the Command Prompt in a DOS session. This command invokes the interpreter.

In the Start In field, as shown in Figure A.19, type `%p`, which designates the directory path of the file currently active in the ConTEXT edit area.

For the Parameters field, this time type `%F`, which designates the name of the file currently open in the ConTEXT edit area. Again, this is a capital "`F`."

Click the control box for the Pause After Execution field.

Do not click the control box for the Capture Console Output field. The reason for this is that you want to view the output of your programs in the DOS window rather than the lower part of the ConTEXT editor. What you see in this way corresponds to what you see in this book.

Click Apply and OK at the bottom of the Execute Keys tab when you finish. This returns you to the ConTEXT editor.

Testing F10

After you configure the F10 key, to test it, begin in the ConTEXT editor with the HelloWorld.java file active in the editing area. Press the F10 key. ConTEXT invokes the `java` command and your Java file is interpreted.

As Figure A.23 illustrates, you see the output in a DOS window that automatically opens when you invoke the F10 key. To close the window, click on the control in the upper right of the DOS window. Alternatively, press the Enter key.

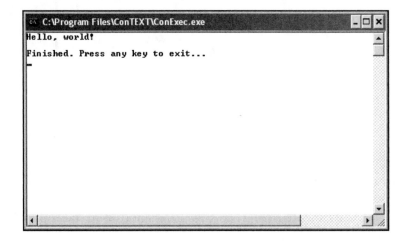

FIGURE A.23

A DOS window opens, and you see the execution of the Java file.

Index